Male Menopause

Male Menopause

Jed Diamond

Sourcebooks, Inc.
Naperville, IL

Published by Sourcebooks, Inc.
P.O. Box 4410
Naperville, Illinois 60567-4410
(630) 961-3900
FAX: 630-961-2168
www.sourcebooks.com

Library of Congress Cataloging-in-Publication Data
Diamond, Jed
    Male Menopause / Jed Diamond
        p.   cm.
    Includes bibliographical reverences and index.
    ISBN   1-57071-397-9
    I. Climacteric, Male.   I. Title
RC884.D5   1997
616.6'93—dc21   97-26509
                                           CIP

Printed and bound in the United States of America
10 9 8 7 6 5 4 3 2

Contents

Acknowledgments

My wife, Carlin, children, Jemal, Angela, Aaron, Evan, Dane, and grandchildren, Jacob, Cody, Shelby, Sierra, and Teanna. And to my mother and father. I couldn't have done it without you.

My agent, Nancy Ellis, a truly dedicated, creative, and persevering presence throughout. You made it happen and kept it going.

The men's group: John Robinson, Dick Ridenour, Ken Petron, Tom Sipes, Denis Sutro, and Tony Black.

The Sterling Men's community: Howard La Garde, Randy Listman, James Thomas, Justin Sterling, Peter Rosomoff, Dave Masciorini, Jeff Franklin, Mitch De Armon, John Fleishhauer, Don Wolff, Mike Frey, Roy Cornett, Mike Street, Phil Chapman, Scott Banks, Jeff Crawford, Doug Firefeather, Carl Pinsky, Ben Troedell, Ron Woolsey, and many others.

The Asian-American men's group: Lindsey Jang, Mike Wong, John Oda, Steven Suzuki, Prahlada, and Ray Chung.

Mentors, teachers, and pioneers in men's work: Robert Bly, Robert Moore, Warren Farrell, Angeles Arrien, Douglas Gillette,

Theresa Crenshaw, Helen Fisher, Mark Gerzon, David Gilmore, Ken Goldberg, John Gray, Germaine Greer, David Gutmann, Richard Strozzi Heckler, Richard Heinberg, Joseph Jastrab, Sam Keen, Bert Hoff, Aaron Kipnis, Shepherd Bliss, Michael Kimmel, John Lee, George Leonard, Daniel Levinson, Gail Sheehy, Malidoma Somé, James Hillman, John Enright, Bob Frenier, Herb Goldberg, Will Courtenay, Bill Kauth, Daniel Quinn, John Stokes, Betty Friedan, Sidney Kramer, John Robbins, Marilyn Milos, Peter Alsop, John Bradshaw, and many others.

Book preparation and production: Dominique Raccah, publisher, visionary, and guiding light. Karen Bouris, who believed in the vision and helped bring it into form. Todd Stocke, whose superb editing made the book better than it might have been. Renee Calomino, who believed the book should be read by everyone in the world. Michael Ritter, who did everything to make the book available to everyone. Connie Fritsche, for editorial guidance and meticulous research. Scott Theisen, for cover design and other artistic work on the book. Beth Peluso, for internal page layout. Lisa Boehm, for research and fact checking. Peter Carni, for photographic excellence. Elizabeth Deahl, for worldwide research, Barbara Taylor, for bibliographic and technical support, Laurie Gann, for help with questionnaires, and The Media Consulting Group (Jeff Harris, Jim Johnson, Peggy Parlee, and Virginia Avery), for media consulting and training.

Introduction to the Paperback Edition:
Latebreaking Data on Viagra, Hormone Replacement Therapy, and Other Men's Health Issues

When I first began writing *Male Menopause* over five years ago, very few people were aware that men, like women, experience physiological changes that affect all aspects of their lives. My goal in the book was to show that male menopause is a multidimensional life transition and can only be treated effectively by focusing on the physical, hormonal, psychological, social, spiritual, and sexual changes that occur in all men's lives, generally between the ages of forty and fifty-five.

This book draws on the latest information from my own clinical experience over the last thirty-five years, as well as from worldwide studies on sexuality, longevity, and vitality medicine. In late 1997, this book was among the first to introduce you to a new medication, *sildenafil citrate*, being tested in the United Kingdom, Europe, and the United States. It was hoped that this new drug would help the more than thirty million men in the U.S. and hundreds of millions of men throughout the world who were suffering from erectile dysfunction (ED).

When I wrote *Male Menopause*, few took note when I reported the results of my colleague, Stephen M. Auerbach, M.D., on a new medication being developed by the pharmaceutical company, Pfizer. "Thus far, the research has been very positive," said

Dr. Auerbach when I interviewed him three years ago. "It has helped 90 percent of my patients who have taken it, and there seems to be few side effects." Few knew then, though most know now, that *sildenafil citrate*, being marketed under the name Viagra, would become, perhaps, the most important medical breakthrough on male sexuality of the century.

I told you then that research on male menopause was just beginning and that we would know much more over the next few years. I am pleased to be able to give you the most up-to-date information available on this emerging new field of study. Specifically, included here are six new areas of research that will affect the lives of men and women around the world:

1. The latest information for men and their partners in treating erectile dysfunction, including the most recent findings on Viagra, Vasomax, and other new medications being researched.

2. New information on enhancing sexuality for men and women over forty, including studies on Viagra for women.

3. Hormone replacement therapy for men, including the latest research on testosterone replacement therapy for men experiencing male menopause.

4. New approaches for understanding and treating depression in men, including studies that show that male and female depression are often quite different.

5. Findings from the emerging field of vitality and longevity medicine, including research showing that we may soon be able to halt or reverse the aging process.

6. News from the front line from those who have been living with male menopause, including a major shift in the way male menopause is seen by the medical profession.

Better Erections Through Chemistry: The Viagra Story

As Bruce Handy said in his cover story for *Time* magazine, "The Viagra Craze," "What else can one say but *Vrooom!* Cheap gas, strong economy, erection pills—what a country! What a time to be alive!"[1]

When did the world begin to pay attention to erectile dysfunction?

A new chapter in the history of treating erectile dysfunction began in 1983, when a fifty-seven-year-old British physician named Giles Brindley stepped from behind the lectern at a Las Vegas medical conference, dropped his pants, and showed his erect penis to hundreds of colleagues. Brindley had just presented work on injectable drugs to treat erectile dysfunction and was displaying an erection he had induced by injecting his own penis. Brindley knew he was making medical history. But he couldn't have foreseen that his dramatic demonstration would eventually trigger a stampede to create better medications to help men keep their sexuality alive and active into their sixties, seventies, eighties, and beyond. Viagra is the most recent medication to capture the attention of the world.

What is Viagra?

Viagra is a small blue pill used to treat ED in men. It can be taken orally in doses of 25, 50, or 100 mgs.

Who will it help?

Viagra is effective in treating ED caused by organic problems (such as diabetes or prostate cancer), psychological problems, or mixtures of organic and psychological problems.

What does it do?

In clinical studies, Viagra was shown to be effective in helping men improve their sexual lives, specifically to help them *achieve* and *maintain* an erection sufficient for satisfactory sexual activity. According to Dr. Harin Padma-Nathan, associate professor in the University of Southern California Department of Urology, and a key researcher in the Viagra clinical trials, it also improves orgasms and enhances the overall quality of sexual intercourse.[2]

How natural is the arousal?

Unlike earlier procedures such as injection therapy, which produced an erection whether the man felt sexy or not, Viagra only works if the man feels aroused. Thus, erections occur "the old-fashioned way" and feel more natural. Steven Lamm, M.D., calls these medications "romance pills." He says, "the ED medications are able to tap into the emotional experience of sex....The fact is that without desire and erotic stimulation, the drugs won't work; they're not aphrodisiacs. These amazing medications restore the natural sequence of events that is unique to each couple. Without doubt, they are the closest thing I have seen to normal erectile function."[3]

Can it enhance as well as restore erections?

According to Stephen M. Auerbach, M.D., who conducted clinical trials on Viagra, "Not only were patients able to become erect, maintain erections, and enjoy successful intercourse, a number were able to enjoy multiple erections and orgasms."[4] A forty-nine-year-old patient of Dr. Lamm, who was having great difficulty dealing with ED caused by his diabetes, reported, "I view the pill as a way to express my love for my wife, who has been so incredibly supportive and loving all these years. We can have extended sex that goes on longer than it ever did—even before my illness. I can hold off and maintain or even regain an erection. The medication has returned something precious to us that I thought was lost forever."[5]

How effective is it?

Sixty-three percent, 74 percent, and 82 percent of the patients on 25 mg, 50 mg, and 100 mg of Viagra, respectively, reported an improvement in their erections. "The evidence that Viagra is an effective treatment is overwhelming and ushers in a whole new era," said Raymond C. Rosen, professor of psychiatry and medicine and co-director of the Center of Sexual and Marital Health at the Robert Wood Johnson Medical School. "Millions of men will be helped."[6]

How well was it tested?

Viagra was shown to be effective in twenty-one randomized, double-blind, placebo-controlled trials of up to six months in duration. It was administered to more than three thousand patients aged nineteen to eighty-seven years of age in the United Kingdom, France, Sweden, and the United States.[7] Dr. Tom Lue, an expert in sexual medicine who directed the clinical trials in the U.S., presented the results of his study to a packed audience at the annual meeting of the American Urological Society. He said, "Sildenafil [the clinical name for Viagra] is an effective, well tolerated oral treatment for patients with ED associated with a broad range of etiologies."[8]

How is it taken?

For most patients, the recommended dose is 50 mg taken, as needed, approximately one hour before sexual activity. However, Viagra may be taken anywhere from four hours to half-an-hour before sexual activity. Based on effectiveness and toleration, the dose may be increased to a maximum recommended dose of 100 mg or decreased to 25 mg. The maximum recommended dosing frequency is once per day.[9]

How does it work?

Viagra prolongs the effects of a chemical, cyclic guanosine monophosphate (cGMP), by blocking an enzyme that breaks it down. It allows the smooth muscles in the spongy erectile tissues of the penis to relax, causing blood to enter the penis and produce an erection.[10]

How long does it last?

In clinical trials, the effects lasted up to four hours, but individual variation is great.[11] A number of clients at our clinic say that they become easily aroused a second time within an hour after ejaculating. Some report still feeling sexy the next morning and being able to develop and maintain an erection "the day after," without taking additional medications.

What are the side effects?

Though side effects were few, the following were reported, along with the percentage experiencing the problem:

Headaches (16%)
Flushing (10%)
Digestive problems (7%)
Nasal congestion (4%)
Urinary tract infection (3%)
Abnormal vision (3%)
Diarrhea (3%)
Dizziness (2%)
Rash (2%)

Warning: Viagra should not be taken by anyone who is also taking nitrate-based medications such as nitroglycerin. It should always be taken under the supervision of a competent medical doctor.[12]

How many people are taking it?

It is difficult to estimate the total number of people taking Viagra, but there is clearly a tremendous interest throughout the world. Three weeks after it was introduced, it became the fastest-selling new drug in the U.S., outstripping such best-sellers as the antidepressant Prozac, and the hair-restoring drug, Rogaine. According to the May 3, 1998, issue of the *New York Times*, since Viagra's introduction in March 1998, twenty thousand prescriptions were being written each day.

*Should a man take it to improve erections even if he doesn't
think he has ED?*

Although researchers warn that taking Viagra when there is no ED may be a waste of money and could cause harm, this is an area of medicine that is sure to become controversial as more people learn about the drug and hear reports in the media and from friends about how good it is. Should it be used by men, and possibly women, as a recreational drug to enhance pleasure?

How will it affect relationships? Will people become "hooked" on the effects and have difficulty making love without the drug? Will a black market develop for those who want to use it?

Researchers, doctors, and patients are confronting such issues. Dr. Lamm reports that one of his patients, a forty-two-year-old man with no erection problems, was insistent in his desire to try Viagra. According to Dr. Lamm, "he stated categorically that he wanted to see if he could turn back the clock and regain the rocklike hardness he had when he was twenty." Dr. Lamm said that his rationale was direct. "If it's available," said his patient, "why shouldn't I use it, as long as it won't hurt me?"[13]

How was it discovered?

In 1991, a pair of seemingly unrelated studies were separated by the Atlantic Ocean, one in the United States, the other in Britain. When they discovered their synergism, medical history was made.

In the U.S., Dr. Solomon Snyder, a neurobiologist at Johns Hopkins University School of Medicine, was studying the effect of nitric oxide on laboratory rats. His team discovered that the common gas transmitted signals between nerve cells, but dissipated so quickly that it was difficult to see which nerves use it.

"We looked all over the body," Snyder said. He found that not only did nerve cells in the brain use the gas, but those in the penis did also. Snyder's team published their results in the journal *Science* in 1992. [14]

Meanwhile in Britain, Dr. Ian Osterloh was developing a heart medication named Viagra for pharmaceutical giant Pfizer. Viagra was originally intended to help men with heart disease who were experiencing chest pains, but was not working for those purposes. The men in Osterloh's experiment did, however, report erections as a curious side effect. Nonetheless, Pfizer was ready to pull the plug on Viagra.

But in a fortunate stroke of luck, Osterloh read the *Science* report by Snyder's team and suddenly understood the correlation between the drug and the men's erections. While nitric oxide led to an erection, Viagra was, in fact, blocking an enzyme that causes the erection to go flaccid.

Once submitted, it took just six months for the U.S. Food and Drug Administration (FDA) to give its approval for the drug. The field of male sexual health—and the lives of millions of men with erection dysfunction—would never be the same.[15]

Where does Viagra fit into a total program for sexual health?

We are a quick-fix society. We all want the magic pill that will make everything right in our world. Viagra's popularity taps into the belief that we can improve our sexual lives quickly and easily. In the thirty-five years I have been working with men and women, there have been many "magic sexual potions" trumpeted in the media.

There seem to be an equal number of "magic new diets" that are sure to melt the fat right off our bodies without pain or strain. I've learned that there is no free lunch, no instant cures for a lifetime of poor eating and exercise practices, and no way to regain a healthy sex life overnight.

Viagra, and any other drug that will be touted as the new "passion pill," is not magic. Though there are indications that it is safe and effective, we do not yet have long-term results. We have only to remember thalidomide, which was first deemed safe and later shown to cause serious birth defects, or more recently fen-phen which was thought to be a miracle drug for losing weight and was later withdrawn because of fears that it caused heart problems.

I recommend caution to those who would jump on the technology bandwagon—for Viagra or for any of the upcoming bio-tech breakthroughs.

Viagra won't repair a relationship torn apart by shame, fear, anger, and doubt. It takes time and often professional counseling to rebuild a damaged relationship. Many men, overjoyed with the possibility of getting back what they have lost, often leave their partners out of the discussion. When they come home with the little blue pill, they are often surprised their partners are not as excited about Viagra as they are. One woman told me, "I feel left out of the discussion. It's the same old story with Jack. He seems more concerned with *his* needs than with *our* needs."

The pill will not make a self-centered man more sensitive to his partner. But what the pill does offer is a new beginning. For many men and their partners who had given up on their sex lives, the pill can give them a new lease on that part of their lives.

Calling it "a great drug," former Senator Bob Dole says he was among the men who took part in the original clinical trials on Viagra. Dole, age seventy-four, was diagnosed with prostate cancer in 1991 while serving as a senator from Kansas, and underwent surgery. Dole's wife, Elizabeth, shared his enthusiasm. Viagra is a boon to couples like the Doles and millions of others who no longer have to worry about losing their sex lives as a result of ED.

Before Viagra was introduced, less than 5 percent of the thirty million men suffering erectile dysfunction sought help. Now the issue of sexual dysfunction has surfaced and can be discussed openly.

At our clinic, the Third Age Wellness Center, we offer a program for the whole person, including the new ED medications, hormone replacement therapy, help with food, exercise, and supplement therapy, herbal healing, acupuncture, massage, stress reduction, counseling, job guidance, and mentoring. The new ED medications won't solve all of a man's problems, but they can offer *hope* for a man and his partner. They are not the be all and end all, but rather are often the first step for sexual health and a return of intimacy.

L-arginine and Ginkgo Biloba— The Natural Alternatives to Viagra

Those working in the field of natural health have also been aware of the importance of nitric oxide in promoting sexual well-being. "Recent studies have confirmed that [nitric oxide] exercises considerable control over blood pressure, boosts immune function, kills cancer cells and microorganisms, and helps control muscular activity, balance, and coordination," say John

Morgenthaler and Dan Joy, authors of *Better Sex Through Chemistry: A Guide to the New Prosexual Drugs.* "Scientists also came to recognize [nitric oxide] as *the primary mediator of penile erection.*"[16]

What does nitric oxide have to do with arginine and sex? "Quite simply, dietary arginine is the primary source of nitrogen molecules for [nitric oxide]," say Morgenthaler and Joy. "Without arginine in the diet, there would be no [nitric oxide], and without [nitric oxide] there would be no erections."[17] To maintain strong levels of arginine, vital to the sexual health of men and women, Morgenthaler and Joy recommend you either consume foods containing arginine, such as dairy products, nuts, chicken, turkey, and other fowl, or take dietary supplements.[18]

In addition to L-arginine, the healing powers of the ancient ginkgo tree are well-known to holistic health practitioners such as Andrew Weil, M.D. In addition to being a powerful antioxidant that can help keep us healthy by scavenging "free radicals," reactive molecules that are implicated in developing various diseases, gingko biloba (which is made from the leaves of the tree) may also help circulation to the brain and the penis.[19] Perhaps all those jokes about a man's brain and his penis have some basis in fact.

"Because of their ability to stimulate vascular flow to the penis, yohimbe and ginkgo biloba are two herbs that are often used to treat impotence," says nutritionist Ann Louise Gittleman. (Yohimbe is discussed on page 23 of this book.) "Ginkgo biloba extract was given to a group of men who had been unresponsive to traditional drug therapy," Gittleman reports. "In a six-month period, half of the group regained potency. One 40 mg capsule taken daily can produce results in two months, though it may take up to six months to regain full potency," she concludes.[20]

John Morgenthaler believes that L-arginine, along with ginkgo biloba, can be very helpful in treating the millions of men suffering from ED. He also believes they may be helpful for improving a woman's sexual pleasure.[21] Although herbs and natural substances are not as widely advertised as the latest "miracle drugs," they have been around a lot longer, and generally have proven themselves to be both effective and safe. As alternatives to the "drug-of-the-week," they should be given careful consideration by men and their partners who want to improve their sex lives.

New Advances in Sexual Medicine—What's Next?

At the forefront of forthcoming drugs is Vasomax (phento-lamine), being developed by Zonagen, another medication that can help with erectile dysfunctions. The drug has completed clinical testing and been submitted to the FDA. Originally, this drug was given as injection therapy for impotency, and it has now been reformulated into an oral preparation. Like Viagra, Vasomax causes corporal smooth muscle relaxation and penile erection; it is also taken as needed prior to intended sexual activity. Vasomax could be approved for use during 1998.

According to Raymond Rosen, Ph.D., who reviewed the preliminary data from the most recent clinical trials, "If you're looking for an on-demand erectogenic agent, Vasomax is close to the perfect formula. The drug is well tolerated, and with the exception of a stuffy nose, there are no noticeable side effects."[22]

One of Dr. Lamm's patients summed up his experience this way: "When I left your office after taking Vasomax for the first time, Amy and I went to dinner. I started to feel differently. I became acutely aware of how lovely she looked, and, all of a sudden, my emotional response to her was matched by a really powerful physical urge. I was overcome with desire for her. In fact, we skipped dessert in the restaurant—and had it at home, if you know what I mean."[23]

Dr. Steven Lamm has had experience using both Vasomax and Viagra. He says, "I use Vasomax for those men who clearly have psychological and early mild erectile dysfunction." He considers Viagra to be a "more powerful and effective medication" which is effective in men with moderate to severe ED.[24]

Beyond Vasomax, there are many other medications now being tested to help men experiencing ED.

Spontane (apomorphine) is being developed by TAP, a joint venture between Abbott Laboratories and Takeda Chemical

Industries of Japan. Apomorphine works through the central nervous system to help with erections. It seems to work best in men with psychogenic ED. Clinical trials are nearing completion.

Topiglan is a gel being developed by MacroChem which contains alprostadil, one of the drugs used for penile injections. Clinical trials are now underway.[25]

Postaglandins are hormone-like substances that help to relax capillaries, decrease cholesterol levels, and lower blood pressure. Creams containing them are being developed that are applied to the surface of the genitals to stimulate blood flow. Clinical trials are underway.

And the story with Pfizer and Viagra is not over yet either. For those who don't even want to wait an hour for Viagra to take effect, Pfizer has begun development on a new version, using the delivery agent Zydis, which would take effect in just minutes.[26]

According to Dr. Stephen Auerbach, there is a revolution occurring in sexual medicine, and he expects that there will be newer and better formulations similar to Viagra as well as new combinations of medications that, taken together, can heal many of the sexual problems that men face today. Perhaps in the future men will be able to take a specifically formulated "love cocktail" that can help improve his sexual well-being. "The main thing I want people to know," says Dr. Auerbach, "is never lose hope. If one approach doesn't work, try another."[27]

The New World of Third Age Sexuality: ED Drugs May Benefit Women As Well As Men

At the Third Age Wellness Center, we talk about the First Age being the years from birth to twenty-one, the Second Age being the years from twenty-one to forty, and the Third Age being the years from forty to one hundred and over. The introduction of the birth control pill revolutionized sexuality for Second Age men and women. So, too, will the introduction of the new ED drugs change the way men and women experience sexuality in the Third Age. It will require men and women to open lines of communication that have often closed down due to fear, anger, and disappointment. The coming of Viagra is a hopeful beginning.

But many doctors report that Viagra also holds great potential for women, and that has piqued the interest of women worldwide. "A lot of women are interested," said Dr. Myron Murdoch, a urologist in Greenbelt, Maryland, and national medical director for the Impotence Institute of America. "If you think there's a big demand for male sexual dysfunction medicine, wait until women find out they can have some sort of sexual dysfunction medicine."

Dr. Murdoch believes that the drugs being used for male dysfunction can increase vaginal and clitoral blood flow for women, and also help women who are experiencing a lack of vaginal lubrication.[28]

Dr. Auerbach was among the one hundred university and drug company scientists who gathered recently to talk about the value of the new ED drugs for women. "Although there are similarities between female and male sexuality," he said, "there are also important differences. We can't assume what will work for men will also work for women."[29]

Laurie Kline, a forty-one-year-old Baltimore woman, very much believes that the new ED drugs can be of help. She feels Viagra gave back her orgasms which she had lost since having a partial hysterectomy when she was thirty-five. "It's a miracle pill," says Kline. "I can't believe how it worked. For so long I didn't have any nerves down there, and it was like that part of me just woke up."[30]

Kline is enrolled in a United States clinical study to determine whether women can and should use Viagra. Dr. Jennifer Berman, a University of Maryland urologist heading the study, believes that the time has come for the study of female sexual dysfunction, after many years in which male research has dominated the field.[31]

Berman believes that there are as many women suffering from dysfunction as there are men, and believes that Viagra might be of help. "It makes sense it would work in women. Blood flow equates with sexual arousal in them too," she says.[32]

Many women aren't waiting for the results to come in before trying Viagra. In May of 1998, near the beginning of the Viagra craze, the *New York Times* reported on women experimenting with the drug outside of clinical studies or the care of a doctor. Their reports tell much about both Viagra's potential usefulness for women and its side effects.

The women interviewed chose to try Viagra for a variety of reasons, including decreased sexual drive due to the use of Prozac, occasional lack of lubrication, and difficulty reaching orgasm. Their sexual results were largely positive. They reported greater sensitivity and reduced time to orgasm. One even referred to it as an "animalistic" experience.

The side effects they reported mirrored some of those in men, including a flushed face, slight bluish tint to the vision, and headaches. These similar effects, however, only scratch the surface of the concerns over women utilizing Viagra.

Although studies are underway, doctors warn against women of childbearing age taking the drug, and both researchers and the experimenting women expressed fears about unknown long-term effects. The psychological effects, particularly with a lack of professional guidance, are also a necessary concern about this kind of experimentation—interestingly, two of the four women cited in the story chose not to tell their partner they had taken the drug.

Nonetheless, many women feel left out of the loop amidst all the furor over Viagra and male potency problems. As one of the experimenting women said, "Look at men. The wind changes direction and they have an orgasm. What about us? Why isn't anyone paying attention to our sexual feelings?"[33]

Theresa Crenshaw, M.D., an expert on male and female sexuality, says we are at the beginning of a whole new area in sexual pharmacology. She believes that many drugs will become available that will not only improve sex, but help us live longer, healthier, and happier lives. She has found, for instance, that Wellbutrin

(Bupropion), a relatively new antidepressant, can cause weight loss, increase sex drive, and promote orgasm.[34]

We are clearly at the beginning of a new era in mind-body medicine. New biological agents will change the way we feel, think, and interact sexually. Our changing perceptions about sex can actually alter the way our brain chemistry works. It is an exciting time to be a man or a woman in the world.

His and Hers Hormone Replacement Therapy: The Wave of the Future?

When I first began doing research for the book, hormone replacement for men seemed about as strange a concept as male menopause. As with male menopause, male hormone replacement therapy is much more widely understood in Europe than it is in the United States.

According to a recent national survey conducted by Roper Starch Worldwide, most men are unaware of the key role testosterone plays in their health and have little knowledge about the symptoms of low testosterone. The survey, sponsored by ALZA Corporation and conducted in February 1998, asked more than one thousand adult men in the U.S. to discuss their knowledge of testosterone and hormone replacement therapy.[35]

The survey showed that 68 percent of men cannot name a single symptom or condition associated with low testosterone. Only 15 percent cited a decreased sexual drive, 6 percent named fatigue, and 3 percent cited a decrease in lean muscle mass as symptoms associated with low testosterone. Less than one percent linked low testosterone levels to a loss of bone density.[36]

The male survey respondents also proved largely unaware of the availability of hormone replacement therapy, with over half saying they had never heard of it. Interestingly, of those who had heard of it, more than one-quarter knew hormone replacement therapy was available for women, but only 7 percent knew that it could also be used for men.[37]

"Traditionally, hormone replacement therapy has been a women's issue, but men need to know it's important for them as well," said Melvin Duckett, M.D., director of the Maryland Urology Group. "For men who are testosterone deficient, hormone replacement therapy can make a significant difference, relieving symptoms of fatigue and depressed mood and increasing sexual drive. In addition, the importance of testosterone to men's health is gaining increased recognition within the medical community."[38]

Dr. Malcolm Carruthers, a specialist in treating male menopause in England, has been carrying out research for the past twenty years on the key role of testosterone in keeping men healthy, happy, and sexually active.

He recently completed a study of one thousand men going through male menopause, perhaps the largest study in the world. He presented his findings at the *First World Congress on the Aging Male* held in Geneva, Switzerland, in February 1998. His research findings need to be understood by men and women going through this change of life, as well as the medical profession who must become partners in treating them.

"The Change"

Every adult woman in North America and other industrialized countries knows what "The Change" refers to: the "change of life" that occurs with menopause. There is great controversy about hormone replacement for women—whether it is helpful in treating symptoms of menopause and preventing other diseases, or if it represents the medicalization of a normal life change for women. There are also disagreements about what kinds of hormones to take, if replacement is needed.

Up until now, men have been left out of the dialogue. Since it was assumed that male menopause was primarily psychological rather than physical, it was thought that aging men need not consider replacing testosterone as that hormone drops. We now know that men go through a "change of life" that is as real and hormonally based as menopause is for women.

Men and women in the United States are just beginning to learn what has been known in Europe for some time. A recent poll in a major British national newspaper established that 97 percent of its readers believed that the male menopause was a fact and should be treated.[39]

If male menopause is real and hormone replacement therapy (HRT) can help men going through this change of life, why haven't we heard more about it? The reason I've found has more to do with current trends and beliefs than with scientific facts. I believe Dr. Carruthers' work is the most soundly based medical information available and I want you to be aware of his findings so you can judge for yourself whether or not HRT may be of value.

Similarities and differences between male menopause and female menopause

Female menopause usually happens in the limited age range of about forty-five to fifty-five years old. For men, the often insidious onset can be any time from age thirty onwards, Dr. Carruthers found. One of the reasons it is often missed is that it is usually more gradual in onset than menopause in the female. Dr. Carruthers believes it can be even more severe in its long-term consequences. It is a crisis of vitality, just as much as virility, even though its most obvious sign is loss both of interest in sex and of erectile power.

Symptoms of male menopause found in one thousand men studied by Dr. Carruthers

1. **Fatigue** was present in over 80 percent of the cases studied. The men experiencing it suffered from an overall loss of vitality.[40]

2. **Depression** was present in 70 percent of the cases. Dr. Carruthers concluded that among all the symptoms of male menopause, depression was one of the most difficult for the men and their families to deal with. As I will show later, I believe that men and women express depression differently, and that it is often underdiagnosed in men.[41]

3. **Irritability** and **anger** were prominent symptoms, present in over 60 percent of the men he saw. Dr. Carruthers' experiences are similar to my own, though I think there is a much higher percentage of men in the U.S. with these symptoms, perhaps as high as 80 to 90 percent.

"Trivial issues will irritate the man as much if not more than important ones," says Dr. Carruthers. "At work, the firm starts to recruit nothing but idiots, then trains them to work against him....At home the whole family deliberately tries to annoy him and succeeds brilliantly! They do all the wrong things at all the wrong times in all the wrong ways.

"Without having to try, he gets into endless arguments with them and ends up infuriated, his patience, like the rest of him, utterly exhausted. He may be aware that he is being unreasonable and be ashamed of it, but still be unable to do anything about it."[42]

Seeing so many men who are perpetually angry during this time of life goes against the frequently held belief that testosterone is the hormone responsible for male aggression. "Usually what is often described all too literally as 'impotent rage' is associated with *low* levels of testosterone activity," says Dr. Carruthers. "When they are restored to normal by treatment the man feels more confident and assertive, and this doesn't seem to overshoot into aggression."[43]

4. **Reduced libido** was present in 80 percent of the cases. "Libido" refers to sex drive or sexual appetite. Waning libido usually comes on gradually over months or years, as active testosterone levels drop in the body. "It affects every aspect of a man's sex life," says Dr. Carruthers, "reducing the frequency of sexual thoughts, fantasies, and even dreams. The number of times he feels in the mood for sex goes down."[44]

5. **Reduced potency**—the ability to obtain or maintain an erection—occurs in about 80 percent of cases. It is perhaps the most troubling symptom of male menopause for a man to deal with, often leading to sexual anxiety which causes premature ejaculation. A full one-quarter of Dr. Carruthers' patients complained of premature ejaculation due to the rush to completion while still erect.

   On the flip side, another quarter of the men experienced delayed ejaculation due to the decreased sensitivity caused by low testosterone.[45]

6. **Premature aging** is often a symptom of male menopause. Dr. Carruthers believes that drops in testosterone that occur as men age can increase the risk of heart problems. Recent studies in Britain and the U.S. have found that low testosterone levels, and sometimes high estrogen levels, may be a precursor to heart disease.

   Lowered testosterone levels also affect circulation, causing cold hands and feet in some men, as well as "hot flashes" in others. Dr. Carruthers found that although less than 25 percent of the men in his study reported hot flashes, over 50 percent experienced increased sweating, especially at night.

   In the background of the specific symptoms of premature aging is an overall feeling of a body losing its vigor and flexibility. Men don't feel like their old selves. They often feel old and creaky. Dr. Carruthers believes that this is caused by a reduced level of testosterone activity resulting in diffuse aches, pains, and stiffness. He concluded that the two primary factors controlling muscle mass and strength in men are testosterone and exercise.[46]

Interestingly, Dr. Carruthers found that 250 out of the one thousand men he treated for male menopause have had vasectomies. He reports on studies throughout the world that show a relationship between vasectomies and many of the symptoms associated with male menopause. Since the symptoms do not appear until many years after the surgery, they are often overlooked. "Vasectomy is, after all, a major surgical insult to a very sensitive, delicate, and highly tuned organ," says Dr. Carruthers.[47] Considering the findings on vasectomies, I can't help but wonder what effect *circumcision* may have on male menopause. If vasectomies are traumatic for the male system, what does it do to the male to have an important part of his sexual anatomy cut off? The studies have yet to be done, but I'll bet they show that men who have been circumcised show more later-life problems than men who have been left intact.

Testosterone Replacement Therapy (TRT):
Promising Results

Some proponents of TRT feel that it is *the* answer to preventing and treating male menopause. Dr. Carruthers' findings are similar to my own in recognizing that TRT can be helpful to some men as a part of a total program for hormonal, physical, mental, interpersonal, and spiritual health. "TRT is but one of a broad range of methods for preventing and treating [male menopause]," says Dr. Carruthers. "Often, however, it proves the key to the door to recovery and puts men in a more positive frame of mind to undertake the other necessary steps, such as managing stress, drinking less, losing weight, and exercising."[48]

The age of the patients that were given TRT by Dr. Carruthers ranged from thirty-one to eighty, the mean being fifty-four. Testosterone can be taken as an injection, pill, pellet, cream, or patch.

Carruthers reported the following findings:

- An overall feeling of increased vitality and well-being.

- Drive and assertiveness increased in both the patients and their partners, but not to the point of aggression.

- Patients became happier, less irritable and easier to live with. They also felt they were coping better at work and in their family lives.

- Increased hair growth, especially in the chest and pubic region.

- Many men noticed improved condition of hair and scalp, and some found a return of color to their hair.

- Penile enlargement and increased genital sensitivity were reported by some.

- In general, there was improvement in all symptoms, and total sexual activity, including intercourse and masturbation, increased.[49]

TRT: is it safe?

Side-effects reported in the study were minimal, mostly limited to mild gastric irritation. Concerns about the safety of the treatment focus mainly on the prostate gland, the liver, and the heart. "Blood pressures were unchanged or even fell slightly," Dr. Carruthers found. "There were no adverse changes in blood fat patterns, glucose, liver function tests, or any part of the detailed blood profile."[50]

The main concern I have heard about TRT focuses on the possibility of an increased risk for developing prostate cancer. Dr. Carruthers findings are reassuring. "The early warning sign for prostate cancer, the prostate specific antigen (PSA), did not change at repeated tests up to five years, there were no signs of enlargement of the prostate clinically or on ultrasound scanning and no tumors developed," he reports.[51]

We know that testosterone can cause prostate cancer to grow more rapidly. One of the treatments for this kind of cancer is to block testosterone. This has lead to a concern that taking testosterone might cause cancers to develop. Dr. Carruthers has found no evidence to support that concern. In fact, he believes that treating men with testosterone has a long history of safety and success: "Fifty years' treatment of hypogonadal patients with testosterone implants and thirty years of treatment with injections of testosterone enanthate do not show any rising incidence of prostate cancer or even benign hypertrophy."[52]

A recent review article on androgens and carcinoma of the prostate summarized the current informed view by stating: "It is extremely unlikely that androgens play a role in the initiation of prostate cancer."[53]

HRT for men, Dr. Carruthers believes, is as safe, if not safer, than HRT for women. He notes that the prostate is the size of the thumb and ultrasound pictures give a very clear view of wherever cancer might arise. By contrast, the breasts are much more difficult to screen; X-rays, which may themselves be harmful, have to be used and there is no sensitive blood test like the PSA which can be used to exclude breast cancer.

Who should consider taking testosterone replacement therapy?

The answer would seem simple: anyone who is experiencing symptoms and who has a low testosterone level. The problem is that we are just beginning to learn what the normal range of testosterone is in men as they age. The generally accepted normal range of all testosterone in the blood is 250 to 1200 ng/dl.[54] Professor Alex Vermeulen from the University of Ghent in Belgium is one of the worldwide leaders in research on male menopause and testosterone deficiency. He recently concluded that there is no real agreement about what the so-called normal range actually is, particularly in men over forty.[55]

Dr. Carruthers' research has helped bring some answers by making clear the importance of measuring the levels of free testosterone not just the overall levels.

Free testosterone: the key to understanding testosterone deficiency in men

Many clients come to our clinic after having been to a number of other doctors with many of the symptoms of testosterone deficiency. Doctors would do a testosterone level check, find the patient had normal levels, and tell them the problem was not related to testosterone deficiency and must, therefore, be totally psychological.

I have heard many so-called medical experts say that there cannot be a hormonal basis for male menopause because testosterone levels fall only slightly up to the age of seventy. They often compare the change to a woman's, where there is a measurably precipitous drop in estrogen levels.

To understand why men can have symptoms of male menopause and still have normal levels of testosterone, we need to understand how testosterone works in the male body. The small but vital amounts of testosterone produced by the testes are immediately swept into the bloodstream and are mainly bound to a special carrier protein called sex hormone binding globulin (SHBG). The more SHBG there is, the less free, active, bio-available testosterone is able to get out of the blood into the cells to do its job.

The availability of the testosterone can be measured as the "free androgen index" (FAI), which is the total testosterone level in the blood divided by the SHBG level, then multiplied by one hundred. The result is usually between 70 and 100 percent. According to Dr. Carruthers' findings, it is when the FAI falls below 50 percent that symptoms of male menopause usually appear.[56]

The importance of measuring the free testosterone, a test many doctors still fail to make, was verified in Dr. Carruthers' research. "Only 13 percent showed abnormally low total testosterone levels in the blood, but...about 75 percent had a low free androgen index." About 70 percent also showed raised levels of the pituitary hormones which stimulate the testes, the LH and FSH, "which confirms that the level of testosterone activity is insufficient for the body's needs."[57]

Testosterone Plus Viagra: A Giant Leap For Mankind

Dr. Carruthers has found that using both testosterone and Viagra can be very helpful for men going through male menopause. "Viagra," he says, "treats one symptom of the male menopause, that of erectile dysfunction. The others of low sex drive, reduced mental and physical energy, irritability, and night sweats would go untreated by Viagra alone, but would be helped by adding testosterone."[58]

Any man considering testosterone replacement therapy or Viagra treatment should consult a physician trained in treating male menopause, have a complete physical and psychological examination to accurately diagnose the problem and rule out other causes, have a prostate exam including a PSA test, and be well-versed on the pros and cons of replacement therapy. The choice is not an easy one. For some time, women have been going through a similar process in deciding whether to take hormones as they age. Perhaps soon there will be "his and hers" menopause clinics with clinicians trained to assist men and women going through the menopause period of their life.

Though it is clear that testosterone levels, including the levels of free testosterone, fall as men age, there is an even more serious threat to men's virility and vitality—the increase of estrogen activity in men.

The Feminization of the World's Men: Why We Are Drowning in a Sea of Estrogens

Some men believe that the problems men are experiencing these days are the result of the rise of feminism and the women's movement. In this way of thinking, women's demands for equality have caused men to lose their old sense of power and with it their feelings of virility. I don't believe that has been the case. Despite a minor, but vocal, group of feminists who feel all the problems in the world are caused by men and masculinity, I believe the women's movement has been liberating for both men and women.

However, a very real loss of masculinity has resulted from biochemical assaults on a man's testosterone. Dr. Carruthers describes the problem this way: "As well as the decreasing amounts and activity of testosterone, the threat to male fertility and virility can be explained by increasing exposure to xeno-estrogens, chemicals in the environment, with actions similar to those of the female hormone estrogen."[59]

Just as testosterone is needed by women, estrogen is also needed by men, but in small amounts. Too much can be devastating. "Estrogens, though essential for the development of female characteristics, seem to work against the action of testosterone in the male. Derived from everything from plastics to pesticides, they are thought to have a harmful effect on fertility and the sexual development of male offspring, and to be even contributing to rising testicular and prostate cancer rates," Dr. Carruthers concludes.[60]

When Dustin Hoffman was told in the movie, *The Graduate*, "Plastics, my boy, plastics," little did he realize that he may have been hearing a warning to protect his future sex life. Some might say there is a poetic justice in the captains of industry creating products that destroy the testosterone levels of all the males on the planet.

But there is a threat even closer to home, the feminization of men by our own misguided practices. "In most middle-aged men, the ratio of testosterone to estrogen is significantly altered," says Eugene Shippen, M.D., a specialist in hormone replacement therapy. "In a young man, a ratio that might have been fifty to one is now twenty to one, or even seven or eight to one. Normal, age-related testosterone decline is partly responsible for these transformative ratios, but increases in estrogen are frequently even more significant."[61]

According to Shippen, alcohol use and obesity contribute to the increasing imbalance in testosterone/estrogen ratio as men get older. Large amounts of alcohol cause a significant rise in estrogen in both women and men. According to Dr. Shippen, a woman's estrogen level can triple after just one drink. "The rise in men is less dramatic but very significant nonetheless," he says.[62]

In addition, when men put on weight, more of their testosterone is converted to estrogen. "Whatever your sex," says Dr. Shippen, "plumpness will tend to estrogenize you."[63]

So listen guys, next time you have a thick steak with baked potato smothered in butter and sour cream and have a few cold ones to wash it all down, you may be giving away your manhood.

Androstenedione: An Alternative to Testosterone Replacement Therapy

Recently, a new dietary supplement has come of interest to those who want to stay strong and sexy as we age. Androstenedione is a metabolite of DHEA (the most abundant steroid in the human body) and a natural precursor of testosterone.[64] It was first synthesized in 1935, but has only recently been shown to be of importance in helping with mid-life changes in vitality and sexuality.

Ward Dean, M.D., has been actively engaged in gerontological research for over ten years, and has published more than fifty articles and reviews in professional journals. Dr. Dean is one of the experts in the clinical use of androstenedione. He quotes a German patent that says that 50 mg of oral androstenedione can raise plasma testosterone levels in men from 140 percent to 183 percent of normal.[65]

"Thus, we may now have arrived at a truly physiologic (natural) way to restore flagging testosterone levels in aging men to those of young, healthy adults," says Dean.[66]

One of the concerns many physicians have in offering testosterone replacement therapy is that it artificially raises the level of testosterone in a man's body and may adversely influence the natural production of testosterone that the man makes himself. Dr. Dean has found that this does not occur in taking supplemental androstenedione.

Proper levels of androstenedione "taken at bed-time, and perhaps again first thing in the morning will mimic the body's normal diurnal rhythms," says Dr. Dean. "Serum levels of testosterone start rising about fifteen minutes after oral administration and stay elevated for around three hours. Blood testosterone levels usually peak in around one to one and one-half hours after ingestion. Because the elevated testosterone levels swiftly return to normal baseline levels, there is little risk of negative feedback suppression of the hypothalamus, pituitary, or testicles."[67]

As I show later in the book, women also need to have a healthy level of testosterone for their general and sexual health (although much less than what men need). Dr. Dean feels that women going through menopause would also find this supplement helpful. He feels that androstenedione may positively affect bone density, thus reversing osteoporosis, and may also act as a "libido-enhancer" in women.[68]

Androstenedione has been garnering much attention lately, particularly with the revelation that baseball slugger Mark McGwire has used the supplement. To date, it remains legal in the U.S., and studies on its short- and long-term effects continue.

Depression: The Silent Killer of Men

Depression is one of the most common symptoms of male menopause and is closely related to the lowering of sexual desire and function that are also hallmarks of male menopause. A man whose sex life is on the rocks is likely to be depressed, and a man who is depressed is likely to have serious problems with his sex life.

Yet most men who suffer from depression aren't even aware that they have it. They often don't recognize themselves when they hear the classic symptoms of major depression such as persistent sad mood, recurrent thoughts of death, diminished ability to think or concentrate, feeling worthless, sleeping too much, low energy, loss of pleasure in life's activities, and significant weight loss or gain.

I believe too many men, particularly in the male menopause years, are suffering and dying from unrecognized depression. I find the following facts disturbing:

- Eighty percent of all suicides in the United States are men.[69]

- The rate of suicide for men forty-five to sixty-four is *three* times higher than the rate for women of the same age. For men over sixty-five, the rate is nearly *seven* times higher.[70]

• A large Swedish survey found a history of depression made the risk of suicide seventy-eight times greater than in those with no history of depression.[71]

• Demetri Papolos, M.D., and Janice Papolos call mood disorders the "common cold" of mind/body illnesses. More than twenty million Americans will suffer an episode of some form of depression at some point in their life.[72]

• Since the beginning of the twentieth century, each successive generation has become twice as likely to suffer from depression.[73]

• In a random sampling of thirty-nine thousand subjects from several countries, researchers recently found more suffering from depression—and at earlier ages—than ever before.[74]

• Sixty to 80 percent of people with depression never get professional help for the disease.[75]

• It can take up to ten years and three doctors for health professionals to make the correct diagnosis of depression.[76]

• Eighty to 90 percent of those seeking help can get relief from depression.[77]

• Men often think of depression as a "woman's ailment" and are reluctant to seek help even when they know they suffer from depression.

• Most men are not aware that they are depressed and so never have the opportunity to get help.

What is depression?

The *American Medical Association Encyclopedia of Medicine* defines depression as "feelings of sadness, hopelessness, pessimism, and a general loss of interest in life, combined with a sense of reduced emotional well-being."[78]

Depressed people have often been told to "just cheer up." But we know now that such an easy answer is not possible because depression is caused by a disruption in the chemistry of the brain. Only by restoring chemical balance can we truly hope to cure depression. We know that there is a strong in-born component to depression and that the susceptibility to depression runs in families.

Over the years I have been a therapist, I have found a real difference between the way women and men experience depression. For women the predominant feeling is sadness, but for men the predominant feeling is often *anger*. "Men often don't even recognize that they are depressed," says Theresa Crenshaw, M.D. "More often it masks itself as chronic anger, irritability, and hostility."[79]

Two kinds of depression

Just as there are two life forces in the natural world, the outer-directed *dynamic* and the inner-directed *magnetic*, I believe there are *dynamic depressions* which are expressed by "acting out" our inner turmoil and *magnetic depressions* which are expressed by "acting in" our pain. Men are more likely to experience dynamic depressions and women are more likely to experience magnetic depressions.

Women often express their depression by blaming themselves. Men often express their depression by blaming others—their wives, bosses, the economy, the government—anyone or anything *but* themselves. This was true in my own life. It was not until I recognized that my irritability, anger, and blame were manifestations of depression that I was finally able to ask for help and receive treatment.

"Girls, and later women, tend to internalize pain," says psychotherapist, Terrence Real. "They blame themselves and draw distress into themselves. Boys, and later men, tend to externalize pain; they are more likely to feel victimized by others and to discharge distress through action."[80]

Symptoms of magnetic depression	Symptoms of dynamic depression
1. Blame themselves for problems	Feel others are to blame for problems
2. Feel sad, apathetic, and worthless	Feel angry, irritable, and ego-inflated
3. Feel anxious and scared	Feel suspicious and guarded
4. Avoid conflict at all costs	Create and thrive on conflict
5. Always try to be nice to people	Overtly or covertly hostile to people
6. Withdraw when feeling hurt	Attack when feeling hurt
7. Have trouble respecting themselves	Demand that others give them respect
8. Feel they were born to fail	Feel the world was set up to fail them
9. Slowed down and nervous	Restless and agitated
10. Chronic procrastinator	Compulsive time keeper
11. Sleep too much	Sleep too little
12. Have trouble setting boundaries	Need control at all costs
13. Often feel guilty for what they do	Often feel ashamed for who they are
14. Uncomfortable receiving praise	Frustrated if not praised enough
15. Find it easy to talk about weaknesses and doubts	Terrified to talk about weaknesses and doubts
16. Strong fear of success	Strong fear of failure
17. Need to blend in to feel safe	Need to be "top dog" to feel safe
18. Use food, friends, and "love" to self-medicate	Use alcohol, T.V. sports, and sex to self-medicate
19. Believe their problems would be solved if only they could be a better _____ (spouse, co-worker, friend, parent)	Believe their problems would be solved if only their _____ (spouse, co-worker, friends, family) would treat them better
20. Constantly wonder, "Am I lovable enough?"	Constantly wonder, "Am I being loved enough?"

Many of us will find we have symptoms of both "magnetic" and "dynamic" depressions. Most will find that they have a tendency towards one or the other. Most men will find they lean towards dynamic depressions. Because we have focused more attention on magnetic or "sad" depressions, the dynamic or "angry" depressions have often gone untreated.

Depression is devastating to men as well as our families. Too many men suffer in silence because they don't know they have a treatable illness. The good news is that we need suffer no longer. At our clinic we use a combination of medications, cognitive restructuring therapy, meditation, exercise, diet, and perhaps most importantly, we teach men how to re-create the social supports that many of us have lost or never had. The best treatment for depression is recognizing that we are unique, important, and necessary in each others' lives.

New discoveries are being made all the time. We know that the new anti-depressant drugs that inhibit the reuptake of the neurotransmitter serotonin, such as Prozac and Zoloft, have had a major impact on treating depression. But we also have learned that there are many ways of changing our brain chemistry in addition to drugs. As Dr. Joel Robertson, author of *Natural Prozac: Learning to Release Your Body's Own Anti-Depressants* reminds us, "Our brain chemistry is altered by food, exercise, thoughts, emotions, and actions."[81]

A new substance which you will likely be hearing about is 5-hydroxytryptophan (5-HTP), a naturally occurring amino acid that not only helps with depression but also with anxiety, insomnia, weight problems, obsessive-compulsive disorder (OCD), premenstrual syndrome (PMS), and even migraines. The underlying problem with all these seemingly unrelated syndromes may be serotonin deficiency, which 5-HTP appears to help restore.[82]

"The general effect of both 5-HTP and [Prozac-like] drugs," say John Morgenthaler and Lane Lenard, authors of *5-HTP: The Natural Alternative to Prozac*, "is to increase the availability of serotonin at specific sites in the brain, known as 'serotonin receptors.'"[83]

"Although 5-HTP and Prozac-like drugs both tend to increase the availability of serotonin at serotonin receptors, they work in different ways," say Morgenthaler and Lenard. "The drugs act by interfering with a natural process—the reuptake or recycling of released serotonin molecules."[84]

"5-HTP raises serotonin levels by enhancing a natural process—the synthesis of new serotonin molecules. This difference in mechanism of action may be the primary reason why 5-HTP, at reasonable doses, produces far fewer side effects, including loss of libido," Morgenthaler and Lenard conclude.[85]

So which is best, the Prozac-like drugs or the natural alternative? I've found that each person is different. As with all the new substances, people need to evaluate choices. The *bad* news is that with so many choices, we can feel overwhelmed. The *good* news is that with so many choices, we need never give up hope of having a life free of anxiety, worry, and depression.

Sex and Life on the Second Mountain: Baby Boomers Want to Keep It Going Forever

When older men talk about their sex lives, they often complain about a loss of desire or their *ability* to develop and maintain erections. When women complain about their sex lives they often say there is a lack of *opportunity*.

Maggie Kuhn, feisty founder of the Gray Panthers, got a rise out a women's conference in Washington, D.C., when she wondered aloud who women were going to have sex with into their eighties and nineties, with so many men their age dead: ten widows for every widower. Well, now we know men, as well as women, can live longer and healthier lives. And with a new emphasis on what I call "Sex on the Second Mountain," men and women can enjoy an active sex life into their seventies, eighties, nineties, and beyond.

At fifty, our parents often felt that their sexual lives, if not over, were not that important. Boomers today, as the Viagra story has shown, are just beginning to develop new aspects of their sex and love lives. In fact, there seems to be a strong relationship between a long and healthy *life* and a healthy *sex life*, though studies have been few and far between.

A Duke University study on aging in the 1970s found a correlation between the *frequency* of sexual intercourse and lower death rates in men. For women, the *enjoyment* of intercourse was correlated with longer life.[86]

Other similar studies of the era came to similar conclusions. Today, these types of studies are being undertaken with new vigor.

A new study published in the *British Medical Journal* suggests that men who have frequent sex are less likely to die at an early age. In a long-term study, the authors studied the health of nearly one thousand men aged forty-five to fifty-nine. The men were asked about the frequency of sexual intercourse. After studying the men, and their frequency of intercourse, over a period of ten years the findings were impressive:

The risk of death in men who had sex twice or more a week was half that of men who had sex less than once a month.[87]

With all the recent studies and advancement, it is joked that you will eventually get the following prescription from your doctor on your one hundredth birthday (and of course on all your birthdays previously):

1. Eat a low fat diet every day.
2. Exercise three times per week.
3. Anti-oxidant vitamins and minerals once per day.
4. Sexual intercourse, at least twice a week.

Healthy sex and a healthy prostate go hand in hand and both are enhanced by a low fat, fruit-and-vegetable-rich diet. Researchers from Harvard Medical School and Harvard School of Public Health evaluated over fifty-one thousand men over a four-year period. They found that the men who ate the most fat were nearly twice as likely to develop prostate cancer as the men who ate the least.

But the publication *Harvard Men's Health Watch* summarized that "animal fat was linked to the disease, but vegetable fat was not. Red meat was the chief culprit; men who ate the most beef, bacon, pork, and lamb were 2.6 times more likely to develop prostate cancer than men who ate the least."[88]

So, listen guys, let's cut down on the meat, keep our prostates healthy, our sex lives active, and our attitudes positive.

Our parents never dreamed they would be enjoying sex in the second half of life, and most didn't believe they would live long either. I remember my mother telling me at my college graduation that she thought she'd be dead by the time I graduated high school (I was born when she was thirty-seven). She couldn't imagine living past sixty.

New research in longevity and vitality medicine may soon extend our healthy lifespan beyond anything we can now imagine. After reviewing the latest research findings, Marvin Cetron and Owen Davies, experts on the new science of aging, conclude:

The most profound transformation in history, the most fundamental change that humanity ever will experience, is as near as next week. It may already have begun. From this decade onward, the years of our lives will not be threescore and ten, but far longer. The Baby Boom generation, and perhaps its parents, can expect to live healthy, active lives that stretch to between 110 and 120 years. It is even possible that some of us may never die, save by accident or choice. Medicine, government, economics, religion—no single facet of human existence will remain the same.[89]

I describe male menopause as the transition between the first half of life and the second. With new research findings helping us understand why we die, we may be able to affect life and death itself. Male menopause may not be the beginning of the end, as many fear, but merely the end of the first act and the beginning of many more to come, each one more interesting and challenging than the one before.

News from the Front-Line: What People Are Saying About Male Menopause Treatment

Jeremy, a good looking forty-five-year-old Vietnam vet, had been coming to our center for the past six months to treat symptoms of male menopause. When he first came to see us, he had multiple problems. "My life, just seems to have gone off track," he told me with real worry in his voice. "I've been drinking too much and I'm getting a paunch. I feel tired all the time and I can't seem to get up the energy to force myself out of this rut." As we talked more, it was evident that he was depressed, but it was expressed more outwardly than inwardly. "I'm pissed at the damn system. I served my country and I deserve the aid that I'm getting, but they treat me like I was some kind of thief. Life sucks!" He said his sex life was non-existent. "I'm interested, but there aren't any women in this town that I'd even go out with. All the good women are married." When I asked him why he didn't make the half hour drive to the next town, he sighed and said, "I don't know. It just seems like too much trouble."

After a complete physical and mental examination, we determined that his basic health was good. His total and free testosterone were within normal limits. We initially worked on getting him off of alcohol and helped him change his diet. He began to feel better physically and his self-esteem improved. When he began running on his lunch hour he said he felt even better. He felt stuck in a dead-end job and we worked with him to re-train for a new career.

The key for Jeremy was when he joined the men's health group and was able to establish new relationships with men: "I realized since coming back from 'Nam, I haven't been able to trust a man. Over there, every man that I trusted ended up dead." Even men who had never been in the service could identify with the isolation and anger that Jeremy was feeling. Getting support from other men gave him the courage to begin dating again.

He confided his fears about seeing Jennifer, a woman he had grown close to, and had come to like a lot. "Our relationship has gotten sexual," Jeremy said in the group, obviously pleased, but shy about talking so intimately. "You know, its wonderful, but...pretty often I lose...you know, I lose my erection before being able to complete having sex."

I suggested he try Viagra the next time he and Jenny were planning to be sexual and the group was excited to hear him report back the results of their experience with the little blue pill.

When Jeremy arrived for the group, he had a smile that he was having trouble controlling. "So, tell, tell, tell!" Jim another member with a similar problem blurted out before everyone could get seated. "Does it work?"

"It didn't make me feel like a twenty-year-old again, but, yes, it works," Jeremy said with a chuckle. He went on to describe the evening. "After a nice dinner together, I took the pill, after Jenny blessed it with a kiss. They said it would take about an hour to begin working. We were both a little nervous so Jenny decided to run down to the store to get some ice-cream."

"I gave her a hug and a long kiss as she was leaving, and Oh, Boy, I felt things starting to happen. She could feel it too. She laughed and gave me a sexy, mischievous look. 'I better hurry back,' she said, and flew out the door."

"How long had it been since you took the pill?" Jim wanted to know.

"It had only been about thirty or forty minutes. It kind of surprised me. The feeling was wonderfully natural. I didn't end up with an instant woody, but when she got back, touching and playing brought all the feelings back and the love-making was great. Even the sensations of pleasure seemed better than before. I not only lasted through to the end, but we made love again, a half-hour later."

Jim jumped up and started to leave the group. "Where are you headed?" I asked.

"I'm going to get me a subscription, I mean a prescription." Everyone laughed.

"I'm coming with you," said George, another group member.

"You don't have erectile problems," I reminded him. George, a good-looking man in his fifties, was happily married and had talked about how his sex life had improved since being treated for depression. "I don't care," he said, "I want some, just in case. Our sex life is great, but maybe it could be even better."

"Well, don't run off too fast," Tony jumped in. "I had the same idea. I wasn't having erection problems, but thought I'd try it. I bought one pill from my buddy and Judy and I gave it a try. For me, our love-making didn't feel any different on Viagra than it did before. The only difference was that I had a splitting headache in the morning."

"I've always believed that you don't put oil in your car without checking the dipstick to see if you are low, and you don't add oil if its already full," I reminded the group. "It's going to be an interesting time as men and women expand their options for staying healthy and sexually active in the second half of life," I concluded. "Amen," Jeremy intoned. The group ended with cheers, slaps on the back, and "see you next week."

Feedback from around the Country and around the World

Most people don't live close enough to come to our clinic for treatment, but many have sent letters telling us about the benefits of putting the information in the book into action.

"I just read your book *Male Menopause* and would like to thank you for writing about a subject no one seems to know anything about. I have been looking everywhere for a book on male menopause and recently found your book in my local bookstore. I held on to your book so tightly, not wanting to let go, my emotions confused, but needing answers so much. Not just any answers, the right answers no matter how much it hurt. I needed to know."

This was the beginning of a letter from a mid-life woman, one of hundreds I have received since *Male Menopause* was first published.

She goes on to describe what she and her family have been going through. "Last month my husband of twenty-eight years left me for another woman much younger than I. He was fifty and I was forty-six. He told me he had found someone else who was more fun and wanted to do all the things he wanted and liked to do. He was very cruel and spared no one, not even our four grown children or five grandchildren. Our family fell apart. He walked away from a business he had started several years ago and totally cut off all communications with anyone in the family.

"I only wish I could have found out about your book sooner, or had learned anything that would have brought to my attention what my husband was going through and about to destroy. You see, for the past two years he has had all the symptoms mentioned in your book. He became more and more irritable, self-centered, and easily fatigued. He complained about being so lonely even though I was always there for him."

But this woman, like so many others, did not know the warning signs and didn't recognize her husband was going through male menopause until it was too late. "It was over, that fast," she continues. "We are now divorced. I have been through so much heartbreak and pain, at times I never thought I'd get through it. Who is this man that I married and loved for so many years? No one knows him anymore, not even his own children. Unfortunately, he has two sons that are described perfectly in your book. The one who was shamed and turned to drugs and the other who doesn't think he's worth anything because he spent his whole life trying to make his dad happy.

"We will pick up the pieces and become a family again. 'If I had only known.' That's what I keep telling myself. What makes a man throw away his whole life, all he's worked for and nurtured for a chance at being an adolescent again? Male menopause."

Although devastated by the loss, this woman finds strength to carry on. "I will treasure your book like a woman's bible for getting through the next passage in life, with or without him."

Reading these letters, I am saddened that it has taken us so long to recognize that men *do* go through a male menopause, that it can be treated, and that families do not have to look forward to stagnation or disintegration as men and women move into this stage of life.

The good news is that I have been getting an increasing number of letters like the following: "I want to thank you for helping me to save my marriage. After twenty-eight years of marriage, my husband said, 'I don't love you anymore,' 'Life is passing me by,' 'The children don't need me, now that they're grown,' and other such phrases.

"Sound familiar? He behaved exactly like the men you describe. Fortunately for me, he agreed to read your book. He truly related to what you talked about. He was able to overcome his reluctance to seeing a doctor and was able to find one who understood male menopause. He changed his diet, began an exercise program that he said makes him feel strong and vital again, and, following your directions, is taking an anti-oxidant vitamin and mineral formula. He also had his hormone levels checked and found that his testosterone level was low. He has started using a testosterone patch and says it has restored his vital energy. I can say that it has certainly helped our sex life. He seems more alive, more vibrant than I have seen him in years. Thank you."

Though most of the feedback has been from men and women in their mid-thirties and older, a significant number of younger men and women have responded. The following letter shows that men and women of all ages want to understand the changes they will go through as they reach mid-life.

"I just finished reading *Male Menopause*," wrote one younger respondent, "and I must say it was incredible. I am a wife and mother, and although I am twenty-one and my husband is twenty-three, I felt this book calling my name.

"I have loved my husband wholeheartedly, and earnestly longed to learn more about him, his health, and what role I will play later in life. As I have read this book, I have discussed what I've learned with my husband. Even though I didn't think it was possible, we have become so much closer. We have agreed to welcome the 'menopause passage,' and embrace the fantastic changes of our lives.

"You have helped someone understand that you can conquer 'Second Adulthood,' and survive. If [age] thirty is as good as you say it is, then over forty must kick ass!"

Men, too, have found the plan we offer in the book to be of help. I have received letters from men from all over the world. A forty-eight-year-old man from Venezuela had this to say: "I enjoyed your book immensely along with some friends and acquaintances who are also undergoing this not-so-easy phase of life. Your book definitely clarifies many misconceptions and myths about the aging process that, unfortunately, everybody must undergo and accept (like it or not) as part of his/her natural development. I particularly liked the resource section that has allowed me to follow-up on information you discussed in your book."

Another man felt he was able to deal with changes he had not understood before.

"I have re-read your book a number of times and wish to thank you! It was just what I needed. I am a fifty-six-year-old gay man in a ten-year monogamous relationship and have been in crisis because I felt so helpless until I read your book. My belly was expanding, my energy was declining, my libido and potency were disappearing.

"I felt terrified and didn't know what to do. I was ashamed to talk about it with my partner and tried to cover over the feelings by working long hours and withdrawing when I got home. Your book had the answers I needed."

The Medical Community Comes to Understand Male Menopause

When I began the research for the book over five years ago, many physicians I talked with were quite skeptical about the concept of male menopause. The responses I received since publication have convinced me that the medical community is recognizing the reality of male menopause and many are ready to make this information available to people throughout the world.

Just one example of the countless responses I have received from doctors across the world is from Stephen B. Strum, M.D., co-director of Healing Touch Oncology, who specializes in treating men with prostate problems. "In the years that I have been going through male menopause and at the same time treating men with prostate cancer with drugs that exaggerate and amplify symptoms and signs of male menopause, it has become shatteringly clear to me that men are solitary creatures that do not share or perhaps are not aware of their bio-psychologic changes," he says.

"It is my belief that changes in DHEA, testosterone, melatonin, and other hormones underlie many of the symptoms we see in male menopause and that the future will find us establishing endocrine profiles to allow us to start replacement hormone therapy early and delay these biologic changes."

Although there are still those who believe that male menopause does not exist, I believe more and more medical professionals will recognize this emerging field of medicine. Until then, as one of the letter writers reminds us, "All I have to do is educate my doctor."

Let Us Hear from You

Letters have been heartening. I am busy at work on another book about male menopause. I would very much like to hear your experiences of what has worked for you, what hasn't worked, and what information you'd like to know more about. If you are a health care professional that works with male menopause, let us know. I am continually being asked for referrals.

Send letters to: Jed Diamond
Third Age Wellness Center
34133 Shimmins Ridge Rd.
Willits, CA 95490

or e-mail me: jedd1221@aol.com

Notes for Introduction to the Paperback Edition

1. Bruce Handy, "The Viagra Craze," *Time* (4 May 1998), 50.

2. Steven Lamm, M.D., *The Virility Solution* (New York: Simon & Schuster, 1998), 65–66.

3. Ibid., 78–79.

4. Personal conversation with Dr. Auerbach, 28 April 1998.

5. Steven Lamm, *Virility Solution*, 79.

6. Ibid., 67.

7. Information received from Pfizer company, 16 May 1998.

8. Steven Lamm, *Virility Solution*, 67.

9. Information received from Pfizer company, 16 May 1998.

10. Ibid.

11. Ibid.

12. Ibid.

13. Steven Lamm, *Virility Solution*, 135.

14. Gina Kolata, "Drugs That Deliver More Than Promised," *New York Times* (5 April 1998).

15. Ibid.

16. John Morgenthaler and Dan Joy, *Better Sex Through Chemistry* (Petaluma, CA: Smart Publications, 1995), 33.

17. Ibid.

18. Ibid., 31–32.

19. Andrew Weil, *Ask Dr. Weil: Vitamins and Minerals* (New York: Ivy Books, 1997), 40.

20. Louise Ann Gittleman, *Super Nutrition for Men* (New York: M. Evans 1996), 106.

21. Personal discussion with John Morgenthaler, 19 May 1998.

22. Steven Lamm, *Virility Solution*, 70.

23. Ibid., 78.

24. Ibid., 80–81.

25. Larry Katzenstein, *Viagra: The Potency Promise* (New York: St. Martin's Press, 1998), 128.

26. Reported by Third Age Media, 6 May 1998.

27. Personal conversation with Dr. Auerbach, 28 April 1998.

28. Maggie Fox, Reuters News Service, 28 April 1998.

29. Personal conversation with Dr. Auerbach, 28 April 1998.

30. Jenifer Joseph, ABCNews.com, 29 April 1998.

31. Ibid.

32. Susan C. Vaughan, M.D., *Viagra: A Guide to the Phenomenal Potency Promoting Drug* (New York: Pocket Books, 1998), 205.

33. Alex Kuczynski, "Curious Women Are Seeing if Viagra Works Wonders for Them," *New York Times* (16 May 1998).

34. Personal conversation, 13 May 1998.

35. Reported in Third Age Media, Thirdagemedia.com, 13 March 1998.

36. Ibid.

37. Ibid.

38. Ibid.

39. E-mail from Dr. Carruthers, 2 May 1998.

40. Dr. Malcolm Carruthers, *Maximising Manhood: Beating the Male Menopause* (London: HarperCollins, 1997), 42–43.

41. Ibid., 46–49.

42. Ibid., 49.

43. Ibid., 51.

44. Ibid., 51–53.

45. Ibid., 54–57.

46. Ibid., 58–61.

47. Ibid., 106-116.

48. Ibid., 130.

49. Ibid., 149-52.

50. Ibid., 151.

51. Ibid., 151–52.

52. Ibid., 156.

53. F. H. Schroder, "Androgens and carcinoma of the prostate," in *Testosterone: Action, deficiency, substitution*, eds. E. Nieschlag, H. M. Behre (Heidelberg: Springer Verlag, 1990), 245-60.

54. Theresa Crenshaw, M.D., *The Alchemy of Love and Lust* (New York: G.P. Putnam's Sons), 241.

55. Dr. Malcolm Carruthers, *Maximising Manhood*, 148.

56. Ibid., 88.

57. Ibid., 90.

58. Personal discussion with Dr. Carruthers, 13 May 1998.

59. Ibid., 91.

60. Ibid.

61. Eugene Shippen, M.D., and William Fryer, *The Testosterone Syndrome* (New York: M. Evans and Company, 1998), 48.

62. Ibid., 51.

63. Ibid.

64. Ward Dean, M.D., *Vitamin Research Update*, 1 February 1998, 1.

65. Ibid., 3.

66. Ibid.

67. Ibid.

68. Ibid.

69. Robert Ivker, M.D., and Edward Zorensky, *Thriving*, (New York: Crown Publishers, 1997), 13.

70. United States Department of Statistics of the United States, National Center for Health Statistics, *Vital Statistics of the United States*, Table 8-5.

71. Peter C. Whybrow, M.D., *A Mood Apart* (New York: HarperCollins, 1997), 61.

72. Demitri Papolos, M.D., and Janice Papolos, *Overcoming Depression* (New York: HarperCollins, 1997), 3.

73. Terrence Real, *I Don't Want to Talk About It* (New York: Scribner, 1997), 34.

74. Ibid., 34

75. Ibid., 23.

76. Peter C. Whybrow, *A Mood Apart*, 7.

77. Ibid., 23.

78. Joel Robertson, *Natural Prozac* (San Francisco: HarperSanFrancisco, 1997), 10.

79. Theresa Crenshaw, M.D., *The Alchemy of Love and Lust*, 239.

80. Terrence Real, *I Don't Want to Talk about It*, 24.

81. Joel Robertson, *Natural Prozac*, 3-4.

82. *Life Enhancement News* (December 1996), 1.

83. John Morgenthaler, *Smart Publications Update*, (18 May 1998), 15.

84. Ibid.

85. Ibid.

86. *Mind/Body Health Newsletter* VII, no. 1 (1998): 1.

87. Ibid.

88. *Harvard Men's Health Watch* 2, no. 10 (May 1988): 1.

89. Marvin Cetron and Owen Davies, *Cheating Death* (New York: St. Martin's Press, 1998), 5.

Hot Flash

Facts and Figures on Male Menopause

What Is Male Menopause?

Male menopause (also called viropause or andropause) begins with hormonal, physiological, and chemical changes that occur in all men generally between the ages of forty and fifty-five, though it can occur as early as thirty-five or as late as sixty-five. These changes affect all aspects of a man's life. Male menopause is, thus, a physical condition with psychological, interpersonal, social, and spiritual dimensions.

The purpose of male menopause is to signal the end of the first part of a man's life and prepare him for the second half. Male menopause is not the beginning of the end, as many fear, but the end of the beginning. It is the passage to the most passionate, powerful, productive, and purposeful time of a man's life.

More information in chapters 1 and 2.

How Many Men Are Going through the Male Menopause Passage?

In the United States, there are 25,172,000 men between the ages of forty and fifty-five who are now going through the Male Menopause Passage.[1]

In less than twenty-five years, by 2020, the number of men in the United States going through the Male Menopause Passage will grow to approximately 57,500,000.[2]

Worldwide, there are approximately 408 million men between the ages of forty and fifty-five who are going through the Male Menopause Passage.[3]

By the year 2020 the worldwide number will grow to approximately 690 million men.[4]

The seventy-six million baby boomers in the United States born between 1946 and 1964 are changing the way everyone views midlife and aging. They are the first to recognize the importance of male menopause.

Baby boomers and their children now comprise about 50 percent of the United States population. They control an estimated 55 percent of consumer spending, head roughly 44 percent of the households, and make up most of the electorate. Better educated than any previous generation, they are the first to understand the importance of the mind/body connection in moving through the Menopause Passage.[5]

More information in chapters 1 and 3.

What Do Other Experts Think about the Idea of Male Menopause?

An increasing number of experts, both male and female, believe that male menopause is a significant life transition for men.

Dr. Ronald Klatz, president of the American Academy of Anti-Aging Medicine says, "One of the best-kept secrets is that men go through a male form of menopause called andropause."[6]

Marc Blackman, M.D., chief of endocrinology and metabolism at Johns Hopkins Bayview Medical Center says, "The male menopause is a real phenomenon and it does similar things to men as menopause does to women, although less commonly and to a lesser extent."[7]

Theresa Crenshaw, M.D., author of *The Alchemy of Love and Lust* says, "In the case of male menopause, we are still in the Dark Ages. Men have fewer guideposts to help them today than women had a generation ago. Only recently have we begun to understand the biochemistry of these events, tilting the scales toward a physiological explanation."[8]

Aubrey M. Hill, M.D., author of *Viropause/Andropause* says, "My experience has now convinced me that most men undergo what could be called male menopause and that many men suffer acutely and needlessly."[9]

More information in chapters 4, 5, 6, and 8.

What Are the Symptoms of Male Menopause?

The most common physical symptoms of male menopause include:

- Taking longer to recover from injuries and illness
- Less endurance for physical activity
- Feeling fat or gaining weight
- Difficulty reading small print
- Forgetfulness or memory loss
- Loss or thinning of hair

The most common psychological symptoms of male menopause include:

- Irritability
- Indecisiveness
- Anxiety and fear
- Depression
- Loss of self-confidence and joy
- Loss of purpose and direction in life
- Feeling lonely, unattractive, and unloved
- Forgetfulness and difficulty concentrating

The most common sexual symptoms of male menopause include:

- Reduced interest in sex
- Increased anxiety and fear about sexual changes
- Increased fantasies about having sex with others
- Increased relationship problems and fights over sex, love, and intimacy
- Loss of erection during sexual activity

More information in chapters 2, 4, 5, 6, and 8.

Is Impotence a Problem for Men Going through Male Menopause?

Impotence is defined as the persistent inability to attain and maintain an erection adequate to permit satisfactory sexual performance.

According to results from the *Massachusetts Male Aging Study* that studied a large sample of men between the ages of forty and seventy, the combined prevalence of minimal, moderate, and complete impotence was 52 percent.[10]

Although the study found that psychological factors play a role as men age, physical factors are more significant.

There was a high correlation between erection dysfunction and heart disease, hypertension, diabetes, as well as with the medications that are often taken to deal with these problems.

Since the physical, psychological, and sexual aspects are interconnected, most all these symptoms can be prevented and treated by concentrating on the whole man.

More information in chapters 4, 5, and 8.

What Sexual Changes Can Men Expect as They Move through the Menopause Passage?

Seven sexual changes that occur in healthy, normal males as they age include the following:

- Erections take longer to occur.
- A man more often requires direct physical stimulation to get an erection; a sexy sight or fantasy may not arouse him as it did before.
- The full erection doesn't get quite as firm as it used to.
- His urge to ejaculate is not as insistent as before. Sometimes he doesn't feel like having an orgasm at all.
- The force of ejaculation isn't as strong as it was in the past. The amount of his ejaculate is less, and he may have fewer sperm.
- The desire for and frequency of masturbation may drop, but in some men it may increase.
- The testicles shrink some, and the scrotal sack droops. The sack doesn't bunch up as much during arousal.[11]

More information in chapters 5, 6, 7, and 8.

What Are the Effects of Hormonal Changes on Men Going through Male Menopause?

Lowered levels of hormones at midlife are central to the changes associated with male menopause. Recent research indicates that lowered levels of the following hormones may decrease sex drive, increase depression and weight gain, and contribute to a general decrease in well-being and health: dopamine, oxytocin, vasopressin, growth hormone, melatonin, DHEA, pregnenolone, thyroid hormone, and testosterone.[12]

Although these hormones tend to decrease with age, each man is unique and individual levels vary widely.

In one study, for instance, the average level of testosterone for men in their fifties was 600 ng/100 ml. However, individual levels ranged from 200 ng/100 ml. to 1,000 ng/100 ml.[13]

Some researchers now believe that giving men replacement hormones may allow them to remain vital and healthy into their sixties, seventies, eighties, nineties, and beyond.[14]

Since significant research on hormone replacement therapy for men is new, men should be cautious about taking hormones and should only do so under supervision of a physician trained in this medical speciality.

Men, like women, experience complex hormonal rhythms that affect their sexuality, mood, and temperament. For instance, researchers have found five different testosterone cycles in men:

- Rhythmic fluctuations three to four times an hour.
- Daily changes with testosterone higher in the morning and lower in the afternoon.
- Monthly fluctuations that are rhythmic, but different for each man.
- Fluctuations throughout the year with levels higher in October and lower in April.

- Decreasing hormone levels associated with the Male Menopause Passage.[15]

Men have physical and emotional reactions to hormonal fluctuations throughout the month, similar to PMS in women.

In a recent study, when men were given the same checklists of symptoms from a typical PMS questionnaire—omitting the female specific symptoms, such as breast tenderness—men reported having as many premenstrual type symptoms (reduced or increased energy, irritability, and other negative moods, back pain, sleeplessness, headaches, confusion, etc.) as women do—when the symptoms aren't called PMS.[16]

"The morning highs, daily fluctuations, and seasonal cycles whip men around," says Dr. Crenshaw. "Think about the moment-to-moment impact of testosterone levels firing and spiking all over the place during the day, and what this must be doing to a man's temperament."[17]

More information in chapters 4, 5, 6, and 8.

What Serious Health Problems Are Uniquely Associated with Men Going through Male Menopause?

Though we enjoy one of the highest standards of living in the world, American men rank only fifteenth in the world in longevity.[18]

Eighty percent of all suicides in the United States are men.[19]

The rate of suicide for men forty-five to sixty-four is three times higher than the rate for women of the same age. For men over sixty-five the rate is nearly seven times higher.[20]

The prostate gland is the most frequently diseased organ of the human body, and all men are susceptible to contracting the three major diseases of the prostate: prostatitis, benign prostatic hyperplasia (BPH), also called enlarged prostate, and prostate cancer. According to Bradley R. Hennenfent, M.D., one of the leading authorities on prostate problems, "A man's odds of getting one of these three diseases approaches 100 percent."[21]

Prostate cancer afflicts one out of nine men and kills forty thousand each year. The death rate for this most common cancer in men has grown at almost twice the death rate of breast cancer in the last five years.[22]

More information in chapters 2, 4, 5, and 8.

How Does Male Menopause Relate to the Need for Male Mentoring?

The Male Menopause Passage is a time when men can commit to becoming mentors to young men and reverse the destructive patterns that are destroying our youth and ravaging our society.

For the first time in history, more teenagers are dying from gunshots than by natural causes.[23]

Fourteen children a day are killed by other children, and one hundred children a day are wounded by other children in this country.[24]

When a man denies this period of his life, or is unable to negotiate the transition effectively, he never really grows up. When a whole society denies this stage of life or is unable to master it, we create a world dominated by "Monster Boy Masculinity."[25]

Without a successful completion of the Male Menopause Passage with men moving into the role of elders, we become a society of siblings, says author Robert Bly. "In a Sibling Society adults regress toward adolescence," says Bly "and adolescents—seeing that—have no desire to become adults."[26]

Without men who have successfully completed the Male Menopause Passage and become true elders, fathers will not have the support necessary to return to responsible parenthood. Without the active involvement of fathers in our society, children will continue to feel lost and increasingly ashamed to be part of the human race.

"In the absence of elders," says author Malidoma Patrice Somé, "the impetuosity of youth becomes the slow death of the community."[27]

More information in chapters 3, 7, and 10.

What Can a Man Do to Successfully Complete the Male Menopause Passage?

1. Eat right. The traditional Asian diet, with its foundation of rice or other grains, an abundance of vegetables, fruits, beans, tofu, and legumes, a limited amount of meat and other animal foods, and virtually no dairy products, is a good foundation for healthy eating.[28]

2. Stay physically fit. Engage in regular exercise that includes the following components: cardiorespiratory (aerobic) endurance, muscular strength, and flexibility.[29] "In my twenty-five years as a health care practitioner," says Robert Ivker, M.D., "I have found nothing that contributes more to optimal health than regular exercise."[30]

3. Take vitamins and supplements for health. Andrew Weil, M.D., recommends the following anti-oxidant formula:
- 10,000 international units (IU) of mixed carotenoids (including lycopene)
- Vitamin E (800 IU)
- Selenium (200 mcg)
- Vitamin C (2,000 mg two or three times a day)
- Zinc (30 mg a day)
- Coenzyme Q (80 mg a day)[31]

4. Take herbs to balance the system and protect the prostate. "While a male's menopause is not as hormone altering as the female's," says herbalist James Green, "it can call for similar herbs to facilitate rebalance during these changes in life. A combination of herbs for a man experiencing male menopause will do well to include:

- Wild Yam for hormone building assistance
- Black Cohosh for a relaxant and normalizer
- Damiana as a prostate tonic, anti-depressant, and nutrient for sluggish sexual organs
- St. John's Wort and Oat for nerve tonics to help deal with any depression and other stress due to the changes
- Saw Palmetto for the prostate and reproductive system."[32]

5. Get regular health checkups. Regular health care visits and screenings are important contributors to men's health and longevity, yet according to Kenneth Goldberg, M.D., men make 130 million fewer doctor visits a year than women.[33] Find health practitioners you trust, and see them regularly.

6. Check hormone levels as you get older. Generally between forty and fifty-five a number of important hormones in a man's body begin to decline.[34] A number of researchers believe that by replacing hormones such as DHEA, pregnenolone, testosterone, thyroid hormone, human growth hormone, and melatonin, men can stay healthier and live longer.[35] Research findings are just now becoming available, and there is still controversy about hormone replacement. Explore the pros and cons with a health care provider who specializes in this area of medicine.

7. Reduce stress and worry in your life. Stress is a major source of trouble for men at midlife. Ways to reduce stress and worry include: living life in the present, letting go of control, dealing with negative emotions, and learning to prepare for what is expected, as well as for what is unexpected.[36]

8. Embrace a sexuality appropriate to the second half of life. In the first half of life, men are often focused on a kind of sexuality that is based on immediate attraction to people who are young, attractive, and "sexy." In the second half of life, our sexuality expands to include more emphasis on friendship, love, intimacy, and spirituality.

9. Become initiated into elderhood. Ideally, all boys between eleven and fourteen would undergo an initiation during early adolescence that would prepare them for the journey into manhood. All men need an initiation as they move into midlife, which prepares them for the journey into elderhood. Programs like those offered by New Warriors and the Sterling Institute of Relationship provide an excellent foundation for adult initiations.[37]

10. Join a men's group. In traditional societies throughout the world, boys were initiated into manhood with their peers and formed life-long support groups with those men. Men today need that kind of ongoing support, particularly as they move through the Male Menopause Passage.

11. Explore and engage your life-work or calling. Most men seek careers in the first half of their lives, often out of the necessity to make money and support their families. In the second half of life, the desire to pursue their life-work or calling pulls men in a new direction. Our calling comes from the deepest part of who we are, what we love, the core of our spirit, and the need of our community. Finding and engaging your calling will make the second half of your life meaningful and joyful.

12. Become a mentor to young men. In the first half of life, men often move out in the world and find that their self-esteem and value rests on their ability to be successful doers. In the second half of life, their developing life-work often involves giving back to the community. One of the primary community roles that elder males must engage if they are to be successful is to be mentors to young men. Without elder males committed to the well-being of younger males, the society falls apart.

More information in all chapters.

What Can Women Do to Help Their Men?

Recognize that male menopause is real.

Understand that male menopause is more than a "midlife crisis" and involves real hormonal and physiological changes in a man's body.

The physical changes of male menopause interact with personal, interpersonal, family, career, and other life changes to affect how a man feels about himself and others. Encourage him to share his feelings, even when his feelings make you uncomfortable.

A man often feels a loss of power, purpose, passion, and potency during this time of life and sometimes feels it is the beginning of the end for him. Let him know you love and appreciate him just the way he is and trust that he will come through this period of life stronger and more compassionate.

Rather than the beginning of the end, male menopause is actually the end of the beginning—a preparation time for the second half of life. Take joy in your own midlife changes and encourage him to do the same.

The most fearful change for a man involves his sexuality. Many feel they are losing the very basis of their manhood. Let him know you will stand by him and help him talk about his fears and desires. Men need to know that sexual change is not the same as sexual dysfunction. If there are problems that persist, don't be ashamed. Talk to an expert. Get help together.

Although there are differences between male and female menopause, there is much that is the same. Learn to talk together and support each other.

A man needs a woman who can take his changes seriously, not ridicule or make fun of him, and support him to become the man he has always wanted to be. He also needs a woman who can recognize when he needs support that a woman cannot give.

A man needs support from other men so that he knows he is not alone and that other men are going through similar changes. A woman can help by encouraging and supporting the man to join a men's group and be part of a community of men.

More information in chapters 2, 6, 9, and 10.

Hot Flash Notes

1. Bureau of the Census, *Statistical Abstract, 1996* (Washington, D.C., 1996), 16.

2. Ibid., 17.

3. Bureau of Census, Dept. WP/94, World Population Profile (Washington, D.C., 1994), 16.

4. Ibid., 16.

5. Gary R. Collins and Timothy E. Clinton, *Baby Boomer Blues* (Dallas: Word Publishing, 1992), 4.

6. Ronald Klatz and Carol Kahn, *Grow Young with HGH: The Amazing Medically Proven Plan to Reverse Aging* (New York: HarperCollins, 1997), 123.

7. Quoted in Klatz and Kahn, 123.

8. Theresa Crenshaw, M.D., *The Alchemy of Love and Lust: Discovering Our Sex Hormones and How They Determine Who We Love, When We Love, and How Often We Love* (New York: G. P. Putnam's Sons, 1996), 210.

9. Aubrey M. Hill, *Viropause/Andropause: The Male Menopause: Emotional and Physical Changes Mid-Life Men Experience* (Far Hills, NJ: New Horizon Press, 1993), xiv.

10. Henry A. Feldman, et al., "Impotence and Its Medical and Psychosocial Correlates: Results of the Massachusetts Male Aging Study," *Journal of Urology* 151 January 1994: 54–61.

11. Crenshaw, 218.

12. See Crenshaw, *The Alchemy of Love and Lust* and William Regelson, M.D., and Carol Colman, *The Super-Hormone Promise.*

13. Winnifred Cutler, Ph.D., *Love Cycles: The Science of Intimacy* (New York: Villard Books, 1991), 89.

14. See Crenshaw, *The Alchemy of Love and Lust,* and Regelson and Colman, *The Super-Hormone Promise.*

15. Cutler, 87–109.

16. Carol Tavris, *Mismeasure of Woman: Why Women Are Not the Better Sex, the Inferior Sex or the Opposite Sex* (New York: Simon and Schuster, 1992), 148.

17. Crenshaw, 10.

18. Robert Ivker, M.D., and Edward Zorensky, *Thriving: The Complete Mind/Body Guide for Optimal Health and Fitness for Men* (New York: Crown Publishers, 1997), 12.

19. Ibid., 13.

20. United States Department of Statistics of the United States, National Center for Health Statistics, *Vital Statistics of the United States*, Table 8–5.

21. Bradley R. Hennenfent, M.D., *The Prostatitis Syndromes* (Bloomington, IL: The Prostatitis Foundation), 2.

22. Ivker and Zorensky, 13.

Thomas M. Bruckman, presentation at Men's Health Conference, Scottsdale, Ariz., 18–19 November 1996.

23. June Stephenson, *Men Are Not Cost-Effective* (New York: HarperCollins, 1995), 34.

24. Ibid., 34.

25. The term first used by the Robert Moore to describe a society where fatherhood has been devalued and adolescent male rites of passage no longer exist. First heard by author in discussions with Dr. Moore at Wingspan Leadership Conference, Chicago, Ill., November, 1995.

26. Robert Bly, *The Sibling Society* (Reading, MA: Addison-Wesley, 1996), vii.

27. Malidoma Patrice Somé, *Of Water and the Spirit: Ritual, Magic, and Initiation in the Life of An African Shaman* (New York: G. P. Putnam's Sons, 1994), 310.

28. Ivker and Zorensky, 67–83.

29. Bert Trott, "Flex Appeal," *Men's Confidential: Health, Sex, and Fitness News for Men*, August 1994, 1.

30. Ivker, and Zorensky, 84.

31. Andrew Weil, M.D., "Protecting Your Prostate," *Andrew Weil's Self Healing Newsletter* 1, no. 4, 1995, 2–3.

32. James Green, *The Male Herbal: Health Care for Men and Boys* (Freedom, CA: The Crossing Press, 1991), 41.

33. Kenneth Goldberg, *How Men Can Live As Long As Women: Seven Steps to a Longer and Better Life* (Fort Worth, TX: The Summit Group, 1993), xix.

34. Regelson and Colman, 18.

35. Ibid., 24–28.

36. Brian Chichester, Perry Garfinkel, and the Editors of Men's Health Books, *Stress Blasters: Quick and Simple Steps to Take Control and Perform under Pressure* (Emmaus, PA: Rodale Press, Inc., 1997), 10–18.

37. Information on New Warriors can be obtained by writing to:

Drury Heffernan, New Warrior Network, Box 230, Malone, New York, NY 12953-9230. Information on the Sterling Institute can be obtained by writing to: Sterling Institute of Relationship, 695 Rand Avenue, Oakland, CA 94610.

Male Menopause

Part I

Male Menopause:
Men, Women, and Society

I

Putting the Men Back in Menopause

When I began researching this book, I was skeptical about the concept of "male menopause." I had been a therapist for over thirty years and had worked with thousands of midlife men and women. Most of the women who were approaching menopause experienced marked changes that were clearly related to physiological and hormonal shifts in body chemistry. It was clear to me that something was also going on with the men, but I assumed that men's changes were more psychological than physical.

I had heard a number of men talk about "male menopause" but wondered if they were just complaining about the difficulties of being a man or trying to justify their irresponsible midlife behavior. In a society where more and more people see themselves as victims, "my hormones made me do it" is not a surprising excuse. As a therapist, I have little tolerance for men (or women) who bemoan their lives or blame bad behavior on something other than themselves.

After completing four years of research, I concluded that midlife men have significant hormonal and physiological changes and that "male menopause" was the proper name to describe what all men experience as they move from the first half of life to the second.

Though there are still those who find the idea of "male menopause" about as ludicrous as "male menstrual cramps," more and more people are coming to recognize the reality of this universal male life passage.

My first experience with male menopause occurred the day I was born, on December 21, 1943. When my mother announced "it's a boy" and lifted me up for my father to hold, he was thirty-seven years old and in the midst of a major life crisis. Over the next five years, he became increasingly depressed and withdrawn. He had what my mother called "a midlife nervous breakdown" and left before I was six. I grew up wondering what had happened to him.

I was twenty-five years old when I held my own son moments after his birth. I vowed that I would be a different kind of father than my father had been. I had already been a practicing psychotherapist for two years, but with Jemal's birth, I began to focus my professional interest on men's issues.

Over the next twenty-five years, I worked with thousands of men, many who were going through their own midlife changes. These men shared common concerns about loss of sexual function and fears about getting old.

While browsing through my local bookstore, I was drawn to a copy of *Vanity Fair* magazine. Well, to be absolutely honest, I was drawn to the cover photo of Sharon Stone, nude to the waist, with her hands cupping, but only partially covering, her breasts. Sharon was staring seductively into the eyes of the reader, with two inch letters emblazoned across her bare midriff proclaiming, "WILD THING!" I was sure there was something important Sharon had to tell me.

However, I never read the article to find out, because just to the left of Sharon's blond hair, right below the April 1993 dateline, were the words that grabbed me by the throat (actually a bit farther south than my throat)—"Male Menopause: The Unspeakable Passage by Gail Sheehy." Those words spoke in a quiet but insistent voice. Inside, I devoured the article "Is There a Male Menopause?" I knew I couldn't turn away from the journey.

I needed to find answers for myself and for the thousands of men and women who struggle to make sense of their lives at midlife.

Is There a Male Menopause?

Most men suspect they are going through a major transition during the midlife years but question whether it is "real." Many only recognize the change after they have gone through it. All the men I interviewed could relate to the response of Dave Frishberg, a sixty-year-old songwriter and piano player, "Gee, I hope there's such a thing as male menopause."

"Because if there isn't...what was that?"[1]

Before I began my own research, I believed that whatever "that" was, it was radically different than what women went through. I could not imagine the term "menopause" being applied to both women and men going through the change of life. By the time I completed my study, my initial perceptions had changed.

The information that convinced me that male menopause is real has come from a variety of clinical, academic, and personal sources.

I reviewed my experiences with clients over the last thirty-two years, many who had been or were going through midlife changes. I discussed their experiences with them and learned that many men felt they were going through a change they identified as "male menopause."

I developed a questionnaire that I gave to one hundred men and one hundred women—gay and straight, married and unmarried—from various backgrounds and age groups in order to get more definitive answers. I followed the questionnaire up with personal interviews in order to get a clearer picture of what was going on with midlife men and the women who know them well.

I interviewed experts throughout the country. I scoured the literature, both popular and scientific, from around the world.

I was surprised to find that there was actually a great deal of information in the scientific and medical literature on male menopause, most written in the last ten years. The problem was that it was spread out and not easily accessible. I found information in articles from Russia, Germany, Italy, Poland, Denmark, Israel, the Netherlands, Spain, Great Britain, and France, but little published in the United States. I discovered that European researchers have been studying male menopause for many years; the United States is just now beginning to catch up.

I sought out and listened to women who had experienced their own Menopause Passage and who had reflected deeply on this time of life. I reasoned that thoughtful women would have a great deal to teach men about the changes in our bodies, minds, and spirits. I found unexpected similarities and surprising differences between what males and females go through during the change of life.

I spoke to elders, who had long since passed through the menopause years, to discover what was on the other side and what joys and challenges awaited us in the second half of life.

I discussed the issues and listened to the responses from the men in my men's group—men ranging in age from forty-eight to sixty-six. I met with my wife's women's group and listened to their experiences of menopause and how they felt about the men in their lives.

I had hours of discussions with my wife, Carlin, sorting out what changes were hers, which ones were mine, and how much our individual changes influenced each other.

Though all the information was helpful and validated what I had been seeing in my clinical practice, there was little agreement on the definition of terms. Many professionals felt that the field of male menopause was about twenty years behind that of female menopause. All acknowledged that a great deal more work was needed before we would have definitive answers to many of the questions that people had about male menopause.

But most of us cannot afford to wait until the research has been concluded and there is general agreement on what male menopause is and how to best support men going through it. Millions of baby boomers are at this stage now and are looking for help and support.

Male Menopause, Midlife Crisis, and Aging Men: Defining Our Terms

We are just beginning to understand male menopause, and a great deal more will be learned as more attention is focused on the second half of life. When a new field of knowledge is being developed, terms and definitions are loosely used, and there is often a great deal of confusion. It is vital, therefore, that we define our terms clearly, so that when we talk about these issues, we will be "on the same page."

I offer the following definitions to aid us in our journey together:

Male Menopause begins with hormonal, physiological, and chemical changes that occur in all men generally between the ages of forty and fifty-five, though they can occur as early as thirty-five or as late as sixty-five. These changes affect all aspects of a man's life. Male menopause is, thus, a physical condition with psychological, interpersonal, social, and spiritual dimensions.

Andropause is a term synonymous with male menopause and has been used in Europe to refer to this transitional experience. The root of andropause, *andro*, comes from the Greek, meaning man. Andropause has been used in medical literature throughout the world.

Viropause, another term for male menopause, has been used more often in Great Britain to refer to this period of a man's life. *Vir* is the Latin prefix for man.

I have intentionally used the term "male menopause" as the title of this book to emphasize what I believe are the important similarities in hormonal, physiological, and chemical changes that both men and women experience during this midlife transition.

One of the major dissimilarities, which I will discuss in future chapters, is that for women, menopause means the biological end of their ability to bring new life into the world. Men at midlife still have a biological choice.

The fact that men do not have a clear, biological marker that signals the end of their reproductive years is both a blessing and a curse. Reproductive choice into their sixties, seventies, and eighties allows men to feel the draw of youthful sexuality and allows them to stay, at least in fantasy, "forever young." It also contributes to sexual frustration when they cannot live up to their "potential" and often keeps men from growing up. Many men over fifty are, emotionally, still boys.

Menopause is the cessation of menstruation in the human female. It has also been called the climacteric. The root of the word, "meno," comes from the Greek word *menses*, referring to the female's monthly menstrual cycle. "Pause" refers to the stopping of that cycle.

Some older women mourn the loss of their youthful looks and abilities. Others experience a "postmenopausal zest" and more easily make the transition into Second Adulthood. Many women over fifty have reclaimed their power and, emotionally, are mature, life-giving elders.

"Aging...is the effect of an energy flow on matter over time. It is inevitable." It is said that time heals all wounds. But time leads to the gradual accumulation of waste products that eventually wears out the body, even in the absence of disease.[2]

Male Menopause Passage is the period of a man's life when he moves from First Adulthood to Second Adulthood. The changes that bring about this passage involve biological, psychological, interpersonal, social, and spiritual transformations.

Midlife Passage, often used interchangeably with "Male Menopause Passage," is brought about by the recognition that we may be halfway through our lives, that there are more years behind us than ahead of us. We learn that the skills needed to navigate the second half of life are radically different than those we used in the first half.

"We yearn to remember the parts of ourselves that we have forgotten," says author Mark Gerzon, "to nourish those we have starved, to express those we have silenced, and to bring into the light those we have cast into the shadows."[3]

Midlife Crisis is a reaction to the perceived changes of the Male Menopause Passage. For those who feel that the changes occurring in the second half of life are to be feared and avoided, who try and cling to youthful ways, this period of life will be seen as a crisis.

For those who understand that the physical, emotional, and spiritual changes are helpful in preparing us for the second half of life, this time will be seen as an adventure rather than a crisis.

What Men Are Saying about Male Menopause

I talked to hundreds of men—friends, clients, and people attending my workshops nationwide. I handed out questionnaires to men I knew, and friends gave them to their friends. Three age groups of men responded: men in their twenties and thirties, who had not yet gone through the Male Menopause Passage; men in their forties and fifties, who were in the midst of the change; and men in their sixties and seventies, who felt they had already gone through this stage of life.

I was surprised that every man who responded felt that male menopause is real and important for men. Nearly all felt the changes men went through were as significant as what women experience. Though they acknowledged there were psychological changes that had to do with aging and midlife, most felt there were actual physical and hormonal shifts that were occurring.

I was astonished at the number of changes men associated with male menopause. From a list of sixty-five symptoms I had discovered after talking with thousands of men in my counseling practice, the men I interviewed had experienced fifty-five of them. The following general symptoms were the most common:

- Taking longer to recover from injuries or illness

- Less endurance for physical activity

- Feeling fat or gaining weight

- Difficulty reading small print
- Forgetfulness or memory loss
- Loss or thinning of hair
- Concerns about aging parents
- Feeling depressed or withdrawn
- Often feeling lonely
- More frequent need to urinate

Changes in sexuality was the area of most concern to the men. The following experiences were the most common:

- Reduced interest in sex
- Increased anxiety or fear about sexual changes
- Reduced interest in sex with usual partner
- Increased masturbation
- Anxiety about loss of sexual appetite
- Increased concern about not satisfying partner
- Reduced force of ejaculation
- Loss of erection during sexual activity
- Failure to achieve orgasm
- Increased fantasies about having sex with others
- Obsessing about younger partners and "getting away from it all"
- Increased relationship problems and fights over sex, love, and intimacy

After talking to hundreds of men, what stood out was how few of the men had ever talked to anyone about these changes and how hungry the men were to talk with other men about them. Most were greatly relieved to know they were not the only ones dealing with uncomfortable changes. A lot of the guilt and shame so many men felt lifted visibly as each man heard his own story through the mouths of other men.

What Menopausal Women Can Teach Men

Scientific understanding of a subject always seems to follow the passionate interest of those who are dealing, in their own lives, with the subject matter of science. Though women have been going through menopause since the beginning of time, specific scientific study has occurred only recently; and it was not until women began talking openly about "the change" that real understanding began to occur. Men can learn a lot about their own midlife process by reflecting on what women have been through.

It was in Rosetta Reitz' book, *Menopause*, that I first read a sensitive account of male menopause. Reitz' book was one of the early books on menopause, published in 1977. In it, she describes her interviews with women from twenty-five to ninety-five years of age who spoke out on sex and aging, lovemaking, hormones, nutrition, and male midlife changes.

Reitz points out that the term "menopause" applies to the ending of a woman's monthly menstrual cycles, but it is really much more than that. "Menopause has come to mean a combination of elements a woman experiences at the same time her menstrual flow stops."

"We can apply the term to men, too, even if they don't menstruate," says Reitz. "For it is more the combination of life's circumstances that occur around the age of fifty, sometimes beginning as early as forty for some, that creates the condition labeled menopause."[4]

But it is not just the life changes that similar for men and women as we approach fifty, our hormones are also undergoing parallel changes. Reitz feels that both women and men experience physical and hormonal changes, as well as psychological and social dislocations.

In doing research for her book, Rosetta Reitz met Martha Weinman Lear, who she describes as "a brilliant writer who understands male menopause." Writing in the *New York Times Magazine*, Lear lists the symptoms that she has observed in men going through the menopause passage:

- Nervousness
- Decrease or loss of sexual potential
- Depressions
- Decreased memory and concentration
- Decreased or absent libido
- Fatigue
- Sleep disturbances
- Irritability
- Loss of interest and self-confidence
- Indecisiveness
- Numbness and tingling
- Fear of impending danger
- Excitability.[5]

Lear continues, with wit and understanding, to connect the symptoms seen in men to the life-changes that so many men go through at midlife:

- The hormone-production levels are dropping
- The sexual vigor is diminishing
- The children are leaving
- The parents are dying
- The job horizons are narrowing
- The friends are having their first heart attacks
- The past floods by in a fog of hopes unrealized, opportunities not grasped, women not bedded, potentials not fulfilled, and the future is a confrontation with one's own mortality.[6]

In her 1993 *Vanity Fair* article, "The Unspeakable Passage," author Gail Sheehy concluded:

If menopause is the silent passage, 'male menopause' is the unspeakable passage. It is fraught with secrecy, shame, and denial. It is much more fundamental than the ending of the fertile period of a woman's life, because it strikes at the core of what it is to be a man.

The Medical Community Recognizes Male Menopause

"RESEARCHERS CERTAIN OF MALE MENOPAUSE AND ITS TREATMENT!" CNN prime-time news headlined the story coming up next. Anchor Natalie Allen introduced the subject. "Age and time steal hormones away from women during menopause. For many, medication is the answer." Coanchor Lou Waters continues the dialogue. "But do men go through menopause? Polls show a lot of men think they do, and one doctor is trying to come up with a treatment."

The camera cuts to Medical News Correspondent, Dan Rutz. "In menopause, women's sex hormones fall rapidly over several years. Sex hormones decline in men as they age, too, but much more gradually. As one doctor puts it, women fall off a cliff. Men sort of roll down the hill. Even so, many people believe there's a true change of life for men."

The camera hones in on a good-looking man on the street who looks to be in his fifties. "Well, I do," he says. "I do simply because the older you get, the more it takes for you to deal with life."

Now a woman joins in. "They go through mood swings. They go through changes like we do."

Another man gets the camera's attention. "I think that many men experience a midlife crisis, which may be triggered by an imbalance or modification of male hormones. Testosterone, I suppose, in particular."

Now the camera focuses on Dr. Lisa Tenover from Emory University who is seen talking with a patient in her office. She describes the kind of hormone replacement therapy she gives to men in their forties, fifties, sixties, and seventies. "The problem is we're about twenty years behind learning what male hormones will do in older men," says Dr. Tenover, "relative to what we know about what lack of estrogens do with postmenopausal women."[7]

It would be nice to think that men would wait to get the answers before they rushed into action, but that is not likely. As more and more men confront midlife changes, they come demanding solutions for the problems they are having with their health and sexuality. According to Census Bureau figures, the number of men in the United States between forty and fifty-five is just over twenty-five million. In less than twenty-five years, the numbers will more than double, increasing to over fifty-seven million by the year 2020.[8]

How do we separate fact from fiction? It is useful to listen to medical professionals who have had a long history of working with the changes women and men experience at midlife.

Psychiatrist Helen Singer Kaplan was a world renowned expert on human sexuality and a professor at Cornell University College of Medicine. She believed there may be physiological changes that occur for men at midlife, but since the change is gradual, most men handle it without problems. "A well-integrated man adjusts to the decline in control and sexual power," she concluded.[9]

One of Kaplan's colleagues, Theresa L. Crenshaw, M.D., an expert on male and female sexuality, sheds new light on these issues and helps clarify the meaning of the hormonal changes men go through during this period of their lives. Dr. Crenshaw believes that both men and women go through menopause. She describes men's change this way:

"Men experience a 'lite' version of menopause—physically, that is—called viropause. Their hormones and neuropeptides diminish, albeit less abruptly. Their bodies sag and change shape. Characteristic medical conditions like an enlarged prostate develop. Sexual functioning is often compromised by hormonal imbalance, disease, medications, mind, or mood. Their stamina and temperament alter as well. Emotionally, like their female counterparts, men can have repercussions from viropause of catastrophic magnitude—including severe depression and suicide. Yet often they are less well equipped to deal with these extremes than women."[10]

The truth is that for many men, male menopause is anything but "lite." These men experience a dramatic shift in their hormone balance. According to Herbert S. Kupperman, M.D., associate professor of medicine at New York University Medical Center, who has spent two decades studying the male climacteric, a small percentage of men between forty-one and sixty experience a complete physiological cessation of testicular function. This change is accompanied by the following symptoms:

- A loss of potency, which can be either premature ejaculation or inability to have an erection

- Hot flashes, similar to but generally less severe than those associated with menopausal women

- A tendency to be nervous, indecisive in actions, and prone to angry outbursts[11]

Physicians who treat prostate cancer have long known about the effects of male menopause. Since the male hormone testosterone causes prostate cancer cells to grow, treatment often involves methods that dramatically lower testosterone levels or block the effect of testosterone.[12] A large percentage of the men undergoing such treatment experience impotence or loss of sexual desire and up to 40 percent experience hot flashes. According to David G. Bostwick, M.D., Gregory T. MacLennan, M.D., and Thayne R. Larson, M.D., authors of *Prostate Cancer: What Every Man—and His Family—Needs to Know*, "These are the same types of hormonal events that women experience at menopause or following removal of the ovaries."[13]

Yet men are often not aware of the effects of changing hormones on their bodies, minds, and spirits. "In the years I have been going through male menopause and at the same time treating men with prostate cancer with drugs that exaggerate and amplify symptoms and signs of male menopause," says Stephen B. Strum, M.D., "it has become shatteringly clear to me that men are solitary creatures that do not share or perhaps are not aware of their bio-psychologic changes."[14]

Studies of men undergoing treatment for prostate cancer show what happens when male hormones are artificially cut off. Though not as dramatic, these same changes can occur naturally as men go through the change of life. "The male menopause is a real phenomenon," says Marc Blackman, M.D., chief of endocrinology and metabolism at Johns Hopkins Bayview Medical Center, "and it does similar things to men as menopause does to women, although less commonly and to a lesser extent."[15]

Just as there are a significant number of women who experience few physical problems as they go through the Menopause Passage, there are a significant number of men who have severe problems. Even so, not all medical professionals are convinced that male menopause is an accurate description of what men experience at midlife.

In November, 1992, the prestigious *Journal of the American Medical Association (JAMA)* published the article, "Is 'Male Menopause' Real or Just an Excuse?" by Andrew A. Skolnick. "It's becoming popular to blame 'male menopause' for the strange behavior of some middle-aged men during their so-called 'midlife crisis,'" the article states.[16]

"However, the changes that occur in men as they age have little in common with the changes that women experience when they go through menopause," says Christopher Longcope, M.D., professor of obstetrics and gynecology and medicine at the University of Massachusetts Medical Center, in the *JAMA* article. According to Longcope, "midlife crisis in men is not a menopausal analogue."[17]

As Dr. Crenshaw. notes in discussing her fellow medical professionals: "Most physicians today do not believe male midlife crisis has a physical basis, and treat it with psychotherapy and antidepressant medication—the same approach they used for female menopause decades ago."[18]

Yet the medical community's understanding of male menopause continues to shift dramatically. Some researchers believe that testosterone may be important in stimulating the nerves and muscles that are required to develop and maintain erections in men, though the precise mechanism is still being sought.[19] "We know more about sending a rocket to the moon than we actually understand about the physiology of erection," says Dr. Kaiser, a professor at St. Louis University School of Medicine. "It appears as if testosterone is a major regulator, probably via a whole slew of other neurotransmitters, most of which we haven't yet identified."[20]

As in many aspects of preventive medicine, the United States lags behind other countries in addressing male menopause. In Great Britain and Europe, a great deal of attention has already been focused on male menopause, both in the medical literature and in clinical practice.

In the 1980s, while United States researchers were still debating whether men experience a significant decline in hormone levels, British physicians were already beginning to use hormones to treat men who showed symptoms of testosterone deficiency.[21]

John Moran, M.D., of the Hormonal Health Care Center in London, and one of the earliest proponents of male menopause, recognized that men experienced many of the same emotional upheavals when their testosterone levels declined in midlife as did women going through menopause. "Men still often experience a mild depression that is quite similar to the type of depression we see in women," Dr. Moran observed. "On testosterone, that depression will lift. They will become less irritable, happier, and more content."[22]

In 1990, another British physician, Dr. Malcom Carruthers opened a therapy clinic in London offering hormone replacement for men. Carruthers claims dramatic results in treating men with depression, lack of sexual and emotional drive, impotence, and poor self-image.[23] One prominent member of Parliament even suggested England's National Health Service should make testosterone replacement therapy available to all older men.[24]

In Europe, many physicians have launched "andropause" clinics that offer various combinations of hormone replacement therapy, including giving testosterone. Danish researcher Dr. Jens Moller has studied male menopause and the changes that men go through as their hormones begin to decline. He found that a large majority of men with lowered testosterone levels experienced a loss of libido, difficulty with developing and maintaining erections, and a feeling of sexual dissatisfaction. He also noted that the men reported greater levels of fatigue, depression, irritability, aches and pains, and stiffness.[25]

One of the first male medical professionals in the United States to focus on male menopause is Dr. Aubrey M. Hill. "Though I did not believe it at the outset," says Hill, author of *Viropause/Andropause*, "my experience has now convinced me that most men undergo what could be called male menopause and that many men suffer acutely and needlessly because they don't have access to the information they need to understand their symptoms."[26]

Dr. Hill, an active family physician in private practice for many years, was surprised when he found amazingly similar symptoms among his male patients in their forties and fifties. "My medical training had not prepared me for finding a connection between men's physical symptoms and the period of life in which they occur. When I searched the medical literature for information about midlife changes in men, I found almost nothing on the subject. Medical science has been conspicuously silent about the changes that I see men commonly experiencing during midlife."[27]

In looking at a range of midlife men, Hill concludes, "Male menopause is a condition that affects both married and single men, heterosexual and homosexual men. I find nothing in the scientific literature to suggest that any man, regardless of orientation or relational status, is immune to the viropause/andropause syndrome."[28]

"As a gynecologist, I hear many concerns about 'Male Menopause' from my patients," says Marshall E. Noel, M.D., codirector of the Canterbury Women's Health Care Center. "Despite my training in many aspects of female menopause, I could many times only be sympathetic to my patients' perceptions." After reaching this stage of life himself and experiencing many of the symptoms of male menopause firsthand, Dr. Noel concludes, "an understanding of menopause for both sexes is necessary for successful coping and graceful aging."[29]

There are numerous studies that show that testosterone and other hormones decline as men age. Yet many men continue to deny that they undergo such changes. Dr. John E. Morely, chairman of the Department of Geriatric Medicine at St. Louis University School of Medicine says, "Men don't like to admit that they may actually decline; it's not a sort of 'male' thing to do."[30]

Loss of testosterone not only affects men's sexual potency, but other body systems as well. Jane Brody, health columnist for the *New York Times*, says, "there is no question that aging is accompanied by changes that can be signs of insufficient testosterone: muscle size and strength decline, body fat increases, bones slowly lose strength-giving calcium, and sexual performance wanes."[31]

"Here is a case," says Brody, "where far more is known about women's health than that of men. In women, the hormonal change at menopause is abrupt and its adverse effects on body organs are well documented. In women, both the immediate and the long-term benefits of providing hormonal supplements are also fairly well established, although possible risks are still incompletely explored.

"But for men it will probably be years before doctors know whether they, too, can profit from hormone replacement and at what price. Well-designed studies of hormone replacement for normal, healthy aging men are just getting under way."[32]

Male Menopause: Better Sex through Chemistry

No one wants to have a problem for which there is no cure. For a long time we assumed that loss of sexual function was just a part of men getting older. If there was a male menopause, you just had to accept your losses.

However, recent research offers hope that there is something men can do to stay healthy and sexually vital into their fifties, sixties, seventies, and beyond. We are starting to recognize that male menopause, rather than signaling the beginning of the end, actually signals the end of the beginning. It tells us we are finished with First Adulthood and ready to embark on a trek up a new mountain to Second Adulthood.

Some believe that male menopause is the road to oblivion, the end of our sexual power. But for those who have the courage to take that road, male menopause is the passage to the most passionate, productive, and purposeful time of a man's life.

The greatest concern most men have as they enter the Menopause Passage is the loss of sexual functioning. Many men cling to memories of the rock-hard-fire-hose penis of their youth. They are unprepared for the normal changes associated with Second Adulthood. Dr. John Medina, author of *The Clock of Ages* says that maximum "ejaculatory distance" declines from roughly one to two feet in young men to three to five inches in the elderly.[33] Many men become terrified, sure that the next step may be no ejaculation at all.

For some time now, doctors have given men testosterone when there were medical problems that caused blood levels of the male hormone to be abnormally low. Yet, testosterone levels decrease for all men as they get older, and hormone replacement studies that focus on normal healthy men are just beginning. Endocrinologist Peter Snyder, M.D., a professor of medicine at the University of Pittsburgh School of Medicine, is currently leading a study of one hundred men aged sixty-five and older who were randomly treated with either a testosterone patch or a placebo patch.

"If we prevent the decline in testosterone with age, will that do more good or more harm?" questioned Dr. Snyder. "[By 1998] we'll have the beginning of an answer."[34]

Research is also taking place on other hormones associated with sexuality. DHEA—short for dehydroepiandrosterone—which is produced by the adrenal glands (located on the kidneys), as well as by the brain and the skin, is the most abundant steroid in the human body. Like testosterone, it also declines as we age. According to Dr. Samuel Yen, a reproductive endocrinologist and principal investigator of a major DHEA study at the University of California at San Diego, DHEA is "a drug that may help people age more gracefully."[35]

"In particular, Dr. Yen's group found that the men and women on DHEA experienced increased energy and better sleep; they felt more relaxed and were better able to handle stress. Those with a history of arthritic symptoms also reported less joint pain. Moreover, none of the study participants experienced any negative side effects."[36]

Many doctors are so encouraged by the results of DHEA research that they are not waiting until final results are in before offering DHEA to their patients. William Regelson, M.D., author of *The Super-Hormone Promise*, has been prescribing DHEA to patients for many years and has also been taking it himself. His conclusion:

I think that just about every adult age forty-five or older can benefit from taking DHEA.

"One of the most constantly repeated comments I hear from patients as well as colleagues and friends who are taking DHEA," says Dr. Regelson, "is that it has renewed their interest in sex. Men, particularly, report that it has revived their sexual interest."[37]

DHEA's effect on male sexual function was documented in the groundbreaking "Massachusetts Male Aging Study," which investigated, among other things, sexual function and activity in men aged forty to seventy. The researchers sought to determine whether there was any correlation between health or personality changes and impotence, which the study showed was a problem for over half of all males. Of the seventeen hormones measured in each of the men, only one showed a direct and consistent correlation with impotency: DHEA. As DHEA levels declined, the incidence of impotency increased.[38]

With so much media hype on the benefits of taking the latest hormone that will return men to the sexual vigor of their youth, it is easy to overlook those who counsel caution. In the July, 1997, issue of *Harvard University's Men's Health Watch*, the authors concluded:

It's clear that much more information is needed before DHEA can be recommended to men of any age. Testimonials notwithstanding, it is unlikely to be the fountain of youth; unfortunately, it's already out of the bottle, being widely available before scientific studies have evaluated its efficacy and safety.

Men's Health Watch also reviewed the findings on three other hormones that decrease with age: growth hormone, testosterone, and melatonin. Although there were some studies indicating the benefits of these substances, they concluded that more scientific study was needed before it was clear whether the benefits outweighed the risk.[39]

Men have finally come out of the closet in acknowledging problems with sexual arousal and functioning. There are now an increasing number of options for help becoming available. Upjohn, a leading pharmaceutical company, is selling the world's first commercial erection injection. Instead of activating a spring-loaded implant or applying a vacuum pump (which are methods that have been used for some time), the user injects a fifth of a teaspoon of prescription medication into the side of the penis.

If getting a shot in the shaft gives men the shivers, other solutions will soon be available. A Menlo Park, California, company called VIVUS recently received FDA approval on a system called MUSE (Medicated Urethral System for Erection), which uses a disposable applicator to squirt a premeasured dose of alprostadil—the main drug used in injection therapy—into the opening at the tip of the penis. This causes only minimal discomfort. Just as with injections, the drug relaxes penile arteries and increases blood flow, beginning an erection. Clinical trials show that it works for approximately 60 percent of men.[40]

Other companies, including the drug giant Pfizer, are scrambling to license what could be the ultimate erection aid: a pill taken an hour before sex. The Pfizer remedy uses a drug called sildenafil, which has been studied in England and seems to improve erections in men who have no physical cause for difficulty with erections or illnesses such as diabetes. The drug, which is being tested under the name Viagra, increases blood flow to the penis, enhancing a man's normal response to stimulation.

According to one of the leading researchers in the field, Stephen M. Auerbach, M.D., interviewed at the recent National Conference on Men's Health, "thus far, the research on Viagra is very promising. It has helped 90 percent of the patients who have taken it, and there seem to be few side effects."[41]

Steven Lamm, M.D., author of *Younger at Last*, says, "another drug, phentolamine mesylate, which has been used for over forty years to treat hypertension, is currently undergoing human trials as an impotence medication. It will be submitted soon to the FDA for approval under the brand name Vasomax. It, too, will be in pill form."[42]

Pausinstalia yohimbine (also called yohimbe), an herb obtained from the inner bark of the yohimbeh tree that grows in Africa, has been used throughout the world to stimulate and restore sexual functioning.[43]

A study, conducted by Dr. Robert Margolis and published in the journal *Current Therapeutic Research*, of ten thousand impotent patients who took yohimbine, said that 80 percent of them reported good to excellent results. According to Robert Ivker, M.D., who quoted the study in his book *Thriving*, "most patients using yohimbine reported that overall sexual pleasure increased with more intensive orgasms. It also decreases the latency period between ejaculations and can stimulate blood flow to the penis."[44]

After extensive testing of yohimbine, A. J. Riley, M.D., a specialist in sexual medicine, has concluded that "it is now possible to restore usable erections for up to 95 percent of men with erectile inadequacy."[45]

With new technologies becoming available nearly every year, however, there is a tendency to focus on specific problems, such as impotence, and ignore the health of the whole man. One person who has pioneered a comprehensive program is Kenneth A. Goldberg, M.D., founder and director of the Male Health Center in Dallas, Texas. Goldberg's center, established in 1989, was the first facility in the country to focus on all men's health issues.

Though he acknowledges that the new medical interventions becoming available seem miraculous, he recognizes that complex sexual problems associated with male menopause are not so easily handled. "We need to deal with the whole man—his diet and exercise habits, his other physiological problems, his relationship with his partner, his ability to communicate, and indeed, sometimes his hormone levels."[46]

It seems clear that continuing scientific discoveries will allow men to live longer, healthier, and sexier lives than ever before. The more important question, which science cannot answer, is "what will men do with these added years?" Without a strong purpose for the second half of life, men begin to feel unnecessary and useless. To survive and prosper in the second half of life, men need a different kind of motivation.

Male Menopause, Sex, and Mentoring: New Pathways in the Second Half of Life

According to Dr. Jonathan Kramer and Diane Dunaway, authors of *Why Men Don't Get Enough Sex and Women Don't Get Enough Love*, "men think about sex an average of six times an hour, that's 750 times a week, not counting dreams." In my own survey, I found that men of all ages report that they would like to have sex about three times a week. By sex, they usually mean sexual intercourse. Almost all are disappointed that the actual times they have sex are much less and that sexual play often decreases with age.

Men's "preoccupation" with sex should not be surprising. From an evolutionary perspective, all humans alive today have evolved from ancestors who were reproductively successful. That is, whatever else they may have done or failed to do, all our ancestors managed to reproduce. Men's focus on sexual intercourse served the evolutionary function of getting more babies produced and insured the survival of our species.

For most of human history, all male sexuality occurred between age fourteen or fifteen, when men became biologically mature, and forty-five or fifty when they died. As recently as 1900, the average life expectancy in the United States for men was 46.3 years.[47] For millions of years, we only needed a sexuality that would get us through the first half of our lives.

But things are changing dramatically. Children born today can expect to live well into their seventies, and if current health trends continue, the average life span of men in America may soon be one hundred years. If we have evolved to reproduce, raise children to reproductive age, then die, what kind of lifestyle is appropriate for men and women who now live twice the average life span of their grandparents?[48]

I began to get clues to the answer when I interviewed men for this book. I was surprised to hear man after man say that as he got older he was much less interested in "sex" and much more interested in "intimacy." George Miller, a fifty-three-year-old contractor said it this way: "When I was young, I liked it fast and furious. Anytime, anywhere, with anyone—I was ready. Now, I want to take my time. I want to touch and be touched. I want a partner I can grow with. I want sex to be an expression of my whole being, not just my penis. I want us to be a team so we can raise healthy children."

Though promising breakthroughs in medical technology will undoubtedly allow men to maintain their sexual vitality into later life, this alone will not satisfy most men.

At age forty-nine, Robert Jessup was at the top of his profession as the CEO of a large computer company. He has an even more expansive view of his sex role. "Since I cut back on my practice and became a 'big brother' to a teenage boy, my whole life seems to have grown larger. In the past, my main satisfactions came from sexual conquests and business takeovers. I got a similar physical rush from both."

"It's kind of strange..." Robert hesitated, looking for the right words. "But I feel that I get a new kind of satisfaction from being a mentor to a young man. In my younger years, my body seemed to want to make babies. Now, it seems to want to nurture, protect, and teach."

Just as men's desire for sexual intercourse is part of the evolutionary drive in the first half of life, so too is men's desire to mentor younger men part of our evolutionary nature. According to David Gutmann, professor of psychiatry and education and director of the Older Adult Program at Northwestern University, "The same evolutionary design that has made the presence of elders a permanent feature of our species is recapitulated in individual lives, as aging men and women develop new, hitherto-unclaimed capacities that enlarge their lives and that fit them for their special social and species assignments."[49]

Psychologist James Hillman in his book *The Soul's Code* describes the shift of perspective that occurs as we become mentors to the younger generation. "Something moves in the heart....Mentoring begins when your imagination can fall in love with the fantasy of another."[50]

Michael Gurian, author of *The Wonder of Boys*, says that boys need the kind of nurturing and support that can only come from an older man. "They need training in sexuality, self-discipline, spirituality, and morality. This is the job of elder males."[51]

Eldering is not only necessary for the well-being of younger males, it is a vital practice for midlife men as well. If men in their fifties, sixties, and seventies do not become elders, they lose their passion, retire from life, and become old and useless.

"Elders are not 'senior citizens' who get gold watches at retirement, move to Sunbelt states, and play cards, shuffleboard, and bingo ad nauseam," says Zalman Schachter-Shalomi, a preeminent rabbi, teacher, and professor emeritus at Temple University.[52]

"Then what are elders? They are wisdomkeepers," says Schachter-Shalomi, "who have an ongoing responsibility for maintaining society's well-being and safeguarding the health of our ailing planet Earth."[53] The purpose of the Male Menopause Passage is not for men to reclaim their lost childhood. Rather, its function is for men to claim the passion and power of elderhood.

Many men fear that elderhood is a time when they must give up the sexual joys that make life worthwhile. Their image of an elder is some kind of sexless saint. The truth is that elders are some of the sexiest people alive. They are filled with creative passion, though it is a different kind of passion than the one that drove them in their younger years.

Male Menopause forces men to confront their changing sexuality. Rather than being a time where sexuality drops off, it can be a time where sexuality expands and takes on new dimensions. No longer restricted by the constant desire to bed beautiful women, it can include the intimacy that comes from loving deeply and well, passing on wisdom to the next generation, and being a force for planetary healing.

Notes Chapter 1

1. Quoted in Cyra McFadden "Is There Really a Male Menopause?," *New Choices,* July–August 1994, 45.

2. Walter M. Bortz II, M.D., *Dare to Be 100* (New York: Fireside Books, 1996), 31.

3. Mark Gerzon, *Listening to Midlife: Turning Your Crisis into a Quest* (Boston: Shambhala, 1996), 5.

4. Rosetta Reitz, *Menopause: A Positive Approach* (Radnor, PA: Chilton Book Co., 1977), 226.

5. Martha Weinman Lear, "Is There A Male Menopause?," *New York Times Magazine,* 28 January 1973, 19.

6. Ibid.

7. "Researchers Certain of Male Menopause and Its Treatment," *Early Prime,* CNN, 27 November 1995.

8. Bureau of the Census, *Statistical Abstract, 1996* (Washington, DC, 1996), 16–17.

9. Quoted in Reitz, 227.

10. Theresa L. Crenshaw, M.D., *The Alchemy of Love and Lust: Discovering Our Sex Hormones and How They Determine Who We Love, When We Love, and How Often We Love* (New York: G. P. Putnam's Sons, 1996), 205.

11. Reported in Patricia Skalka, *The American Medical Association Guide to Health and Well-Being after Fifty* (New York: Random House, 1984), 88.

12. David G. Bostwick, M.D., Gregory T. MacLennan, M.D., and Thayne R. Larson, M.D., for the American Cancer Society, *Prostate Cancer: What Every Man—and His Family—Needs to Know* (New York: Villard, 1996), 148.

13. Ibid., 154.

14. Stephen B. Strum. M.D., correspondence with author, 5 June 1997.

15. Quoted in Ronald Klatz and Carol Kahn, *Grow Young with HGH: The Amazing Medically Proven Plan to Reverse Aging* (New York: HarperCollins, 1997), 123.

16. Andrew A. Skolnick, "Is 'Male Menopause' Real or Just an Excuse?," *JAMA,* no. 18 (1992): 2486.

17. Quoted in Skolnick.

18. Crenshaw, 212.

19. William Regelson, M.D., and Carol Colman, *The Super-Hormone Promise: Nature's Antidote to Aging* (New York: Simon and Schuster, 1996), 131–32.

20. Quoted in Regelson and Colman, 132.

21. Regelson and Colman, 133.

22. Quoted in Regelson and Colman, 133.

23. Reported in Thomas D. Fahey, "The Male Mid-Life Crisis: Viropause: Myth or Reality?," *Muscle and Fitness*, May 1994, 216.

24. "Do Men Go Through Menopause," *Consumer Reports on Health*, October 1993, 105.

25. Reported in Klatz and Kahn, 182

26. Aubrey M. Hill, M.D., *Viropause/Andropause: The Male Menopause: Emotional and Physical Changes Mid-Life Men Experience* (Far Hills, NJ: New Horizon Press, 1993), xiii.

27. Ibid., xiv.

28. Ibid., ix.

29. Marshall E. Noel, M.D., correspondence with author, 9 June 1997.

30. Quoted in Regelson and Colman, 128.

31. Jane E. Brody, "Hormone Replacement for Men: When Does It Help?," *New York Times*, 30 August 1995, sec. C, p. 8.

32. Ibid.

33. John J. Medina, *The Clock of Ages: Why We Age—How We Age—Winding Back the Clock* (Cambridge: Cambridge University Press, 1996), 223.

34. Quoted in Brody, "Hormone Replacement for Men" sec. C, p. 8.

35. Quoted in Benedict Carey, "Hooked on Youth: The Latest Anti-Aging Drug is Cheap, Convenient, and Makes Some People Feel Like Kids Again. So What's the Catch?," *Hippocrates*, February 1996, 40.

36. Regelson and Colman, 47-48.

37. Ibid., 48.

38. Henry 8A. Feldman et al., "Impotence and Its Medical and Psychosocial Correlates: Results of the Massachusetts Male Aging Study," *The Journal of Urology* 151 (January 1994): 54–61.

39. "The Aging Male: Can Hormones Help?" *Harvard University Men's Health Watch* 1, no. 12 (July 1997): 1–3.

40. Richard Berger, M.D., "New Name, Treatments for Impotence," *Health News* 2, no. 17 (1996): 3–4.

41. Stephen M. Auerbach, M.D., presentation at Men's Health Conference, Scottsdale, Ariz., 18–19 November 1996.

42. Steven Lamm, M.D., and Gerald Secor Couzens, *Younger at Last: The New World of Vitality Medicine* (New York: Simon and Schuster, 1997), 59.

43. Ibid., 64–65.

44. Robert Ivker, M.D., and Edward Zorensky, *Thriving: The Complete Mind/Body Guide for Optimal Health and Fitness in Men* (New York: Crown Publishers, 1997), 218.

45. Quoted in Ivker and Zorensky, 218.

46. Kenneth Goldberg, *How Men Can Live as Long as Women: Seven Steps to a Longer and Better Life* (Fort Worth, TX: The Summit Group, 1993), 169.

47. Frank Kendig and Richard Hutton, *Life Spans: Or How Long Things Last* (New York: Holt, Rinehart and Winston, 1979), 11.

48. Ronald Klatz and Robert Goldman, *Stopping the Clock* (New Canaan, CT: Keats Publishing, Inc., 1996), 5.

49. David Gutmann, *Reclaimed Powers: Toward a New Psychology of Men and Women in Later Life* (New York: Basic Books, 1987), 4–5.

50. James Hillman, *The Soul's Code: In Search of Character and Calling* (New York: Random House, 1996), 120–21.

51. Michael Gurian, "The Wonder of Boys: An Interview with Michael Gurian," interview by Bert H. Hoff, *M.E.N. Magazine*, October 1996.

52. Zalman Schachter-Shalomi and Ronald S. Miller, *From Age-ing to Sage-ing: A Profound New Vision of Growing Older* (New York: Warner Books, 1995), 12.

53. Ibid.

2

The Personal Side of Male Menopause: Listening to Men and the Women Who Love Them

Denial and Discovery:
My Own Male Menopause Passage

The beginning of my own Male Menopause Passage—though I would never have called it that at the time—was both subtle and dramatic. The drama began when I got the call from my doctor. "Jed, we've got the results of your tests, and I'd like to see you in my office as soon as possible." Dr. Volen's voice was calm. My heart seemed to stop, then tried to escape through my throat.

Just moments before the attack that had sent me to the doctor for tests, I was on top of the world. I was forty-seven years old, had just signed a major book contract, was traveling all over the country giving workshops and lectures, and was happily married and looking forward to more time with my wife now that our last two children had left home.

Feeling more physically fit than I ever had, I was doing my daily three-mile run. The sky was sparkling blue, and the summer heat caused a satisfying sweat to cover my body. Suddenly, my heart began pounding wildly, and my head felt like it was about to explode. The pain brought me to my knees, and I sat on the ground stunned and shaken. Within hours, however, the pain had disappeared, and I felt like my old self. I decided to ignore whatever it was, figured I was fine, and kept the experience to myself. I didn't want to worry my wife, I told myself. The next day, I had another attack. Something was happening that I couldn't ignore.

Even seated in the doctor's office, I was sure the concern was unwarranted. I had convinced myself that I was having a drug reaction to the prednisone I had recently taken to heal poison ivy blisters—the result of a tracking-skills course at Tom Brown's wilderness training camp. I had prided myself on using only natural remedies for healing and figured the drug was causing problems with my super-clean immune system.

"The tests indicate that you've got an adrenal tumor," the doctor said, looking me straight in the eye. "It will need to come out as soon as possible." I couldn't believe what I was hearing. I couldn't have a tumor. I was too young. I was too healthy. I was doing all the right things. There must be some mistake.

I checked with other doctors. I looked for natural alternatives to surgery. There was no mistake. The tumor had to come out, and my life would never again be the same.

The other changes were less dramatic. They nibbled at the edges of my consciousness, easier to push away, but like mosquitoes at nightfall, more pesky and persistent. My mother had died when I was forty-three, and since then, thoughts about death found their way into my awareness at the most unexpected times.

Even though our three oldest children were launched, I now found myself worrying about whether they would make it. The world seemed so much more chaotic and dangerous than when I left for college at age seventeen. The two youngest had recently left home: Aaron to live with his father, and Angela to live with an older friend a hundred miles south of where we lived. I missed them, wished they would visit more, and worried about their health and safety.

I felt finished with the day-to-day responsibilities of raising children but was concerned about the increasing levels of violence, particularly among young males, in our society. Young men seemed to need the guidance of older males. Was I ready to be one of those "older males?" Having grown up without the presence of a father, I was afraid there was some critical male wisdom I had never gotten myself and so would not be able to pass it on to my sons.

I loved my work as a therapist but began wondering whether there was more I should be doing. Was it enough to help one person or one family at a time? So many of the problems seemed to be related to the stresses coming from the larger society. I saw more and more single mothers with teenage sons they did not know how to handle, boys who hungered to be men but were starving from a lack of male guidance.

I saw these boys growing up with deep-seated confusion and rage, which I knew was going to blow up when it was least expected. I saw fathers who had lost faith in their ability to be role models for their sons—men worn down by a society that increasingly told them men were a menace and fathers were unnecessary.

Helping people adjust to a dysfunctional culture seemed irresponsible and immoral. More and more, I wanted to change the society. But how was I to do that? There was so much that needed to be done, and time was running out.

I felt restless and irritable. I wanted to do something new, but I had no idea what it might be.

My male friends suddenly seemed less interesting. It didn't seem like we had much in common, and they often appeared immature and foolish. They were never available when I needed them and were always in my face when I wanted to be alone.

I was a city boy, born in New York, raised in Los Angeles, and living near San Francisco. I loved the urban diversity and excitement but had fantasies of living in the country where things were slower and quieter.

Emotionally, I seemed to be riding a rollercoaster. When I was "up," I wanted to work for days on end. My energy was endless, and I gloried in the vision of taking life by the tail and swinging it wildly over my head. I was supremely confident that I could make a real difference in the world. But then, the dark moods would come over me, and I wanted to kill something or at least beat the hell out of it. "What" or "why" was a complete mystery to me. On the other side of anger was the depression, a beast I needed to keep at bay.

Things with my wife, Carlin, were good, better than they had ever been. Yet I felt uneasy and confused. I had expected that when the kids were gone we would be closer, more intimate, and would finally have more time for each other, more time for sex.

But within a week after our last child left home, Carlin went on a retreat and returned to announce she was starting a school—The Diamond-Wise School for Sacred Living and Joyful Action. She seemed on fire with passion, but it didn't seem directed at me.

Five-and-a-half years my senior, she had been going through menopause, a change neither one of us understood. For me, it was a time of longing and disconnection. Just when I would be feeling close to Carlin, a hot flash would roar through her body like a wild fire in a forest, and she would descend into an under-world where I could not follow and did not belong. I wanted to reach out and hold her and be held, but I was not sure she still wanted me.

There was something both wonderful and unsettling about her postmenopausal zest. She had an "edge" about her that gleamed like a diamond and brightened my world, but her decisiveness and honesty could also be frightening. I longed for greater intimacy but was afraid of being hurt.

Lovemaking was less frequent and less enjoyable. I was sure it was the beginning of the end of our sex lives. At times, Carlin seemed happy enough to avoid sex altogether. I tried to be under-standing, but my mind kept screaming, "I'm too young to stop having sex." I thought about finding a younger partner, but I love my wife. I considered having an affair, but it seemed more fun in fantasy than reality. What I really wanted was my wife back.

It wasn't until after Carlin had gotten through her own menopause that I gradually suspected I was going through mine.

Letting the awareness in was not easy. Her changes were so much more dramatic that they easily eclipsed my own. Besides, the very idea that a man could go through menopause seemed ludicrous and unseemly, about as likely as a man having a baby, monthly periods, or menstrual cramps.

Midlife crisis, yeah, I could accept that. Fear of getting old, uh huh, maybe so. But male menopause? Give me a break. The concept must have been hatched by radical feminists, I thought, to make men suffer for ten thousand years of patriarchal oppression.

But I couldn't dismiss the physical and emotional changes I was experiencing. My body was clearly going through a transformation. My emotional state was extremely volatile, going from the depths to the heights so fast I knew there had to be some physiological cause. It was difficult for me to slow down enough to recognize that all the changes were related and that they were part of male menopause.

Even more troubling and difficult to accept than the physical and emotional symptoms were the sexual symptoms associated with male menopause:

- The times we would make love, and I would lose my erection
- The times I found it difficult to keep an erection even when I desperately wanted to make love
- The times the orgasm was not as strong or enjoyable as it used to be
- The times I would have to fantasize about some sexy scene in order to have an orgasm at all

I remembered the medications they had given me prior to my surgery. They were supposed to regulate my blood pressure, but as a side effect, I lost all, and I do mean all, my sexual feelings. God, what if that was what was in store for me? I did my best to push the fears out of my consciousness and keep the focus on Carlin's changes. I had trouble accepting that something real was going on in my own body.

I read the books Carlin was reading on menopause. I told myself (and her) that it was so I could better understand what she was going through. The deeper truth was that I was looking for something that would answer my own questions.

As Carlin began to emerge on the other side of her Menopause Passage, she gently suggested that maybe the tension we were experiencing in our sex lives might have something to do with what was going on with me. "Perhaps the frustrations and anger you are feeling about sex could be a part of your own midlife changes," she offered with a supportive smile.

I listened intently but thought to myself, "Nonsense. The only problem with our sex life is that you're not interested enough. And the reason I'm upset all the time is because we don't have enough sex. I'm busting my butt trying to make a living and damn it, I don't get the appreciation I deserve....And besides, I'M NOT FRUSTRATED AND ANGRY!"

Yet no matter how I tried to deny my own changes, uncomfortable questions kept bubbling up into consciousness. Was the problem her lack of sexual interest or could it really be that I was losing my own sexual power? Could there really be something going on physically? Were there hormonal changes going on in my body? Could there be something called "male menopause" that would explain these changes? If I am going through menopause, does that mean I am losing my manhood? And the bottom line question, was there something I could do to reclaim my power and revive my flagging sexuality?

Overcoming Fear and Isolation: Guys, We Are Not Alone

As I listened to the men who came to see me for therapy, I began to hear similar concerns about sexual, physical, and emotional upheavals. "I feel like I'm losing interest in sex," Roger, a tall, good-looking stockbroker in his forties confided. "When Judy and I were first together, the sparks would fly when we'd get within thirty feet of each other. Now, we feel more like friends than lovers. We still make love, but it isn't as often and isn't as exciting as it once was. I miss what we had."

George, a fifty-four-year-old, single, medical doctor came to see me when, for the first time, he "failed" with a woman. "I never had a problem sexually in *that* way before," George said, remembering the confidence he felt in the past. Though I've felt a slight flagging of my libido over the years, I never came close to failing."

George paused, and I saw the shame and embarrassment I was seeing on the faces of more and more men, married and single, living alone and cohabiting. "This absolutely gorgeous, young woman, was looking up at me with lust and excitement in her eyes," George continued, the pain evident as the words rolled out. "I was absolutely terrified. I could feel myself losing it, even as I tried desperately to hold on. As my erection wilted away, it felt like all the life was flowing out of me."

Heterosexual or homosexual, men going through the Menopause Passage face similar challenges. Jack is a friendly, good-looking man who appears much younger than his fifty-two years. He has been with his partner, Bryce, for the last sixteen years, and both describe the relationship as joyful and satisfying.

"I'm finding I'm having a renewed vitality and sense of adventure," says Jack, "that comes into conflict with longtime patterns in my relationship with my partner."

Jack goes on to acknowledge that he has been having both sexual and emotional attractions to people outside his committed relationship, an experience very common to men at this stage.

"Sometimes I feel that time is running out," Jack says wistfully. "I'm feeling 'last chance' anxiety about my being able to find work that is creative, life goals that are satisfying, and a sex life that I can live with."

Jack continues, "I'm at a transition period with my partner, and we're both looking for ways to move together into the future in a way that meets both our needs. Becoming an effective and valued elder is becoming increasingly important to me."

When I asked Jack about differences between heterosexual and homosexual men at midlife, he said, "the main difference is that people assume there must be a difference. As I spend more time in men's groups with heterosexual men, I find we are much more alike than different."

One thing Jack does remember is how differently his priest viewed sexuality for boys who were attracted to other boys, as opposed to boys who were attracted to girls. "I grew up Catholic," Jack recalls. "When we were about thirteen years old, the boys and girls were separated. The girls got a lecture about the sins of lusting after the boys, and the boys got a similar lecture about the dangers of letting their sexual desires lead them to a path of sin. As the priest was leaving, almost like a tag line that was not worth really mentioning, he said, 'and the idea of being attracted to a boy is a sin beyond sin.' He said it in such a way that I felt I was being told I was somewhere between a foul toad and an insignificant turd."

In a society where heterosexuality is the norm, boys who grow up gay take on the fear of the dominant culture. They are forced to hide who they are, and the resulting shame can cause wounds long after gay men "come out."

Straight men are also deeply wounded by the homophobia present in society. Heterosexual men are afraid of acting "unmanly" and being accused of being a "foul toad," an "insignificant turd," or something even worse. One of the greatest barriers that keeps men from talking about male menopause is the fear of being less than manly. Many would rather die than admit that their erections are no longer rock hard, that they can't get it up whenever they want, or that they are afraid they no longer satisfy their partners. The terror of being seen as a "queer" or a "pussy" causes millions of men to deny the changes that are going on as they reach midlife. In a way, all men—heterosexual or homosexual—face a "coming out" about their Male Menopause Passage.

Though women have come a long way in the last ten years in bringing menopause out of the closet, it has not been easy for them either. The experiences of thoughtful women, who have experienced their own Menopause Passage can be of great help to men.

What Men Can Learn from Menopausal Women about Male Menopause

Author Germaine Greer does not believe in male menopause, yet her insights can be helpful to men going through this period of their lives. In her book, *The Change*, Greer remembers sitting with her friend Sandra a few months after her fiftieth birthday, enjoying a day to themselves in Beaubourg, France, when they began to reflect on the middle years:

"'I won't live like that,' said Sandra. Her eyes were fixed on a little gray lady with a plastic shopping basket apologetically threading her way through the gaudy prostitutes and lounging boys on the pavement opposite. 'I won't live in some bedsit with a plate and knife and a fork and creep out to the market each day for a slice of cheese and baguette. I won't become gray and invisible.'"

Greer comments on the experience:

"Sandra's anxiety, with its telescoping of the next thirty years into a single grim tomorrow, is typical of the climacterium. We had both sailed through our forties with very little awareness of growing older. We had each buried a parent; she had shed a husband, but we had both remained at the center of the life we had built. Suddenly something was slipping away so fast that we had not had time quite to register what it might be. All we knew was that it was irreplaceable. The way ahead seemed dark. Somewhere along the line optimism seemed to have perished. Neither of us could identify this feeling of apprehensive melancholy."[1]

Most men don't read books like Greer's *The Change* that have subtitles like "*Women, Aging and Menopause,*" but if they did, they would find kindred spirits. What man, as he approaches fifty, has not been aware of something slipping away that he could not quite identify or has not felt his heart grow numb as "optimism seemed to have perished?" What man has not tried to wrestle with ghosts he could not quite grasp and struggled to "identify this feeling of apprehensive melancholy?"

Since I had learned so much from my wife, Carlin, about men and menopause, I thought I might learn more from some of her female friends. I asked if she would invite some of them to discuss men and menopause and let me be "a fly on the wall" and listen.

We met on a sweltering Monday night in July. The first arrival joked that if I wanted the responses of some hot, menopausal women, this was the time. Another said she had just seen the best bumper sticker in town. "It was on a truck driven by a tough, hard looking woman, with a bunch of kids in the car," said Susan who identifies herself as a lesbian feminist activist. "Clearly she had a husband. I mean she wasn't one of my 'dyke' sisters. The bumper sticker said, 'I have PMS and a handgun.'" All the women laughed uproariously. "Now that's a woman no one is going to mess with," Susan mused. I thought, this is going to be an interesting evening!

Carlin began by having the ten women introduce themselves. They were a mixed group: Black, White, and Hispanic; heterosexual and lesbian; radical feminists and conservative homemakers. The youngest was forty-six, and the oldest was sixty-five. Carlin asked the questions that I had prepared.

She began, "What's your general impression of men you know who are forty to fifty-five? How do you feel about these guys? Do you think they are going through 'male menopause'?"

Theresa, a forty-seven-year-old homeopath and therapist, jumped right in. "I felt I didn't know anything about men, but...when I went to see *Men Alive,* I thought, fuckin-a, I'll become a lesbian separatist because men are hopeless, ABSOLUTELY HOPELESS. They can do one emotion, and that's anger. And they're just hopeless!" The other women chuckled in the background. Theresa seemed to be voicing words that other women feel but don't say out loud.[2]

Theresa touched right into the major fear and frustration I had heard men voice over and over again. All the men who had participated in the *Men Alive* production felt that they had been more honest about their true feelings than they had ever been. Although the men expressed joy and tenderness, love and longing, passion and playfulness, there was also a great deal of rage and frustration.

Men have heard for years from women, "Tell us how you really feel. We want to know. Let it out." We felt we had finally let it out and the response we got was, "You're hopeless." Men have had difficulty telling their emotional truth, and women have had equal difficulty hearing it when it was spoken.

As Theresa talked about her own midlife changes, her voice began to soften. "So when I thought about all this...what do I know about male menopause...? All I can think of, as a woman getting menopausal, is that my level of grief is titanic." Theresa's voice got low and her pain showed. "I mean I have three people who are dying. I've lost four friends to cancer in the last few years. For me, the pain is overwhelming. And what becomes apparent with men of any age, with few exceptions, is their inability to express deep feelings."

She continued with real sadness in her voice. "They can't deal with fear, and they can't deal with grief...and they can't deal with loneliness." There was a great deal of compassion in the room as Theresa talked about the men she knows.

"I was thinking about men losing their power at this stage," said Celia, a former school teacher. "It must be so much more devastating for them because they put so much stock in it. I mean it defines their whole existence."

"I taught junior high for eleven years," Celia continued, "and when their testosterone comes in, these guys were no better than rams butting heads. It was ridiculous to watch what they'd go through to see who was at the top and who had it over who in arm wrestling. Men are constantly defining themselves through their force and power. It's all physical. There is little understanding of spiritual power. It's very rare to meet the male that understands the power of the spirit."

"And if that's all you have," Lisa, a fifty-three-year-old artist, picked up the thread of conversation, "and you start to feel your power easing away, as you do in middle age, if you don't have another force, you're going to feel at a great loss. It would be healthy if men had a vehicle for expressing that loss, where they could say 'I'm in menopause and it's time to let go of the old stuff.'"

"I'm just recently in a relationship," said Nel who teaches at the local college. "I just turned fifty, and I've been dating for four decades." The women laughed. "I found that the younger men I dated were reasonable, and the older men I dated were reasonable, but there are real problems with the men forty to fifty-five years of age. They're spoiled!"

"Testosterone poisoning," Susan interjected.

Nel continued, "They're unmanly, not terribly sure who they are as men, and just really waiting for women to take care of them. At times you feel like you don't have a mate—you have a son." Nods and "uh huhs" from the women. "And then it feels kind of incestuous."

"But sex seems to be a big thing for these men," Marlena, a fifty-one-year-old counselor said. "They're concerned about the changes they're going through, the loss of sexual desire. I'm going through that too." Marlena paused and searched for the right words to convey her feelings. "But in some way, for me, it is a great relief that I don't want it the way I used to. Thank God, you know?" All the women nodded and laughed.

Nel added that the shift to a more mature sexuality seemed more difficult for the baby boomer males. "One thing that is happening," she said, "is that we have a whole generation of children who were raised by clearly unhappy mothers. I think the women were resentful of their place. I think they were in many cases mean-spirited. They were unhappy, and they legislated that unhappiness upon their children. And I think what we ended up with was women who became feminists and men who became frail."

Nel continued, her voice strong and confident. "My feeling is that the whole menopausal thing is very real for men, and I think that the forty- to fifty-five-year-old men are more impacted. I feel they were not given a very good 'head set.' They were a handicapped generation from the beginning. And then when you add the complexity of menopause on top of that, you get wounded and crippled men, cut off from their bodies, their sexuality, and their emotions."

"For me, there is a difference between menopause and midlife crisis," said Vi, who is a professor of languages. "Menopause is dramatic. Midlife crisis is a gradual thing. The body is telling a woman she better not have more babies. It will be dangerous for her and the babies too. It serves the biological purpose of ending the time of reproduction so women can do other things. Giving birth is a function that only belonged to the woman. That's why menopause is not a male thing. It's only a female thing."

"It's the term itself," said Celia, "that's where I feel the rip-off. It's one of those oxymorons. There's no such thing as 'male menopause' because they don't have the 'meno' in the first place, but if it helps men open up, if that's what they want to call it...I'm O.K. with it."

"What I need to know," said Susan, bringing the question to a head, "if men have a menopause, what are the symptoms? I want to know if men have headaches? I want to know if men think they're crazy because they don't go to sleep? I want to know if men are restless? I want to know if men have hot flashes? I want to know if they feel their lives are coming apart?"

"I'm from Missouri," Susan concluded. "I'm waiting. Is the idea of male menopause just another excuse so men can deny responsibility for their destructive behavior, or are there real, physiological changes men go through?"

As I listened to Susan, I wished she could be "a fly on the wall" at one of my men's groups and listen to what men are saying about their lives. Women can't understand what men are not willing to voice, and men are just now beginning to talk about the changes of male menopause.

Twenty Years in the Life of a Men's Group

We had been meeting together for nearly twenty years, seven men who were committed to giving each other support and learning about what it means to be a man at midlife and beyond. We ranged in age from forty-eight to sixty-six. The seven of us were sitting around a table at a wonderful restaurant in the wine country of northern California, enjoying good food, good wine, and the company of men who knew each other well.

"Listen, I know the perfect place to have our twenty-year celebration," said Harry, a community activist and tour guide. "We ought to go to India."

"I like it," said Bob, age fifty, the founder of a private elementary school. "We need to go someplace exotic and exciting, find an elder who can teach us something about the life of spirit."

"We could stop in Thailand for something truly exotic," said Ben, a business consultant and a young-looking fifty-six.

"I don't know," I said, "I like the idea of having a spiritual experience, but I don't feel drawn to India. I feel more connected to American Indian traditions than India Indians."

"What about a monastery in France?" Ralph asked. A community health planner, now age sixty, he had just returned from Europe with his wife and teenage daughters, his second family.

"What's the goal here?" Alvin, a fifty-one-year-old computer specialist asked. "Do we want to have a spiritual experience or just have fun?"

"Why do we have to leave home to celebrate and have a spiritual experience that will carry us through the second half of our lives?" Dave joined in, his voice quiet, yet firm. The eldest at age sixty-six, he always offered a different perspective from those of us who were younger. "If we want a spiritual experience," Dave said seriously, "why don't we go to New York and spend some time in a hospital holding crack-addicted babies?"

In the nearly twenty years we had been meeting together, we had gone through a lot of life changes together—births of children, divorces, marriages, retirement, and new career starts. At this meeting, we had spent the day talking about health issues, the changes we were going through as we aged, and the commitments we had made to each other to keep ourselves in good shape physically, mentally, and spiritually.

The worries we were having seemed fairly typical of men I knew. Though we had been together for a long time and knew each other well, it was still difficult to be honest about our feelings and fears about aging. "I'm concerned about chronic pain in my lower back and the knee injury that never healed properly," said Bob, who still looks like he could be a star tackle for his high school football team. "My skin's showing the wrinkles, and I can't see well."

"What's the problem with your eyesight?" Harry wanted to know. "You already wear glasses."

"I probably need bifocals," Bob admitted with a sheepish grin, "but I don't want to get them. I'm afraid they'll make me look...old." We all nodded and chuckled, both at the physical changes we all identify with and the worries about how we look to others.

"I don't like seeing the wrinkles either," said Harry, "but I'm much more concerned about my heel spurs. They're so painful at times, I can't even walk. Also, I'm putting on weight and don't seem to be able to get it off."

"Hey, as long as you're getting it on," Ben joked, "you're all right."

"Don't laugh," Harry continued seriously. "I feel like my sexual energy is diminishing. I worry about my loss of sexual appetite."

"Yeah, I joke about it," said Ben, "but it's a problem with me too. The last two years I feel like I have weaker erections and sometimes can't get it up at all. I also forget things more, and my mental quickness seems to have diminished."

"Are you coloring your hair," I wanted to know.

"I am!" Ben responded almost proudly. "Just the over-the-counter stuff. I feel like it looks better as my hair thins, and now that I'm doing consulting, it may make a difference."

"Last week I was doing a consultation, and right in the middle of the discussion, I forgot the name of the CEO I was talking to," Ralph admitted, the embarrassment still evident in his voice. "I worry about Alzheimer's." We all nodded.

"How are you doing keeping the weight down?" Dave asked.

"Well, I lost close to thirty pounds but have put some back on," Ralph said. "I really need to start riding my bike again, though it does seem to irritate my prostate, which has been giving me some trouble."

"The doctor says mine is slightly enlarged," I joined in. "About typical for my age he says, but it accounts for why I wake up every two or three hours to pee."

"Speaking of prostates," I continued. "We've all had the exam, right? Bend over, drop your drawers, gloved finger up the butt, twist and push, Ouch!" Nods all around. "No one likes it, feels invasive, reminds us of adolescent fears...but, the American Cancer Society estimates that 317,000 men will be diagnosed with prostate cancer this year, far outdistancing the 184,000 women who will find out they have breast cancer.[3] So, the over-the-table exam is necessary, right?" The men shook their heads in agreement.

"Well, not quite," I said. "In the past, I have always been examined by a male doctor. But, when I had my last checkup at the clinic, a woman doctor did the prostate exam, and rather than bending over the table, she had me lie on my side on the table. It didn't hurt at all. I didn't feel invaded. Next time, when my doctor asks me to bend over, I'm going to request he do the exam the other way, with me relaxing on my side. Maybe if men were examined more respectfully, fewer of us would suffer needless illness because we refuse to see a doctor until there's a real medical emergency."

"It's true," Alvin joined in. "Most of the guys I know would rather eat hot coals than go see a doctor. Unfortunately, too many are dying because they haven't gotten the support to move beyond their fears."

"So what are your health concerns, Dave?" I asked our elder.

"To tell you the truth, I feel better now than I did in my forties and fifties," Dave said with a smile. "I'm under less stress and I'm clearer now about what's really important in life. I do forget things more often, lose my balance occasionally, and get out of breath more easily. But all in all, I feel great."

"So, we're all aging and are going through, or have gone through, a midlife transition," I said. "But do you believe there really is a specific physical change you would call 'male menopause?'" Though all the men knew the focus of my book, I hadn't given them any details about my beliefs or my findings.

Every man said that male menopause was real for them. All felt it had something to do with reduced vitality and sexual potency with significant, and sometimes serious, emotional, interpersonal, and spiritual changes.

"I'm convinced there is a significant hormonal component," said Ben. "After feeling a continuing loss of sexual desire, I finally went to my doctor and asked him if it could be related to hormone deficiencies. He tested me and found that my testosterone level was below normal."

"What did you do?" Harry asked with obvious interest.

"I started taking testosterone shots, and they really helped," Ben said, his voice rising with excitement.

"Where do they give you the shots," Bob wanted to know. Most of us had heard of a shot in the penis to restore erections, and we all had some fear of that.

"In the butt," Ben said. "It definitely seemed to help my feeling of sexual interest and vitality. But I found my prostate was beginning to enlarge, so I stopped awhile. Now, I'm taking a medication to keep the prostate from growing, and I'm trying the new testosterone patches that you put on each day. Hey, if women can take estrogen for their menopausal symptoms, why can't men take testosterone for ours?"

"My problems seem more emotional than sexual," Harry said sadly. "I can't seem to end the battle that rages inside me. I feel like I'm on an emotional teeter-totter. I go up and down and up and down. I know I love Rita, but I can't stop wondering if I really should be married. I've got a good life here, and I like what I'm doing, but I'm not really sure it's my life-work." Many in the group nodded with understanding.

"The books tell us to 'follow your bliss, pursue your passion,'" Harry continued, "but I feel I've lost my sense of passion and purpose." Then, with a pause and shake of his head, "maybe I never had it. If this is what male menopause is…it's rough."

The Seasons of a Man's Life

Listening to Harry, I remembered one of the first discussions we had as a men's group shortly after we began meeting. Alvin had brought a copy of a new book by Daniel Levinson, *The Seasons of a Man's Life*.

"What does it mean to be an adult?" Levinson asked in the book's first line. "What are the root issues of adult life—the essential problems and satisfactions, the sources of disappointment, grief and fulfillment?"[4] His questions were our own. As we devoured Levinson's book, it felt like he was another member of our group.

I felt a close kinship with Dan Levinson, though we never met. Like Levinson, my ancestry is Jewish. My family came from Russia and emigrated to New York to create a better life for their children. Like Levinson, my mother and father had children late in life, and both parents shared a passionate interest in personal transformation and social justice.

When Dan Levinson died on April 12, 1994, I felt the men's group had lost one of its own. He had just completed *The Seasons of a Woman's Life*, which updated and expanded his original research on men to focus on changes in women's lives.

Levinson's findings about midlife paralleled our group's experiences. "Adults hope that life begins at forty—but the great anxiety is that it ends there. The result of this pervasive dread about middle age is almost complete silence about the experience of being adult."[5] We were meeting to break that silence.

Like many men, we had a vision of life as a mountain with forty being the peak. We liked the journey getting to the top but were not crazy about going down the back side. We hoped there might be another mountain we could climb called "Second Adulthood" but were still fearful of going down the first mountain. What if we found nothing at the bottom but impending death?

Although much has changed since Levinson did his research on men in the 1970s, our difficulties accepting aging are still pervasive. "The widespread fears about old age have been widely recognized," Levinson reminds us. "Long before old age is imminent, however, middle age activates our deepest anxieties about decline and dying. The most distressing fear in early adulthood is that there is no life after youth."[6]

We often find the best descriptions of this time of life in great literature. In his Pulitzer Prize winning novel, *Independence Day*, Richard Ford describes what his middle-aged protagonist Frank Bascombe is going through following his divorce. He says it is "maybe a kind of major crisis or the end of something stressful followed by the beginning of something indistinct."[7]

Bascombe, like many men of this age, feels he must make a change. "I one day simply quit my job at a large sports magazine in New York and moved myself to Florida, and then in the following year to France, where I had never been but decided I needed to go."[8]

But escaping to France, even in the company of a woman twenty years younger than he, does not quell the uneasiness. "Though what I in time began to sense in France was actually a kind of disguised urgency (disguised, as urgency often is, as unurgency), a feeling completely different from the old clicking, whirly, suspenseful perturbations I'd felt in my last days as a sportswriter: of being divorced, full of regret, and needing to pursue women just to keep myself pacified, amused and slightly dreamy."[9]

But something more profound is calling to us at midlife, something more personal, with lessons that can be powerful and enlightening. "This new variety," Bascombe continues, "was more a deep-beating urgency having to do with me and me only, not me and somebody. It was, I now believe, the profound low thrum of my middle life seeking to be seized rather than painlessly avoided."[10]

"There's nothing like spending eight weeks alone with a woman two decades your junior," Bascombe concludes, "to make you wise to the fact that you'll someday disappear, make you bored daffy by the concept of youth, and dismally aware how impossible it is ever to be 'with' another human being."[11]

Like Frank Bascombe, middle-aged men often learn their most important lessons in the company of youth. It was certainly true for me.

When my son, Jemal (who was eighteen at the time), spent his birthday with me and my father (who was eighty-one), we all received a great insight. After my father had read some of his poems, put on a puppet show, and did a little dance, Jemal began to smile, and his whole face lit up. "I just realized, for the first time, that I don't have to worry about growing up. I thought getting older meant losing vitality, excitement, and love of life. You've shown me I was wrong." He gave his grandfather a big hug. The crinkly, rough, old man and the peachy-smooth, young man gave each other the great gift of life-wisdom passed on and received.

As the "man in the middle," I also learned something vital about my place in the cycle of life and death. I felt Dan Levinson was present with us as I read his words. "Our overly negative imagery of old age," says Levinson, "adds greatly to the burden of middle age. It is terrifying to go through middle age in the shadow of death, as though one were already very old; and it is a self-defeating illusion to live it in the shadow of youth, as though one were still simply young."[12]

One of the joys of midlife is to be able to look back along the road from which we have come and to catch a glimpse of the road ahead. Having made it to the bottom of the "First Adulthood mountain," I can now report confidently that there is another mountain waiting.

Many of us would like to go directly from the summit of the first mountain to the summit of the second mountain. Life doesn't work that way, however. The path up the mountain of Second Adulthood can only be reached by going down the mountain of First Adulthood. The journey down that mountain and through the valley below is what I call the "Male Menopause Passage."

The primary purpose of the Male Menopause Passage is to prepare midlife men to take their position as elders so they can nurture and guide younger men. Poet and author Robert Bly calls this archetypal process becoming a "male mother" and says that it is vital to the well-being and growth of our youth.

Bly reminds us that elders have certain rights and obligations. "One obligation is if a young man asks you how you've kept your heart alive up to this age, you have to have an answer."[13] Only a successful completion of the Male Menopause Passage will allow men to have the wisdom to respond to the hopeful questions of youth.

If men deny the Menopause Passage, they create a world without elders, a world where adults regress to the level of adolescents, and adolescents, sensing that they have been abandoned, take out their rage on everyone around them. Men create, in short, a world ruled by what Jungian psychoanalyst and psychologist Robert Moore calls, "Monster Boy Masculinity."[14]

1. Germaine Greer, *The Change: Women, Aging and the Menopause* (New York: Ballantine, 1991), 11–12.

2. *Men Alive* was a theater production that a number of men in the community and I had put on (partially in response to a performance that Carlin had produced with women) to tell the truth about our experiences as men. Many of the women had seen it and had strong reactions, both positive and negative.

3. American Cancer Society, "Facts on Prostate Cancer," Booklet no. 2654, 1996.

4. Daniel J. Levinson, *The Seasons of a Man's Life* (New York: Ballantine, 1978), ix.

5. Ibid.

6. Ibid.

7. Richard Ford, *Independence Day* (New York: Alfred A. Knopf, 1995), 91.

8. Ibid.

9. Ibid., 92.

10. Ibid., 92–93.

11. Ibid., 93.

12. Levinson, x.

13. Robert Bly, "The Gifts of Growing Old: An Interview with Robert Bly," interview with *Utne Reader*, May–June 1996, 60.

14. The term first used by the psychologist Robert Moore to describe a society where fatherhood has been devalued and adolescent male rites of passage no longer exist. First heard by author in discussions with Dr. Moore at Wingspan Leadership Conference, Chicago, Ill., November 1995.

3

The Denial of Male Menopause and the Rise of "Monster Boy Masculinity"

Elders and mentors have an irreplaceable function in the life of any community. Without them, the young are lost—their overflowing energies wasted in useless pursuits. The old must live in the young like a grounding force that tames the tendency towards bold but senseless actions and shows them the path of wisdom. In the absence of elders, the impetuosity of youth becomes the slow death of the community.

—*Malidoma Patrice Somé*
Of Water and the Spirit

If we think of male menopause as a disease that afflicts men in their forties, fifties, and sixties, we will avoid it like the plague. In truth male menopause is not a disease, but the passage to the most passionate, powerful, productive, and purposeful time of a man's life.

The primary purpose of Second Adulthood for men is to become elders—to stand for something, to have a vision for the second half of their lives, to be the kind of men young men would want to look up to and follow.

When a man denies this period of his life or is unable to negotiate the transition effectively, he never really grows up. He remains a perpetual adolescent, a flying boy, a Peter Pan. When a whole society denies this stage of life or is unable to master it, we create a world dominated by "monster boys," the chilling term used by psychologist Robert Moore.

The rule of society by so called "monster boys" is the inevitable result of a culture where parents and grandparents have abandoned their adolescent children. "The popular official and media distortions of adolescent experience in 1990s America," says Mike A. Males, author of *The Scapegoat Generation*, "define a generation of parents and grandparents that seem not to know our own youth and, at worst, not to care what happens to them. The relentless defunding and dismantling of public and private support for the young by the richest generations of middle-aged and elders in American history is extreme and dangerous."[1]

Without male elders, young men try to initiate themselves into manhood. But young men cannot initiate each other. The young man's process becomes addictive and fails. Whether addicted to drugs or to behavior, actions become increasingly compulsive, out of control, and continue to escalate despite problems that are caused.

The more a young male tries to initiate himself, the more frustrated he becomes, and the more extreme are the measures he uses in his attempts to "prove" himself a man. Trying harder and harder to get the feeling of manhood he lacks, he becomes hooked on behaviors that don't work. Increased rage and violence is the inevitable result.

The Spread of "Monster Boy Masculinity"

It was a hot summer evening in Philadelphia as Mohammed maneuvered his truck through the streets. He hummed along with the music as he drove and smiled at the children who clamored around him when he stopped. He loved the look in their eyes when they handed up their money and he handed down the deliciously cool Mister Softee ice cream cones.

Suddenly, a young man appeared at the truck window demanding money. Mohammed quickly shut the window. The young man disappeared but did not leave. Instead, he went around to the back of the truck, entered quietly, and shot Mohammed in the head.

Staggering out on the pavement, Mohammed called for help. Witnesses said that teenagers stood around and laughed at him as the music from his truck played on. Rather than give aid, they taunted him. They made up songs about his dying: "Mister Softee is dead. He didn't give out enough sprinkles." A sixteen-year-old boy was arrested two days later. The victim, Mohammed Jaberipur, father of three, had been on the job only a week.[2]

Youth violence continues to escalate, and the attackers and the victims are getting younger and younger.

After receiving a slight reprimand while playing at a neighbor's house, ten-year-old Joseph ran home and took the key to his father's ten-rifle gun cabinet from its hiding place under a bedside lamp. He then unlocked the ammunition drawer, loaded the 20-power scope rifle with a single Remington cartridge, opened the window, removed the screen, and fired a single fatal shot at the seven-year-old neighbor girl. Later, the boy lied at first about the cut over his eyebrow, which was determined to be an injury from the gun's scope. He was read his *Miranda* rights sitting on his mother's lap.[3]

Not a day goes by that we don't hear of some horribly violent and senseless crime, each one seemingly more violent and more senseless than the previous one. It is becoming increasingly evident that most of these crimes are committed by young males. The grim statistics bear this out:

- Fourteen children a day are killed by other children, and one hundred children a day are wounded by other children in this country.[4]

- Black teens are 1100 percent more likely to die of gunshot wounds than white teens.[5]

- For the first time in history, more teenagers, white and black, are dying from gunshots than by natural causes.[6]

"Young American males are our biggest national tragedy," a major American study concludes. "Males between the ages of

eighteen and twenty-five are the real cause of our crime problem."[7] Comparing young males in America to their counterparts
throughout the world, one study offers the following statistics:

- The United States has twenty times the number of
  rapes reported in Japan, England, and Spain.[8]

- Young males in Harlem are less likely to survive to the
  age of forty than are their counterparts in Bangladesh.[9]

- The homicide rate among young American males is
  twenty times that of Western Europe and forty times
  the Japanese rate.[10]

Many researchers have sought to understand the violence of
American young men and have come up with reasons that range
from poor family values to America's wild-west tradition. One of
the most consistent correlations found, however, is between male
violence in America and the conditions of poverty that so many
of our children are subjected to:

- The United States has the highest rate of children and
  adolescents living in families with incomes below
  poverty guidelines ($11,522 per year for a family of
  three in 1993) in the industrial world, the result of
  spending fewer public resources on children than any
  other industrial nation.[11]

- The rate of child poverty in America is 50 percent
  higher than those of fellow frontier cultures Australia
  and Canada, and two to eight times higher than those
  of Europe.[12]

- The United States ranks third from the bottom in
  percent of our wealth spent on education, topping
  only impoverished Ireland and non-secular and war-
  torn Israel.[13]

When I look in the eyes of young males today, I am frightened.
I used to see a lot of confusion and rage. Now, more often than
not, the rage seems to have gone underground. What I see now is
numbness and death. Thinking about young males today takes

me back to an interview I had with a fourteen-year-old boy, named Jeffrey, who was incarcerated at the Tracy facility of the California Youth Authority. The boy had been found guilty of killing a twelve-year-old neighbor in a dispute over money. I was looking forward to learning about what had happened so I could help young men like Jeffrey.

When I entered the facility, I was outraged at the prison atmosphere I encountered. "These are just kids," I thought. "Why are they locked up like they were some kind of animals?" Thinking about some of the things I did in my wild youth, somewhere deep inside I thought, "but for the grace of God...I could be a resident here, not just a visitor."

After I had been properly searched and given instructions about what I could and could not do, I settled in with Jeffrey. He was tall and thin, dressed in jeans and t-shirt; just a regular kid, I thought. That perception didn't last long.

"What made you want to kill him?" I asked, truly wanting to understand.

"I don't know," he replied and shrugged indifferently. "I guess I wanted his money, and he mouthed off at me."

"How much did you take?"

"About 60 cents." Another shrug. Jeffrey never looked at me when he talked. He didn't seem, really, to be looking at anything. His voice was robot-like.

"Do you feel bad that he's dead?" I asked, sure I would get some kind of a rise from him.

"I never gave it much thought," he said coldly. "I never gave much thought to killing flies either."

"Are you saying that killing a human being isn't any different for you than killing a fly?" Despite attempts to keep my feelings under lock and key, my voice was rising. I had lost my cool inter-viewer tone and wanted to shake him until his teeth fell out. "Don't you feel anything?" I wanted to shout.

I realized I had begun to shake, not noticeably, mostly inside. I got a funny feeling at the back of my neck, like when you sense some unseen danger. I knew, though I couldn't have articulated it at the time, that I was in the presence of a person who was dead. Not totally dead exactly, but like a zombie, the kind we used to see in the movies, a creature who used to be human but had been transformed into something else.

As I learned more about people like Jeffrey, my initial perceptions were borne out. "Looking at the gate leading into the Massachusetts prison you do not see inscribed over it Dante's motto, 'Abandon all hope ye who enter here,' but it does not need to be, for most of those whom I see there had already abandoned all hope."[14] These are the words of James Gilligan, M.D., a psychiatrist who has devoted most of his professional life to understanding what makes men violent. As director of the Center for the Study of Violence at Harvard Medical School, his experiences can help us understand people like Jeffrey.

"To speak of these men as 'the living dead' is not a metaphor I have invented," says Gilligan, "but rather the most direct and literal, least distorted way to summarize what these men have told me when describing their subjective experience of themselves....Some have told me they feel like robots or zombies, that they feel their bodies are empty or filled with straw, not flesh and blood....Another murderer I worked with says he is a 'vampire.'"[15]

As a kid, I believed that zombies were make-believe, created by Hollywood to give us a good scare. When I met Jeffrey, I changed my thinking and concluded that zombies might be real but were very rare and lived behind bars. As I look around me now, I see a world full of young, male zombies. They are no longer rare, they are no longer locked up, and we are no longer safe.

What happened? How did we create a world of disinterested, detached, deadly males? Robert Moore, who has done extensive work on the evolution of the male psyche, says we have moved from "healthy masculinity" to "monster boy masculinity." The work of researchers like Dr. James Gilligan can give us a clue about how we have created monster boys and why they become such vicious murderers.

Shame: The Root Cause of "Monster Boy Masculinity"

I have yet to see a serious act of violence that was not provoked by the experience of feeling shamed and humiliated, disrespected and ridiculed, and that did not represent the attempt to prevent or undo this "loss of face"—no matter how severe the punishment, even if it includes death.

—James Gilligan, M.D.
Violence

We live in a shame based culture where more and more of us feel a loss of respect. Many sell their souls to get or hold a job, and others have no hope of ever finding work that can give their lives meaning.

Many men approaching midlife feel disheartened about the changes they experience in their bodies, minds, and souls. They often feel over-the-hill and useless. Instead of being proud mentors and guides to younger men, they hang their heads in shame. Yet more and more young men are starving for the care and respect only elders can give them. Many young males would kill to get respect or to keep from losing the little they have. Many do.

"The prison inmates I work with have told me repeatedly, when I asked them why they had assaulted someone," says Gilligan, "that it was because 'he disrespected me.'....The word 'disrespect' is so central in the vocabulary, moral value system, and psychodynamics of these chronically violent men that they have abbreviated it into the slang term, 'he dis'ed me.'"[16]

"For we misunderstand these men, at our peril," says Gilligan, "if we do not realize they mean it literally when they say they would rather kill or mutilate others, be killed or mutilated themselves, than live without pride, dignity, and self-respect. They literally prefer death to dishonor."[17]

During the thirty-two years I worked with clients with drug abuse problems, I found that the core experience driving their hunger for drugs was shame. Most all felt there was a deep wound, a "black hole," at the center of their being. Shame was the feeling associated with this loss. "There is a hole at my core," said one addict, "where my self ought to be."

Drugs were often used in a futile attempt to fill the void. We see the same dynamic with violence. "The emotion of shame is the primary or ultimate cause of all violence," says Gilligan, "whether toward others or toward the self."[18]

For most men, shame is deeply hidden, and the things that trigger shame often seem insignificant. For many men, shame is triggered by experiences that seem so minor few people would believe a person is affected. A "funny look," a tone of voice, or a forgotten item from the grocery store can set a man off.

The shame, that many men will do anything to hide, is how easily they are shamed. "This is a secret that many of them would rather die than reveal," says Gilligan. "The secret is that they feel ashamed—deeply ashamed, chronically ashamed, acutely ashamed, over matters that are so trivial that their very triviality makes it even more shameful to feel ashamed about them."[19]

Many young men today grow up in families and communities that put them down and undermine their self-respect so often and so consistently that it takes almost nothing to push them over the edge. They hunger for a kind word—to be told that they are smart, or good, or needed, or appreciated—they are like homeless beggars. They are deeply ashamed, both of their neediness and the ease with which their hunger can be triggered. "Often violent men will hide this secret behind a defensive mask of bravado, arrogance, 'machismo,' self-satisfaction, insouciance, or studied indifference," says Gilligan.[20]

Gilligan sums it up this way: "Behind the mask of 'cool' or self-assurance that many violent men clamp onto their faces— with a desperation born of the certain knowledge that they would 'lose face' if they ever let it slip—is a person who feels vulnerable not just to 'loss of face' but to the total loss of honor, prestige, respect, and status—the disintegration of identity, especially their adult, masculine, heterosexual identity; their selfhood, personhood, rationality, and sanity."[21]

If this is true for adult men, it is even more real for young men who have not yet developed their identity and sense of self. They are just beginning to separate from their mothers and find their place in the world. They are even more vulnerable to a loss of face, more susceptible to shame, more unsure of their manhood, and more ready to become violent in a losing battle to feel the self-worth that can only come when they are honored, recognized, and appreciated by an older male. They desperately need men who have completed the Male Menopause Passage and can honor their emerging manhood.

Monster Boys and Frightened Women

A report from the Senate Judiciary Committee depicted violence against women as one of the fastest rising crimes in the nation, with twenty-nine states reporting record numbers of assaults.[22] Although our fears of violence conjure up images of assaults by violent strangers, in fact, most violence occurs between people who know each other. Domestic violence and date rape are two of the most prevalent forms of violence.

Of the women interviewed in a recent survey, 20 percent reported that they had been raped on a date, though less than 5 percent say they reported the crime. As one woman says, "I never told anyone I was raped. I would not have thought that was what it was. It was 'unwilling sex.' I just didn't want to, and he did. Today, at twenty-nine I know it was rape."[23]

Most date rapists are not Jack-the-Ripper types. Most women report that the men who raped them were intelligent, attractive, and kind. There was nothing about their exterior behavior that would indicate a tendency toward sexual violence. What does not show on the surface, but is true of most date rapists, is that they grew up in violent families. Their training led them to believe that sex is a form of combat, and women who resist need to be subdued with force.

Once men and women pass the dating stage, violence does not decrease. Sociologist Myriam Miedzian reports that 1.8 million women a year are physically assaulted by their husbands or live-in boyfriends.[24]

Why are men so violent towards women? We can begin to understand the underlying causes when we note that the condition that most often fosters battering in a relationship is a situation where a man comes to expect that a woman should serve him and do as she is told. In order for a relationship like this to develop, there has to be a collusion (i.e., co-illusion) that both the man and woman buy into.

In this scenario, the woman learns as part of her social development that her primary role in life is to please her man. He comes to expect her to serve him and becomes emotionally dependent on this giving to such a degree that any deviation is seen as a threat to his masculinity.

This adolescent way of relating is typical of boys who never grew up and girls who are so hungry for male companionship, and so lacking in adult male modeling, that they settle for boys, hoping they can mother them into becoming men. The problem is that the more mothering they get, the more shame they feel for needing it, and the more they have to "prove" their manliness by showing that no woman is going to tell him what to do. It's a double bind that women know all too well.

Robert Bly meets a lot of women like this in his workshops. "As the supply of adult men lessens," he explains, "fewer daughters grow up experiencing the adult male presence, so they choose a mate without reference to any standard of maturity. Some women speak with surprise of a lover: 'He looked so good at first—he let his feelings show, he didn't have all these hard edges that the corporate clam-men have, he talked about his childhood, he made me feel needed, wasn't afraid to say he is scared.'

"Then what?" Bly asks. "'All of a sudden he doesn't do his share, he leaves his clothes everywhere. He quits his job because there's too much hassle, and he doesn't try for another; if I tell him I'm feeling sad or lonely, his eyes look somewhere else in the room. Then I feel like a mother! An unsuccessful mother, at that.

And as soon as that happens, he doesn't make love much anymore: we end up as brother and sister. That's it. It's over."[25]

Elizabeth Janeway, in her book, *Man's World, Woman's Place*, explains this male dependence as arising from the early parent/child relationship. The experiences we have with our mothers get transferred to our mates. Janeway says these feelings might be stated this way: "I want a woman of my own, whom I can command, and who will respond willingly, to comfort me in my lack and loneliness and frustration as my mother did long ago."[26]

Whether mother was there for us as we had wished or not, we have a life-long belief that she should have been.

We can all identify and empathize with such a plea. Yet beyond the desire comes the belief that, as Janeway says, "a man does not just need a woman, he has a right to her and that right is part of the order of the world."[27] Couple this mythic belief with the shame and rage that men feel for needing women so much, for feeling unmanly and childish, and we have the ingredients for violence.

Successful completion of the Male Menopause Passage allows a man to feel proud, strong, and loving. It allows him to be with a strong woman without having to beat her down or weaken her power. He can be an equal partner with her rather than a needy child.

Monster Boys and the Attack on Men

One out of three black men are in the criminal justice system in some form. Their despair is beginning to resonate through the entire culture; that is why suburban children want rap music.

—Robert Bly
The Sibling Society

Every year, Malik Smith went to Utah to enjoy some of the best skiing in the world. He loved the outdoors and appreciated the serenity of the slopes. On his last trip, during his annual vacation, he went into a suburban nightclub. On his way back to his table, he was accosted by an eighteen-year-old stranger, John Tavo Leota. Leota beat Malik Smith into unconsciousness, and Smith died a day later from brain injuries. After the murderer was arrested, a police sergeant said, "The real tragedy is that the suspect just went around and picked fights and this guy Smith just happened to be the target. It was an unprovoked attack."[28]

When we think about male violence, we often think about men as the perpetrators, with women and children as the victims. Because male violence towards other men has become such an expected behavior in the culture, we are often blind to it. When we think of date rape, for instance, we often think about what men do to women. In the same study that revealed that a surprising 20 percent of the women surveyed had been date raped, it was found that 37 percent of homosexual or bisexual men had been raped by men they knew.[29]

Although women are often hurt and killed by men, the most likely victims of male violence are other men. Each year about three times as many men as women are murdered.[30] All men are not at equal risk, however. For every white male killed each year, seven African-American males die violent deaths.[31]

Violence has become so prevalent in our communities that many have come to accept it as a fact of life. We continue to seek simple solutions to complex problems. Some hope that gun control will solve the problem, others are sure that outfitting the police with the latest automatic weapons will help.

Rarely are significant questions being asked. Why is violence increasing? Why is most of the violence caused by young males? Is there a relationship between young male violence and the absence of caring fathers and other male mentors in the lives of the young? Without answers to these questions, violence continues to escalate. The only remedy seems to be to build more prisons and lock these young men up. But putting young men in prison doesn't teach them to become less violent, it causes violence to escalate.

Department of Justice statistics estimate there are 135,000 rapes of women a year, nationwide, though many groups believe the number is higher.[32]

According to James Gilligan, M.D., the number of males raped in prisons is as high as eighteen every minute, roughly one thousand per hour, or just under nine million rapes per year.[33]

If you are as shocked by the enormity of the figures as I was, consider these two facts: (1) "There are close to two million men in various penal facilities of this country on any given day....And since the turnover of those awaiting trial and those sentenced to short-term incarceration is especially high, the total number of men in custody for at least part of the year, in any one year, comes to more than ten million, with a near equal number released back into our communities." (2) Rape is a fact of life for nearly all men in prison.[34]

According to one study, "So prevalent was the issue of sexual assault that one correction officer quoted in a report to a state legislator said that a young inmate's chances of avoiding rape were 'almost zero....he'll get raped within the first twenty-four to forty-eight hours. That's almost standard.'"[35]

"But those guys being assaulted in prison are criminals," some might say. "Maybe they don't deserve to be raped, but they broke the law and deserve to live with the consequences of their actions." We would like to distance ourselves from these men and close our eyes to what is happening to them every day in our prison system. The truth is difficult to accept. Stephen Donaldson is one of those who can never distance himself from those men and has accepted the truth. "Twenty years ago," he says, "I was gang raped while in jail on a charge for which I was later acquitted."[36] For those who think it could never happen to us or any of the men we know, rape may be as close as a false charge for protesting war and violence.

For many women, sexual assault is a two step process. First they are free, living their lives in the world, then they are assaulted and their lives change forever. For many men in our society, the process is the same. They, too, are assaulted by family members, raped on dates, and sometimes by strangers. But, for most men who are raped, sexual assault is a three step process. First they are free, then they are put in jail, and finally they are raped. Since they are out of sight and out of mind, few people are aware that it even occurs.

There are no rape crisis centers for men and boys, no public protests to "take back the night," and few advocates to wake us up. As the government defines it, rape can't even happen to males. The Federal Bureau of Investigation defines the crime of rape as: "the carnal knowledge of a female forcibly and against her will,"—a formulation that, in effect, defines the phenomenon of male rape out of existence.

I have focused attention on men being raped for three reasons: First, to show that sexual assault is not just a problem facing women. It is also a "men's issue." Second, to show the kind of rage that builds up in men when their needs for love and respect are not met. Third, to show that male violence will not be curbed by hiding it in prisons. Male violence results when men are shamed and abused. It will only be healed when all men, even those in prison, are treated with care and respect.

Monster Boys and the Environment

Feminist scholars have long recognized that the violence perpetrated on vulnerable men and women is related to the violence that is done to the earth. "The physical rape of women by men in this culture is easily paralleled by our rapacious attitudes toward the Earth itself," says Arisika Razak writing in *Reweaving the World*. "She, too, is female. With no sense of consequence and scant knowledge of harmony, we gluttonously consume and misdirect scarce planetary resources."

"With unholy glee," Razak continues, "we enter 'virgin' territory. Nature is naturally threatening—she must be conquered, reduced, put in her place."[37]

Although women have also participated in the behaviors that are ultimately destructive of the planet—the overconsumption of goods, the increasing use of fossil fuels for automobile and air travel, and the destruction of animal and plant habitat to make room for the human population explosion—men are less connected to the natural rhythms of life. As a result, men are more likely to try to control and dominate nature.

In describing the different focus that women and men have in our culture, author Sam Keen says, "No matter how she might participate in a consumer culture, her primal psychological identity was with the biological order. Her bottom line was not profit and loss, but birth and nurturance. Men's identity since the industrial revolution, on the other hand, has been so closely bound up with exploiting natural resources that creation of an earth-honoring ethic will require men to make a fundamental change in our self-understanding. Not just our actions must change. Our identity must also change."[38]

In many ways, we have been acting like children in our relationship to the earth. We treat the earth like an all giving mother whose only purpose is to meet our every need. "We have been behaving like a five-month-old infant who doesn't want to grow up," a psychologist said recently. "In his narcissistic babyhood, the baby sees its mother as existing only to look after him. She has no being, no purpose, other than that. She comes and goes when he demands comfort, or food, or warmth, as far as the baby is concerned. He is the be-all and end-all of the universe."[39]

Most children grow up to realize that their mothers are separate people and have needs of their own. They learn to respect the needs of others and take care of themselves. "Unfortunately, not every baby learns this lesson," the psychologist concludes. "There are quite a few middle-aged men around who haven't stopped tyrannizing the provisioning mother."[40]

As Sri Lankan writer and psychotherapist Anuradha Vittachi reminds us, "What humans are beginning to realize—or rather, to remember—is that we are not infant gods who own Mother Earth and can scream for unlimited sustenance from her as our right."[41]

However, when boys don't get the support necessary to grow up to be men, they continue their childish demands. They expect women to serve them, getting angry when they find women have their own needs. They also make similar demands on the environment, expecting the world to be a perpetual sugar tit. They feel it is their right to get everything they want, when they want it.

A key reason why we are facing an environmental crisis is that we live in a world where many men have yet to grow up. If men do not successfully complete the Male Menopause Passage, they continue to act like hungry, demanding children who feel they deserve to be fed. We know that young men cannot grow to become responsible adults without the involvement of strong, caring fathers.

Male Menopause and the Undoing of the American Father

In 1993, we saw his picture on the cover of *Newsweek*. He is the middle-aged, frustrated, emotionally wounded, out-of-work, divorced father who finally comes unglued under the strain of modern life. The face on the cover was Michael Douglas, who played the character in the movie *Falling Down*. But we all recognized him as the guy next door, perhaps even the guy we see in the mirror each morning when we shave. He's the Menopause Man, and things are not going well for him.

Critics weren't sure how to take the movie or the message it was giving us about society, but in reviews from *The National Review* to *Rolling Stone*, there was agreement that the movie reflected an important trend toward greater conflict and violence in American society and the frustration that was being felt by white, middle-class, middle-aged men.

We've all had the desire. Weighed down by increasing feelings of anger and isolation, sweating in traffic in the smoggy glare of an L.A. morning, the "hero" of *Falling Down*, who remains nameless through most of the movie, bolts from his car. "Where do you think you're going?" an angry motorist yells after him as he begins to climb the freeway embankment. "Going home,"

Menopause Man replies simply, pointing vaguely in the direction he's heading.

Later, the cops, led by Detective Prendergast (Robert Duvall), on his last day before retirement, will call him D-FENS, after the vanity plate on the car he ditched, another displaced worker from one of local defense plants. It soon becomes clear that Prendergast, as the savvy elder, is the only hope for Menopause Man and his family, if disaster is to be averted.

Menopause Man heads for a pay phone to call his ex-wife (Barbara Hershey) and tell her he's on his way home for his daughter's birthday party. For Menopause Man, the journey home becomes a nightmare as his personal pain mixes with hopelessness and rage of other men he encounters on the way.

As we see his humanity deteriorate before our eyes and dread the inevitable confrontation with his ex-wife and daughter, we wonder whether he was a madman masquerading as loving father or a loving father driven mad by the loss of his wife, his family, his job, and his self-respect. When Prendergast finally confronts him with the truth of how far he's fallen—"You were going to kill your wife and daughter, then turn the gun on yourself"—Menopause Man is stunned. In a bewildered whisper he asks, "I'm the bad guy? How did that happen? I did everything I was told to do."

"They lied to you," Prendergast says simply.

In reviewing the film *Falling Down*, most social critics focused on racial conflicts the film highlighted and the fear many middle-class whites have about non-white minorities. The *Newsweek* cover story, for instance, headlined "WHITE MALE PARANOIA: Are They the Newest Victims—or Just Bad Sports?"[42]

But others also recognized the significance of the fatherhood issue and the importance of men who have completed the Menopause Passage. David Blankenhorn, in his book *Fatherless America*, describes the Michael Douglas character in the movie this way: "Removed from his home, estranged from his child, denied the role of husband and father, his life ceases to make sense. He is lost. He feels castrated, unmanned, unfathered."[43] He feels deeply ashamed, the "fuel" we have seen, which leads to violence.

The loss of fatherhood in our culture is spreading like wildfire, and the results are devastating to the family and the society. "Fatherlessness is the most harmful demographic trend of this generation," says Blankenhorn. "It is the leading cause of declining child well-being in our society. It is also the engine driving our most urgent social problems, from crime to adolescent pregnancy to child sexual abuse to domestic violence against women."[44]

It was not so long ago that fathers were an important presence in the family, but now they are disappearing daily. "The United States is becoming an increasingly fatherless society," says Blankenhorn. "A generation ago, an American child could reasonably expect to grow up with his or her father. Today, an American child can reasonably expect not to."[45]

What's even more damaging to the culture is that we have come to accept the absence of fathers as the norm. We have come to believe that fatherhood is superfluous, and the need to teach fathers about fatherhood, the prime purpose of those who have completed the Male Menopause Passage, is unnecessary.

When society goes after "dead-beat" dads to force them to pay child-support but does little or nothing to provide support for fathers to stay involved with their children, a message is sent that fathers are needed only for their money. If a father is out of work or doesn't have enough money for his family, he often feels hopeless, helpless, and useless.

Male Menopause and the Economic Shame of the Father

I still remember the fear in our family. I was five years old and my father was forty-two. He was in the midst of the Menopause Passage, though he was not aware that it even existed. He had been unemployed for over a year. His career as an actor and writer was stalled, and my mother had gone to work to try and support the family. Though there was always enough to eat, I was afraid that my family was falling apart.

My five-year-old mind had no idea what was going on. It was only in recent years, when I came across a journal my father had kept at the time, that the true nature of what he was going through was finally revealed to me.

June 4th:

"Your flesh crawls, your scalp wrinkles when you look around and see good writers, established writers, writers with credits a block long, unable to sell, unable to find work, yes, it's enough to make anyone, blanch, turn pale and sicken."

August 15th:

"Faster, faster, faster, I walk. I plug away looking for work, anything to support my family. I try, try, try, try, try. I always try and never stop."

November 8th:

"A hundred failures, an endless number of failures, until now, my confidence, my hope, my belief in myself, has run completely out. Middle aged, I stand and gaze ahead, numb, confused, and desperately worried. All around me I see the young in spirit, the young in heart, with ten times my confidence, twice my youth, ten times my fervor, twice my education. I see them all, a whole army of them, battering at the same doors I'm battering, trying in the same field I'm trying. Yes on a Sunday morning in early November, my hope and my life stream are both running desperately low, so low, so stagnant, that I hold my breath in fear, believing that the dark, blank curtain is about to descend."

As a midlife man myself I can feel my father's pain as his self-esteem slowly eroded away, the fear and frustration of trying to support a family took its toll, and the tide of shame began to envelop him.

Six days after his November 8th entry, my father tried to kill himself. Though he survived physically, emotionally he was never again the same. Over the last thirty years, I've treated more and more men who are facing similar stresses to those my father experienced. The economic conditions and social dislocations that contributed to his feelings of shame and hopelessness continue to weigh heavily on men today, particularly those going through the Menopause Passage.

"Recent economic trends have left millions of men permanently unemployed or underemployed....College-educated men over forty-five have...seen their yearly pay descend by 18 percent over the last five years."[46] More than forty-three million jobs have been erased in the United States since 1979, according to a *New York Times* analysis of Labor Department statistics.[47] In the last twenty years, the United States has transformed itself into a postindustrial society. The result has been good for big business and bad for men and their families.

As America's economy becomes even more high tech and specialized, traditional blue-collar male jobs (i.e., factory, construction, and transportation) have become scarce. During the 1980s, the number of men who were working full-time, year-round, declined by over 10 percent. By 1991, the number of men working full-time, year-round, was declining by 1.2 million each year.

Nearly three-quarters of all households have had a close encounter with layoffs since 1980, according to a new poll by the *New York Times*. In one-third of all households, a family member has lost a job, and nearly 40 percent more know a relative, friend, or neighbor who has been laid off.[48]

When a man cannot support his family, he feels ashamed and finds it difficult to hold on to his manhood. When he loses his job and the prospect of finding suitable work at the same time he is going through the Menopause Passage, it can be devastating.

Many fathers take out their frustrations in violent ways, directed at themselves and those around them. They become impotent with rage. Unable to assume their positions as men, more and more are left in limbo. Just when they feel they should be passing on the fruits of their successes to the next generation, being men of pride and substance, they are cut off at the knees. Instead of being able to give to their adult children, they feel like they have become children themselves. Instead of feeling they can pass on the fruits of their labors, they find their trees no longer bear fruit. Instead of becoming elders in their families and communities, they find they have become aging children.

Without a Successful Menopause Passage We Become a Society of Siblings

---

[In a Sibling Society] adults regress toward adolescence; and adolescents—seeing that—have no desire to become adults.

—Robert Bly
The Sibling Society

As Robert Bly puts it, without the presence of fathers in the society, "we are all fish swimming in a tank of half-adults."[49] Without strong, loving fathers to look up to, we forever feel like frightened, competitive siblings. Without the presence of men who complete the Menopause Passage and act as role models and mentors, more and more young males and females lose interest in becoming adults at all.

Simply put, for a society to function effectively, children need to be parented by males and females. In ever increasing numbers, children are being raised in families without fathers. Fathers cannot learn the skills and courage to remain in their families without the support of elder males who have successfully completed the Male Menopause Passage.

When Betty Friedan wrote *The Feminine Mystique* in 1963, she started a women's revolution. That same year a little-known German psychiatrist, Alexander Mitscherlich, wrote *Society Without the Father*, which lays the foundation for an understanding of why males in our society are so troubled, ineffectual, and violent.

"Mass society, with its demand for work without responsibility," says Mitscherlich, "creates a gigantic army of rival, envious siblings. Their chief conflict is characterized, not by Oedipal rivalry, struggling with the father for the privileges of liberty and power, but by sibling envy directed at neighbors and competitors who have more than they."[50]

As a psychotherapist who has practiced in the sixties, seventies, eighties, and nineties, I have seen major changes in individuals, families, and society. During this time, I have seen the demise of what we might call "the old father." This was a guy who equated fatherhood with "bringing home the bacon," thought that women's place was in the home, felt that he was "king of his castle" and his word must be obeyed without question, distanced himself emotionally, believed that women and children should be seen and not heard, and generated more fear than love in his family.

The women's movement helped free women from the domination of the old father and allowed them to expand their role in the world. It also helped focus attention on the restrictions in the male role that kept men bound to an old model that was as confining and deadly for men as the old feminine role was for women.

However, we have not developed a new fatherhood role to replace the old one. Rather, we have simply gone in the other direction and replaced "the old father" with the "opposite of the old father." Thus, we now have men who become fathers who have no intention of supporting their children financially, who have given their power over to women and act more like children themselves than equal partners, who are emotional and weepy to the extreme, who believe that "mother knows best," who have become serfs in their own homes, and who are sensitive and kind but lack backbone and courage.

Women, seeing this kind of man around the house, decide that they better take care of things themselves. They try to become both mother and father to the children, an act that is not possible. Since only men can become fathers, mothers end up burning themselves out, and the fathers end up feeling useless.

Without the presence of strong nurturing fathers, the children lose respect for men. The boys grow up being pulled in two directions. Some decide that the best way to become "manly" is to act like their mothers. They grow up with a feminine view of maleness. Others decide to reject anything that is the least bit feminine and become "super-manly."

These young men are the ones, who in the extreme, become the monster boys of the society. They become more and more violent in the futile attempt to become manly without the presence of strong men in their lives. Those boys who try to find their missing manhood by acting like "strong women" are equally lost. Both groups grow up to become "pseudo-men." They develop an "act-as-if" manhood and at midlife feel they have little true manliness to pass on to younger men.

Society is, thus, caught in a vicious cycle. Many midlife men are still looking for the fathering they never received. They feel they must first find the missing ingredient of manhood before they can turn around and give something to younger men.

Young men, hungering for recognition and respect, feel rejected. When they look towards the older men, all they see are their backs. The truth is that midlife men will not feel manly until they turn towards younger men. In the act of facing the young men they long to nurture but also fear will not accept them, midlife men become the fathers they have been seeking and move a step closer to becoming the men they have always wanted to be.

Robert Bly concludes his book, *The Sibling Society*, by having us imagine a field with youth on one side and elders on the other, each group looking into the eyes of the other. There is a line drawn on the earth between the two groups. "The adult in our time," says Bly, "is asked to reach his or her hand across the line and pull the youth into adulthood....If we don't turn to face the young ones, their detachment machines, which are louder and more persistent than ours, will say, 'I am not a part of this family,' and they will kill any real relationship with their parents."[51]

It is the midlife men who must turn around, even though they are not sure they can do it, and face the younger men. "The hope lies in the longing we have to be adults," says Bly. "If we take an interest in younger ones by helping them find a mentor, by bringing them along to conferences or other adult activities, by giving attention to young ones not in our family at all, then our own feeling of being adult will be augmented, and adulthood might again appear to be a desirable state for many young ones."[52]

Notes Chapter 3

1. Mike A. Males, *The Scapegoat Generation: America's War on Adolescents* (Monroe, ME: Common Courage Press, 1996), 4–5.

2. June Stephenson, *Men Are Not Cost-Effective* (New York: HarperCollins, 1995), 40.

3. Ibid., 39–40.

4. Ibid., 34.

5. Ibid.

6. Ibid.

7. James Patterson and Peter Kim, *The Day America Told the Truth: What People Really Believe about Everything That Really Matters* (New York: Prentice Hall Press, 1991), 6.

8. Ibid., 120.

9. Ibid.

10. Ibid.

11. T. M. Smeeding "Children and Poverty: How the U. S. Stands," *Forum for Applied Research and Public Policy*, Summer 1990, 65–70.

12. Males, 7.

13. Ibid.

14. James Gilligan, M.D., *Violence: Our Deadly Epidemic and Its Causes* (New York: G. P. Putnam's Sons, 1996), 32.

15. Ibid., 33.

16. Ibid., 105–6.

17. Ibid., 110.

18. Ibid.

19. Ibid., 111.

20. Ibid.

21. Ibid., 112.

22. From Gannett News Service, reported in *Marin Independent Journal*, 22 March 1991.

23. Quoted in Patterson and Kim, 129.

24. Myriam Miedzian, *Boys Will Be Boys: Breaking the Link Between Masculinity and Violence* (New York: Doubleday, 1991), 5.

25. Robert Bly, *The Sibling Society* (Reading, MA.: Addison-Wesley, 1996), 49.

26. Elizabeth Janeway, *Man's World, Woman's Place: A Study in Social Mythology* (New York: Dell, 1971), 44.

27. Ibid., 45.

28. Quoted in Stephenson, 37.

29. Patterson and Kim, 130.

30. Ibid., xxiv.

31. Department of Justice, Federal Bureau of Investigation, *Uniform Crime Reports, 1989.*

　　Bureau of the Census, *Statistical Abstract of the United States, 1985, 1990.*

32. Department of Justice, Federal Bureau of Investigation, *Uniform Crime Reports, 1996.*

33. Gilligan, 175.

34. Ibid.

35. Ibid., 174.

36. Stephen Donaldson, correspondence with author. Donaldson is a writer and president of Stop Prisoner Rape, a national organization.

37. Ariska Razak, "Toward a Womanist Analysis of Birth," in *Reweaving the World: The Emergence of Ecofeminism,* ed. Irene Diamond and Gloria Feman Orenstein (San Francisco: Sierra Club Books, 1990), 165.

38. Sam Keen. *Fire in the Belly: On Being a Man* (New York: Bantam Books, 1991), 120.

39. Quoted in Anuradha Vittachi, *Earth Conference One,* 18.

40. Ibid.

41. Vittachi, 18.

42. "White Male Paranoia," *Newsweek,* 29 March 1993, cover.

43. David Blankenhorn, *Fatherless America: Confronting Our Most Urgent Social Problem* (New York: Basic Books, 1995), 142.

44. Ibid., 1.

45. Ibid.

46. Andrew Kimbrell, *The Masculine Mystique: The Politics of Masculinity* (New York: Ballantine, 1995), 9.

47. New York Times, *The Downsizing of America: The Reporters of the New York Times* (New York: Random House, 1996), 4.

48. Ibid., 5.

49. Bly, *The Sibling Society,* viii.

50. Alexander Mitscherlich, *Society Without the Father: A Contribution to Social Psychology*, trans. Eric Mosbacher (New York: HarperCollins, 1969), 269–70. Originally published in Germany, 1963.

51. Bly, *The Sibling Society*, 237.

52. Ibid.

Part II

Understanding the Biological, Psychological, Interpersonal, and Social Realities of the Male Menopause Passage

4

It Doesn't Work the Way It Used To: A Man's Body at Midlife

The Loss of Power, Passion, Potency, and Purpose

Men at midlife often experience a lapse in virility and vitality, a discontent with their lives, and a decline in well-being. Yet most men will talk about most anything else other than their concerns about sexuality. When Robert, a forty-five-year-old accountant, first came to see me, he complained about a lack of energy and increasing stress at work.

It was only after three months of counseling that Robert began talking about his relationship with his wife, Susan. They had been married for two years, the second marriage for Robert, the first for Susan. He talked about their fights and frustrations over his long working hours, his conflicts with his ex-wife, and Susan's spending habits. Finally, he talked about what was happening in the bedroom.

"It's the damnedest thing," Robert said with a laugh, though it was obvious that he was quite frightened. "Everything's fine and we're in bed together and she's really ready and wants me and I want her and then the damn thing just doesn't work." He was talking fast now, like he was trying to get it all out before the roof caved in on him.

"How often has this happened?" I wanted to know. "More than once," was Robert's anguished reply. Like most men, Robert believed that a single lapse was an uncomfortable, but acceptable phenomenon. But more than once was intolerable.

Robert's story was a common one. I'd heard it from hundreds of men at various ages, and it was becoming an increasingly common complaint men in their forties and fifties were voicing. Most all the men initially feel like Robert—shock and disbelief hit first, then they try to ignore it and hope the problem will just go away. When it doesn't, fear and finally panic sets in.

What often made it even worse was the shame so many men felt. They were sure they were the only ones going through this and "knew" they were losing their manhood along with their erections. The most difficult step men like Robert take is acknowledging the problem, talking to someone they trust, and coming for help if problems continue.

Too many men, however, deny the problem, refuse to talk about it with anyone, blame their partner or themselves, begin withdrawing, and finally find reasons to avoid having sex. The problem that "doesn't exist" eats away at their self-esteem, their relationships deteriorate, and their lives go downhill fast. It doesn't have to be that way. Erection dysfunctions are very common and very treatable.

Equally treatable and particularly common with many men in midlife are problems associated with a lack of sexual desire. A man who is losing his sexual interest often loses his erections, and a man who is having difficulty "getting it up" often loses his desire for sexual activity. That raises fears and conflicts.

"I just don't feel as turned on as I used to," says John, a fifty-four-year-old school superintendent, married for twenty-five years. "In my twenties and even into my thirties, I thought about sex nearly all the time. It was almost like an obsession. Now I think about it less often, and I don't feel much sexual energy in my body. Sometimes I just accept it as a 'fact of aging,' but mostly I miss the juicy sexual feelings I used to have."

For many men, sexual desire and performance has been the one constant in their lives. They may get married, have children, lose a job, get divorced, watch their children grow up and leave, move to a new town, put on weight, start dating, remarry, etc. Their lives may be in continual flux, but their sexual desire and performance are like old and trusted friends, a constant companion, a part of themselves. When these friends desert them, they often come undone.

Though most of these men can't articulate the fearful questions, they can be read in their eyes. "If I'm not able to perform and I even lose my sexual desire, what else am I about to lose? Is this the beginning of the end? Is death around the corner?"

Changes in men's sexuality often force them to confront other questions associated with the Male Menopause Passage. How do we make sense of the changes that occur at this stage of the journey? What can we expect? How much of the change is due to the inevitable effects of aging, and how much can we control? In order to begin to answer these questions, we need to understand aging and the changes that occur naturally in men's bodies.

Aging Is Not a Disease

To understand aging, it is necessary to distinguish between aging and the diseases people get as they age. Both aging and disease can produce impairments or deficits in optimum functioning, but it is important to make the distinction between the two. For instance, a healthy, physically fit man of fifty is not able to run as fast as he could at twenty. Loss of running speed is due to the inevitable changes of the body as it ages. It is not a disease. Neither is gray hair, wrinkled skin, balding, or loss of bone mass.

Yet we live in a culture that is so fearful of age that we are more frightened of our normal body changes than we are of most diseases. At least you have a chance to recover from disease, we think, but aging is a one-way ticket to pain and oblivion.

Dave Barry's best-seller, *Dave Barry Turns 40*, is full of hilarious stories, but the humor becomes dark when he looks ahead to the later years:

Is there something you can do about [aging]? You're darned right there is! You can fight back. Mister Old Age is not going to get you, by golly. All you need is a little determination—a willingness to get out of that reclining lounge chair, climb into that sweatsuit, lace on those running shoes, stride out that front door, and hurl yourself in front of that municipal bus.

The diseases associated with old age are not part of the normal aging process. Cancer, heart disease, Alzheimer's disease, and strokes become more prevalent as we age because of our reduced capacity to repel them. Erectile dysfunctions and other types of sexual problems also become more prevalent as we age, but they are no more inevitable than is heart disease.

In fact, most of what we think of as aging is actually disease. Many of us are afraid of aging because we think it means inevitable decline and dysfunction. The bad news is that all systems in the human body slow down over time. The good news is that healthy slowing is so gradual that we can keep most of our important functions intact until we die at a ripe old age.

No matter what we do to stay healthy, most of our body functions will deteriorate about 1/2 percent per year.[1] However, this reality should not cause us to accept the inevitability of frailty in old age. Walter M. Bortz II, M.D., who is on the faculty of Stanford University Medical School and the author of *Dare to Be 100*, says that though the loss of 1/2 percent per year is inevitable, anything faster than that is not aging, but the result of negative lifestyle practices that can be prevented.[2] "At this rate" says Dr. Bortz, "at age sixty-five you have surrendered only 15 percent of original vitality, and virtually full functional capacity is assured. Extrapolation of these figures indicates that frailty might never be encountered before age 120."[3]

Aging from Head to Toe:
Normal Body Changes over Time

There are three early signs of old age. The first is loss of short-term memory, and...I don't remember the other two!

—*Anonymous*

Roger Morris was ninety-six when he was asked to join one of the most important and ambitious studies on aging ever undertaken. The Baltimore Longitudinal Study of Aging, commonly known as the BLSA, was started in 1958.[4] More than one thousand five hundred, "healthy community-living," males were recruited.[5] Since the study began, they have come in every two years for two and a half days of testing that involves over one hundred procedures. At ninety-six, Roger was the oldest. Joe Firestone, a seventeen-year-old teen-ager, was the youngest.[6]

The results, thus far, have yielded information about what really happens to healthy people when we age and has already destroyed a number of myths about aging. One of the first myths to go was the belief that "all old people are essentially the same." Another one was that "old age is a time of inevitable decline."

The study found that "older humans show a greater range of individual variation in many physiological and psychological measurements than do younger adults....The BLSA scientists have found extraordinarily (young) eighty-year-olds and extraordinary (old) forty-year-olds."[7]

So, knowing that your path through Second Adulthood will be unique, let's take a look at some of the changes you might expect along the way.[8]

In over fifty measurements of age changes, graying of the scalp hair was the most reliable indicator of the aging process. Yet graying is by no means universal and occurs in men at different ages. Later in life, slower growth and loss of hair frequently occur in men, but, like graying, it is not universal.

Although scalp hair generally diminishes as we age, hair in the ears, nostrils, and eyebrows may undergo a burst of continuous growth. Armpit and pubic hair may change in color and texture and lessen as we age.

Several studies have shown that both the nose and ears elongate with age. Other facial dimensions do not appear to change significantly. The sense of hearing changes with age in most people, and there is often a loss in ability to hear the higher frequencies.

Some gerontologists believe that changes in the lens of the eye come closest to being a universal change associated with human aging. In humans, the lens becomes thicker and heavier with age, reducing the ability to focus on close-up objects.

Older people have increased amounts of wakefulness, and the number of times they wake up after first falling asleep increases. According to Dr. Leonard Hayflick, author of *How and Why We Age*, "the number of midsleep awakenings is much greater for men than for women."[9] Hayflick believes that this may be related to the fact that men are more likely to snore than women.

"Recently, it has been found that disturbances in breathing or respiration during sleep increase greatly with age....In a group of healthy men and women ranging in age from sixty-two to eighty-six, one-third experienced five to ten interruptions per hour in their sleep caused by disordered breathing."[10]

"Snoring almost always indicates an abnormality somewhere in the breathing airway....The frequency of snoring increases with age; almost 60 percent of men in their sixties and 45 percent of similarly aged women are habitual snorers."[11]

No one dies of old skin, but the skin does show dramatic changes with age. Wrinkles are a result of losses of the protein collagen as we age. The two layers of the skin, the epidermis and the dermis, get thinner in old age. Males have a thicker dermis than do females, which may be why female facial skin seems to deteriorate more quickly with age. Most skin damage is not normal but is caused by the ultraviolet component in sunlight. People who worship the sun in their youth will pay the price with deeper and earlier wrinkling in later life.

"Virtually every study done [on weight and aging] has shown that weight increases in the middle years and decreases in old age."[12] Yet, "we know much less about the nutritional requirements of the elderly than about those of infants, children, and young adults. We don't even know whether the natural tendency of older people to eat less puts them at or below safe nutritional levels."[13]

Internal organs such as brain and kidneys decrease in size as we age. The heart, the lungs, and, unfortunately for many men, the prostate all increase in size. Skin folds deepen, and muscle mass decreases. "Seventy-year-old men have about twenty pounds less muscle mass than they had when they were forty and about seven and a half pounds more fat and connective tissue. Bone mass is also commonly lost with age."[14]

"Exercise tolerance and performance usually decrease with age....Between the ages of thirty and eighty, muscle strength decreases 30 to 40 percent in men and to a lesser degree in women....Maximum aerobic capacity generally decreases with age. However, older people who are physically active have aerobic capacities far greater than do similarly aged, or even younger, sedentary people, and their reaction and movement times are also superior."[15]

Until recently, it was believed that with age came an inevitable decline in cardiovascular function. However, Edward G. Lakatta and his colleagues, researchers in the BLSA, have found that in subjects who are free of cardiovascular disease, age does not cause a decrease in functioning. Once again, if men stay free of disease, aging causes a minimal loss of functioning.

"Normal aging produces loss of bone tissue in everybody, but the rate of loss varies in each of us. Bone loss seems to begin in the fifties for both sexes, but then proceeds more rapidly in women than in men. In women, the rate of loss is highest during the five- or ten-year period after menopause. Men lose 17 percent of the bone mass that they had as young adults, women about 30 percent."[16]

Autoimmune diseases, including certain types of arthritis, increase as people age. The job of the immune system is to detect, inactivate, and remove microorganisms and other foreign materials from the body. As we age, some of our normal "self" proteins incur minor changes and are then seen by the immune system as "foreign." They are then attacked as "foreign invaders."

Even before physical changes remind us that we are getting older, changes in mental state become evident. Short-term memory declines with age. When you begin to write yourself reminder notes for things you used to remember easily, the process is beginning. "It is firmly established that older people do not perform as well on memory tests as do younger people. Retrieving proper names seems to be particularly troublesome." Verbalizing a word that is "on the tip of the tongue" was found by one researcher to be the most common complaint of subjects over the age of sixty-four who were concerned about memory failure.[17]

Many fear that these normal changes of aging are signs of Alzheimer's disease, but they are not. From 1906 when Alois Alzheimer, a German neurologist, first described this form of mental impairment, until less than ten years ago, the belief that "senility" was a normal consequence of aging was widespread. We now know that Alzheimer's is a disease and not part of the usual aging process.

Though both men and women age, men seem to get more of the diseases associated with aging and die of these diseases more often than women. Men going through the Menopause Passage need to understand why this is if we are to learn how to prevent these problems.

Why Men Die Sooner and Live Sicker

"Men in the United States suffer more severe chronic conditions, have higher death rates for all fifteen leading causes of death, and die seven years younger than women," says Will H. Courtenay, founder of Men's Health Consulting and a psychotherapist in Berkeley, California.[18]

Although a variety of psychosocial factors have been found to influence health, including access to medical care, economic status, and race, biologic sex consistently emerges as the strongest predictor of health and longevity.[19]

Until recently, most people accepted the fact that men's bodies break down sooner than women's. We believed it was merely a part of men's nature. Though some of the difference may result from simply being male, a great deal results from the way men live.

Based on recent research, Will Courtenay found ten key factors that contribute to men's loss of health as they age:[20]

1. Men visit physicians less and have far fewer health checkups than women.

Regular health care visits and screenings were found to be important contributors to men's health and longevity, yet according to Kenneth Goldberg, M.D., men make 130 million fewer doctor visits a year than women. Regular screenings, for instance, can detect a variety of cancers at an early stage, when successful treatment is more likely. Ninety percent of cancers that are found when they are still localized are curable.[21]

2. Men are less likely to practice self-care.

One recent study of a random sample of six thousand health maintenance organization members found that 77 percent of the women conducted self-screenings for cancer compared to 45 percent of the men.[22]

Sleep is another form of self-care, and men get far less sleep than women. Even among a national sample of eleven thousand health-conscious respondents, the men reported sleeping an average of six hours to women's eight.[23]

The fact that men sleep fewer hours than women contributes to their significantly higher injury rates. Each year, sleepiness is believed to cause seventeen thousand nighttime injury deaths, three thousand five hundred unintentional injury deaths, and over half of all work-related injury deaths.[24]

Additionally, there is growing evidence that immune functioning decreases with even modest sleep deprivation. Men's poorer quality of sleep also increases their health risks. For example, sleep apnea (often associated with snoring) increases the risk of heart attack twenty-three times in men.[25]

3. Men's diets are worse than women's.

Males consume more saturated fat and dietary cholesterol than females do, even when sex differences are adjusted for body size. Men are less likely than women to limit fat or red meat in their diets.[26]

Men eat far fewer fruits and vegetables than women and consume less fiber. [27]

Men more often skip breakfast and are less likely to limit sugar and sweet foods in their diets. They also drink far more coffee than women and are more likely to drink at least five cups each day.[28]

The "male American diet" is a major contributor to heart disease and cancer, the leading killers of men in the United States. As much as forty percent of cancer among men may be linked with diet.[29]

4. More men than women are overweight.

Contrary to popular belief, men have more problems with weight than women. The Department of Health and Human Services defines being significantly overweight as weighing at least 20 percent above ideal body weight. One-third of adults nationally are, by this definition, overweight, and the majority of these are men.[30]

Furthermore, only half as many men as women, at most, attempt to lose weight.[31]

Maintaining desirable weight is unequivocally associated with better health and lower mortality rates. In one recent study, men with waists of at least 40 inches were nearly three times as likely to develop heart disease as men with 34-inch waists.[32]

5. Men are less physically active than women.

Among those aged thirty-five to fifty-four, far more men than women engage in little or no physical activity. Among those who are active, women are more likely to engage in light to moderate exercise, which experts agree, and research shows, is optimal for the body's well-being.[33]

Men who are active are more likely to be "weekend warriors" who engage in infrequent but strenuous physical activity such as jogging, playing tennis, shoveling snow, or mowing the lawn. In one recent study, these individuals increase their risk of heart attack one hundred times.[34]

There is overwhelming and consistent evidence that physical activity significantly reduces the risk of major chronic diseases and premature death. Twelve percent of all deaths are attributable to lack of regular physical activity.[35]

Inactive men are two to three times more likely to die from any cause than their more active peers, and over one third of all heart disease deaths are attributed to physical inactivity, more than those attributed to smoking, excess weight, or hypertension.[36]

6. Men drink more and use more drugs.

The use of alcohol and other drugs is far greater among men than women. For example, over twice as many men have used cocaine, and five times more men than women drink an average of two or more alcoholic drinks per day. Research consistently reveals greater heavy and problem drinking among men and a higher prevalence of alcohol abuse and dependence.[37]

Tobacco use accounts for roughly one in five deaths overall, and one in four deaths among those aged thirty-five to sixty-four years. Twice as many male as female deaths are attributed to smoking, and men's higher lifetime use of tobacco is considered a primary reason for their higher rates of cardiovascular disease and stroke.[38]

Each year, nearly one-half million people die of cancer due to tobacco use, and the majority of them are men. Three of four men who get any kind of cancer are smokers.[39]

7. Men engage in more risk-taking than do women.

Men are more likely than women to drive dangerously. Motor vehicle-related fatalities account for nearly half of all unintentional injury deaths, and men are two and a half times more likely to die in accidents than are women.[40]

Men are far more likely than women to participate in risky sports and recreational activities. It has been suggested that sports injuries pose a greater public health risk than many reportable infectious diseases. It is estimated that three to five million sports injuries are sustained annually in the United States, the great majority to males.[41]

Men begin sexual activity earlier than women and are more likely to engage in high-risk sex. Each day, thirty-three thousand Americans become infected with STDs (sexually transmitted diseases), and sexual behavior accounted for an estimated thirty thousand deaths in 1990.[42]

Based on a variety of behaviors, including condom use and number of sexual partners, men are much more likely than women to be in the highest risk group for AIDS and other STDs.[43]

8. Men engage in more violence.

Men's willingness to engage in overt physical aggression contributes to their health risks. Men are much more likely than women to be both the perpetrators and the victims of violence. For example, nearly one half of men nationally have been punched or beaten by another person, compared to one quarter of women.[44]

Fighting is the most immediate antecedent behavior for a great proportion of homicides. The homicide death rate is four times greater for men than women.[45]

Firearm-related injuries are seven times greater among males than females. Nearly forty thousand deaths a year are due to firearms. Ninety percent of these are male, including the nine of ten deaths that are considered accidents.[46]

9. Men have fewer social supports than women.

Men have fewer, less intimate friendships than women and are less likely to have a close confidant, particularly someone other than a spouse. Some researchers have even concluded that most men have no close friends at all.[47]

There is consistent evidence that the lack of social relationships constitutes a risk factor for mortality—especially for men.

Men with the lowest levels of social relationships are two to three times more likely to die from all causes.[48]

In one study of heart disease patients, 50 percent of those without a confidant were dead after five years compared to only 17 percent of those with a spouse or confidant.[49]

People with higher levels of social support also maintain more positive health practices. They are likelier to modify unhealthy behavior and adhere to medical treatment. Their immune systems function better and react to stress more efficiently.[50]

10. Men have higher risks on the job than women and may suffer more when they lose their jobs.

Most jobs in America are demarcated by sex. While most women in America's workforce are employed in fairly risk-free environments, many high-risk jobs such as construction and farming are still primarily done by men. For instance, 95 percent of all local and state police officers are male, as are the vast majority of firefighters. These higher risk jobs lead to a greater number of work-related deaths among men than women.[51]

While males constitute 56 percent of the workforce, they account for 94 percent of all fatal injuries on the job. The five occupations with the greatest percentage of workers exposed to hazardous chemicals, for instance, are construction, agriculture, oil and gas extraction, and water transportation—all jobs held primarily by men.[52]

Unemployment is consistently linked with a variety of negative health effects, and there is evidence that these negative effects are greater for men than women. Suicide rates, for instance, are linked with unemployment and economic depression for men, but not for women.[53]

As men move through the Menopause Passage they have the opportunity to reexamine what it means to be a man. Many, for the first time in their lives, can decide to change those behaviors they had once associated with manliness.

Josh, a forty-eight-year-old attorney, remembered the "health practices" of his youth. "As a young man, I ate my prime-rib and potatoes (with lots of sour cream and chives), drank great quantities of alcohol and caffeine, played hard, slept little, and took pride in the idea that I would 'die in the saddle,' probably before I was fifty."

In his research on men and health care practices, Will Courtenay found that poor health care practices are built into our cultural definition of what it means to be a man. A man who acts in accordance with what a real man is supposed to be like does things that will undermine his health. "He would think of himself as independent, not needing to be nurtured by others," says Courtenay. "He would have difficulty developing friendships, and his social networks would be small. He would be unlikely to ask others for help....He would see himself as invulnerable to risks commonly associated with unhealthy behavior."[54]

But recently, Josh felt like blinders had been removed from his eyes when he began to make a concerted effort to take better care of himself. "Hell, now I see there is nothing manly about killing yourself, and there's nothing unmanly about eating well, drinking less, exercising regularly, and being in a men's group."

Just as men like Josh were taught that taking care of themselves is unmanly, so too, many men believe that hormones are associated with women, not men. In order for men to understand this time of their lives, they need to learn about the way hormonal changes effect them.

Men, Sex, and Hormones

The endocrine system, which is composed of the cells and tissues that produce hormones, plays a key role in the aging process. A hormone is a substance produced in the body, usually in a gland, that is secreted into the bloodstream, travels through the body, and exerts its effects on some other gland or tissue of the body. The profound effect that hormones have on virtually all cells of the body, and the fact that the level of several hormones drops with age, explains why hormone replacement therapy has often been suggested as a means of turning back the clock.[55]

The secretion of many hormones—including insulin, various growth hormones, thyroid hormone, aldosterone, melatonin, DHEA, pregnenolone, and testosterone—decrease with age. To complicate the picture, hormones act by first attaching to a receptor site on their target cells, and research has shown that these receptors decrease in number and efficiency as we age. It is possible, therefore, that changes that have been attributed to decreases in hormone production are really due to decreases in ability of target cells to respond to hormones.[56]

Do hormones make a difference in male sexuality? Though we have tended, in the past, to assume that the main engine driving sexuality is in the mind, an increasingly respected body of research shows that male hormones play a significant role.

One researcher who believes that hormones play an important part in men's lives is Dr. Theresa L. Crenshaw, past president of the American Association of Sex Educators and an expert in the field of male and female sexuality.

She points out that testosterone levels in men oscillate every fifteen to twenty minutes throughout the day and speculates about its relationship to male sexuality. "Is this constantly surging testosterone responsible for the sexual thoughts and impulses men are reputed to have every twenty minutes throughout the day? It would make sense."[57]

Since testosterone is so crucial in understanding male sexuality and the changes that occur during the Menopause Passage, let's look at it in more detail.

Testosterone: The Good, the Bad, and the Ugly

It has been called the "hormone from hell" and "the fountain of youth." It is blamed for wars, gang violence, rape, and the monosyllabic grunts of Sylvester Stallone. It is credited with making men strong, shrinking their bellies, protecting their heart, and boosting sexual desire in both men and women. It is perhaps the most misunderstood player in the human sexual symphony. It is what makes those born with an XY chromosome male. It is testosterone. Here's how it works. In the first weeks in the womb, the tiny fetus is neither male nor female. It has all the basic equipment to develop as either sex. At around six weeks, the sexual identity is finally determined when the special cells in the testes produce male hormones, the main one being testosterone. "It usually does a nice job," says Dr. Crenshaw, "crafting the penis and its neighbors, the scrotum and testicles, along with the requisite body contouring."[58]

We don't get much action from this hormone until it is awakened with a bang when the boy reaches puberty and testosterone levels rise 400–1000 percent. "Teenage boys become walking grenades, just waiting for someone to pull their pin," says Dr. Crenshaw. "As production kicks into high gear, the psychological and physical impact of testosterone is overwhelming. More than any other substance, testosterone controls the development and maintenance of masculine characteristics. Facial hair sprouts, competing with crops of acne. The voice cracks and deepens. Shoulders broaden, hips narrow. Muscles become lean and powerful. Body hair and body odor make fine companions. Sperm gets produced and wants release, often."[59]

Men are not the only ones who feel the effects of testosterone. Though present in much smaller amounts, women too, have testosterone in their bodies. Those women who feel that the world would be a much better place if testosterone were eliminated are probably not aware of recent research that shows the importance of testosterone to the developing female. "Although it is only about 10 percent of the amount circulating through teenage boys," says Dr. Crenshaw, "it is this testosterone, not estrogen, that causes the heightened erotic sensitivity of the clitoris, breasts, and nipples. It maintains the fullness, thickness, and health of her genital tissue as well."[60]

There is also evidence that satisfactory levels of testosterone are necessary if a woman is to have a healthy sexual life through the Menopause Passage. The introduction to Susan Rako's *The Hormone of Desire* states, "The fact is, that female sexuality without testosterone is a house without a foundation."[61]

For a man, testosterone fluctuations are crucial throughout his life. As a young man moves through puberty, his testosterone levels off and things quiet down, until there is another major change at midlife when testosterone, together with other hormones, begins to drop.

Testosterone and Male Menopause

In the case of male menopause, we are still in the Dark Ages. Men have fewer guideposts to help them today than women had a generation ago. Only recently have we begun to understand the biochemistry of these events, tilting the scales toward a physiological explanation.

—*Theresa L. Crenshaw, M.D.*
The Alchemy of Love and Lust

There is increasing evidence in the scientific community that there is a biological basis for the male midlife potency crisis. This has paralleled findings that other diseases such as Alzheimer's and depression have a biological base, as well as a psychological and social component.

For women at midlife, emphasis has often been placed on hormonal shifts while psycho-social changes have been neglected. For men the reverse has been true. The psychological and social aspects of the male "midlife crisis" have been emphasized, and less attention has been focused on male hormonal rhythms.

That is beginning to change now. After reviewing recent research studies, Theresa L. Crenshaw, M.D., author of *The Alchemy of Love and Lust*, says, "...hormones and related molecules are wreaking havoc with men as well as women....The information that results from these studies may just reverse the way we have traditionally viewed midlife male behavior, revealing a depth of chemical complicity about with we can now only hypothesize."[62]

So what happens to men's reproductive system as we age? Compared to the conspicuous reproductive aging that occurs in women, the aging of the male reproductive system is a more gradual affair, and the end result is not the end of reproductive capability as it is in women. Clearly, some men retain full reproductive capacity into extreme old age.

Nevertheless, reduced reproductive capacity and sexual drive have been clearly demonstrated in older men, and these changes are related to hormonal shifts.

"For every major hormone system that's been studied, we find age-related changes that suggest they could have meaning to the aging process," said Dr. Marc R. Blackman, chief of endocrinology at the Johns Hopkins Bayview Medical Center in Baltimore. Loss of muscle mass and strength, an increase of body fat, particularly around the abdomen, a weakening of the bones, a decline in immune responses, a general loss of energy, and a lessening of sexual response are among the recognized attributes that loss of hormones may bring.[63]

In her book *Love Cycles*, Winnifred Cutler reports on her research showing the general decrease in testosterone levels as men age. What's interesting about her findings is that there is a great deal of variation in testosterone levels between men at all ages. For instance, some men in their twenties have blood levels as low as 300 ng/100 ml. and as high as 1100 ng/100 ml. Men in their fifties have levels that range from a low of 200 ng/100 ml. to a high of 1000 ng/100 ml.[64]

Though the average levels of men drop steadily as we age, the research shows the importance of knowing our individual levels if we are to understand what is going on in our own bodies.

"Is a decline in testosterone inevitable? Apparently yes," says Dr. Cutler. "In all but one of the many studies, systematic decline with age has been reported. We have as yet no way of predicting how steeply a man's hormones will decline as he ages."[65]

The change in hormone levels parallels changes in sexual functioning. Dr. Cutler notes that research on the relationship between male sexuality and hormonal changes is in the early stages. "Even so," she says, "with only these crude hormone measurements a number of very significant relationships between a man's testosterone levels and his sexuality have already been demonstrated in healthy men as they age."[66]

Cutler's research showed that with decreases in hormone levels as men age, there is also an age-related decline in frequency of orgasm, morning erections, and sexual thoughts (frequency of thinking about sex).

Men in their sixties, for instance, show a much lower incidence of monthly orgasm than younger men, and men in their seventies show an even more drastic reduction. When you compare the decline in sexual behavior with the decline in the average testosterone levels at these same ages, the relationship is clear.

Male Menopause and Loss of Erections

One of the most devastating problems men experience at midlife is an inability to attain and maintain an erection adequate to permit satisfactory sexual performance. This is what medical professionals term "impotence" and I call erection dysfunction.

I believe the word impotence is inaccurate and misleading. The definition of "impotent" is "powerless to act or accomplish anything, physically weak." This view of a man only adds to his fear and shame. Erection dysfunction says what the problem is without adding all the extra baggage that makes a man feel like he is good for nothing. An inability to keep an erection adequate for sexual intercourse is baggage enough for the millions of men who are affected. According to Donvan Webster in his June 1996 *Men's Health* article "Erections 'R' Us":

Impotence affects eighteen million American men, with as many as thirty million suffering its occasional effects.

Despite the prevalence of the problem and the importance to men and their partners, little attention has been paid to the causes of erection dysfunctions. Until recently, the Kinsey survey, which was conducted more than forty years ago in a social and medical context vastly different from that of the present day, provided the only reliable data we had on erection dysfunction.[67]

Yet that neglect is beginning to change as greater attention is focused on male sexuality. Many clinicians and researchers are now beginning to recognize the biological basis of erection dysfunction, particularly in older males.

Some important findings on erection dysfunction are being reported now from the federally financed Massachusetts Male Aging Study, the largest study on male sexuality since the Kinsey Report. Over seventeen hundred men between forty and seventy years of age took part in the study. Blood samples, physiological measures, sociodemographic variables, psychological indexes, and information on health status, medications, smoking, and lifestyle were collected by trained interviewers in the subject's home. A self-administered sexual activity questionnaire was used to characterize erectile potency.

Startlingly, the study revealed that erection dysfunction had occurred in more than half of all American men over the age of forty. The study also found that the prevalence of complete erection dysfunction tripled from 5 percent in subjects in their forties to 15 percent in subjects in their seventies.[68] The good news, of course, is that the vast majority of men, even in the older age groups, maintain their potency and enjoyment of sex.

Although the study found that psychological factors play a role as men age, physical factors are more significant. There was a high correlation between erection dysfunction and heart disease, hypertension, diabetes, as well as with the medications that are often taken to deal with these problems. Of the seventeen hormones measured in the study, only the adrenal androgen DHEA showed a correlation with impotence. The age-adjusted probability of complete impotence increased from 3.4 to 16 percent as DHEA decreased from 10 to 0.5 mg/ml.[69]

Interestingly, there was no significant correlation found between impotence and lowered testosterone levels.

"DHEA drops precipitously as men age," according to Dr. Crenshaw. "By the time they are eighty, it is almost undetectable. When sixty healthy men twenty to eighty-four years old were compared with sixty healthy women in one study, DHEA was significantly lower in the men."[70]

Male Menopause and the Wisdom of the Penis

Though erectile dysfunction is not a normal part of aging, we need to accept the fact that our sexuality does change as we age. We no longer experience the same kind of erections that embarrassed us when we were young but often miss as we get older.

A man often treats his penis like an unruly servant who must be at his beck and call every moment and who must be whipped into shape so he is always ready, willing, and able to perform any duties asked of him. Like most masters, men fail to understand the changing needs of those who serve them. Men would save themselves a great deal of grief if they understood the normal changes that occur in our sexuality over time.

Seven Changes That Occur in Healthy, Normal Males as They Age:

1. Erections take longer to occur.

2. Men more often require direct physical stimulation to get an erection; a sexy sight or fantasy may not arouse him as it did before.

3. The full erection doesn't get quite as firm as it used to.

4. His urge to ejaculate is not as insistent as before. Sometimes he doesn't feel like having an orgasm at all.

5. The force of ejaculation isn't as strong as it was in the past. The amount of his ejaculate is less, and he may have fewer sperm.

6. The desire for and frequency of masturbation may drop, but in some men may increase.

7. The testicles shrink some, and the scrotal sack droops. The sack doesn't bunch up as much during arousal.[71]

Although recent research shows there is more of a physical basis to sexual problems than we once thought, the intimate connection between mind and body is nowhere more obvious than in the expression of our sexuality. We now know, for instance, that changes in hormone levels affect our sexuality and that changes in sexuality affect our hormone levels.

"The androgens do stimulate sexual behavior," says Dr. Cutler, "but sexual behavior in turn seems to stimulate the production of sex hormones. The testosterone levels before, during, and after sexual intercourse are usually higher than they are during times of celibacy."[72]

How does the relationship between the mind and body effect men's health, sexuality, and the Male Menopause Passage? We will deepen and expand our understanding in the next chapter.

Notes Chapter 4

1. Walter M. Bortz II, M.D., *Dare to Be 100* (New York: Fireside Books, 1996), 46.

2. Ibid.

3. Ibid.

4. National Institute of Health, *Older and Wiser: The Baltimore Longitudinal Study of Aging*, NIH publication no. 89–2797 (Washington, DC: U. S. Government Printing Office, September 1989).

5. Starting only in 1978, seven hundred women were enrolled. So unfortunately, less information is available on the female volunteers.

6. Names of participants have been changed.

7. Reported in Leonard Hayflick, *How and Why We Age* (New York: Ballantine, 1994), 140–41.

8. Much of the information on the following body changes comes from Leonard Hayflick's fine book *How and Why We Age*; John Medina's equally fine *The Clock of Ages: Why We Age, How We Age, Winding Back the Clock*; and *Older and Wiser: The Baltimore Longitudinal Study on Aging*.

9. Hayflick, 180.

10. Ibid.

11. Ibid.

12. Ibid., 167.

13. Ibid., 181.

14. Ibid.

15. Ibid., 184.

16. Ibid., 160.

17. Ibid., 165.

18. Will H. Courtenay (in review for publication), "Behavioral Factors Associated with Male Disease, Injury, and Death: Evidence and Implications for Prevention," *American Journal of Preventative Medicine*.

19. Ibid.

20. The data for the following ten factors that contribute to men's loss of health as they age are from the article by Will H. Courtenay (in review for publication), "Behavioral Factors Associated with Male

Disease, Injury and Death: Evidence and Implications for Prevention," *American Journal of Preventative Medicine*. The sources in notes 22–54 were cited in this article.

21. American Cancer Society, *Cancer Facts and Figures: 1994* (Atlanta: American Cancer Society, 1994).

Kenneth Goldberg, *How Men Can Live as Long as Women: Seven Steps to a Longer and Better Life* (Fort Worth, TX: The Summit Group, 1993).

S. J. Winawer and M. Shike, *Cancer Free: The Comprehensive Cancer Prevention Program* (New York: Simon and Schuster, 1995).

22. J. S. Rossi, "Stages of Change for 15 Health Risk Behaviors in an HMO Population," (paper presented at the 13th annual scientific sessions of the Society of Behavioral Medicine, New York, NY, March 1992).

23. National Stress Survey, March 1995.

M. H. Redaihs, J. S. Reis, and N. S. Creason, "Sleep in Old Age: Focus on Gender Differences," *Sleep* 13, no. 5 (1990): 410–24.

A. Reyner and Horne, "Gender- and Age-Related Differences in Sleep Determined by Home-Recorded Sleep Logs and Actimetry from 400 Adults," *Sleep* 18, no. 2 (1995): 127–34.

L. M. Verbrugge, "Unveiling Higher Morbidity for Men: The Story," in *Social Structures and Human Lives*, ed. M. W. Riley (Newbury Park, CA: Sage, 1988).

24. D. Leger, "The Cost of Sleep Related Accidents: A report for the National Commission on Sleep Disorders Research," *Sleep* 17, no. I (1994): 84–93.

25. J. Hung et al., "Association of Sleep Apnea with Myocardial Infarction in Men," *The Lancet* 336 (1990): 261–64.

M. Irwin et al., "Partial Sleep Deprivation Reduces Natural Killer Cell Activity in Humans," *Psychosomatic Medicine* 56 (1994): 493–98.

H. Moldofsky et al., "Effects of Sleep Deprivation on Human Immune Function," *Federation of American Societies for Experimental Biology Journal* 3 (1989): 1972–77.

26. American School Health Association, *The National Adolescent*

Student Health Survey: A Report on the Health of America's Youth (Oakland, CA: Third Party Publishing, 1989).

G. Block, W. F. Rosenberger, and B. H. Patterson, "Calories, Fat and Cholesterol: Intake Patterns in the U. S. Population by Race, Sex, and Age," *American Journal of Public Health* 78, no. 9 (1988): 1150–55.

Centers for Disease Control, *Hepatitis Surveillance*, Report No. 56 (Atlanta: Centers for Disease Control, 1995).

Centers for Disease Control, "Selected Tobacco-Use Behaviors and Dietary Patterns Among High School Students: United States, 1991," *Morbidity and Mortality Weekly Report* 41, no. 14 (1992): 760–72.

D. Gilroy, ed., *How Men Stay Young* (Emmaus, PA: Rodale Press, 1991).

W. Rakowski, "Personal Health Practices, Health Status, and Expected Control over Future Health," *Journal of Community Health* 11, no. 3 (1986): 189–203.

J. S. Rossi, "Stages of Change for 15 Health Risk Behaviors in an HMO Population."

L. V. Van Horn et al., "Diet, Body Size, and Plasma Lipids-Lipoproteins in Young Adults: Differences by Race and Sex," *American Journal of Epidemiology* 133, no. 1 (1991): 9–23.

27. J. P. Leigh and J. F. Fries, "Associations Among Healthy Habits, Age, Gender, and Education in a Sample of Retirees," *International Journal of Aging and Human Development* 36, no. 2 (1993): 139–55.

T. R. Prohaska et al., "Health Practices and Illness Cognition in Young, Middle Aged and Elderly Adults," *Journal of Gerontology* 40 (1985): 569–78.

M. K. Serdula et al., "Relationship Between Drug Use and Sexual Behaviors and the Occurrence of Sexually Transmitted Diseases Among High-Risk Male Youth," *Sexually Transmitted Diseases* 20, no. 6 (1993): 307–13.

L. V. Van Horn et al., "Diet, Body Size, and Plasma Lipids-Lipoproteins in Young Adults: Differences by Race and Sex."

28. Department of Health and Human Services, *Highlights from*

Wave 1 of the National Survey of Personal Health Practices and Consequences: United States, 1979, DHHS Publication No. [PHS] 81–1162 (Hyattsville, MD: Public Health Service, 1981).

Department of Health and Human Services, *Vital and Health Statistics: Health Promotion and Disease Prevention, United States, 1990,* DHHS Publication No. [PHS] 93–1513 (Hytattsville, MD: Public Health Service, 1993).

D. Gilroy, ed., *How Men Stay Young.*

J. D. Lane et al., "Cardiovascular Effects of Caffeine and Stress in Regular Coffee Drinkers," *Psychophysiology* 24 (1994): 157–64.

P. J. Pascale and W. J. Evans, "Gender Differences and Similarities in Patterns of Drug Use and Attitudes of High School Students," *Journal of Drug Education* 23, no. 1 (1993): 105–16.

29. R. Altman, *The Prostate Answer Book* (New York: Warner Books, 1993).

American Cancer Society, *Cancer: What You Eat Could Put You at Risk* (Atlanta: American Cancer Society, 1993).

American Heart Association, *Heart and Stroke Facts* (Dallas: American Heart Association, 1994).

M. A. Denke, C. T. Sempos, and S. M. Grundy, "Excess Body Weight: An Underrecognized Contributor to High Blood Cholesterol Levels in White American Men," *Archives in Internal Medicine* 153 (1993): 1093–1103.

J. M. McGinnis and W. H. Foege, "Actual Causes of Death in the United States," *JAMA* 270, no. 18 (1993): 2207–12.

M. Oppenheim, *The Man's Health Book* (Englewood Cliffs, NJ: Prentice Hall, 1994).

S. J. Winawer and M. Shike, *Cancer Free: The Comprehensive Cancer Prevention Program.*

30. Department of Health and Human Services, *Vital Health and Statistics: Health Promotion and Disease Prevention, United States, 1990.*

D. Gilroy, ed., *How Men Stay Young.*

C. E. Ross and C. E. Bird, "Sex Stratification and Health Lifestyle: Consequences for Men's and Women's Perceived Health," *Journal of Health and Social Behavior* 35 (1994): 161–78.

C. A. Schoenborn, "Health Habits of U. S. Adults, 1985: The 'Alameda 7' Revisited," *Public Health Reports* 101, no. 6 (1986): 571–80.

31. S. N. Blair et al., "Body Weight Change, All-Cause Mortality, and Cause-Specific Mortality in the Multiple Risk Factor Intervention Trial," *Annals of Internal Medicine* 119, no. 7 (1993): 749–57.

J. Rossi, "Stages of Change for 15 Health Risk Behaviors in an HMO Population."

32. R. Andres, D. Muller, and J. D. Sorkin, "Long-Term Effects of Change in Body Weight on All-Cause Mortality," *Annals of Internal Medicine* 119, no. 7 (1993): 737–43.

N. B. Belloc, "Relationship of Health Practices and Mortality," *Preventive Medicine* 2 (1973): 67–81.

N. B. Belloc and L. Breslow, "Relationship of Physical Health Status and Health Practices," *Preventive Medicine* 1 (1972): 409–21.

L. F. Berkman, L. Breslow, and D. Wingard, "Health Practices and Mortality Risk," in *Health and Ways of Living,* ed. L. F. Berkman and L. Breslow (New York: Oxford University Press, 1983).

L. Breslow and J. E. Enstrom, "Persistence of Health Habits and Their Relationship to Mortality," *Preventive Medicine* 9 (1980): 469–83.

J. E. Enstrom, L. E. Kanim, and L. Breslow, "The Relationship Between Vitamin C Intake, General Health Practices, and Mortality in Alameda County, California," *American Journal of Public Health* 76 (1986): 1124–30.

G. A. Kaplan et al., "Mortality Among the Elderly in the Alameda County Study: Behavioral and Demographic Risk Factors," *American Journal of Public Health* 77 (1987): 307–12.

E. B. Rimm et al., "Body Size and Fat Distribution as Predictors of Coronary Heart Disease among Middle-Aged and Older U. S. Men," *American Journal of Epidemiology* 141, no. 12 (1995): 1117–27.

33. A. Blair et al., "Physical Fitness and All-Cause Mortality: A Prospective Study of Healthy Men and Women," *JAMA* 262, no. 17 (1989): 2395–2401.

Centers for Disease Control, "Prevalence of Sedentary Lifestyle: Behavioral Risk Factor Surveillance System, United

States, 1991," *Morbidity and Mortality Weekly Report* 42, no. 29 (1993): 576–79.

J. L. Weissfeld, J. P. Kirscht, and B. M. Brock, "Health Beliefs in a Population: The Michigan Blood Pressure Survey," *Health Education Quarterly* 17, no. 2 (1990): 141–55.

34. Mittleman et al., "Triggering of Acute Myocardial Infarction by Heavy Physical Exertion: Protection against Triggering by Regular Exertion," *New England Journal of Medicine* 328, no. 4 (1993): 253–56.

S. N. Willich et al., "Physical Exertion as a Trigger of Acute Myocardial Infarction," *New England Journal of Medicine* 329, no. 23 (1993): 1684–90.

35. J. A. Berlin and G. A. Colditz, "A Meta-Analysis of Physical Activity in the Prevention of Coronary Heart Disease," *American Journal of Epidemiology* 132 (1990): 612–28.

C. Bouchard et al., *Exercise, Fitness and Health: A Consensus of Current Knowledge* (Champaign, IL: Human Kinetics Books, 1990).

J. E. Enstrom, L. E. Kanim, and L. Breslow, "The Relationship Between Vitamin C Intake, General Health Practices, and Mortality in Alameda County, California."

G. A. Kaplan et al., "Mortality Among the Elderly in the Alameda County Study: Behavioral and Demographic Risk Factors."

I. M. Leigh, C. C. Hsieh, and R. S. Paffenbarger, "Exercise Intensity and Longevity in Men: The Harvard Alumni Health Study," *JAMA* 273, no. 15 (1995): 1179–84.

R. S. Paffenbarger et al., "The Association of Changes in Physical-Activity Level and Other Lifestyle Characteristics with Mortality Among Men," *New England Journal of Medicine* 328 (1993): 538–45.

R. R. Pate, Ph.D. et al., "Physical Activity and Public Health: A Recommendation From the Centers for Disease Control and Prevention and the American College of Sports Medicine," *JAMA* 273, no. 5 (1995): 403.

K. E. Powell et al., "Physical Activity and Chronic Diseases," *American Journal of Clinical Nutrition* 49 (1989): 999–1006.

36. L. F. Berkman, L. Breslow, and D. Wingard, "Health Practices and Mortality Risk."

Centers for Disease Control, "Public Health Focus: Physical Activity and the Prevention of Coronary Heart Disease," *Morbidity and Mortality Weekly Report* 42, no. 35 (1993): 669–72.

K. E. Powell et al., "Physical Activity and the Incidence of Coronary Heart Disease," *Annual Review of Public Health* 8 (1987): 253–87.

37. Department of Health and Human Services, *Vital Health Statistics: Health Promotion and Disease Prevention, United States, 1990.*

D. S. Haisin, B. F. Grant, and J. Weinflash, "Male/Female Differences in Alcohol-Related Problems: Alcohol Rehabilitation Patients," *International Journal of the Addictions* 23, no. 5 (1988): 547–48.

R. F. Huselid and M. L. Cooper, "Gender Roles as Mediators of Sex Differences in Adolescent Alcohol Use and Abuse," *Journal of Health and Social Behavior* 33 (1992): 348–62.

R. C. Kessler et al., "Lifetime and 12-Month Prevalence of *DSM-111-R* Psychiatric Disorders in the United States: Results from the National Comorbidity Survey," *Archives of General Psychiatry* 51 (1994): 8–19.

B. W. Lex, "Some Gender Differences in Alcohol and Polysubstance Users," *Health Psychology* 10 (1991): 121–32.

National Institute on Drug Abuse, *National Household Survey on Drug Abuse: Population Estimates 1991,* DHHS Publication No. [ADM] 92–1887 (Washington, DC: U. S. Government Printing Office, 1992).

L. N. Robins et al., "Lifetime Prevalence of Specific Psychiatric Disorders in Three Sites," *Archives of General Psychiatry* 41 (1984): 949–58.

B. S. Thomas, "The Effectiveness of Selected Risk Factors in Mediating Gender Differences in Drinking and its Problems," *Journal of Adolescent Health* 17, no. 2 (1995): 91–98.

38. American Cancer Society, *Cancer Prevention Study 11: Fact Card* (Atlanta: American Cancer Society, 1988).

American Heart Association, *Heart and Stroke Facts.*

C. E. Bartecchi, T. D. MacKenzie, and R. W. Schrier, "The Global Tobacco Epidemic," *Scientific American*, May 1995, 44–51.

Centers for Disease Control, "Surveillance for Smoking-Attributable Mortality and Years of Potential Life Lost, by State: United States, 1990," *Morbidity and Mortality Weekly Report* 43, no. SS-I (1994): I–3,6–7.

J. M. McGinnis and W. H. Foege, "Actual Causes of Death in the United States."

S. J. Winawer and M. Shike, *Cancer Free: The Comprehensive Cancer Prevention Program.*

39. American Cancer Society, *Cancer Facts and Figures:1994.*

40. Department of Health and Human Services, "Advance Report of Final Mortality Statistics, 1991," *Monthly Vital Statistics Report* 42, no. 2 (Hyattsville, MD: Public Health Service, 1993).

J. A. Farrow and P. Brissing, "Risk for DWI: A New Look at Gender Differences in Drinking and Driving Influences, Experiences and Attitudes Among New Adolescent Drivers," *Health Education Quarterly* 17, no. 2 (1990): 312–21.

National Safety Council, *Accident Facts, 1994 Edition* (Itasca, IL: National Safety Council, 1994).

D. F. Preusser, A. F. Williams, and A. K. Lund, "Characteristics of Belted and Unbelted Drivers," *Accident Analysis and Prevention* 23, no. 6 (1991): 475–82.

M. Zuckerman, *Behavioral Expressions and Biosocial Bases of Sensation Seeking* (New York: Cambridge University Press, 1994).

M. Zuckerman, "Sensation Seeking: A Comparitive Approach to a Human Trait," *The Behavioral and Brain Sciences* 7 (1984): 413–71.

M. Zuckerman, "Sensation Seeking and Sports," *Personality and Individual Differences* 4, no. 3 (1983): 285–93.

41. J. F. Kraus and C. Conroy, "Mortality and Morbidity from Injuries in Sports and Recreation," *Annual Review of Public Health* 5 (1984): 163–92.

National Safety Council, *Accident Facts, 1992 edition* (Itasca, IL: National Safety Council, 1992).

F. P. Rivara et al., "Epidemiology of Childhood Injuries," *American Journal of Diseases of Children* 136 (1982): 502–6.

M. Zuckerman, *Behavioral Expressions and Biosocial Bases of Sensation Seeking.*

M. Zuckerman, "Sensation Seeking: A Comparitive Approach to a Human Trait."

M. Zuckerman, "Sensation Seeking and Sports."

42. Centers for Disease Control, "Selected Behaviors that Increase Risk for HIV Infection, Other Sexually Transmitted Diseases, and Unintended Pregnancy Among High School Students–United States, 1991," *Morbidity and Mortality Weekly Report* 41, no. 50 (1992): 945–50.

EDK Associates, *The ABCs of STDs* (New York: EDK Associates, 1995).

K. P. Ericksen and K. F. Trocki, "Behavioral Risk Factors for Sexually Transmitted Diseases in American Households," *Social Science and Medicine* 34, no. 8 (1992): 843–53.

K. P. Ericksen and K. F. Trocki, "Sex, Alcohol, and Sexually Transmitted Diseases: A National Survey," *Family Planning Perspectives* 26 (1994): 257–63.

B. C. Leigh, M. T. Temple, and K. F. Trocki, "The Sexual Behavior of U. S. Adults: Results from a National Survey," *American Journal of Public Health* 83, no. 10 (1993): 1400–8.

J. M. McGinnis and W. H. Foege, "Actual Causes of Death in the United States."

M. Zuckerman, *Behavioral Expressions and Biosocial Bases of Sensation Seeking.*

43. EDK Associates, *The ABCs of STDs.*

K. P. Ericksen and K. F. Trocki, "Behavioral Risk Factors for Sexually Transmitted Diseases in American Households."

K. P. Ericksen and K. F. Trocki, "Sex, Alcohol, and Sexually Transmitted Diseases: A National Survey."

B. C. Leigh, M. T. Temple, and K. F. Trocki, "The Sexual Behavior of U. S. Adults: Results from a National Survey."

M. A. Shafer et al., "Relationship Between Drug Use and Sexual Behaviors and the Occurrence of Sexually Transmitted Diseases Among High-Risk Male Youth," *Sexually Transmitted Diseases* 20, no. 6 (1993): 307–13.

44. Department of Justice, *National Crime Victimization Survey: Criminal Victimization—1993*, Publication No. NCJ-151658 (Washington, DC: U. S. Government Printing Office, 1995).

Department of Justice, *Sourcebook of Criminal Justice Statistics—1993*, Publication No. NCJ-148211 (Washington, D.C.: U. S. Government Printing Office, 1994).

45. Centers for Disease Control, "Physical Fighting Among High School Students: United States, 1990," *Morbidity and Mortality Weekly Report* 41, no. 6 (1992): 91–94.

Department of Health and Human Services, *Healthy People 2000: National Health Promotion and Disease Prevention Objectives*, DHHS Publication No. [PHS] 91-50212 (Washington, DC: U. S. Government Printing Office, 1991).

Department of Justice, *Sourcebook of Criminal Justice Statistics—1993*.

R. J. Gelles and M. A. Straus, *Intimate Violence* (New York: Simon and Schuster, 1988).

46. J. L. Annest et al., "National Estimates of Nonfatal Firearm-Related Injuries: Beyond the Tip of the Iceberg," *JAMA* 273, no. 22 (1995): 1749–55.

Centers for Disease Control and Prevention, "Emergency Department Surveillance for Weapon-Related Injuries—Massachusetts, November 1993–April 1994," *JAMA* 273, no. 22 (1995): 1746–47.

National Safety Council, *Accident Facts, 1994 Edition.*

47. T. C. Antonucci and H. Akiyama, "An Examination of Sex Differences in Social Support Among Older Men and Women," *Sex Roles* 17, no. 11/12 (1987): 737–49.

R. H. Corney, "Sex Differences in General Practice Attendance and Help Seeking for Minor Illness," *Journal of Psychosomatic Research* 34, no. 5 (1990): 525–34.

D. Levinson, *The Seasons of a Man's Life* (New York: Ballantine, 1978).

M. E. McGill, *The McGill Report on Male Intimacy* (New York: Holt Reinhart, 1985).

M. K. O'Neil, W. J. Lance, and J. J. Freeman, "Sex Differences in Depressed University Students," *Social Psychiatry* 20 (1985): 186–90.

L. B. Rubin, *Intimate Strangers* (New York: Harper and Row, 1983).

D. Sherrod, "The Bonds of Men," in *The Making of Masculinities*, ed. H. Brod (Winchester, MA: Allen and Unwin, 1987).

D. Umberson, C. B. Wortman, and R. C. Kessler, "Widowhood and Depression: Explaining Long-Term Gender Differences in Vulnerability," *Journal of Health and Social Behavior* 33 (1992): 10–24.

D. G. Williams, "Gender, Masculinity-Femininity, and Emotional Intimacy in Same-Sex Friendship," *Sex Roles* 12, no. 5/6 (1985): 587–600.

48. L. F. Berkman, "Assessing the Physical Health Effects of Social Networks and Social Support," *Annual Review of Public Health* 5 (1984): 413–32.

L. F. Berkman and L. Breslow, eds., *Health and Ways of Living: The Alameda County Study* (New York: Oxford University Press, 1983).

D. G. Blazer, "Social Support and Mortality in an Elderly Community Population," *American Journal of Epidemiology* 115, no. 5 (1982): 684–94.

T. C. Camaho and J. Wiley, "Health Practices, Social Networks, and Changes in Physical Health," in *Health and Ways of Living*, eds. L. F. Berkman and L. Breslow (New York: Oxford University Press, 1983).

N. H. Gottlieb and L. W. Green, "Life Events, Social Network, Life-Style, and Health: An Analysis of the 1979 National Survey of Personal Health Practices and Consequences," *Health Education Quarterly* 11 (1984): 91–105.

S. C. Ho, "Health and Social Predictors of Mortality in an Elderly Chinese Cohort," *American Journal of Epidemiology* 133, no. 9 (1991): 907–21.

J. S. House, K. R. Landis, and D. Umberson, "Social Relationships and Health," *Science* 241 (1988): 540–45.

J. S. House, C. Robbins, and H. L. Metzner, "The Association of Social Relationships and Activities with Mortality: Prospective Evidence from the Tecumseh Community Health Study," *American Journal of Epidemiology* 116, no. 1 (1982): 123–40.

M. Kandrack, K. R. Grant, and A. Segall, "Gender Differences in Health Related Behavior: Some Unanswered Questions," *Social Science and Medicine* 32, no. 5 (1991): 579–90.

V. J. Schoenbach et al., "Social Ties and Mortality in Evans County, Georgia," *American Journal of Epidemiology* 123, no. 4 (1986): 577–91.

T. E. Seeman et al., "Social Network Ties and Mortality Among the Elderly in the Alameda County Study," *American Journal of Epidemiology* 126 (1987): 714–23.

D. Shye et al., "Gender Differences in the Relationship Between Social Network Suport and Mortality: A Longitudinal Study of an Elderly Cohort," *Social Science and Medicine* 41, no. 7 (1995): 78–80.

D. Umberson, "Gender, Marital Status and the Social Control of Health Behavior," *Social Science and Medicine* 34, no. 8 (1992): 907–17.

49. R. B. Williams, M.D., et. al., "Prognostic Importance of Social and Economic Resources Among Medically Treated Patients With Angiographically Documented Coronary Artery Disease," *JAMA* 267, no. 4 (1992): 522–23.

50. V. E. Bovbjerg et al., "Spouse Support and Long-Term Adherence to Lipid-Lowering Diets," *American Journal of Epidemiology* 141 (1995): 451–60.

J. M. Cwikel et al., "Mechanisms of Psychosocial Effects on Health: The Role of Social Integration, Coping Style, and Health Behavior," *Health Education Quarterly* 15 (1988): 151–73.

R. Fleming et al., "Mediating Influences of Social Support on Stress at Three Mile Island," *Journal of Human Stress* 8 (1982): 14–22.

U. J. Gruninger, "Patient Education: An Example of One-to-One Communication," *Journal of Human Hypertension* 9, no. 1 (1995): 15–25.

H. B. Kaplan, "Social Psychology of the Immune System: A Conceptual Framework and Review of the Literature," *Social Science and Medicine* 33, no. 8 (1991): 909–23.

C. Kirschbaum et al., "Sex-Specific Effects of Social Support on Cortisol and Subjective Responses to Acute Psychological Stress,"

Psychosomatic Medicine 57 (1995): 23–31.

S. J. Lepore, K. A. Allen, and G. W. Evans, "Social Support Lowers Cardiovascular Reactivity to an Acute Stressor," *Psychosomatic Medicine* 55 (1993): 518–24.

L. E. Lonnquist, G. L. Weiss, and D. L. Larsen, "Health Value and Gender in Predicting Health Protective Behavior," *Women and Health* 19, no. 2/3 (1992): 69–85.

D. Meichenbaum and D. C. Turk, *Facilitating Treatment Adherence: A Practitioner's Guidebook* (New York: Plenum, 1987).

A. F. Muhlenkamp and Sayles, "Self-Esteem, Social Support, and Positive Health Practices," *Nursing Research* 35, no. 6 (1986): 334–38.

M. K. O'Brien, K. Petrie, and J. Raeburn, "Adherence to Medication Regimens: Updating a Complex Medical Issue," *Medical Care Review* 49, no. 4 (1992): 435–54.

S. J. Winawer and M. Shike, *Cancer Free: The Comprehensive Cancer Prevention Program.*

51. Bureau of Labor Statistics, *Employment and Earnings: January, 1991* (Washington, DC: Bureau of Labor Statistics, 1991).

Department of Justice, *Sourcebook of Criminal Justice Statistics—1993.*

52. National Institute for Occupational Safety and Health, *Fatal Injuries to Workers in the United States, 1980–1989: A Decade of Surveillance,* NIOSH, No. 93–108 (Cincinnati: National Institute for Occupational Safety, 1993).

53. I. L. Abraham and H. V. Krowchuk, "Unemployment and Health: Health Promotion for the Jobless Male," *Nursing Clinics of North America* 21, no. 1 (1986): 37–47.

M. Boor, "Relationships Between Unemployment Rates and Suicide Rates in Eight countries, 1962–1976," *Psychological Reports* 47 (1980): 1095–1101.

G. H. Elder and J. K. Liker, "Hard Times in Women's Lives: Historical Influences Across Forty Years," *American Journal of Sociology* 88 (1994): 481–89.

A. Hammarstrom, "Health Consequences of Youth Unemployment: Review from a Gender Perspective," *Social Science and Medicine* 38, no. 5 (1994): 699–709.

P. C. Holinger, "Violent Deaths Among the Young: Recent

Trends in Suicide, Homicide, and Accidents," *American Journal of Psychiatry* 136, no. 9 (1979): 1144–47.

G. Vigderhous and G. Fishman, "The Impact of Unemployment and Familial Integration on Changing Suicide Rates in the U. S. A., 1920–1969," *Social Psychiatry* 13 (1978): 239–48.

54. W. H. Courtenay (in revision for publication). "Constructions of Masculinity and Their Influence on Men's Well-Being: A Theory of Gender and Health," *Social Science and Medicine.*

55. Hayflick, 155.

56. Ibid., 156.

57. Theresa L. Crenshaw, M.D., *The Alchemy of Love and Lust: Discovering Our Sex Hormones and How They Determine Who We Love, When We Love, and How Often We Love* (New York: G. P. Putnam's Sons, 1996), 16.

58. Ibid., 123.

59. Ibid.

60. Ibid., 124.

61. Barbara Bartlik, M.D., and Helen Singer Kaplan, M.D., Ph.D., introduction to *The Hormone of Desire* by Susan Rako, M.D. (New York: Harmony Books, 1996), 14.

62. Crenshaw, xviii.

63. Quoted in Jane E. Brody, "Restoring Ebbing Hormones May Slow Aging," *New York Times*, 18 July 1995, sec. B., p. 5.

64. Winnifred Cutler, *Love Cycles: The Science of Intimacy* (New York: Villard Books, 1991), 89. Blood plasma levels of testosterone are graphically shown by Cutler.

65. Ibid.

66. Ibid., 97.

67. A. C. Kinsey, W. B. Pomeroy, and C. E. Martin, *Sexual Behavior in the Human Male* (Philadelphia: W. B. Saunders Co., 1948).

68. Henry A. Feldman et al. "Impotence and Its Medical and Psychosocial Correlates: Results of the Massachusetts Male Aging Study," *Journal of Urology* 151 (January 1994): 54–61.

69. Ibid.

70. Crenshaw, 211.

71. Adapted from Crenshaw, 218.

72. Cutler, 107–8.

5

The Body/Mind/Spirit Link: Getting Back to the Whole Man

I had finally gone to the clinic because I was having difficulty urinating. At times, I would have difficulty getting the stream to start even though I felt I had to go. Other times, I couldn't get to the bathroom fast enough, but once I would start, I felt I had to push to keep things going.

Like most people, though I never enjoyed going to the doctor, I rarely felt uncomfortable. But now I felt uneasy, slightly embarrassed. I couldn't have put words on it at the time, but looking back, it didn't seem manly to be having problems with my penis. In fact, the last time I even thought much about my penis was when my uncle gave me some manly advice when I was six or seven. "Be sure and give it three good shakes before you put it back in your pants," he said with a grin and put his hand on my shoulder. He continued with his instruction as he gave me three good pats to illustrate his point. "Less than three and you end up with a wet spot. More than three and you're playing with yourself."

The doctor's words broke into my thoughts. "It's really nothing to worry about," he said with an authoritative smile. "What you've got is a case of prostatitis. We'll give you some antibiotics, and it should clear right up." I was so relieved, I blurted out my other concern, expecting the same kind of immediate medical attention that would make the problem disappear forever.

"Well, while I'm here..." I began tentatively. The doctor had his head down writing out a prescription, which made it easier for me to begin. He didn't look up. "There's one other thing. I've noticed lately that my erections aren't as hard sometimes." He raised his head and looked at me now, but his blank look didn't give me a clue about what he was thinking. I wished I hadn't said anything and had left while I was ahead. But I plunged ahead, remembering my uncle's advice about playing poker. "In for a dime, in for a dollar. If you can call, you can raise."

"Well, it seems like my ejaculations aren't as strong as they used to be," I rushed rapidly on, "and the lovemaking isn't as much fun." He looked confused, then covering it with a big *smile*, he offered this summary of my problem. "Just need help getting the old woody to work."

I felt a mixture of feelings. I was relieved that whatever I had, it could be joked about and therefore couldn't be too serious. But I also felt uneasy that his diagnosis was so quick and off-the-cuff. I felt confused about what the problem really was. I wasn't sure it was just about "getting the the old woody to work." Would that help the decrease in the force of my ejaculation, and more importantly, the loss of enjoyment I was feeling?

"The medications should help," he said, handing me the white slip of paper. As he went out the door, he called over his shoulder, "If things don't improve, come back in and we'll see what we can do." He said it in such a way that it seemed unlikely that I would need to come back. I put my concerns aside and hurried to the pharmacy to get started on medications that would make my problem go away, whatever it was.

A year later, none of the symptoms had improved. He had tried me on four or five different courses of medications. When I pressed him for answers about my sexual difficulties, which seemed to have gotten worse over the year, he finally admitted that he didn't know too much about the sexual issues but was sure that the right medications would fix the problem. When the medications didn't work, he recommended surgery.

I was confused and my emotions were in turmoil. I felt ashamed that I needed a doctor to "fix me," and having given myself over to him for his magic "cure," I was afraid to let go when it wasn't working. The more things didn't work, the more frightened and inadequate I felt, and the more dependent I felt on the doctor for rescue and support. To admit that the problem was not going away was to admit I couldn't just bring myself into the repair shop, drop off my body, and pick it up after work, good as new. It meant I had to take more responsibility for my own health. It meant I had to deal with what was going on in my mind and how it was affecting my body.

I finally went to see another doctor, who was a urologist like the first doctor, but had a reputation of doing more than "getting the old woody to work." As soon as I walked into the office, I knew I was in for a different kind of experience. He told me he could give no guarantee that my urinary and sexual problems would go away, but if we worked together on learning as much as we could about what was going on, he felt we had a good chance to turn things around.

He began with a complete physical exam, which was much more thorough and gentle than anything the first doctor had ever done. I felt hopeful for the first time in over a year. Next, he asked me to talk about my life in the past few years and seemed interested in everything I said. He nodded when I described the increased pressures at work, my wife's travels, and my fears that she might meet someone else.

After two hours together, the doctor wrote out an unusual prescription. He told me to discontinue all medications. He also suggested that my wife and I take a break from all sexual activity for two weeks. In the meantime, he told me, I needed to drink two gallons of water a day to "clean out my system." He told me the body was made mostly of water and that drinking lots of it was one of the best "treatments" he had ever found for dealing with problems like mine. Even though my past experience said, "give me a drug," his calm and direct approach made me feel that his unconventional approach would work for me.

Finally, he said I should just relax, stop trying so hard to make things right. I should plan a nice, romantic weekend with my wife when the two weeks was up, but not to have any expectations or make any demands. Just enjoy it and see what happens. To my surprise, things began to improve. In discussing my prostate problems, the doctor explained the important links between people's expectations and fears and their physical responses. It was my first experience with mind/body medicine.

Learning about the Prostate: The Key to Men's Sexual Health

In talking with thousands of men over the years, I began to find out how many men have gone to doctors with prostate problems and gotten the kind of response I had received from the first doctor—different kinds of medications and, when that fails, recommendations of surgery.

Since nearly all men will experience some kind of prostate problem during their lives and since prostate health is so intimately connected with men's sexuality, it will serve us well to better understand the structure and function of this important gland.

As we know, the structures of the male urinary system and of the male sexual system are intermingled. The prostate gland is at the center of both systems. The gland is about the size of a walnut and sits beneath the bladder. The urethra, which carries the urine from the bladder to the outside world for elimination, passes through the prostate.[1]

The bulk of the prostate gland, 75 percent or more, consists of glandular tissue. The prostate is divided into front and back by the urethra. First and foremost, the prostate is a sexual organ. It secretes and stores the fluid that makes up about one-third of the semen. This stored fluid is expressed out of the prostate at orgasm by muscular contractions and mixes with the sperm and seminal fluid that allows for new life to form when sperm and egg connect.[2]

Blood flows through the prostate to the penis, and nerves that are vital to sexual feeling run through the prostate. Blood flow is essential for erections, and the nerves provide the sensation necessary for sexual pleasure. A healthy prostate is vital for having a joyful sexual experience.[3]

The prostate is located deep within the male pelvis. The location of the prostate and its relationship as the common conduit for urine, seminal fluid, prostatic fluid, and sperm, helps to explain all the different symptoms that can occur when the prostate begins to cause problems for its owner.[4]

The Big Three Prostate Problems

Author John Irving describes the kind of problems many men experience as they get older.

"Odd and painful peeing is not new to me. Seven times in the last five years, I have suffered this unnameable disorder...Urinating is often a challenge, the sensation's always new and surprising. Also, it's time consuming—your day spent in anticipation of the next time you'll have to pee. Sex, typically, is unmentionable. Orgasm is truly climactic. Coming is a slow experience—the long, astonishing journey of a rough and oversized ballbearing. In the past I had given up the act altogether. Which drives me to drink, which makes the pee burn: an unfriendly circle. And always the non-specific diagnosis."[5]

We now know that the prostate gland is the most frequently diseased organ of the human body.[6] All men are susceptible to contracting the three major diseases of the prostate:

1. Prostatitis

2. Benign prostatic hyperplasia (BPH), also called enlarged prostate

3. Prostate cancer

According to Bradley R. Hennenfent, M.D., one of the leading authorities on prostate problems, "A man's odds of getting one of these three diseases approaches 100 percent."[7] Yet we are just now beginning to understand what these diseases are, how they relate to each other, and why so many men develop them as they get older.

"Prostrate enlargement," says Theresa M. Crenshaw, M.D., "increases urinary frequency day and night, interfering with men's sleep and their ego." She goes on to explain that these changes are important to a man's sense of self. "A busy bladder is second only to baldness as a key marker for 'over-the-hill' thoughts."[8]

"Some enlargement occurs in 10 percent of all forty-year-olds and 80 percent of all eighty-year-olds. Most often the enlargement is due to benign cell growth, but sometimes the growth is cancerous, so the condition should be followed closely by a urologist."[9]

According to Thomas M. Bruckman, executive director and CEO of the American Foundation for Urologic Disease, prostate cancer is second only to skin cancer as the most often detected cancer in the United States and has recently taken center stage as a health topic of national concern and debate.[10]

Prostate cancer has often been compared to breast cancer because of the similarities in structure between the breast and the prostate. Also, the rates at which the diseases kill men and women are similar. In 1996, for instance, 41,000 men died of prostate cancer and 45,000 women died of breast cancer. In the same year, 317,000 cases of prostate cancer were diagnosed, and 184,000 cases of breast cancer were diagnosed. Yet, according to Bruckman, federal research for prostate cancer totaled only $80,000,000 compared to $550,000,000 for breast cancer.[11]

If prostate cancer has been under-researched, prostatitis research has been given almost no attention. "Chronic prostatitis is truly the forgotten disease in this country," says Richard Alexander, M.D. "The state of research in this disease is woefully inadequate."[12]

Noted urologist Thomas Stamey has said that 50 percent of all men will experience prostatitis symptoms, which include pain anywhere in the uro/genital area, urinary flow dysfunction, and sexual dysfunction.[13]

According to a poll by Dr. Alexander at the University of Maryland and the National Cancer Institute, the average patient with symptoms of prostate problems is near the age of forty and 95 to 97 percent of these men will be told, "You have chronic prostatitis," for which there is no known cause or cure.[14]

This is a discouraging response for men to hear. To be told that you have a problem that affects your daily functions and sexuality and that there is nothing you can do about it can cause men to feel frustrated, angry, and depressed.

Recent research, however, is offering new hope to men who suffer from prostate problems. The research indicates that all three prostate diseases may be related and caused by difficult-to-detect viral or bacterial infections. "There is a great deal of evidence," according to Bradley R. Hennenfent, M.D., "that suggests that BPH may simply be chronic untreated infection." He also believes BPH and prostate cancer may be connected to unhealed prostatitis and that more research needs to be done.[15]

As men talk to each other about prostate problems and demand answers from the medical community, who have for too long neglected men's health issues, things will change. However, men must first do a better job in attending to their own health needs.

It seems that men in their twenties neglect their health because they feel immortal, sure they are too young and strong to get sick. In their thirties they feel overwhelmed by work and family responsibilities and neglect their health because they are too busy. In their forties they often feel the effects of this neglect and are reluctant to seek medical attention, fearing they might find something seriously wrong with them. However, as men move through the Menopause Passage, they have a new opportunity to attend to their own health.

Just as research is showing relationships between the different kinds of prostate problems, there is also an increasing body of research that is showing the relationship between the physical aspects of male menopause and the psychological and spiritual aspects.

With my own clients, for instance, I have found that prostate problems increase when there is stress in the marital relationships.

Likewise, having a prostate problem can increase marital discord. Mind and spirit influences the disease process, and physical diseases affect a man's mind and spirit.

Many men, however, don't fully appreciate the value of the psychological and spiritual dimensions of healing. They often believe they must concentrate on the "bottom line" if they are to be successful in life. They don't see how learning about the mind/body/spirit can help them.

But neglecting these dimensions of life is like driving an eight cylinder car with only two cylinders working, or playing a basketball game with a ball that isn't fully inflated. As men move through the Male Menopause Passage, it becomes increasingly important to be in tune with all dimensions of life. To get a better understanding of the power of integrating a mind/body/spirit approach to life, it will be valuable to take a short side trip into the world of professional sports.

The Mind, the Body, the Spirit, and the Bulls

Welcome to the inner sanctum. On one wall hangs a wooden arrow with a tobacco pouch tied to it. On another, a bear claw necklace. The room also contains the middle feather of an owl, a painting that tells the story of the great mystical warrior, Crazy Horse, and photos of a white buffalo calf born in Wisconsin.

What is this place? You might think it was a Native American lodge, a holy dwelling to cleanse and renew the mind, body, and spirit. You would probably not expect to find the room full of bulls, specifically Chicago Bulls, the professional basketball team led by the amazing Michael Jordan and coached by the phenomenal Phil Jackson. In a sport as physical and competitive as basketball, you might not expect the team room of the five-time world champion Bulls to reflect so much emphasis on mind and spirit.

"This is the room where the spirit of the team takes form," says Phil Jackson, the head coach of the Bulls. One of the most successful coaches in NBA history, Jackson has developed a new paradigm of leadership based on Eastern and Native American principles. His approach flies in the face of the egotistic, winner-take-all attitude that has dominated American life as we approach the end of the twentieth century. Rather than winning through intimidation, Jackson—who describes himself as a Zen Christian (he is the son of Pentecostal ministers who learned about Zen Buddhist practice later in life)—stresses awareness, compassion, and, most of all, selfless team play.

During the basketball playoffs, while most coaches are exhorting their teams to "go for broke, kill the enemy" and quoting Vince Lombardi, "Winning isn't everything, it's the only thing," Phil Jackson is telling his players to meditate, visualize, and think of each other. "There's a passage from Rudyard Kipling's *Second Jungle Book* that I often read during the playoffs," says Jackson, "to remind the team of this basic principle:"

> Now this is the Law of the Jungle—
> as old and as true as the sky;
> And the Wolf that shall keep it may prosper,
> but the Wolf that shall break it must die.
> As the creeper that girdles the tree trunk
> the Law runneth forward and back—
> For the strength of the Pack is the Wolf,
> and the strength of the Wolf is the Pack.[16]

Jackson, a superbly conditioned athlete who had spent his life playing sports, was forced to begin dealing with mind and spirit when midlife injuries forced him to stop playing professional basketball. Jackson's experience will be familiar to all men who are forced to leave their job before they are ready.

"To me, this was a kind of death," Jackson says, recalling the day his career ended. "It meant giving up my identity as a warrior, my *raison d'être* since boyhood, and becoming, in my view, a nonperson."[17]

After months of soul searching, Jackson became a coach in the "minor leagues." One of his first tasks was to quiet his chaotic mind, which seemed to race as fast as his players going up and down the court. He needed a different kind of focus on work than he had learned growing up. He got help from an unlikely source, Albert Einstein.

"Einstein once described his rules of work," says Jackson:

  1. Out of clutter, find simplicity.

  2. From discord, find harmony.

  3. In the middle of difficulty lies opportunity.[18]

Michael Jordan and the Warrior's Journey Home

"This is a book about a vision and a dream," says Jackson in his book *Sacred Hoops*. "When I was named head coach of the Chicago Bulls in 1989, my dream was not just to win championships, but to do it in a way that wove together my two greatest passions: basketball and spiritual exploration."[19] Jackson would always remind his players, "not only is there more to life than basketball, there's a lot more to basketball than basketball."

One of the most difficult problems he faced was how to relate to superstar Michael Jordan, who many feel is the greatest player ever to play the game. In fact, he is so good, his teammates have a tendency to stand back and let Michael weave his magic.

The Associated Press reported that in a survey of African-American children, Jordan had tied with God as the person they most admired after their parents. And his greatness goes well beyond the African-American community. Many of my night dreams include my going one-on-one against Michael...and beating him. I know I'm not the only "white boy" who wants to "be like Mike."

To create a team that worked as closely together as five fingers on a hand required new practices, as well as a new philosophy of life. The mind had to be clear, receptive, and connected to everything. The players needed to learn a practice Zen Buddhists call "mindfulness." Its a practice useful not only to professional basketball players, but also to those moving through the Male Menopause Passage.

When Jackson taught these practices to the Bulls, players were at first skeptical. Jordan kept opening his eyes to see if any of the other players were actually doing the meditation. When he saw that most were, he went back and practiced. He learned the lessons. Awareness is everything.

I can still picture Michael Jordan in 1991 holding the long sought after championship trophy as if it were a child in need of love and protection. With tears running down his cheeks, it was clear that this was a man who had embarked on a path that embraced the mind and spirit, as well as the body. "I could imagine a new incarnation of the Bulls," said Jackson, "built around the new Michael Jordan, now an elder statesman, not a young rambunctious warrior."[20]

Perhaps men like Michael Jordan and Phil Jackson can teach us something about the potential of all human beings. They can teach us what it means to be mentors and elder statesmen and to live life fully and well.

If life is like a basketball game, for most of human history, all of us died in the first half. We were born. We matured. We mated. We raised the children to self-sufficiency. And we died, usually before age fifty.

With this historical experience, it is no wonder most of us fear "getting old." What must it be like to "know" in our bones that humans are capable of living to be one hundred, but that most of us will die by age fifty? Perhaps, it is like the terror of trying to get all your scoring done in the first part of a basketball game, because we fear the game will end at halftime.

But for the first time in human history, we have the opportunity to play the whole game, to know that we have time to develop a different strategy for the second half than we have in the first half of the game. Perhaps it will allow us to be less fearful of the psychological changes that occur at midlife.

The Midlife Mind and Menopause

Aubrey Hill, M.D., the author of *Viropause/Andropause*, who has been in practice for over forty years, describes five significant psychological changes that occur during the Male Menopause Passage:

1. Memory Changes

Just as there is a natural decrease in men's physical strength as they age, there is also a decrease in mental functioning. "Forgetfulness tops the list of mental changes in later life," says Dr. Hill.[21] The fact that mental processes are slowing down often is apparent when men notice that it takes them longer to make decisions.

2. Feeling Down and Discontent

"Doctors refer to such an emotional state as dysphoria," says Dr. Hill, "a term derived from the Greek word *dysphoros*, meaning hard to bear. Dysphoria can be described as agitation, excessive psychological pain, or anguish. Medically, it is defined as disquiet, restlessness, and malaise."[22]

Most men who experience these feelings never seek help. Many don't even notice that they are down. Why are men so disconnected and reluctant to seek help? I've found that men are often not aware of their feelings on a conscious level.

From childhood, males are encouraged to think logically and put their emotions aside. Most men feel strongly, but are often ashamed of the loss of control that feelings produce. Even those who accept their feelings often have difficulty naming their emotions and shrug their shoulders rather than say "I feel something, but I don't know what it is or what to call it."

Those who can articulate their feelings and acknowledge that they feel down or depressed are often reluctant to seek help because they have come to believe that "a man should be able to handle his problems himself." The idea persists that it is somehow more masculine to suffer silently than to admit that something is wrong.

3. Anxiety and Sleeplessness

"When a man experiences male menopause," says Dr. Hill, "he has uncertainty about his self-worth and is confused about priorities; therefore, there is anxiety."[23] When people are anxious, they often have difficulty sleeping. A man in his forties or fifties who is otherwise healthy but has difficulty falling asleep or awakens during the night and is unable to return to sleep, could be suffering from male menopause.

Though anxiety and other related symptoms such as headaches, stomach problems, and worry, may be present in a man's life, he may minimize them or deny that anything is wrong. It is often those close to the man who first recognize that something has changed.

"To his family, his friends, or his colleagues at work, it is often obvious [something is wrong]," says Dr. Hill. "They may notice that he is irritable, cranky, short-tempered, or cross when previously he was not. Or they may see him as unusually quiet and withdrawn."[24]

4. Fearfulness

When people arrive at midlife, fears of death may intrude on their thoughts. They may worry about the death of parents, spouse, children, or themselves.

I remember one night, shortly after my fiftieth birthday, my wife, Carlin, was in town visiting friends. When she didn't return by the time I had expected her, I began to worry. The worry soon turned to fear and the fear to panic and terror. Though she was often late, and I had accepted that fact as an irritating reality in an otherwise wonderful marriage, on this night, I was sure that something terrible had happened.

I quickly became unhinged. I called the police, the highway patrol, and every hospital in town. I was sure she was dead, and I became obsessed with how I was going to tell the children. I was sure I would be unable to carry on without her and contemplated my own demise.

When she arrived home, her usual cheery self, I was still sobbing as though my world had ended. I was overjoyed at her "return from the grave" and immediately felt stupid and ashamed for acting like a baby.

5. Inadequacy

No matter how successful men are, at this stage of life, they often feel that they are failures. If the business is going well, they feel they have been poor husbands and fathers. If they focused on their families, they feel they didn't reach their full career potential. They often feel like they didn't provide adequately for their family's future. Often they feel they have failed in all aspects of their lives. Declining sexuality and physical stamina undermine the core of their manhood.

Men of this age may become obsessed with regaining the passion, power, productivity, and purpose that seems to be lost, yet often look for what was lost in the wrong places.

They may feel they have to have a flashy sports car or speed boat. That Harley-Davidson motorcycle they have been eyeing begins to occupy their thoughts, and they begin to tell themselves how much sense it would make to own one. "Think of the gas mileage…no parking problems…the savings on repair bills."

Men often feel like "chucking" their careers or become grimly determined to "make it to the top." Some men feel like running away to some fantasy island where they will stay forever young and live happily ever after. Others buckle down and trudge determinedly up the ladder to success.

Feeling like failures internally, they try to show the outside world that they are a success. Alcohol, drugs, and other forms of escape are often used to hide the fearful truth that many men of this age try to deny. "I feel I have failed at life, and it's too late to start over and do it right."

I have found that there is a sixth psychological change that occurs during the Male Menopause Passage—Sexual Fantasy.

As he notices physical and sexual changes in his body, a man of this age may cling to the sexuality of his youth. He remembers all the fun he had as a young man, when he could party until dawn and have any woman he fancied. Looking back, he usually fancies himself more sexually successful than he actually was. However, whether he has been a Don Juan or a "Don' ever get any women," his fantasies about sexual conquest preoccupy him.

He may spend more time reading pornography, looking at pictures, or surfing the sex sites on the Internet.

He may tell himself that his daughter's friends are coming on to him, and if he is not careful, he may act on his fantasies. He finds himself looking through the personals section of the newspaper and wondering "what it would be like to..."

George, a fifty-two-year-old client going through the Male Menopause Passage, brought the following ad that had caught his eye. He said he knew it was silly, but he couldn't get the image out of his mind. The ad read as follows:

ENERGIZER BUNNY

Slim, pretty, petite, smart, blonde, blue-eyed and bushy-tailed (no garden type variety). EVEREADY for hiking, skiing, diving, travel, theatre, intimate meals a deux, on the town or in the hutch, seeks intelligent well traveled athletic "Bugsbunny" 40–55 for hip hoppity fun and adventures that go on and on and on...[25]

The feelings men have at this age are often confused and they have difficulty making sense of their desires. In many ways, they seem to be going through a second adolescence. If they have teenage children, their own changes may exacerbate the usual tensions between parent and child, particularly if they are in denial, as many men are.

If they are unable to directly confront their own midlife fears, they may project their feelings onto their sons and daughters. When midlife parents become enraged at their teenagers' dress and demeanor, their surliness and sadness, their aggressiveness and sexuality, we can be sure that the parents, too, are having great difficulty with these same feelings.

Dealing with the emerging sexuality of teenage daughters can be particularly difficult for men. Their own confused feelings can cause them to be inappropriately intimate with their daughters. But more often, their fears of their own and their daughters' sexuality causes them to withdraw completely. Most of the women I see in therapy remember with confusion and sadness the time when "my father stopped playing games with me, withdrew contact, and wouldn't hug me anymore."

Midlife: The Best Is Yet to Come

Harry Wilmer is as close to being a Renaissance man as anyone I have ever met. He is a medical doctor, as well as a Ph.D. psychologist and practicing Jungian analyst. He has written over 170 scientific books and publications and has produced plays, films, and PBS documentaries. His understanding of men at midlife can help us all on the path.

"The midlife crisis, even when it brings on depression, anxiety, fear, or despair," says Wilmer, "is a time of great challenge, out of which come symbols of transformation, tinctured with a sweet poison of nostalgia."[26]

Wilmer is well-aware of the lure of escape for men at midlife and helps us understand the root causes. "Midlife depressions," says Wilmer, "are fueled by reawakened adolescent despair and unresolved sexual conflicts." The way through this maze, he says, is by "not running from the reality that actually is one's midlife lot and not seeking:

- intoxication of drugs and alcohol;

- excitement of promiscuous sex;

- greener pastures;

- power, glory, and notoriety;

- new job, new wife, new husband, new lover;

- denial of the humdrum of everyday."[27]

On the positive side, Wilmer counsels the following:
- go towards the inner values;

- seek development of what you have neglected;

- follow the flow of life but do not float passively.[28]

Though we become much more accepting of things as they are, Wilmer reminds us that the special purpose of eldering, which begins at midlife, is to confront those things in the world that threaten life. "Those in the second half of life have a greater responsibility to remedy evils because they have had a longer stake in perpetuating them."[29]

Dr. David Gutmann, who has spent his professional career studying the special meaning of the second half of life, feels that elders are crucial for the survival of the species. According to Gutmann, Second Adulthood, rather than being a superficial add-on to the human life cycle, may well be the evolutionary core of what makes us human.

We recognize that the great length of human childhood is unique to the human species and allows us to educate the young to utilize their full potential. What has not been fully understood is that the years of elderhood are not accidental, but also have an evolutionary purpose. "We do not have elders because we have a human gift and modern capacity for keeping the weak alive," says Gutmann, "instead, we are human because we have elders."[30]

Just as evolution draws men and women together for "pro-creation" in their early years, it calls on them to "co-create" in their later years. Gutmann says that this co-creative process enables men and women to fulfill the most important role of Second Adulthood, that of "emeritus parents."

Recent findings from the emerging field of evolutionary psychology demonstrate that without the active involvement of these elders, even the healthiest nuclear families are doomed to failure. Without the presence of elders, says Gutmann, "the unbuffered nuclear family does appear to be increasingly incapable of raising children who can avoid addictions, who do not need cults or charismatic totalitarian leaders, who can grow up to be parental in their own right."[31]

One of the difficulties in finding positive models for eldering, Gutmann believes, is the mind/body schism in contemporary psychology. "Mind is separated from body," says Gutmann, "and the dynamic, purposeful organism disappears from our theoretical radar screens."

"As we age," says Mark Gerzon, author of *Listening to Midlife*, "we human beings yearn for wholeness. We yearn for the parts of ourselves that have been in the dark to find sunlight, and those that were sunburned to find shade. We yearn for the parts that have been underdeveloped to grow, and those that were over-developed to be pruned. We yearn for the parts that have been silent to speak, and those that were noisy to be still. We yearn for the parts that have been alone to find companionship, and those that have been overcrowded to find solitude."[32]

Gerzon sums up the hunger men have at midlife this way: "We yearn to live our unlived lives."

In the first half of men's lives, they are often focused on "getting the job done." In the second half, they can take time to tune into the less tangible aspects of life and begin to feel the connection between mind, body, and spirit. Probably more than any other man, Dr. Deepak Chopra has popularized this broadened understanding of our human potential in the second half of life.

Ageless Body, Timeless Mind: The World of Deepak Chopra

I first met Dr. Chopra in the dining room at the Omega Institute in upstate New York where we were both on the faculty. He was relaxed and quiet, but gave off an air of youthful vitality. We discussed our workshops, and though he was becoming quite well-known by then, I had to admit that I was not familiar with his work. That soon changed as we began to discuss our ideas of mind/body healing and its relevance to my own focus on men's issues and addiction recovery.

Dr. Chopra is a physician—an endocrinologist who came to the United States in 1970. He is also a practitioner of the spiritual traditions of ancient India and combines the best of ancient and modern practices. Like many of us, his professional journey is intimately related to his personal life.

Chopra's father, a successful British-trained cardiologist, was in England when he learned that his own father was taking Ayurvedic medicine, the traditional Indian herbal healing practice, for a heart condition. The doctor disapproved, and from

London, he demanded that his father "abandon this nonsense and call in a Western-style heart specialist." Chopra wrote in his 1988 memoir, *Return of the Rishi*, that his grandfather "called in the heart specialist, dutifully took the prescribed drugs, and died two weeks later."[33]

Chopra seemed destined to follow in his father's footsteps and become a master of Western medicine. At twenty-three, he was an intern at a small hospital in New Jersey, recruited during the Vietnamese doctor shortage. By thirty-eight, he was chief-of-staff at a large Massachusetts hospital, looking for the next step up the ladder to success. But there were problems. "Chopra, who now says he has an 'addictive personality,' was dismayed at the lifestyle that came with his job: pots of coffee and packs of cigarettes and Scotch each night to come down again."[34]

"'All I was doing was seeing patients one after another, prescribing medication like a legalized drug pusher.' In *Rishi* he suggests that by purveying short-term cures but ignoring long-term prevention, the typical Western physician 'was fostering a diseased system and beyond that, a diseased world, with himself at its center. Like a spider in its web, he gave off something sticky that entrapped his patients.'"[35]

Chopra sought and found a different way, one that could integrate mind, body, and spirit. Based on his clinical studies, Chopra has developed a new paradigm that he feels is particularly useful for dealing with our lives as we age. In his book, *Ageless Body, Timeless Mind*, Dr. Chopra offers the following beliefs about the body, mind, and spirit:

1. "*The mind and body are inseparably one.* The unity that is 'me' separates into two streams of experience. [People] experience the subjective stream as thoughts, feelings, and desires. [They] experience the objective stream as [the physical] body. At a deeper level, however, the two streams meet at a single creative source. It is from this source that we are meant to live.

2. *"The biochemistry of the body is a product of awareness.* Beliefs, thoughts, and emotions create the chemical reactions that uphold life in every cell. An aging cell is the end product of awareness that has forgotten how to remain new.

3. *"Impulses of intelligence create your body in new forms every second.* What you are is the sum total of these impulses, and by changing their patterns, you will change."[36]

Continuing research shows that the old dichotomy between mind and body is inaccurate and offers important understandings that can help us treat and prevent many of the problems men face as we deal with the Male Menopause Passage.

Practicing Mind/Body Medicine: The Core of Our Healing Journey

Dr. Jon Kabat-Zinn, an expert in mind/body medicine, stress reduction, meditation, and yoga, has made a significant contribution to enhancing the quality of life for thousands suffering from chronic illness and disease. His Stress Reduction Clinic at the University of Massachusetts Medical Center has received national recognition and brought mind/body healing to the mainstream medical community.

What he teaches is useful not only for those having chronic medical problems but for anyone who wants to lead a more healthy, less stressful life. Kabat-Zinn, like Chopra, takes ancient practices that have worked for thousands of years and offers them in ways the average person can understand.

He defines "mindfulness" as "moment-to-moment non-judgmental awareness." It is this kind of awareness that seems to work best for healing. Meditation he says is simply "paying attention intentionally."[37]

Kabat-Zinn believes that though the concepts are simple, they take time to master. "You don't just throw a switch and get enlightened. It's more organic than that, requiring years of digging in the dirt, planting seeds, cultivating and weeding."[38]

A colleague of Kabat-Zinn's, Herbert Benson, M.D., has been cultivating mind/body healing for over thirty years. In 1988 he founded Harvard Medical School's Mind/Body Medical Institute, which continues to conduct innovative and scientifically sound research in this emerging field.

Benson has been researching ways to take the over-stressed, pulled-apart, contemporary American and put him back together. "Perhaps my most significant contribution to the field," says Dr. Benson, "was in defining a bodily calm that all of us can evoke and that has the opposite effect of the well-known fight-or-flight response. I call this bodily calm 'the relaxation response,' a state in which blood pressure is lowered, and heart rate, breathing rate, and metabolic rate are decreased."[39] Benson's findings were first documented in his widely read book, *The Relaxation Response*, written in 1975.

The core of mind/body healing is that our beliefs can change the way our bodies function, and changes in our physical being can affect the way our mind works. Since the 1950s, there have been many studies confirming the importance of our beliefs in contributing to our well-being.

Mind/Body Work and Male Menopause

When I spoke recently with Dr. Benson, I asked him about male menopause and the applicability of his work for helping men with problems they are having at this stage of life. "Yes, I believe there is a male menopause," Dr. Benson said, "and the techniques we have developed can be very helpful. Anytime there is stress and anxiety associated with a problem, men can benefit from learning the relaxation response and the process of remembered wellness. Usually men come to our clinic with physical complaints. It's only later that they begin to recognize the influence of their beliefs, values, and emotions."[40]

Yet an increasing body of research is showing the strong connection between psychological and hormonal changes that affect men going through the Menopause Passage. For instance, it has been shown that when a man is depressed, his testosterone levels drop and his sexual drive decreases. Conversely, when testosterone levels drop, as they do when men get older, a man may become depressed and experience less sexual interest.[41]

It has been shown that males who are high in status have higher levels of testosterone in their blood and have more sexual experiences than males who have lower levels of testosterone. Studies show that at football games, fans of a winning team had higher testosterone levels than the fans of the losing team. High status and success seem to cause an increase in testosterone. And the reverse is also true. If testosterone levels in males are raised artificially, they become more assertive and are more successful in attracting sexual partners.

A recent study of adolescent boys showed the connection. "The higher the testosterone," says Dr. Winnifred B. Cutler, one of the nation's experts on hormonal influences on the mind and body, "the more frequently the boy thought about sex, the more easily he was turned on, the more frequently he held hands, hugged with girls, and had intercourse, and the more sexually mature was his physical development."[42]

I first had experienced the mind/body connection when I began talking to doctors about my prostate problems. The first doctor I saw simply viewed the problem as physical. He prescribed medications, and when that didn't work, suggested surgery. The second doctor I saw did a complete physical examination, but then talked with me about my emotional state and the stresses that were going on in my relationship with my wife. He indicated that my prostate problems were caused by the interaction of the physical, emotional, and interpersonal.

His support and understanding allowed my wife and me to talk more honestly about our hopes and fears and about our changing needs at this stage of our lives. She got involved with a women's group. I deepened my involvement with my men's group. The problems I was having with urination gradually went away. My sexual potency and enjoyment returned. We had learned an important lesson about the way the mind interacts with the body.

Many people are not so fortunate. Faced with a similar problem, many men refuse to explore the psycho-social aspects of their lives. They cling, as I did at the beginning, to the belief that there is a simple physical fix that can be employed so that they don't have to look at their lives and confront their feelings.

As the physical problems become more chronic and entrenched, they begin to withdraw from their partner. Since sex is problematic, they avoid it. Hoping to prove that the plumbing has not rusted away, they may seek out a younger, newer partner, and have an affair. Partners, who feel neglected and confused, may also look for solace in the arms of another. Marriages dissolve, and children grow up with part-time parents. Since feelings and the life situations that cause them are denied, they arise again and the problems return, often worse than before.

Once having had the experience of the miraculous effects the mind can have on our healing, some people go to the extreme and assume that every illness the body contracts can be "cured" by focusing the healing power of the mind. If things don't work, they feel guilty and ashamed. "I just don't believe enough. Maybe, unconsciously, I want this illness," they may say to themselves. "I just need to meditate more, focus my mind more consistently, get better at getting better. Mind over matter, I know I can do it."

Although the power of the mind has often been neglected in medicine and its re-emergence as a significant tool for healing is important, we must not throw out the baby with the bathwater.

"It's…very tempting," says Dr. Benson, "to oversimplify this information, to become so impressed with mind/body connections that you attribute any decline in health to spiritual failure. Medical problems are, of course, the result of a number of variables including genetics and family history, environmental causes, personal history, healthy habits, and accidents."[43]

We have to be realistic about mind/body healing Dr. Benson cautions. He calls the power of the mind to heal, "remembered wellness," but acknowledges the limitations. "It can help to the extent that any disease or condition is caused or exacerbated by mind/body interactions. If a disease progresses, despite the best efforts of self-care, it had a life of its own that was beyond the influence of remembered wellness. Sometimes the best medicines and the kindest, most renowned specialists cannot quell disease, and so it is with remembered wellness."[44]

In future chapters, we will see how the mind/body medicine can be applied to healing problems associated with the Male Menopause Passage. But first, we need to explore in more depth the difference between male menopause and female menopause.

Notes Chapter 5

1. See Patrick C. Walsh, M.D., and Janet Farrar Worthington, *The Prostate: A Guide for Men and the Women Who Love Them* (Baltimore: Johns Hopkins University Press, 1995), 1–15.

2. Ibid.

3. Ibid.

4. Ibid.

5. John Irving, *The Water Method Man* (New York: Ballantine, 1972), 12.

6. Quoted in Bradley R. Hennenfent, M.D., *The Prostatitis Syndromes* (Bloomington, IL: The Prostatitis Foundation, 1996), 2.

7. Hennenfent, 2.

8. Theresa Crenshaw, M.D., *The Alchemy of Love and Lust: Discovering Our Sex Hormones and How They Determine Who We Love, When We Love, and How Often We Love* (New York: G. P. Putnam's Sons, 1996), 227.

9. Leonard Hayflick, *How and Why We Age* (New York: Ballantine, 1994), 159.

10. Thomas M. Bruckman, presentation at Men's Health Conference, Scottsdale, Ariz., 18–19 November 1996.

11. Ibid.

12. Richard Alexander, Congressional testimony before the House Subcommittee on Labor, Health and Human Services, and Education, 29 February 1996, quoted in Hennenfent, iii.

13. Reported by Tom Cruse, Director for the Prostatitis Foundation at Men's Health Conference, Scottsdale, Ariz., 18–19 November 1996.

14. Ibid.

15. Hennenfent, 13.

16. Quoted in Phil Jackson and Hugh Delehanty, *Sacred Hoops: Spiritual Lessons of a Hardwood Warrior* (New York: Hyperion, 1995), 18.

17. Jackson and Delehanty, 54.

18. Quoted in Jackson, 70.

19. Jackson and Delehanty, 3.

20. Ibid., 199.

21. Aubrey M. Hill, *Viropause/Andropause: The Male Menopause: Emotional and Physical Changes Mid-Life Men Experience* (Far Hills, NJ: New Horizon Press, 1993), 17.

22. Ibid., 18.

23. Ibid., 22.

24. Ibid.

25. Personal ad, *Pacific Sun*, 17 July 1996.

26. Harry A. Wilmer, M.D., *Practical Jung: Nuts and Bolts of Jungian Psychotherapy* (Wilmette, IL: Chiron Publications, 1987), 199.

27. Ibid., 200.

28. Ibid.

29. Ibid., 201.

30. David Gutmann, *Reclaimed Powers: Toward a New Psychology of Men and Women in Later Life* (New York: Basic Books, 1987), 4.

31. Ibid., 7.

32. Mark Gerzon, *Listening to Midlife: Turning Your Crisis into a Quest* (Boston: Shambhala, 1996), 10.

33. Deepak Chopra, M.D., *Return of the Rishi: a Doctor's Search for the Ultimate Healer* (Boston: Houghton Mifflin, 1988), 24.

34. David Van Biema, "Emperor of the Soul," *Time*, 24 June 1996, 67.

35. Ibid.

36. Deepak Chopra, M.D., *Ageless Body, Timeless Mind: The Quantum Alternative to Growing Old* (New York: Harmony Books, 1993), 6.

37. Quoted in Jon Kabat-Zinn, "Moment to Moment: An Interview with Jon Kabat-Zinn," interview by Virginia Lee, *Common Ground*, Spring 1997, 147.

38. Ibid.

39. Herbert Benson and Mark Stark, *Timeless Healing: The Power and Biology of Belief* (New York: Scribner, 1996), 16–17.

40. Herbert Benson, interview with author, 13 August 1996.

41. Winnifred B. Cutler, Ph.D., *Love Cycles: The Science of Intimacy* (New York: Villard Books, 1991), 101.

42. Ibid., 99.

43. Benson, 264–265.
44. Ibid.

6

His Change/Her Change:
Similarities and Differences
between Female and
Male Menopause

When I began research for this book, I expected I would find major differences between what men and women go through at midlife. I initially envisioned a chart showing menopause on one side and viropause on the other. I envisioned a neat separation, with women having one kind of "change of life," and men having a very different kind. We could each learn about the other, but the "otherness" seemed clear and distinct.

Yet the more I delved into the physical, hormonal, psychological, social, and spiritual changes that men and women experience at midlife, the more similar they seemed. The conclusion is that there are many more similarities than differences.

As we saw in chapter 5, our beliefs have such a strong influence on what we see in the world, they may blind us to the truth. I originally bought books on menopause to help me understand what my wife, Carlin, was going through when she began her Menopause Passage. I have page after page underlined, with notes in the margin reading, "Exactly, right. That's what's happening to Carlin…That's her…She's going through the same thing." At the time, it never occurred to me that anything I read applied to me.

Since I "knew" menopause was something that all women went through and no men experienced, I never saw what was staring me in the face. It reminds me of a story an anthropologist told of encountering natives who had been so isolated they had rarely seen a non-native person. Wanting to know what name they gave to various objects, he placed a number of things he carried in his pocket within a circle he had drawn on the ground. There was some change, a small knife, a cigarette, and a watch. The native man recognized and named all the objects he saw.

Yet, there was still one object left in the circle. The anthropologist kept prodding the man to name the last object. The native man insisted that he had already named everything, that there was nothing left in the circle to name. The anthropologist finally concluded that the man had never seen a watch before, and therefore it didn't register as an object in his brain. For him, the circle was empty.

The story illustrates an important point about male and female menopause. What we believe about these human experiences will determine whether it exists for us and what we may do about it. A psychologist friend reverses the old phrase, "I'll believe it when I see it," and says, "I'll see it when I believe it."

I hope by now you have expanded your beliefs to accept the idea that "male menopause," like the watch in the native's circle, exists. I hope you have also recognized that there are many similarities between what women go through—both emotionally and physically—during menopause and what men go through.

Listening to Carlin's women's group discuss their Menopause Passage and listening to my own men's group go over the same territory, I was struck by how similar the issues were. If someone were reading the transcripts of the two groups and didn't know in advance which was the men's group and which was the women's group, their gender wouldn't be immediately obvious.

Contrary to the myth that men and women are from different planets, we are much more alike than different—the differences are greatest during the reproductive years. The similar changes that men and women experience in midlife can draw us together.

"There are many things women and men of middle age have in common," says Rosetta Reitz, author of *Menopause,* "and to know about the other is to learn more about oneself. A sympathetic viewing of female menopause would teach men a lot about their own."[1]

Earlier, I contrasted "menopause" and "male menopause" in the following way:

Menopause is the cessation of menstruation in the human female. The cessation of menses is an unmistakable biological marker for the ending of a woman's reproductive capacity.

Male Menopause (also called viropause or andropause) begins with hormonal, physiological, and chemical changes that occur in all men generally between the ages of forty and fifty-five, though it can occur as early as thirty-five or as late as sixty-five. These changes affect all aspects of a man's life. Male menopause is, thus, a physical condition with psychological, interpersonal, social, and spiritual dimensions.

Although there are many similarities between male and female menopause, the most obvious difference is that a woman's reproductive ability ends at menopause while a man can continue having children into old age. Yet, the core of the Menopause Passage, for both men and women, has to do with reproduction. Specifically, it involves the shift from the reproductive period to a new period of life. In order to understand the similarities and differences between men and women at this stage, we need to go back to the beginnings and explore the male and female reproductive systems.

On Genes and Gender: Why Males and Females Are More Alike Than Different

Our identity blueprints come to us in the form of forty-six chromosomes, half contributed by our mother, half by our father. The first forty-four team up with one another, forming pairs of chromosomes that determine most of who we are. The last two pairs, called either XX or XY, determine whether we will become a female or a male. With so much emphasis these days on how males and females differ, we often forget how much alike we are.

This first came home to me when I was a medical student at University of California at San Francisco in 1965. Students worked in teams of four to dissect human bodies so that we might learn something about what we were made of. I can still remember the weeks we worked, some teams on male bodies, other teams on female bodies. Yet day after day, what we "discovered" did not differ by sex. The hearts, livers, kidneys, lungs, brains, blood vessels, nerves, lymph nodes, and on and on—all were in the same place, all had the same function. It was very clear how much alike we were.

There was a relatively short period of time spent on the different genitalia that the males and females possessed. Yet even looking at differences and remembering the contribution of the forty-fifth and forty-sixth chromosomes, the structures were so analogous that the underlying similarities were obvious.

In high school biology class, we learn that people who were female had received an "X" chromosome egg from their mother and a "X" chromosome sperm from their father. Those who received an "X" egg from their mother and a "Y" sperm from their father become male.

It wasn't until I entered college and took more advanced classes in embryology that I realized how similar our foundations are, whether we are male or female.

Until the sixth week of development, XX and XY embryos are anatomically identical right down to the core of their developing sexual anatomy. Dr. Anne Fausto-Sterling, professor of biology and medicine at Brown University, describes the embryological development of males and females as follows:

"During this early period each develops an embryonic gonad dubbed the 'indifferent gonad' because of its sameness in both XX and XY embryos. In similar fashion the other internal structures of both the male and female reproductive systems begin to form, so that by the first month and a half of embryonic development all the embryos, regardless of which sex chromosomes reside inside their cells, have a set of female (Müllerian) ducts as well as a set of male (Wolffian ducts)....In XX embryos the female ducts normally develop into the oviducts, uterus, cervix, and upper vagina, while in XY embryos the male ducts usually become the vas deferens, epididymis, and ejaculatory ducts."[2]

In other words, six weeks after fertilization all embryos are sexually bipotential, containing those parts needed to become either a male or a female.[3]

But for those embryos who have a Y chromosome, something new is added. The gonads develop into testes, and the fetus begins to produce the male hormones or androgens, the main one being testosterone. The hormones instruct the body not to bother with developing a feminine set of sexual equipment, while stimulating the development of embryonic male genitalia. At about the same time, if the baby is female, genetically XX, the reproductive machinery develops along female lines, and results in a baby girl.

Yet both males and females retain their ability to produce both androgens ("male" hormones) and estrogens ("female" hormones). The changes in these hormone levels as men and women move through the Menopause Passage proves to be important.

Why Men Have "Female" Hormones and Women Have "Male" Hormones

As a little boy, the main things I learned about males and females was that women had emotional ups and downs at a certain time of the month that were caused by their "hormones." Men, it seemed, had nothing like that. I had no idea what a hormone might be, but it was clear that it was quintessentially female.

When I studied biology in high school, I was shocked to find out that males also had hormones. I thought the changes I was experiencing as an adolescent male were just part of growing up. I had no idea I was under the influence of "raging hormones." "When a boy hits puberty, the influence of testosterone on his body and brain increase manifold," says Dr. Michael Gurian, author of *The Wonder of Boys*. "His testosterone level itself will increase in quantities ten to twenty times more than girls."[4]

After puberty, testosterone levels remain relatively stable in men until they reach midlife when levels begin to drop off. Both males and females must deal with significant hormonal changes during adolescence and again as they approach the Menopause Passage. "The physical phenomenon we obviously share is a diminishing production of sex hormones in the body," Rosetta Reitz reminds us. "In women it's the ovaries, in men it's the testes, which are similar in size and shape to the ovaries."[5]

Testosterone is not the only hormone that is of importance to men. Estrogen is also vital to male well-being and happiness. "Just as women have much less testosterone than men," says Dr. Theresa Crenshaw, "men have considerably less estrogen than women. They do, however, have some estrogen surges of their own during puberty."[6]

Estrogen in the male bloodstream may account for his desire not just for sex but also for love and intimacy. Estrogen promotes receptivity and touching, qualities that both men and women value.

Many Americans remember the outpouring of response when Ann Landers asked whether women preferred hugging and cuddling "to the act itself." Over twenty thousand women responded. Most said they preferred a loving touch to sexual intercourse.

It would have been interesting if Ann Landers could have gotten an honest response from men to the same question. Contrary to the myth that all men want is sex, most men, particularly as they get older, want and need to touch and be touched. They need sensual and emotional intimacy, even more than sexual connection.

When my wife, Carlin, was at the height of her menopause and we were the most distant, I greatly missed our sex life. But even more than sex, I missed the loving touch that usually accompanied it. When I thought that menopause might mean the end of our sex life, it became clear to me that I could survive, and the relationship would survive, without sex, but I could not go on without loving touch. The estrogen (as well as other hormones) circulating in men's blood helps the emotional and receptive aspects of a man's sexuality.

Just as estrogen is important to men, testosterone is a crucial hormone in female sexual well-being. "From our point of view as sexologists," say Barbara Bartlik, M.D., and Helen Singer Kaplan, M.D., Ph.D., "for a woman to live with inadequate levels of testosterone is no small matter....No matter how hard a woman might try to assemble the building blocks of healthy sexual functioning—the required amounts of other hormones, a loving partner, adequate stimulation, possibly a good sexual fantasy—it cannot work if she does not have the basic foundation of enough testosterone."[7]

Susan Rako, M.D., was forty-seven and still having periods, albeit irregularly, as she describes it, when her world began to change. "I could not make sense of the significant loss in general vital energy, thinning and loss of pubic hair, and loss of sexual energy I experienced," she remembers. "To say that I was lacking a feeling of well-being would be an understatement."[8]

Dr. Rako's search led to a surprising finding. "The data was there," she says, "but it didn't say estrogen was what I needed. It said testosterone."

She reported the results of her personal quest and the startling findings that have implications for both men and women going through the Menopause Passage in her book, *The Hormone of Desire*. She discusses three significant findings from her research:

1. A woman's normal physiology includes the production of a critical amount of testosterone, essential to her normal sexual development, to the healthy functioning of virtually all tissues in her body, and to her experience of vital energy and sexual libido.

2. This critical amount of testosterone decreases after menopause, in many women resulting in a loss of vital energy and sexual libido.

3. Supplementary testosterone can be a substantial help in restoring a woman to her familiar level of energy, libido, and well-being.[9]

It makes little scientific sense to look at women as the ones who have hormonal shifts and for whom the decrease of estrogen at midlife is significant and to look at men as the ones who have psychological changes and for whom the decrease of testosterone at midlife is significant. In fact it doesn't make much sense to call testosterone "the male hormone" and estrogen "the female hormone." Men and women have both and need both.

Hormonal Shifts and Sexual Cycles: Men Have Them Too

Although most of us now accept that women and men have "male" and "female" hormones, it is more difficult to accept that men also have hormonal cycles. Yet according to the endocrinologist Dr. Estelle Ramey, professor at Georgetown University Medical School, they do. "The evidence of them may be less dramatic," says Dr. Ramey, "but the monthly changes are no less real."[10] But if men do have hormonal cycles, why don't they recognize them or talk about them?

Dr. Ramey believes it is because men respond to their cycles in a way that is a function of their "culturally acquired self-image. They deny them."[11] This denial is the main reason she feels the largely male scientific and medical communities have taken so long to study male menopause. Men who are out of touch with their body rhythms, afraid that "cycles" are feminine and hence to be avoided at all costs, are unlikely to be aware of the whisperings within until they get very loud.

Dr. Winnifred Cutler is another modern researcher who has found a significant relationship between male sexuality and hormone changes. Like many women I have talked to, she began to recognize the hormonal patterns in men after studying shifts in women's cycles. For over twenty-five years, her research has addressed the nature of the reproductive system of men and women, the effects of male and female hormones, sexual and behavioral implications, and the changes in men and women as they age.

A series of scientific studies in recent years has greatly expanded our understanding of hormonal changes men experience. "Now it is known that men show a hormonal rhythm," says Dr. Cutler, "a rhythm I call the hormonal symphony of men. A man's hormones are intimately linked to his sexuality."[12]

Like the rotation of the earth and ebb and flow of the tides, many of our hormones rise and fall within our bodies in cycles. A cycle might last a few minutes, a day, a week, a month, a season, a year, or a lifetime. There are also cycles within cycles.

"If a young man has blood taken from his arm six times a day starting in the early morning and continuing every four hours thereafter, lab results will tend to show a rhythmic rise and fall of testosterone reflecting the time of the day. When he goes to sleep, his hormone levels will start rising hour by hour until, by the time he wakes, his testosterone levels will have reached the highest they will be for the nighttime sampling. By the early and late morning, he is likely to show his peak levels. In the afternoon, his testosterone will usually fall."[13]

Men's hormones also cycle throughout the year. In studies conducted in the United States, France, and Australia, it was found that men secrete their highest levels of sex hormones in October and their lowest levels in April. There was a 16 percent increase in testosterone levels from April to October and a 22 percent decline from October to the next April. Interestingly, though Australia is in its spring when France and the United States are in their fall, men in all three parts of the world showed a similar pattern of peaks in October and valleys in April.[14]

Men also have monthly hormonal cycles, though there are some interesting differences and similarities between women's and men's cycles. Women's monthly cycles are more predictable and synchronous. Women, for instance, who live in close proximity find that their monthly cycles begin to align. Men's cycles seem to be more unpredictable and individual.

A study of twenty young men showed that the majority had a discernible cycle of testosterone with regularly repeating rises and falls. However, each man who showed a cycle had a cycle unique to himself.[15]

"In other words, men emerged as cyclic, but with unique individuality to their cycles," says Dr. Winnifred Cutler, who reported on the study. "This pattern of individual cycles…is very different from the pattern in women, where the 29.5-day cycle is the universal optimum for fertility….Thus males are hormonally individualistic creatures, whereas females are hormonally harmonic with one another."[16]

Perhaps the least understood and most interesting of men's hormonal cycles is the rapid oscillation of testosterone that occurs three to four times every hour. Not only do testosterone levels cycle in males every fifteen or twenty minutes, the extent of the highs and lows is influenced by a whole host of factors, including the seasons, the environment, the presence of male competitors, and proximity of a desirable sexual partner.

"The morning highs, daily fluctuations, and seasonal cycles whip men around," says Dr. Crenshaw. "Think about the moment-to-moment impact of testosterone levels firing and spiking all over the place during the day, and what this must be doing to a man's temperament. Men who so strongly need to feel in control are in fact in much less control than they realize. No wonder they can be so, well, testy!"[17]

Could men be going through a kind of Premenstrual Syndrome every fifteen or twenty minutes? A number of researchers, including Dr. Crenshaw, feel they do. "The speed or rate at which your blood hormone levels change can be as important or more important than the amount of change," says Dr. Crenshaw. "For example, the man's rapid quarter-hourly surges of testosterone can have more emotional and physical impact than the greater but more gradual changes of some of the hormones that fluctuate during the menstrual cycle."[18]

The hormonal shifts that cause PMS, long associated with women, may be a fact of life for men as well. "One of the most misleading consequences of the popular focus on Premenstrual Syndrome," says psychologist Carol Tavris, "is that it omits men as a comparison group."[19] In a recent study, when men were given the same checklists of symptoms from a typical PMS questionnaire—omitting the female specific symptoms, such as breast tenderness—(reduced or increased energy, irritability and other negative moods, back pain, sleeplessness, headaches, confusion, etc.), "men report having as many 'premenstrual symptoms' as women do—when the symptoms aren't called PMS."[20]

Psychologist Jessica McFarlane and her associates, who conducted a "weekend happiness" study, concludes that "women are not 'moodier' than the men; their moods were not less stable within a day or from day-to-day. Evidence of weekday mood cycles in both sexes suggest that treating emotional fluctuations as unhealthy symptoms, and assuming that only women usually manifest them, is misleading."[21]

The final hormonal cycle that men must deal with, and one which is influenced by all the other shifts, involves the drop in hormone levels that occurs in midlife. This cycle is what we know now as male menopause. It usually begins around age forty and lasts until around age fifty-five, though it can begin as early as thirty-five and last until age sixty.

Male menopause can come on gradually or abruptly. It is triggered by a drop in testosterone, DHEA, and other hormone levels, as well as by life changes such as loss of a job, widowhood, divorce, illness, physical injury, financial setbacks, decrease in sex drive, or impotence. Since mind and body influence each other, decreasing hormones can cause life changes and life changes can cause hormone levels to drop.

Men experience 5 types of hormonal cycles:

1. Rhythmic fluctuations three to four times an hour.

2. Daily changes with hormones higher in the morning and lower in the afternoon.

3. Monthly fluctuations that are rhythmic, but different for each individual.

4. Fluctuations throughout the year with levels higher in October and lower in April.

5. Decreasing hormone levels associated with the Male Menopause Passage.

Research on male hormonal cycles, as well as male menopause, is in its infancy. Yet it is clear that men, too, have hormonal cycles that have a profound effect on their personality, mood, sexual interest, and sense of well-being. Perhaps the proverbial battle of the sexes would produce fewer casualties if men and women recognized how similar they were and how much their emotions fluctuated with the rhythms of their hormones.

The Bottom of the Mountain: Men and Women Face the Future

We see, then, that both men's and women's hormones change during the Menopause Passage. The drop is more rapid for most women than it is for most men. As one doctor described it, women fall off a cliff and men sort of roll down the hill.

But even difference in the speed with which women and men go through the change is not as clear cut as we once thought. "It used to be true that the majority of women began menopause in their mid-forties to early fifties," says John R. Lee, M.D., author of *What Your Doctor May Not Tell You about Menopause*. "In the last generation, however, things appear to have changed. Women now may have anovulatory periods starting in their early thirties and yet do not experience cessation of periods (menopause) until their fifties."[22]

What we generally refer to as menopause in women is not an event, but a gradual shift from one stage of a woman's life to another. "Menopause itself..." says Susan M. Love, M.D., "probably lasts for only a few days, and you can never be absolutely certain when it's occurred. Menopause is usually identified retrospectively, when it's been a year since your last period."[23]

Just as there are hormonal shifts that occur for males and females during puberty, so too are there shifts that occur during the Menopause Passage. However, the similarity in these two stages of life have often been overlooked. "Yet it has seemed obvious to me for quite a while that the time right before menopause is the mirror image of puberty," says Dr. Love. "During puberty, this mechanism is starting up. Then, at the other end, when the process is gearing down, the same things happen again. What these two life stages have in common is big hormonal shifts."[24]

Though Dr. Love's comments referred to the changes that females go through in puberty and again during menopause, it seems clear to me that similar hormonal changes apply to males as well.

Male menopause generally occurs more gradually beginning around age forty, with changes occurring over the next fifteen years. However, for some men, there is a very rapid drop in hormone levels that can bring on male menopause in a matter of months rather than years. For some men, hormonal shifts are so rapid that they experience hot flashes similar to those reported by women.[25]

Yet, however quickly they get there, both men and women eventually find themselves at the bottom of the hill. For most of us the feeling is not a pleasant one.

Being at the bottom feels pretty close to being "six feet under." Death is a visitor we all face as we complete this period of our lives. "In the Midlife Transition the Young/Old polarity is experienced with a special force," says Daniel Levinson in *The Seasons of a Man's Life*. "As early adulthood comes to an end, a man is assailed by new fears of the 'loss of youth.' He feels that the Young—variously represented as the child, the adolescent and the youthful adult in himself—is dying. The imagery of old age and death hangs over him like a pall."[26]

"At menopause as never before," says Germaine Greer, "a woman comes face-to-face with her own mortality. A part of her is dying. . . . The feeling that one's day has passed its noon and the shadows are lengthening, that summer is long gone and the days are growing ever shorter and bleaker, is a just one and should be respected."[27]

Another similarity shared by men and women is that we all live in a society where old age is not valued, and we are bombarded by advertising that tells us of the horrors of aging and absolute necessity of buying this or that product that will keep us young, attractive, and vital. Midlife women have long been a focus of the medical establishment. Many in the medical community have seen menopause as a disease that requires special intervention and cure.

"The midlife woman now has her very own disease—estrogen deficiency syndrome—specific to her sex and time of life," says Sandra Coney, author of *The Menopause Industry*. "Medicine has determined that in her normal state, the midlife woman is sick. The idea of normal aging has been collapsed into a definition of pathology. The menopause is no longer simply the end of periods or a life stage, rather it has been construed as an illness that no woman can escape."[28]

Convincing women that it is a bad thing to look or feel old and that there is a product that can be purchased to prevent it has been the task of the advertising by major corporations that have an investment in selling new and improved products.

As more and more men begin to become aware of their own midlife changes, they too are beginning to be targeted by the medical and pharmaceutical industries. Dr. John B. McKinlay, an epidemiologist at Boston University who has studied aging in both men and women, believes that men will soon be targeted for medical treatment for their midlife changes. "There's a very strong interest in treating aging men for a profit, just as there is for menopausal women."[29]

In our market driven economy, we can be sure that baby boom men will be a prime target for those who would prey on men's fears of aging and loss of sexual function. "Attention all men over 50!" cautions the Center for Medical Consumers. "You are about to be declared an illness. It won't happen overnight, of course, but the pharmaceutical industry has only just begun marketing testosterone replacement therapy."[30]

On the other hand, just because there are huge profits to be made in marketing to midlife men doesn't mean what is offered is not helpful. Like women, men will have to become informed consumers, to separate the facts from the advertising hype.

The Life We Were Meant to Live: Climbing the Mountain of Second Adulthood

We are at a unique stage in human evolution. For most of our three million year history, human beings died once their reproductive peak had passed. According to life expectancy statistics from the National Center for Health Statistics, as late as 1910, the average life expectancy at birth in the United States was fifty years, slightly lower for males, a bit higher for females.[31]

Yet, for the first time in human history, we now have a chance to see the full extent of the human life cycle. Most of us are not prepared for the fact that it may be as long as 120 years. "Virtually everyone has died too soon," says Walter M. Bortz II, M.D., who is on the faculty at Stanford University Medical School, and author of *Dare to Be 100*, "like animals in the wild that rarely have the chance to grow old."[32]

"Ours is the first generation in history, to know what a whole human life can look like," says Dr. Bortz.[33] "There is now a sufficient fund of data and experience to allow baby boomers—and, of course, younger generations—to plan their one hundredth birthday party with calm assurance, prepare the guest list, and muster enough respiratory reserve to blow out all those candles."[34]

And that may be just the beginning. Recent research on aging and longevity has led some in the field to predict that we are just beginning to find out the potential for human life. According to Michael Jazwinski, M.D. a leading researcher on aging at Louisiana State University Medical Center, "possibly in thirty years we will have in hand the major genes that determine longevity, and will be in a position to double, triple, even quadruple our maximum life span of 120 years. It's possible that some people alive now may still be alive 400 years from now."[35]

Our past tells us that once we reach the bottom of the mountain, that's the end of the story. Our future would have us believe that there is another mountain we have an opportunity to climb, the mountain of Second Adulthood.

The purpose of the Menopause Passage, for men and for women, is to prepare them for the journey up the second mountain. Many of the things that men and women experience as negative, such as a loss of strength and physical stamina, actually help prepare them for the second half of life, where more emphasis is placed on the emotional and spiritual issues.

During First Adulthood, physical activities were often engaged in to achieve some goal such as losing weight, winning a race, getting stronger, being the best. In Second Adulthood, more emphasis is placed on doing things simply for the joy of doing them. Since more and more men and women are living longer, more opportunities are available to enjoy the things in Second Adulthood that were missed the first time around. And for those who have been to the top of the Second Adulthood mountain, the view, I'm told, is spectacular.

The sights will not be reserved only for the lucky few or contingent upon new breakthroughs in science. "Using data supplied by the Census Bureau, Paul Siegel and Cynthia Taueber predicted that 'if the average rates of decrease in death rates continue to prevail in the coming years, in 2050 the average life expectancy will be one hundred.' If this is the case, there will be nineteen million centenarians."[36]

"Shirley Potter bungee-jumped 210 feet in Alpine, California, to celebrate his 100th birthday. He lamented, however, that the subsequent publicity was 'killing me.'...Claire Will [was] taking dance classes at 100. Genevieve McDaniel, 102, taught aerobics. David Eldridge of St. Petersburg still umpired at 105. Otto Aster at 103 was said to be America's oldest roller skater. Herman Smith-Johansen cross-country skied five miles at age 100. Harlow Potter, 103, was the oldest of the eight thousand competitors in the 1995 Senior Sports Classic. He took up golf at age 92 and recently shot a ninety-eight."[37]

The experiences of those on the Second Adulthood moutain go beyond recreational activities and include new opportunities for intimacy and sexuality. Many of the sexual difficulties men and women have as they begin the Menopause Passage are not indicators of a downward slide to a sexless old age, as many fear. In fact, they may be transitional changes that are needed to prepare them for a richer and more intimate sex life in later years.

Dr. Bortz and his colleagues at Stanford University recently worked with a group whose average age was sixty-seven and found that they were a sexy lot, "sexier than we would have expected," Dr. Bortz acknowledged. "Fifty-three percent of the men under seventy reported having sex at least once a week, as did 33 percent of those over seventy." The figures were virtually identical for the women.[38]

However, most of the men and women would like to have more sex if given the chance. Bortz found that 98 percent of all the men and women in his group would like to have sex once a week and 66 percent would like sex two or more times a week. There were two issues that kept the members of the group from having the sexual lives they desired. "For the men, the issue was impotence," says Bortz, "but for the women it was opportunity."[39]

The good news for men is that we know a lot more about sexual dysfunction than we did in the past. "Until recently, impotence was thought to be largely psychological in origin," says Dr. Bortz. "Now this opinion has shifted totally as science identifies the mechanics of having an erection and what can go wrong with the apparatus...ill health, medication usage, and lack of a congenial partner are all negative conditions for the aging man. Fortunately, they can be counteracted."[40]

"Various experts report that women's interest and capacity for sexual fulfillment do not diminish, until advanced old age, provided there is opportunity available," says Dr. Bortz. A number of women friends have said that more older women are turning to each other for sexual satisfaction, many because of life-long sexual preferences, others because suitable males just aren't available. "We men simply must do a better job at living longer, and thereby participating in the intimacies of our mates as long as we both shall live."[41]

The Menopause Passage can prepare both men and women for a life where love and intimacy are linked with sexuality in ways that were not possible in the earlier years when sexuality was driven by the desire to reproduce and raise children. In order to understand the opportunities for greater closeness in intimate relationships, it is important to understand the differences between the male path and the female path through the Menopause Passage.

His Change/Her Change: The Differences between Menopause and Male Menopause

Though there are more similarities than differences between "his" and "her" change, what men and women do not share is critical and important. Carlin's women's group, which we met in chapter 2, touched on some of the perceived differences.

"I want to make a distinction between male menopause and midlife crisis," says Susan. "Men in their forties, fifties, and sixties are getting older. Women in their forties, fifties, and sixties are getting older. But women go through a menopause and men do not."

"Now when women go through menopause, this is incredibly dramatic," Susan continues. "Now it's not to say that men don't go through the same thing. But men go through it over a fifty or a forty or a thirty year period. Women go through it in a very short period. Men go through a loss of testosterone just like we go through a loss of estrogen, but women go through it like THAT." Susan claps her hands loudly.

"For a man to experience what a woman experiences at menopause, it seems to me that a man would have to have an ordinary sex life and then be castrated." The rest of the group looks a bit shocked. "Now if he was suddenly castrated, he might begin to have some of the symptoms women have at menopause.

"Women," Susan continues, "have a specific stopping time where they can no longer have children. Men don't. They can have children on and on."

Susan raises two of the crucial differences between menopause and male menopause. First, men can have precipitous changes in their hormone levels—and those who do have dramatic symptoms, including hot flashes—physically, male menopause is usually more gentle and gradual than menopause. Though some women report very few symptoms of menopause due to a very gradual drop in hormones, most women experience changes that are more rapid and the symptoms more dramatic.

In this respect, male menopause and menopause are different in degree but not in kind. However, a second difference is a change in kind and clearly separates male menopause from menopause. This difference has major implications for the ways in which men and women handle this stage in their journey. As women complete menopause, all of them will find that they are unable to have children. As men complete male menopause, most all of them will still be able to reproduce.

The reactions of individual women vary. "I am so happy my reproductive years are over," says Barbara a fifty-two-year-old mother of three. "I don't have to play the mating game anymore. I can finally begin to think about myself and what I want to do with the rest of my life. For the first time ever, I feel free."

For Joan, a forty-eight-year-old single mom whose periods recently ended completely, the feelings were much less positive. "It's been a long time since I have even thought of having more children, but not to be able to have them deeply saddens me. I feel like a big part of my womanhood shut down with my ovaries. I cry at night thinking about what's been lost."

There are also a range of reactions that I hear from men. "I know I don't want more children," says Bill a fifty-three-year-old father of five, "but it just feels good to know that my sperm are alive and well. I like the idea of being able to father children into my nineties. When I heard that Anthony Quinn had a baby when he was in his eighties, a little cheer of joy went off inside me."

"I wish the whole reproductive thing would end for men like it does for women," confided John, a tall, good-looking fifty-six-year-old businessman. "I'm tired of the whole mating dance. I feel like a traitor to the male race by even thinking it, but I wish the constant search for sex and security would just go away. I still get caught up in the flirting game, mostly for my ego satisfaction, I guess. But I just wish young women would stop looking at me as 'daddy material.' If I could, I'd put a sign on my forehead, 'All the sperm have come and left. Daddy has retired and gone fishing.'"

Many couples have a difficult time, particularly those where the woman has had children but the man has not. This is the situation for two men I interviewed. "I love Linda," says George with deep sadness in his voice, "and I know I don't want to leave. But I'm having trouble letting go of the fact that staying with her means I will never have children of my own."

"I'm in the same situation," Joseph laments. "Ellen has four children, and she isn't going to have any more. I'm not sure I do want children, but the thought that I could creates a lot of doubt in me. Is this the right person for me? Is it my destiny to be a stepfather and never have my own children, or am I selling myself out by not keeping my options open?"

With the increase of divorce and remarriage, an increasing number of couples find themselves in this situation. Even for couples where the man has already fathered a child, there is still tension. "I know I'm not getting any younger," says Julia, a woman in her fifties, "and my childrearing years are done. My husband, Jeff, says he is happy, loves me, and wants to spend the rest of his life with me. But the attractions of a younger woman are always there. He knows he is still capable of reproducing, and she knows he still has wild and active sperm. That mixture makes for a powerful aphrodisiac, and it scares me more than I'd care to admit."

I have found that this is one of the taboo topics for middle-age couples. He pretends he doesn't look at younger women, and she fumes, silently, knowing he does. She pretends not to notice that she is living with a man who can still have children, while she cannot. He stews in silent anger, knowing that his commitment to her will forever end his sexual adventuring and possibility of fathering more children.

And even less talked about than these issues are the ones about becoming a mature adult. Men's reproductive freedom allows them the option of staying "forever young" and often keeps them from ever growing up emotionally. Like it or not, the end of a woman's menstrual cycles and the cessation of her reproductive life pushes her towards the next step in becoming a more mature woman.

Men, with their more gradual menopause and open-ended reproductive capability, don't get the same kind of push to assume their mature position in society. His biology pulls him to the past, drawing him towards beautiful young women who are still capable of offering viable eggs for his still mobile sperm. And yet, his deepening spirituality hungers for life in a different direction.

It craves for mature masculinity. It cries out for him to stay with his older partner, to share in her journey and have her be a part of his. His deepening spiritual hunger calls on him to join with a mature partner to become elders to future generations. How a man resolves the conflict will determine whether the second half of his life is deep with meaning or superficial and hollow. To receive the proper guidance at this stage of the journey, we must understand why men are the way they are. To that end, we need to explore the evolution of sex.

Notes Chapter 6

1. Rosetta Reitz, *Menopause: A Positive Approach* (Radner, PA: Chilton Book Company, 1977), 226.

2. Anne Fausto-Sterling, *Myths of Gender: Biological Theories about Women and Men* (New York: Basic Books, 1985), 78–80.

3. Ibid., 80.

4. Michael Gurian, *The Wonder of Boys: What Parents, Mentors and Educators Can Do to Shape Boys into Exceptional Men* (New York: G. P. Putnam's Sons, 1996), 10.

5. Reitz, 226–27.

6. Theresa Crenshaw, M.D., *The Alchemy of Love and Lust: Discovering Our Sex Hormones and How They Determine Who We Love, When We Love, and How Often We Love* (New York: G. P. Putnam's Sons, 1996), 31.

7. Barbara Bartlik, M.D., and Helen Singer Kaplan, M.D., Ph.D., introduction to *The Hormone of Desire: The Truth about Sexuality, Menopause, and Testosterone*, by Susan Rako, M.D. (New York: Harmony Books, 1996), 15.

8. Susan Rako, M.D., *The Hormone of Desire: The Truth about Sexuality, Menopause, and Testerone* (New York: Harmony Books, 1996), 25.

9. Ibid., 25.

10. Quoted in Reitz, 228.

11. Ibid.

12. Winnifred B. Cutler, Ph.D., *Love Cycles: The Science of Intimacy* (New York: Villard Books, 1991), 88.

13. Ibid., 89.

14. Ibid., 90.

15. Ibid., 91.

16. Ibid.

17. Crenshaw, 10.

18. Ibid.

19. Carol Tavris, *The Mismeasure of Woman: Why Women Are Not the Better Sex, the Inferior Sex, or the Opposite Sex* (New York: Simon and Schuster, 1992), 148.

20. Ibid.

21. Quoted in Tavris, 148.

22. John R. Lee, M.D., and Virginia Hopkins, *What Your Doctor May Not Tell You about Menopause: The Breakthrough Book on Natural Progesterone* (New York: Warner Books, 1996), 8–9.

23. Susan M. Love, M.D., and Karen Lindsey, *Dr. Susan Love's Hormone Book* (New York: Random House), 3.

24. Ibid., 4.

25. Reported in Patricia Skalka, *The American Medical Association Guide to Health and Well-Being after Fifty* (New York: Random House, 1984), 88.

26. Daniel J. Levinson, *The Seasons of a Man's Life* (New York: Ballantine, 1978), 213.

27. Germaine Greer, *The Change: Women, Aging and Menopause* (New York: Ballantine, 1991), 124.

28. Sandra Coney, *The Menopause Industry: How the Medical Establishment Exploits Women* (Alameda, CA: Hunter House, 1994), 19.

29. Reported in Natalie Angier, "Male Menopause," *New York Times*, 23 October 1992.

30. Center for Medical Consumers, Inc., 1995.

31. Reported in Frank Kendig and Richard Hutton, *Life Spans: Or How Long Things Last* (New York: Holt, Rinehart and Winston, 1979), 11.

32. Walter M. Bortz, II, M.D., *Dare to Be 100* (New York: Fireside, 1996), 14.

33. Ibid., 16.

34. Ibid., 19.

35. Quoted in John J. Medina, *The Clock of Ages: Why We Age—How We Age—Winding Back the Clock* (Cambridge: Cambridge University Press, 1996), 313.

36. Quoted in Bortz, 21.

37. Bortz, 76–77.

38. Ibid., 56.

39. Ibid.

40. Ibid., 56–57.

41. Ibid., 57.

7

The Evolution of Sex, Men, and Menopause

He who thus considers things in their first growth and origin, whether a state or anything else, will obtain the clearest view of them.

—*Aristotle*

Since sex is such an important aspect of our lives, and concerns about sexual changes such a significant concern for men going through the Menopause Passage, it will serve us well to take an excursion into the new science of evolutionary psychology.

This new discipline draws from and influences such diverse fields as anthropology, psychology, biology, sociology, genetics, politics, sexology, linguistics, philosophy, ethology, and deep ecology. It shows that there is a universal human nature that has developed over millions of years of evolutionary history and also that males and females have different natures based on the different evolutionary challenges that men and women have faced.

Before men can decide what changes, if any, they wish to make to improve their sexuality and health, it is important to fully understand the true nature of male sexuality.

Humans are the sexiest animals on the face of the planet, bar none. We celebrate sex in song, poetry, and advertising. We think about it, worry about it, plot and plan for it. We "just let it happen" and spend days and months getting ready. After years of sexual fidelity, we wonder "is this all there is," and when sexual experiences are few and far between, we cling desperately to whatever we can get. In adolescence, it seems to be busting out all over, and as we age, it seems to come and go, with often more go than come.

"We are a species devoted to sex," says anthropologist Helen Fisher, author of *The Sex Contract* and *The Anatomy of Love*. "We talk about it, joke about it, read about it, dress for it, and perform it regularly. We have legends to explain it, punishments to curb it, and rules to organize it."[1]

Yet contrary to what many would have us believe (and many men are afraid is true), it is the female of the species that makes us the sexiest animal that ever lived. According to Fisher, it is the woman who "is physically able to make love every day of her adult life. She can copulate during pregnancy, and she can resume sexual activity shortly after having a child. She can make love whenever she pleases." Fisher believes this is extraordinary. "No females of any other sexually reproducing species make love with such frequency."[2]

I first met Helen Fisher at the Human Behavior and Evolution Society Conference in Santa Barbara where she was giving a talk on "Future Sex." How could I resist? I was impressed by her passionate interest in all aspects of human sexuality and the breadth of her knowledge. When we talked later, she invited me to co-teach a class entitled: "Women, Men, Sex, and Power: Life in the 21st Century," which she would be doing later that year at the Esalen Institute in Big Sur, California.

Fisher, who is research associate in the department of anthropology at the American Museum of Natural History, has devoted her professional life to understanding why humans mate, marry, stray, divorce, and long to do it all over again. She is one of the leading figures in the emerging field of evolutionary psychology and one of the field's most experienced researchers. Her interest, however, is more than professional. The roots go back to her childhood. "I am an identical twin," she says. "By the time I was four or five, I had begun to notice grown-ups staring at my twin sister and me as they asked us questions. Did I know when Lorna was in trouble? Did we like the same toys? Did I ever think I was Lorna?"

She reflects back on her own thoughts during those early years. "So as a child I started, quite unconsciously, to weigh my behavior: How much of it was inherited? How much of it was learned?"

Her interest continued on through college. "Then, in graduate school, I discovered the 'nature/nurture' debate. John Locke's concept of the 'tabula rasa,' or empty tablet, was particularly troubling. Was every infant really a blank sheet of paper on which culture inscribed personality? I didn't believe it.

"Then I read Jane Goodall's book *In the Shadow of Man*, about the wild chimpanzees of Tanzania. These creatures had different personalities, and they made friends, held hands, kissed, gave one another gifts of leaves and twigs, and mourned when a companion died. I was overcome by the emotional continuity between man and beast. And I became convinced that some of my behavior was biological in origin."[3]

In order to understand menopause, for men and women, we have to understand the human life cycle and cycle of life of which humans are a part. Evolutionary psychology places humans within the context of the entire evolutionary history of the universe and shows where we fit in the life of our home planet.

The Origin of Sex and the Hunger to Come Home

"Fifteen billion years ago, in a great flash, the universe flared forth into being."[4] The earth was formed 4.5 billion years ago, followed soon by the first cell of life a half billion years later. Life flourished on the earth over the next three billion years, cells dividing in two, passing on identical DNA to the next generation. Only rare, random mutations brought about change. Like begat like, and life flourished in the primordial seas.

But a billion years ago, a new type of cell came into being, one which contained two nuclei. When this new cell divided, two different types of cells were formed. For the first time in evolutionary history, a "significant other" was created. Able to nourish themselves, but no longer capable of dividing into daughter cells, these new type of cells could only survive if they were able to "mate."

These two kinds of cells, called Tristan and Iseult by Brian Swimme and Thomas Berry, authors of *The Universe Story*, are our ancestors—the first male and female. To understand our place in the universe, to learn why men and women are the way they are, and the role that menopause plays in our life histories, we must understand the billion year old story of sex.

Here is how Swimme and Berry poetically describe this first act of sexual union:

"A slight, an ever so slight, chance existed that a Tristan cell would come upon a corresponding Iseult cell. They would brush against each other, a contact similar to so many trillions of other encounters in their oceanic adventure. But with this one, something new would awaken. Something unsuspected and powerful and intelligent, as if they had drunk a magical elixir, would enter the flow of electricity through each organism. Suddenly the very chemistry of their cell membranes would begin to change. Interactions evoked by newly functioning segments of her DNA would restructure the molecular web of Iseult's skin, so that an act she had never experienced or planned for would begin to take place—Tristan entering her cell wholly."[5] The beauty and wonder of sex had begun.

Swimme and Berry's book reminds us that humans are an integral part of the universe story. We are not a blight on the planet as some radical environmentalists would have us believe. Nor are we God's gift sent as special messengers to have dominion over land and sea, as some fundamentalists insist.

We are part of the natural world, just as important as the beetles, berries, bears, bushes, boars, and buttercups. Yet we have forgotten our place. We have become estranged from our home.

Lost and alone, our fear turns into pain and our pain into anger. Feeling our life slipping away, we turn our rage both inward and outward.

Not only are we killing off our fellow life forms, but to deal with the pain of our actions, more and more of us are becoming addicts. We use every imaginable drug to ease our pain. We get hooked on our computers, televisions, and videogames. We also escape through gambling, overeating, overspending, and overconsumption of all kinds. We are consuming the very planet that has sustained us for billions of years. We are eating ourselves alive.

After working with addictions for over thirty years, I have concluded that addicts are people who want to go home, but like confused homing pigeons, they fly 180 degrees in the wrong direction. It's as though their homing device was out of whack, and like lemmings, they follow each other over the cliff to their deaths, believing until the very end that they are on the right track.

I believe our homing mechanisms have become dysfunctional because we have cut ourselves off from our internal radar, from the core of our wisdom which is our connection to our biological roots. Yet there is still time to reconnect with our roots and get back on track, but time is running out for us. "We never knew enough," says Thomas Berry. "Nor were we sufficiently intimate with all our cousins in the great family of the earth. Nor could we listen to the various creatures of the earth, each telling its own story. The time has now come, however, when we will listen or we will die."[6]

In order to find our way home, we need to reconnect with our evolutionary roots. To do that, we need to come home to our sexual selves as males and females.

Are Men Really from Mars and Women from Venus?

Humans have become so cut off from nature that we mistakenly believe that we are the measure of all things, that God is dead, and that it is our job now to run the world. As individuals, we have also become ego inflated, thinking that the world revolves around us. It is sobering and valuable to look at individuals the way many evolutionary biologists see us, as a gene's way of getting itself into the next generation. "No matter how much knowledge and wisdom you acquire during your life," says Richard Dawkins, author of *The Selfish Gene*, "not one jot will be passed on to your children by genetic means. Each new generation starts from scratch. A body is the genes' way of preserving the genes unaltered."[7]

Understanding the evolutionary logic of reproduction from a gene's eye view, can help us understand men and women better and the place of menopause in our lives. In chapter 4, we detailed ten reasons men die so much sooner than women. If natural selection is about the survival of the fittest, why do so many people do things that limit their potential for survival?

The answer lies in knowing that from a gene's perspective, it is less important whether we survive to a ripe old age than whether we reproduce. Charles Darwin revolutionized science when he published *On the Origin of the Species By Means of Natural Selection* in 1859. Less well-known than his ideas on how natural selection works to produce species differences were his ideas on reproduction and what he called "sexual selection."

The idea that reproduction was the key to understanding why we do what we do was ignored for many years after Darwin's death and has only recently come back into vogue. "Its principal insight," says Matt Ridley, author of *The Red Queen*, "is that the goal of an animal is not just to survive but also to breed. Indeed, where breeding and survival come into conflict, it is breeding that takes precedence; for example, salmon starve to death while breeding. And breeding, in sexual species, consists of finding an appropriate partner and persuading it to part with a package of genes."[8]

This important insight brings us to the touchy issue of males and females. It has been an accepted belief by many modern, educated people that there are no significant inherent differences between males and females. When I was in school, I was proud that I had learned to overcome the sexist past and could appreciate people for being people. I believed that men and women were inherently equal and any differences were purely the result of cultural and social influences. And yet, like so many of my contemporaries, I couldn't quite shake the belief that biology played a larger role than I was willing to acknowledge.

When my wife and I tried to raise our children in non-sexist ways, there seemed to be some inner force that drew our boy to "boy things" and our girl to "girl things," in spite of our best efforts to give him dolls to play with and teach her the joys of sports.

I didn't want my daughter to be limited in her potential because of beliefs that pushed her towards motherhood. Nor did I want my son to automatically place career goals above family. Yet I was aware that we do live in a dominator culture where differences are often used to put one group down. I was concerned that focusing on differences might support the beliefs that "women's work" was less important than what men did and that men must be competitive and unemotional in order to be successful. Yet I was aware that we do live in a dominator culture where differences are often used to put one group down.[9]

In such a culture where differences have been used to keep certain groups from achieving equality and claiming power, one way for those who have less power in the system to gain power is to assert that there are no differences between groups. "If being different is going to work against me, I am going to believe that differences don't matter and that I am the same as everyone else."

However, another more effective way to achieve social justice is to recognize and accept differences between groups and to commit ourselves to ending the sexism and racism that so deeply divides our culture. This is beginning to happen in the ongoing dialogue on differences between men and women.

Linguist Deborah Tannen, for instance, tells us that men and women have different communication styles, which is why they complain that "You Just Don't Understand," the title of her bestselling book. In their book Brain Sex, geneticist Anne Moir and journalist David Jessel tell us that men and women "are equal only in their common membership in the same species, humankind."[10] Different brains produce different kinds of people, they believe.

Psychologist John Gray goes even farther, suggesting that we are so different it would be better if we accepted that men are from Mars and women are from Venus. Gray believes that we must accept our differences if we are going to get along, and he teaches the skills we need for interplanetary communication.

So what are we to believe? Are we better served by focusing on the real differences between men and women? Or would it be better if differences were downplayed and we focused more on what men and women have in common?

The Roots of Male and Female

Let's start by looking at the biological roots of gender. What does it mean to be male? What does it mean to be female? Are there definitions that are not biased by our dominator culture?

Biologists have a very simple and useful definition of what is male and what is female, whether we are fish, ferns, or human beings. An individual can either produce many small gametes (sex cells) or fewer but larger gametes. The individuals that produce smaller gametes are called "males," and the ones that make larger gametes are called "females." A single human female egg, for instance, though microscopic, is so large it could house 250,000 sperm.[11]

The small gametes are designed to fuse with a large one, and the large ones are designed to fuse with a small one. The female strategy produces gametes that are large and have a high rate of survival and fertilization. The male strategy is to produce as many as possible to increase the chances of finding a large one. Science shows that about four hundred eggs are ovulated in a woman's lifetime. A healthy male produces 185 million sperm per day.[12]

An individual must either invest in a few large eggs or millions of sperm. Thus, there will always be many times more sperm than there are eggs. Consequently, sperm must compete for access to those rare eggs.

Generally, it is easier to move the smaller sperm to the larger egg than vice versa, and so throughout the animal kingdom, it is the male that seeks out the female and the female who makes the selection from those males that come courting.

If you asked the average man or woman today about their life goals, it is unlikely that "reproductive success" would be at the top of the list. With the advent of reliable birth control, we are generally more concerned about limiting births than producing more children. Cut off as we are from the natural rhythms of life, we often forget that the ability to reproduce offspring is basic to all life.

We also fail to recognize how much our lives are driven by our evolutionary desire for reproductive success. Because this need is so important, the desires are built into our minds and bodies and are generally unconscious. We don't have to say to ourselves, "I must be successful at reproduction so that my genes will be passed on to the next generation." Rather, we simply desire to fall in love with an attractive partner, we compete with others for access to possible mates, we become jealous when others are attracted to our mate, and we feel drawn to other attractive people, even when we have a partner at home.

Humans inherit many things from our ancestors—the color of our eyes, our height, whether or not we lose our hair, how to eat, think, and speak. But above all, we inherit a drive to reproduce. "Therefore, anything that increased the chances of a person reproducing successfully was passed on at the expense of anything else. We can confidently assert," says Matt Ridley, author of The Red Queen, "that there is nothing in our natures that was not carefully 'chosen' in this way for its ability to contribute to eventual reproductive success."[13]

There is certainly more to life than reproduction. There are Mozart sonatas and Shakespeare plays. There are walks in the park and sunsets over the ocean. There are lazy summer days and winter snowstorms. There's more to life than sex, but without sex, there would be no life.

The Evolution of Desire:
Are There Two Human Natures?

None of your direct ancestors died childless. Think for a moment of the power contained in that statement. Over a period of three million years, not one of your ancestors dropped the ball. You are a product of their reproductive success, and you can bet that what it takes to pass on your genes to the next generation is built into your intentions, behavior, emotions, heart, mind, and soul.

Though the process is not always conscious, we never choose mates at random. We are all descended from a long and unbroken line of ancestors who competed successfully for desirable mates, attracted mates who were reproductively valuable, retained mates long enough to reproduce, and fended off interested rivals.

The way we carry out these vital functions is what evolutionary psychologists call our "reproductive strategy." It is our characteristic way of doing things, our standard operating procedure. It is what draws us to certain people, "the whisperings within," as evolutionary psychologist David Barash calls them. We don't always follow what we hear, but we must always listen.

Many people are afraid that if we accepted a theory that emphasizes the powerful pull of our genetic desires, it will take away free will and make us slaves to our hungers and sexual biology. I have found the reverse to be true. The more I understand about the forces that pull on me, the freer I am to "go with the flow" and accept my biologically driven desires when that is appropriate for me. It also allows me to choose to go against my genetic hungers when it is in my best interest to resist them.

So, being aware that knowledge brings freedom, let's look more deeply into the ways in which males and females interact in the natural world. In Africa, male weaverbirds build nests and hang from them while singing their courting song. Female weaverbirds inspect the nests of various males and stay to mate with the ones who have the most desirable nests. Women, like weaverbirds prefer men with desirable nests. Throughout the world and across cultures, women are drawn to men who have resources.[14]

I know what some of you are thinking. "Humans are not birds and women, like men, want all kinds of things. You can't make sweeping generalizations." We are not birds, but we are all animals. Forgetting that fact cuts us off from the web of life and blinds us to who we really are. There are individual variations, and generalizations can be misleading, but they can also be helpful. Few would disagree with the statement that men are taller than women, though at five feet five inches (when I tilt my head just right), there are many women taller than me.

Recognizing individual differences is important, but also being aware of group differences can be equally crucial in our understanding of our sexual natures. "Not everything is different; most things, in fact are identical between the sexes," says Matt Ridley. "Much of the folklore about differences is merely convenient sexism."[15] Yet, he goes on to say that those who have studied the differences between men and women, even those who were determined to find none, have concluded that significant differences do exist.

As anthropologist Melvin Konner put it, "Men are more aggressive than women and women are more nurturant, at least toward infants and children, than men. I am sorry if this is a cliché; that cannot make it less factual."[16] So what does evolutionary psychology tell us about gender differences?

Evolutionary psychologist Dr. David Buss and colleagues did a study on 511 college men and women asking if it would be more distressing or upsetting to imagine your mate having sexual intercourse with someone else, or to imagine your mate forming a deep emotional attachment to someone else. The study findings showed that if you are a man, it is likely that you find the idea of your mate having intercourse with someone else far more distressing—indeed, the majority of men in a study conducted by Buss did so, too. Conversely, 83 percent of the women who were posed this question in Buss's study said they found the idea of their mate forming a deep emotional attachment to someone else far more upsetting.[17]

Based on his research findings, Buss found a host of other differences between men and women and concluded that there are actually two human natures, one male, the other female. He believed that both the similarities and the differences could be explained by understanding evolutionary pressures our ancestors faced over the last three million years.

For instance, a man's greater jealousy over his mate's sexual infidelity can be traced, Buss believes, to the uncertainty men have over the paternity of their children. Every woman who gives birth is 100 percent certain that the child carries her genes. For men, on the other hand, there is always a degree of doubt.

In evolutionary terms, the consequence of raising a child that may not carry his genes, but those of another man, is the death of his line. The man who took an easygoing approach to the possibility of his mate being sexual with other men left fewer genes than those men who were sexually jealous.[18]

What makes Buss's findings so compelling is the breadth of his research. "If mating desires and other features of human psychology are products of our evolutionary history," says Buss, "they should be found universally, not just in the United States." To test his theories, he conducted a five-year study working with collaborators from thirty-seven cultures located on six continents and five islands. All major racial groups, religious groups, and ethnic groups were represented. In all, his research team surveyed 10,047 persons worldwide.[19]

What Do Women Really Want?

In Buss's worldwide study, he found that the top three qualities women look for in men are exactly the same as those things that men look for in women: intelligence, kindness, and love. Once again, we see that, at their core, men and women are the same. But then, what women want diverges from what men want. Once they know about a man's intelligence, kindness, and love, women then look at a man's ability to protect her and her children, his capacity to provide, and his willingness to make a commitment to a relationship.

Worldwide, women seek men who are strong and tall. Even women who are quite capable of taking care of themselves are attracted to men of size and strength. Women, as a group, judge short men to be less desirable than tall men. In personal ads in the United States where women mention height, 80 percent want a man 6 feet or taller.[20] Fortunately, not all women follow the trend. If there were not individual differences, all men my height would be celibate loners.

Women are also drawn to men with good earning capacity. This is true worldwide and doesn't seem to depend on whether the women themselves are well-off.[21] Women doctors, for instance, are drawn to even higher paid male doctors, rather than to male nurses.

Worldwide, women are drawn to men who are older than they are, which is not surprising since in most cultures older men have higher status and earn more money. In the United States, thirty-year-old males make, on average, $14,000 more a year than 20 year olds and $7,000 a year less than the average forty-year-old male.[22]

This pattern holds even for women who insist that wealth, status, strength, and height do not make a difference. The "whisperings within," which made for reproductive success through evolutionary history, are often stronger than our logical mind.

Finally, women want men who will commit their resources to the care and support of the woman and her children. In Buss's study, he concluded that the reason women were less concerned about a man's sexual fidelity and more concerned about their mate's emotional fidelity was the fear that an emotional attachment was more likely to lead to abandonment and the loss of the man's resources.[23]

These desires are often not conscious. Women usually don't say to themselves, "I like that guy because he is willing to commit his resources to me and my children, if I decide to have children." She just says, "I like that guy. I can count on him." She doesn't say, "I want a tall strong man who can protect me from wild animals." She just says, "He turns me on. The chemistry feels right."

Likewise, men don't go out looking for a "reproductively viable female who will raise my children, if I decide to have children." He sees a woman at a party and moves towards her thinking, "God, she's beautiful!" He doesn't say, "I want a woman who will protect by genetic investment." He says, "I love how you love me. You make me feel special."

Frustrating as it is for many women, men's desires are different, not because they come from another planet, but because they faced different evolutionary pressures than women on this planet.

What Do Men Really Want?

Like women, men seek love, intelligence, and kindness in a mate. But then a man is drawn to youth and beauty. This interest is not just a modern desire driven by advertising and a male desire to control women. According to Buss, it is a universal desire based on evolutionary pressures for reproductive success.

Men who mated with women who were incapable of bearing children left no ancestors. Every man alive today is descended from men who did not make that mistake. "Ancestral men," says Buss, "solved the problem of finding reproductively valuable women in part by preferring those who are young and healthy."[24] Buss's studies show that worldwide, men are drawn to younger women.

When the anthropologist Napoleon Chagnon asked which females are the most sexually attractive to Yanomamo Indian men of the Amazon rain forest, his male informant replied without hesitation, "females who are *moko dude*." In referring to the life-giving fruits of the jungle, Chagnon was told, *moko dude* means that the fruit is perfectly ripe. When referring to a woman, it means that she is postpubescent but has not yet borne her first child, or about fifteen to eighteen years of age.[25]

Since women's ability to conceive and bear children decreases with age, youth is a direct indicator of reproductive capacity. In most cultures throughout the world, men's attraction to youth has been understood and honored. In our modern dominator societies, men who feel this natural attraction are condemned and shamed.

Buss found that men throughout the world were attracted to beautiful women. "Full lips, clear and smooth skin, clear eyes, lustrous hair, and good muscle tone," he says, "are universally sought after."[26]

Attraction to beauty seems to be built into our biological makeup, according to psychologist Judith Langlois and her colleagues. In one study, adults evaluated color slides of white and black female faces for their attractiveness. Then infants of two or three months of age were shown pairs of these faces that differed in their degree of attractiveness. The infants, both male and female, looked longer at the more attractive faces. "This evidence," says Buss, "challenges the common view that the idea of attractiveness is learned through gradual exposure to current cultural standards."[27]

These sex differences are not limited to the United States, or even to Western cultures. "Regardless of the location, habitat, marriage system, or cultural living arrangement," Buss concludes, "men in all thirty-seven cultures included in the international study...value physical appearance in a potential mate more than women."[28]

History and Herstory: The Evolution of the Family

Humans have lived so long within the confines of a dominator culture we forget that male/female differences evolved for three million years within egalitarian societies because it was the best way of raising children.

Cross-cultural studies demonstrate that children, throughout evolutionary time, must be assured of two kinds of nurturance: the provision of physical security and the provision of emotional security. Throughout our three million year history, although the roles were quite flexible, things seemed to work best when most fathers had roles that differed from those of most mothers.

In studying cultures throughout the world, David Gutmann, professor of psychiatry and education and director of the Older Adult Program at Northwestern University, drew the following conclusions: "The fact of gender captures and memorializes the processes of evolutionary selection whereby the necessary capacities were assorted by sex, so as to assure the provision, to children, of physical and emotional security."[29]

Gutmann offers the following view of the evolutionary advantage to children of having fathers and mothers that assume different roles:

"Let us first consider the masculine responsibility for physical security. In the species sense, there is always an oversupply of males, in that one man can inseminate many females, but women, on the average, can gestate only one child every two years during their relatively brief period of fruitfulness. The surplus of redundant males, those over the number required to maintain viable population levels, can be assigned to the dangerous, high-casualty 'perimeter' tasks on which physical security and survival are based. The more expendable male sex, armed with large muscle and a greater store of intrinsic aggression, is generally assigned to hunt large game; to open, maintain, and defend distant tillage; to guard against human and nonhuman predators or to raid other communities for their wealth.

"By the same token," Gutmann continues, "the sex on whom the population level ultimately depends is less expendable. The sex that has breasts, softer skin, a milder nature, the sex that fashions the baby within its own flesh, is generally assigned to secure areas, there to supply the formative experiences that give rise to emotional security in children."[30]

Gutmann is not saying that all women must stay at home and all men must go out and "bring home the bacon." What he is saying is that someone must be responsible for meeting children's needs for physical security and emotional security. Through evolutionary time, these two needs have been best met when fathers cooperated with mothers, each taking primary responsibility for fulfilling one of the needs.

The division of labor is never totally one-sided. Fathers have always given a great deal of emotional support to children, and mothers have always provided a great deal of protection. But when protection was needed, it was most often the men who left home. When help was needed for the emotional well-being of children, it was most often the women who took on that task.

Support for this evolutionary view of gender differences comes from a surprising source, a freelance philosopher named Ken Wilber. Since he began writing in the 1970s, he has integrated a staggering variety of disciplines. Widely respected, both by Western scientists and Eastern sages, he has been compared to Sigmund Freud, William James, and Albert Einstein. He is the only man I know who could write a book called *A Brief History of Everything* and deliver what the title promises, and more.

"Not only certain sex differences, but certain gender differences, tend to repeat themselves cross culturally," says Wilber. "It's as if the biological sex differences between men and women are such a strong basic platform that these differences tend to invade culture as well, and thus tend to show up in gender differences also. So, even though gender is culturally molded and not biologically given, nonetheless certain constants in masculine and feminine gender tend to appear across cultures as well."[31]

Wilber notes that hormonal differences between males and females are linked to our evolutionary roles—males as hunter/protectors, females as gatherer/nurturers. Testosterone gives males the drive to make love and also to kill wild animals. Oxytocin induces females to mate, but also to care for and mother offspring.

Some believe that the insights of evolutionary psychology are regressive, taking us back to a time where white men tried to rule the world and women and minority men were kept in a place beneath them. I believe there is a much more radical and hopeful alternative.

The insights of evolutionary psychology lead me to the following beliefs:

1. Humans are adapted to a way of life that has worked well for over 99 percent of human history.

2. If males and females are going to conceive children, they have to be prepared to raise them.

3. Children need fully gendered fathers and mothers, not genderless parents.

4. Elders are needed to help parent the parents.

5. Men and women need not live in a world where the battle of the sexes rules our lives, but one where differences can be appreciated and enjoyed.

6. The way home is not to deny our differences, or have us believe that men and women are from different planets, but to create a world where differences can be honored and gender justice becomes our guiding light.

Understanding the evolutionary role of men and women can give us insight into why menopause means the end of reproductive capacity for women, while men retain their reproductive viability into old age.

Why Women Stop at Fifty and Men Go On and On: An Evolutionary Perspective on Menopause

As both Carlin and I have moved into the Menopause Passage, I've felt closer to her. It feels like we are more in sync, dealing with the same life issues. Yet she can no longer have children, and I still can. I've wondered why.

Most wild animals remain fertile until they die. So do most men. There are a number of documented cases of fertile older men, including a ninety-four-year-old, fathering children. However, this is not the case for women. After the age of forty, a human female's fertility declines so dramatically that by her early to mid-fifties she may not be able to produce children.[32]

If evolution favors those who leave the most offspring, why do human females stop reproducing so soon? Is this God's way of punishing women, another patriarchal curse, or is there a more reasonable explanation?

"Along with the big brains and upright posture that every text of human evolution emphasizes," says biologist Jared Diamond, "I consider menopause to be among the biological traits essential for making us distinctively human—something qualitatively different from, and more than, an ape."[33]

In order to offer an evolutionary explanation of female menopause or any other trait that is stable in a population, biologists must show that the trait confers a reproductive advantage to those who possess it. There is an obvious advantage for giraffes who have long necks. Those that do can reach the greenery high up in trees, eat better, and reproduce more than those with shorter necks.

Men who can produce children throughout their lives would have a distinct advantage over those who stopped reproducing at fifty. Through evolutionary time, those who possessed these useful traits reproduced more and passed on these traits to their offspring who kept the ball rolling.

So what reproductive advantage could menopause offer women? To answer that question, we must look to our origins as gatherer/hunters in the savannas of Africa. When we evolved from our primate ancestors, humans developed larger and larger brains that enabled us to have more varied and flexible responses to our environments. It allowed us to create tools that furthered our survival capabilities.

Yet, tool use and other skills of survival must be taught to children, and the teaching takes time. "As a result," says Diamond, "human children in most societies do not become capable of economic independence until their teens or twenties. Before, that, they remain dependent on their parents, especially on the mother, because mothers tend to provide more child care than do fathers."[34]

There are two basic methods that animals can use for securing an evolutionary advantage. The first is to have a large number of offspring—more babies, more parental genes get passed on, greater evolutionary advantage. The other method is to have a smaller number of offspring but to take such good care of them that most of them grow to maturity. Humans, as a species, have opted more for the second method. Fish, who lay millions of eggs at a time, opted for the first.

Women, more so than men, have also opted for the first option. "As a woman ages," says Diamond, "she can do more to increase the number of people bearing her genes by devoting herself to her existing children, her potential grandchildren, and her other relatives than by producing yet another child."[35]

Why haven't men followed that same evolutionary path? Wouldn't there be just as much advantage for men to stop reproducing at fifty and devote more time to raising successful children and grandchildren?

The difference is that men don't birth babies, women do; and birth has always been a risky proposition. "For example, in one study of 401 rhesus monkey pregnancies, only three mothers died in childbirth. For humans in traditional societies, the risk is much higher and increases with age. Even in affluent twentieth-century Western societies," Diamond reminds us, "the risk of dying in childbirth is seven times higher for a mother over the age of forty than for a twenty-year-old."[36]

If a mother dies, any children she has given birth to are at increased risk of not surviving. Thus, paradoxically, evolution would favor human female menopause because, by having fewer children, the chances of survival for her existing children increases.[37]

If a non-menopausal older woman died in childbirth or while caring for her infant child, the repercussions would encompass not only the investment loss to her previous children, but also her grandchildren. Mothers, whose children become mothers, become grandmothers, an important role in most traditional societies.[38]

So it seems that evolution has selected both men and women for their abilities not only to produce children, but to be around to teach those children how to raise children of their own. Since conceiving children is much more dangerous for an older woman than it is for an older man, female menopause marks the end of a woman's reproductive capacity, while male menopause allows for the possibility of additional children.

The Parental Imperative and the Evolution of Grandfathers

Since men don't get the biological push into eldering that women do, there is a need for a special kind of education for males. I first learned about this from Malidoma Somé, whom I met several years ago at a community conference on spiritual eldering. Though much of this wisdom has been lost in our addictive, industrial society, men like Somé are helping us reclaim what was lost.

Somé is a Dagara medicine man and diviner born in West Africa, where the intergenerational connections are still strong. When I first met him, he radiated an air of wisdom well beyond what I had come to expect from a man his age in our Western society. As he spoke of his past, I began to realize the special source of his wisdom.

"My grandfather had been my confident interlocutor for as long as I can remember," he recalled. "There is a close relationship between grandfathers and grandchildren. The first few years of a boy's life are usually spent, not with his father, but with his grandfather. What the grandfather and grandson share together—that the father cannot—is their close proximity to the cosmos."

I could feel the long expanse of intergenerational spiritual wisdom as Somé continued describing his past. "The grandfather will soon return to where the grandson came from, so therefore the grandson is bearer of news the grandfather wants."

How wonderful, I thought, to come into the world feeling that you had a unique gift to offer your elders. Feeling valuable and useful as a child is a wonderful thing. But grandfathers also need to feel useful, and in traditional societies, like those Somé grew up in, they were not only useful, but essential. "The grandfather must also transmit the 'news' to the grandson using the protocol secret to grandfathers and grandsons," says Somé. "He must communicate to this new member of the community the hard tasks ahead on the bumpy road of existence."[39]

Unlike Somé, who grew up in a traditional African society and was educated in the West, David Gutmann grew up in the West but was drawn to the wisdom of traditional cultures throughout the world. Like Malidoma Somé, Gutmann has had a lifelong interest in the human life cycle and the special place of elders in the initiation and teaching of the young.

One of the characteristics that differentiates humans from other animals is our large brain, which has allowed us to adapt to changing circumstances. The problem of being a big-brained species, as every woman who has given birth knows, is the difficulty of getting that large head through a rather small pelvic opening. The result is that, relative to all other animals, human babies are born while still immature. If nature waited until the human fetus was totally formed, its head would be too big for the birth canal. As anthropologist Ashley Montagu concluded about the birth of a baby, "If he weren't born when he is, he wouldn't be born at all."

In order for human children to learn all they need to learn, a prolonged childhood is necessary. This creates what David Gutmann calls the "parental imperative," a genetically programmed commitment that healthy parents make on behalf of their children.

In the I-want-to-have-it-all-now atmosphere that people now accept as normal, many young parents are not willing to sacrifice their own personal growth on behalf of their children. In postmodern jargon, care for others is often seen as "codependency," a disease akin to addiction that must be confronted and rooted out. In their futile attempt to have it all, parents often sacrifice their children's needs on the altar of personal growth and happiness.

Yet Gutmann has found that our evolutionary history demands that adults, in the first half of life, sacrifice their personal needs in the service of raising healthy children who themselves can grow up to raise healthy children of their own. "Until the child's new learning comes on line," says Gutmann, "normal parents must shoulder a chronic and largely unrecompensed burden.

The greater measure of freedom that our species has won from bondage to old learning has been gained at the price of adult bondage to parental tasks."[40]

Gutmann tells us that though the first half of life, for those who choose parenthood, needs to be focused on the children, the second half can be devoted to self-fulfillment and personal growth. However, in the world that glorifies the "now" generation and is distrustful of the future, many in our society feel unwilling and unable to carry out the duties of full parenthood.

The core issue, however, is not that parents are just too selfish to care properly for their children, as some social critics maintain. Parents don't need more shame and blame for not doing better. Most parents want desperately to meet the needs of their kids and are doing the very best they know how. But when we view self-sacrifice as a disease and tell parents they are doing their children harm if parents are unhappy because all their needs aren't being met, we make it nearly impossible for them to act responsibly.

The solution to our dilemma lies in the recognition that it takes more than two parents to raise a healthy child. The belief that "it takes a village to raise a child," is not new age jargon; it is ancient wisdom, known to tribal people throughout human history.

David Gutmann is even more specific about what is needed when he points to the evolutionary importance of elders in the society. "Elders," says Gutmann "are necessary to the well-being of all age groups, particularly the young. They fill unique roles, vital to the continuity of their extended families and larger communities, across the range of human societies."[41]

Gutmann points out that without elders, it is not possible for parents to be successful in their role of raising children. "In order to usher the child successfully through the long period of helplessness," says Gutmann, "human parents also need to be nurtured. In need of special kinds of parenting themselves, these parents receive uniquely important support (beyond mere babysitting) from the older men and women of their communities."[42]

In order for men and women to step into the position of "emeritus parenthood," as Gutmann calls this role, aging men and women must recognize how important they are to the evolutionary success of the human species. Men, in particular, must redefine and rethink their manhood as they move through the Male Menopause Passage if they are to live lives of power, passion, and purpose.

As we will see in the next section, the core purpose for men in the second half of life is to become mentors and elders to younger men. In order to do so, we need to learn how to stay vital and healthy in the second half of life and how to develop a new kind of sexual power.

Notes Chapter 7

1. Helen Fisher, Ph.D., *The Sex Contract: The Evolution of Human Behavior* (New York: William Morrow and Company, 1982), 23–24.

2. Ibid., 24.

3. Helen Fisher, Ph.D., *Anatomy of Love: The Natural History of Monogamy, Adultery, and Divorce* (New York: W. W. Norton and Company, 1992), 11.

4. Brian Swimme and Thomas Berry, *The Universe Story: From the Primordial Flaring Forth to the Ecozoic Era, A Celebration of the Unfolding of the Cosmos* (San Francisco: Harper San Francisco, 1992), 7.

5. Ibid., 107.

6. Thomas Berry, interview with author, 24 June 1996.

7. Richard Dawkins, *The Selfish Gene* (Oxford: Oxford University Press, 1976), 24–25.

8. Matt Ridley, *The Red Queen: Sex and the Evolution of Human Nature* (New York: Macmillan Publishing Company, 1993), 20.

9. See Riane Eisler, *The Chalice and the Blade* (San Francisco: Harper and Row, 1988) for a discussion of dominator cultures.

10. Anne Moir and David Jessel, *Brain Sex: The Real Difference Between Men and Women* (New York: Carol Publishing Group, 1991), 5.

11. Kalman Glantz and John K. Pearce, *Exiles from Eden: Psychotherapy from an Evolutionary Perspective* (New York: W. W. Norton and Company, 1989), 93.

12. Meredith F. Small, *What's Love Got to Do with It? The Evolution of Human Mating* (New York: Doubleday, 1995), 110–11.

13. Ridley, 4.

14. David M. Buss, *The Evolution of Desire: Strategies of Human Mating* (New York: Basic Books, 1994), 7.

15. Ridley, 248.

16. Quoted in Ridley, 249.

17. Buss, 128.

18. Ibid., 130–31.

19. Ibid. 4.

20. Ibid., 39.

21. Ibid., 22–25, 46.

22. Ibid., 28.

23. Ibid., 41–43.

24. Ibid., 51.

25. Ibid.

26. Ibid., 53.

27. Ibid., 54.

28. Ibid., 58.

29. David Gutmann, *Reclaimed Powers: Toward a New Psychology of Men and Women in Later Life* (New York: Basic Books, 1987), 190.

30. Ibid., 190–91.

31. See Ken Wilber, *Sex, Ecology, Spirituality: The Spirit of Evolution* (Boston: Shambhala, 1995), 153–62, and Ken Wilber, "World According to Wilber," interview by David Guy, *New Age Journal*, July/August 1995, 76–79.

32. Jared Diamond, "Why Women Change," *Discover*, July 1996, 131, 132.

33. Ibid., 131–32.

34. Ibid., 135.

35. Ibid.

36. Ibid.

37. Ibid.

38. Ibid., 136.

39. Malidoma Patrice Somé, discussions with author, 1995, and *Of Water and the Spirit: Ritual, Magic, and Initiation in the Life of an African Shaman* (New York: G. P. Putnam's Sons, 1994), 19–20.

40. Gutmann, 7.

41. Ibid., 4.

42. Ibid., 7.

Part III

Second Adulthood or Die:
How to Keep What You Have,
Regain What Was Lost, and
Find the Fountain of Life

8

Maintaining Health and Sexual Vitality into Your Sixties, Seventies, Eighties, Nineties, and Beyond

Death Comes Home to Rest

Carlin had gone to Portland to join two of her oldest friends at their fortieth high school reunion. When she left, I jokingly told her not to have a fling with any of her high school sweethearts. I trusted her completely, but I'll probably never be so secure that I don't have a little bit of insecurity when my wife is having fun with friends and I'm not around.

Since it was a quick trip, fly up, class bash, and fly back, I hadn't expected to hear from her. But when I heard her voice on the phone, I knew something was wrong. She had said she was going to stop to see her Mom who was recovering from a bout of food poisoning, and I had a quick flash that maybe her Mom had gotten worse. I wasn't prepared for what I heard.

"Mom has cancer," Carlin said, her voice sad, but strong. "We're doing some more tests tomorrow, but it looks like it's spread. The doctors don't think its curable."

I was stunned and scared about what I would hear next.

"I want to bring her back with me and have her stay with us."

I swallowed hard.

"What do you think?"

There wasn't time for me to think. All I knew was that there was an emergency, and my wife needed me. Somewhere at the back of my mind, I sensed her mother needed me too.

"Of course," I said. "Bring her as soon as you're ready. I'll start getting the house fixed up."

"I love you," she said.

"I love you, too. Tell Bess I'll be thinking about her."

When I was younger, I dreaded the thought of taking care of an older person. I was glad my mother had insisted that she never wanted to be a burden, and when it was her time to go, she died very quickly.

As the reality began to sink in, I remembered Carlin's words, "what do you think?" I realized I was thinking a lot. What if her mother is in pain? How will I deal with that? What if she is bedridden and I have to feed her, bathe her, deal with her toilet needs? What if she goes on and on, losing more of her humanity day by day, while her body is kept alive? I've dealt with death, but what will it be like if I have to deal with prolonged illness in my own life? I'm not sure I'm ready for that. I realized I was thinking myself into a frenzy.

A wise friend gave me some sound advice. "Don't worry about what you are going to do in the future. Wait until she gets there and just bring who you are to each situation that arises. You've got a lot to give to Bess, and she has a lot to give to you." I felt calmer immediately. I realized that the Menopause Passage to Second Adulthood was first about confronting death, but more importantly, it was about the courage to engage life fully.

The Last Resort:
Our Modern Fear of Aging and Death

Some time ago, the well-known French author Simone de Beauvoir published an impressive and well-documented study of aging. After a long and detailed analysis of the biological, ethnological, historical, and phenomenological aspects of aging, she concluded: "The vast majority of mankind looks upon the coming of old age with sorrow or rebellion. It fills them with more aversion than death itself."[1]

This view is embedded in our social and religious traditions. In the thirty-first Psalm of the Bible, we hear the lament of an old man who could be speaking for many today:

> Take pity on me, Yahweh,
>> I am in trouble now.
> Grief wastes away my eye,
>> my throat, my inmost parts.
> For my life is worn out with sorrow,
>> my years with sighs;
> my strength yields under misery,
>> my bones are wasting away.
> I am contemptible,
>> Loathsome to my neighbors,
> to my friends a thing of fear,
> Those who see me in the street
>> hurry past me;
> I am forgotten, as good as dead in their hearts,
>> something discarded.[2]

In a society like ours that values people, particularly men, for what they do more than for who they are, those who can no longer produce in the market economy are viewed as useless. "I have learned that a culture which equates material possessions with success," says Sharon Curtin, author of *Nobody Ever Died of Old Age*, "and views the frantic, compulsive consumer as the perfect citizen, can afford little space for the aged human being. They are past competing, they are out of the game. We live in a culture which endorses what has been called 'human obsolescence.' After adolescence, obsolescence. To the junk heap, the nursing home, the retirement village, the 'Last Resort.'"[3]

It's no wonder that most of us are terrified, not so much of death, as of aging. We cling to youth like a terrified child to his mother's apron strings. When adolescence and obsolescence are the only two stages of life, young people lose the will to become adults and adults become aging children.

The Fountain of Youth or the Joy of Eldering: Which Is Worth Seeking?

More than anything else, Robert wanted the red sports car he had been eyeing for more than a year. "I deserve it," he told me during one of our recent therapy sessions. "I've been working hard on my business. We just closed the biggest deal of my career, and I want a reward."

Robert has the boyish good looks of the perpetual adolescent, though he just turned forty. He and his girlfriend, Judith, have been going together for two years, but Robert has been unable to commit. "Women are so unpredictable," he told me, "and I'm not sure she's the one. As soon as I think it might be great to settle down and get married, she starts to get closer and I begin to feel smothered."

Robert had been concerned about his greying hair, the difficulty he was having keeping off weight, and a general feeling of lethargy. He had heard about a health clinic in Palm Springs, California and had brought in their literature before deciding to go.

The first sheet out of the packet was a reprint from the magazine *Hippocrates* with an article about "the new anti-aging drug." The cover had a picture of sixty-six-year-old Bob Jones in shorts and running shoes looking confident and vigorous atop a rocky mountain peak. The headline for the article said a lot about what is being sold to older men:

"The Latest Anti-Aging Drug Is Cheap, Convenient, and Makes Some People Feel Like Kids Again."[4]

Although the article discussed some of the pros and cons of modern anti-aging drugs, there was no discussion of the underlying premise that it is a blessing to prevent aging and feeling like a kid again is a worthy goal for our later years. Certainly, the director of the Palm Springs clinic, Edmund Chein, doesn't seem to question this assumption. He is described by the magazine article as "a good-natured, almost jolly, proponent of youth preservation by pill, injection, lozenge—any means available."[5]

If a picture is worth a thousand words, the sight of Dr. Chein speaks volumes about the focus of the clinic. "The doctor himself is a sight to behold: an L.A. character from his goldrimmed glasses down to his white cowboy boots, Chein has the smooth-skinned countenance of an oversized boy, even at forty-five. Give him a backpack and a Lollapalooza T-shirt and he'd pass for a medical student."[6]

There are many things we can do to make the second half of our lives joyful and productive. I don't believe that one of them is to return to our youth. In fact, as long as we seek youth as the goal of Second Adulthood, we sacrifice the joy of being real men. There is something much finer that lies ahead for us than perpetual youth. What the world does not need is a few good boys.

We now have the knowledge to live well to our one hundredth birthday and beyond. But why would we want to live that long? Is it just so that we can enjoy the toys of adolescence for a longer time, or is there something more? Dr. Walter Bortz, a member of the teaching faculty at Stanford University Medical School and author of the book *Dare To Be 100*, says that we need both "smarts" and "guts" to live a long and healthy life. "Guts means having the valor of purpose necessary to tackle the *why* [of life]. The capacity to search steadily for a significance in life represents the highest nobility," says Bortz. "The *why* is finding a meaning for all of the expanded living and also the energy and involvement necessary to make it happen."[7] According to Bortz:

For the flame of life to burn brightly for all your days, a steady supply of active participation is essential. If apathy, discontent, and boredom are given room to thrive, your chances of seeing one hundred are slim to none.

Those who focus on staying young easily become addicted to the next product that seems to offer an image of youth. One of my fifty-year-old clients who found himself continually seeking the thrill of fast cars, fast women, and fast money finally came to the conclusion that "my drug of choice is more." No matter how much he had, he was never satisfied. There seemed no end to his desires, and satisfying them never seemed to offer contentment and joy. Though we wish it weren't so, the nutrients of life that we need for the second half are different than those that nourished us in the first.

That's why those who cling to youth in the second half of life often become hooked on trying to stay forever young. Rather than find what is truly satisfying, many keep trying to fill the void with more of the same. For these men, too much is never enough.

Seeing men in the second half of their lives desperately holding on to the glories of youth is like watching animals in the zoo. There is a compulsive restlessness about their behavior. They go back and forth from one side of their cage to the other, anxious and at the same time bored.

There is a parable in the Talmud in which a traveler comes upon an old man planting a carob tree. "When will the tree bear fruit?" asks the traveler. "Oh, perhaps in seventy years," replies the old man. "Do you expect to live to eat the fruit of that tree?" "No," says the old man, "but I didn't find the world desolate when I entered it, and as my father planted for me before I was born, so do I plant for those who come after me."

Many of us have come to feel that we have nothing worth giving, no nourishment that anyone really needs. If you believe this, you are mistaken. I tell you truthfully, you are needed. There is no one else on this earth that can give what you can give.

We are each put on the planet to offer our special gifts, and what we have to offer is unique and precious. "What we do is nothing but a drop in the ocean," Mother Teresa reminds us, "but if we didn't do it, the ocean would be one drop less."[8]

Albert Schweitzer, who spent fifty years of his life serving his fellow man in the oppressive heat of the African jungle, providing medical aid to those most desperately in need, said something which can guide us all at this time of our lives:

I don't know what your destiny will be, but one thing I do know; the only ones among you who will be really happy are those who have sought and found how to serve.

Another Albert, the one named Einstein, wrote, "Only a life lived for others is a life worthwhile."[9]

Perhaps Martin Luther King, Jr., summed it up best when he observed, "Every man must decide whether he will walk in the light of creative altruism or in the darkness of destructive self-ishness. This is the judgment. Life's most urgent question is, what are you doing for others?"[10]

Many of us hold ourselves back because we feel inadequate to the task. We compare ourselves to others and find that we fall short. "If I had the compassion of a Schweitzer, I'd have some-thing to give," we tell ourselves. "If I had the courage of King, I'd have something worthy to offer others."

The truth is, we have the only gift we will ever need, the gift of ourselves. All of our heroes have flaws. So do we. But we can all give of ourselves to those who need the special gift that only we can offer. Shortly before his death, Rabbi Susya, a great Hasidic master, confronted the question we must all ask our-selves. "In the coming world, they will not ask me, 'Why were you not Moses?' They will ask me 'Why were you not what you, Susya, could have been?'"[11]

Men, your family needs you, your friends and community need you, the planet needs you. If you are willing to be you and give what only you can give, the modern world has some exciting tools to enhance your health and vitality from now until the end of your time.

Erections Return:
There's a Whole New Sexual Revolution Going On

"It's early Wednesday morning at the Urology clinic of Irwin Goldstein, M.D., and the patients are lining up to get inside. By

9 A.M., these two waiting rooms in Boston University Medical Center are packed with men, blocking each other out for available chairs, like slow-motion NBA rebounders. They're three-deep at the registration window, flipping through sports sections and outdoor magazines, wondering where they should put their overcoats. And yet, despite the men and activity, the rooms resonate with an awkward silence. Except for the crackling of magazine and newspaper pages, the men aren't making a sound."[12]

In his article "Erections 'R' Us," this is how the health writer Donovan Webster describes his first visit to one of the many new clinics opening up throughout the country that specialize in helping men with sexual dysfunction. Impotence, technically a consistent inability to have or maintain a satisfactory erection, is one of the most common problems men face. Today there are estimated eighteen million men, most over the age of forty, who have problems with impotence. There are another twelve million men who have occasional problems.[13]

According to Wilhelm Stekel, M.D., author of *Impotence in the Male*, "In men love-inadequacy is increasing to an alarming degree, and impotence has come to be a disorder associated with modern civilization. Every impotent man forms the nucleus of a love tragedy. For impotence makes marriage impossible, or may be the cause of an ill-fated one; it also undermines the health of the woman, and has an equally pernicious effect upon the mental life of both husband and wife."[14]

Dr. Stekel could be speaking today, and his book could be on the *New York Times* best-seller list, but in fact, he wrote those words seventy years ago when his book was first published in 1927. The problem is not new, but the treatments are.

Stekel, one of the preeminent psychiatrists of his time, believed that practically all cases of impotence could be traced to psychological inhibitions. The treatment of choice, he believed, was psychotherapy. That has continued to be the view until quite recently, when scientific research found that most cases of impotence were based in the body, not in the mind.

Researchers found that 80 to 90 percent of all chronic potency problems were based on physical imbalance caused by a variety of stressors. Medical conditions including diabetes, heart disease, and hypertension play a role, as well as many of the medications taken to treat these diseases. Cigarette smoking has a significant effect, as does excessive alcohol consumption.[15]

Physical injuries can cause impotence in young men, as well as older men, particularly sports- or work-related injuries to the penis or perineum. (The perineum is the area between men's legs from the base of the scrotum to the anus, where critical blood vessels pass unprotected into the penis.)[16]

Though we now know that a great deal of erection dysfunction has a physical basis, psychological factors also play a key role. Men who hold their anger in, as well as men who are often angry at others, have more difficulties maintaining erections. Men who are depressed and feel unable to control their life circumstances are also at higher risk.[17]

Whatever the origins of sexual dysfunction, once it begins, psychological, physical, and interpersonal factors interact to make it difficult to return to full function. If a man loses erections due to a medication he is taking, for instance, he may begin to worry about whether his penis will work the next time he makes love. The more he worries, the more stress he feels, and the less his body is able to respond to sexual stimuli. His partner may feel that there is something wrong with her, that she is no longer attractive to her mate. She may withdraw, which adds to his feeling of low self-worth. This vicious cycle can go on and on with both partners feeling more and more ashamed, fearful, and frustrated.

The way out of these downward cycles is to be able to risk talking to each other. No one is to blame when there is a sexual impasse. Breaking the silence is the first step to breaking out of the shame that so many men feel when they are having difficulties with sexuality.

It is often necessary to get help from those who specialize in treating sexual dysfunction. There are a number of new approaches that have recently become available. One involves insertion into the urethra of one or two drugs that bypass damaged nerves. The drugs, alprostadil and prazosin, relax smooth muscles and dilate blood vessels, allowing the penis to fill with blood. Within ten minutes, the drug, inserted with a tiny plunger, produces an erection that lasts up to an hour.[18]

Another increasingly popular external method is vacuum therapy. Just before sexual activity, a cylinder is placed over the penis and an attached hand pump is used to create negative pressure inside the cylinder, causing blood to flow into the penile cavities. A soft rubber ring is then slipped over the base of the penis, which helps to maintain the erection for about thirty minutes.[19]

An third method, which is still in the testing phase, involves taking a pill an hour before sex. The drug, sildenafil, has been studied for some time in Great Britain. The drug, which is being tested under the name Viagra, increases blood flow to the penis, enhancing a man's normal response to stimulation. The result is an increase in blood flow to the penis, which enhances a man's normal sexual response.[20]

Alan P. Brauer, M.D., director of TotalCare Medical Center, (a comprehensive clinic focusing on total health care), uses these and many other approaches for restoring men to full sexual functioning. "We offer comprehensive treatment for erectile dysfunction," Dr. Brauer says, "including penile injections, non-needle penile injections, vacuum therapy, prescriptive medications and a wide range of natural and herbal interventions."[21]

Dr. Brauer's clinic does not limit its approach to physical interventions, but also includes a full interview and evaluation process with the man and his family to explore all aspects of a man's health needs. "We use biofeedback, hypnosis, individual and couples counseling, as well as both traditional evaluation and treatment as well as alternative, complementary and integrated therapies. We do whatever it takes to return a man to full function and enhanced health."[22]

Men tend to be reluctant to see doctors at all, and they are even more reluctant to talk about their own bodies. When it comes to talking about sexual anatomy and dysfunction, men become panicked. The fear of being shamed keeps millions of men away who need help. It takes a lot of courage to "put your balls on the line," so to speak. But more and more men are stepping forward. They are not willing to sacrifice their sex lives on the altar of their fears.

Research focusing on male sexuality is making more advancements than ever before. New methods are coming on the market all the time. The main things to remember are the following:

1. No man needs to live with sexual dysfunctions

2. All sexual problems are treatable.

3. New approaches are rapidly emerging.

4. There is an approach that is right for you.

5. Don't hide the problem, talk to someone, get help.

6. Don't be frightened into drastic measures such as surgery until you have checked the alternatives.

7. As Franklin Delano Roosevelt said, "The only thing you have to fear, is fear itself."

But erectile dysfunctions aren't the only aspects of men's sexual lives that can be enhanced by the findings of modern medicine, new evidence indicates that hormone replacement may be of benefit to some men.

Hormone Replacement for Men: Getting Back What's Been Lost

Researchers are exploring the beneficial effects of several hormones that are known to undergo rather striking declines with age. There have been three areas of hormone research that have often been operating separate from each other. One group of researchers has been focusing on things that will enhance sexuality. Another group has been focusing on things that will help us live longer. A third group has been looking for ways to enhance the quality of our lives, however long we live.

Although much of the research is new and a great deal is yet to be learned, there are strong indications that some of the same hormones that enhance sexuality will help us live longer, as well as healthier.

Theresa Crenshaw, M.D., whom we met earlier, is an active clinician and researcher specializing in enhancing human sexuality. In looking for substances that would improve people's sex lives, she made some interesting discoveries. "I noticed a recurring relationship between the drugs of interest to me and those receiving the most attention from longevity researchers."[23]

"In fact," says Dr. Crenshaw, "a striking percentage of these drugs all:

• Increased sex drive;

• Had an antidepressant effect;

• Facilitated weight loss;

• Were targeted for study by longevity researchers."[24]

So, let me get a show of hands. How many of you would like to increase your sex drive, be less depressed and more joyous, lose weight and keep it off, and live longer and healthier? Keeping in mind that the research on hormone replacement for men is in its infancy, let's look at some of the substances that might be of help.

Dopamine

Dopamine is a neurotransmitter produced by specialized nerve cells located in the arcuate nucleus of the brain. "Dopamine is essential to our happiness, our ability to pursue whatever we enjoy....Deprenyl is a prescription drug that works through promoting dopamine" says Dr. Crenshaw. "According to *Medical World News*, a researcher, Jozsef Knoll, claimed that Deprenyl 'can shift the life span of the human from one hundred fifteen years to one hundred forty-five years.'

"His series of studies [on rats] showed that the Deprenyl-treated old rats recovered full sexual activity and maintained this activity for an extended life span. Placebo-treated rats continued to be sexually sluggish or became completely inactive....It will come as no surprise that Deprenyl-treated rats were also thinner!"[25]

"Pretty impressive, I'd say," comments Dr. Crenshaw after examining the research. "Other drugs that boost dopamine include L-dopa and Wellbutrin," continues Dr. Crenshaw. "The same holds true for them: they have antidepressant properties, tend to thin you down, and are of interest to longevity research."[26]

Oxytocin

Oxytocin is a peptide secreted from the posterior lobe of the pituitary gland. It flows to receptor sites in various parts of the brain and throughout the reproductive tract of both men and women. In women with newborn babies, it assists in the bonding process. According to researcher Dr. Joan Borysenko, author of *A Woman's Book of Life*, oxytocin helps a woman to become "totally infatuated with her newborn, doting on every movement, every look."[27] Does it also help men bond with their babies? The research hasn't been done, but I expect it would.

We do know that oxytocin contributes to the infatuation men and women feel when they fall in love. "Apparently, whether you raise oxytocin a few times a week with touch...orgasm, intercourse, or by injection, it is good for you," says Dr. Crenshaw. "So good you may actually live longer because of it." Crenshaw continues. "Oxytocin is also a mood elevator in the respect that it creates or promotes the euphoric state that results from holding someone you love. Does it make you thinner? I am not sure, but I bet it does. Wouldn't it be remarkable if constant physical contact with someone you love worked better than diet pills?"[28]

Vasopressin

Vasopressin is a peptide much like oxytocin and one of its closest neighbors, secreted from the same general area of the brain. While it resembles oxytocin structurally, its metabolic impact is quite different.

"One of vasopressin's most captivating qualities is its influence on how we think," says Dr. Crenshaw. "It focuses a person on the pragmatics of the 'here and now,' helping us to notice sexual cues, and to pay attention to what we are doing."

For the same reasons, Dr. Crenshaw feels that it may be a particularly good antidepressant/antianxiety drug. "With its focus on the present, as opposed to the past or the future, it makes depression and anxiety difficult to sustain." Dr. Crenshaw concludes with these comments. "Here again is a drug, also a naturally occurring substance, that promotes sex, happiness, and longevity. If the pattern is consistent, we will also discover that it thins you down."[29]

Human Growth Hormone (HGH)

Although the research studies are just coming in, giving human growth hormone (HGH) to the elderly seems to be generating a lot of positive interest. "In one small study, twelve older men were placed on growth hormone. After taking it over six months, they averaged a 14 percent decrease in body fat while lean muscle mass increased by 9 percent. They also showed a 7.1 percent increase in skin thickness."[30]

Ronald Klatz, President of the American Academy of Anti-Aging Medicine and author of Grow Young with HGH says, "There is no reason to wait until you are a senior citizen to enjoy the benefits of HGH replacement. In fact there is every reason to believe it is better to start at a much younger age when the levels of your own hormone have already begun to decline."[31]

"Treatment with human growth hormone may enable people to retain a more youthful and vigorous body state as they get older," says Richard Cutler, Ph.D., a gerontologist at the National Institute of Aging. "If we find that it also lengthens life span, that would be icing on the cake."[32]

Other researchers are more cautious. "In my opinion the people who will benefit the most from growth hormone are the sickest," says William Regelson, M.D.[33] For most people, he feels that other hormones are more helpful. "I believe it is possible to obtain many of the same beneficial effects of growth hormone by using the other super-hormones, particularly DHEA, melatonin, estrogen, and testosterone, all of which are inexpensive and easily available, and have no untoward side effects."[34]

Dr. Regelson's credentials are impressive. He is a professor of medicine at the Medical College of Virginia, Virginia Commonwealth University. A specialist in medical oncology, with joint appointments in microbiology and biomedical engineering, he has been a leading researcher in the field of aging for over twenty years. In his recent book *The Super-Hormone Promise*, he discusses the latest research on the positive potential of hormones.

Though Dr. Crenshaw is optimistic about the possibilities of growth hormone, she is also cautious. "Growth hormone is not an innocent substance," she says. "Bear in mind that growth hormone makes things grow. That can include tumors. Also, too much growth hormone can be deadly, leading to enlargement of the heart and congestive heart failure."[35]

That's why its so important to get accurate and complete information before we decide to take any of the "miracle" substances we hear about. It is also vital that we get our information from those who do not have a vested interest in selling us these substances. As my father once told me, "In the world of business, benefits are always trumpeted loudly, and risks, if they are mentioned at all, are always whispered softly."

Melatonin

This is one of the "miracle" drugs that many people have heard about because it has received a great deal of media attention, but sound research findings have been slow to reach the public.

Melatonin is produced in a tiny organ at the very center of your brain called the pineal gland. It is the first gland in your body to be formed, and can be seen as early as three weeks after conception. Yet its secrets have only recently become known. Thirty-two years ago when I began medical school, I was taught that the pineal gland served no known function in human beings, that it was merely left over from our evolutionary past.

Today, it is being said that the pineal gland and the hormone it produces are vital to human well-being. "Melatonin is one of the most versatile and potent substances in the body, a principal player in the maintenance of health and well-being in all stages of life," says Dr. Russel Reiter. "Not only does this amazing hormone counteract stress, fight off viruses and bacteria, improve the quality of sleep, minimize the symptoms of jet lag, reduce the risk of heart disease, and regulate biological rhythms, it may even help protect against cancer, and play a role in determining how long we live."[36]

I am used to reading claims like these in magazines given away in health food stores to promote the latest "fountain of youth" formula. But I was surprised to hear it from one of the most respected scientists in the world.

For more than thirty years, Dr. Russel Reiter has been a dominant force in pineal/melatonin research. He is called by many the godfather of melatonin research and is respected by scientists all over the world. His recent book, *Melatonin Revolution*, was recommended by one of my own mentors, Dr. Andrew Weil, who called it "*the* book on the subject, written by one of the world's leading melatonin researchers."

The book offers many insights relevant to the Male Menopause Passage. In addition to the benefits already mentioned, Dr. Reiter believes that melatonin may play an important role in improving men's sex lives. There is preliminary evidence that giving males melatonin may increase production of testosterone. "Another way that melatonin may enhance male sexuality is by increasing the firmness and frequency of erections.... Melatonin may protect the health of the arteries leading to the penis through its antioxidant and cholesterol-lowering effects."[37]

"Antioxidant" is a word you will hear more and more about in the future. It may be the key to prolonged health and well-being. Antioxidants help protect us from disease disabling certain types of molecules in the body called free radicals, which in overwhelming quantities can cause extensive damage to the body.

"More than sixty diseases, from rheumatoid arthritis to herpes zoster, are now believed to be caused or exacerbated by free radicals," says Dr. Reiter. "Antioxidants stop free radicals in their tracks, helping to preserve the integrity of our cells and protect our overall health."[38]

In 1993, Dr. Reiter and his colleagues at the University of Texas Health Science Center at San Antonio discovered that melatonin is the most potent and versatile of all the known antioxidants. "This discovery has profound implications for human health and longevity," Dr. Reiter concluded.[39]

Another respected researcher, William Regelson, M.D., also feels melatonin is important for health. "Our landmark experiments with melatonin demonstrated that it is possible not only to halt the downward spiral that far too many of us have come to accept as a normal part of aging," Regelson says "but also to actually extend the length and to improve the quality of our lives."[40]

DHEA (Dehydroepiandrosterone)

DHEA is the most abundant hormone in the human body, which both men and women can transform into almost any other hormone. It is a steroid hormone, manufactured mainly in the adrenals, but also by the ovaries, testicles, and brain. It is the only hormone that peaks around age twenty-five and declines steadily thereafter. Dr. Crenshaw feels it may be a key factor in producing the symptoms associated with male menopause.

"DHEA drops precipitously as men age (about 3 percent per year)," says Dr. Crenshaw. "By the time they are eighty, it is almost undetectable."[41] In reviewing recent research studies on impotence in older men, Crenshaw made the following conclusion: "Much of the sexual dysfunction was correlated with disease," she says, "but impotence was inversely correlated with DHEA levels, meaning the lower your DHEA the more likely you are to become impotent."[42]

In his book, *The Super-Hormone Promise*, Dr. Regelson says, "Within the past decade, researchers (myself included) have discovered some amazing things about this super-hormone that not only makes people feel terrific but does some pretty terrific things to virtually every important body system."[43] Regelson says:

DHEA rejuvenates the immune system, improves brain function, relieves stress, and may prove to be the most potent anti-cancer drug of all time.

Dr. Crenshaw's findings also show the importance of DHEA. "The importance of DHEA in men is not so much the immediate effect on their sex drive, but the indirect effects on other aspects of their health that ultimately influence their sex drive, such as stress, heart disease, midlife changes, their sexual attractiveness, and quality of life."[44]

Pregnenolone

Pregnenolone is a steriod hormone precursor that the body normally manufactures using cholesterol as the primary raw material. It is then converted into other steroids that the body can use. As is the case with the steroid-hormone precursor DHEA, pregnenolone levels also decline with age.

In 1995, researchers studying the effects of various steroids found that pregnenolone enhanced memory in rats running a maze. The researchers found that many steroids helped in memory, but pregnenolone was effective at doses one hundred times lower than any of the other compounds.[45]

In reviewing the recent research, Will Block, executive editor of the magazine *Life Enhancement* says, "At low doses (10–30 mg/day), pregnenolone has been shown to be a powerful memory enhancer. On the other hand, at high doses (400–500 mg/day), pregnenolone has been shown to have anti-inflammatory properties that can help with arthritic conditions. It also helps with energy levels, helps to balance hormone levels, and may help to repair the myelin sheath which covers neurons in the central nervous system."[46]

"Some scientists believe it is the most potent memory enhancer of all time," Dr. William Regelson concludes. "Perhaps what is even more amazing are the studies that demonstrate pregnenolone enhances our ability to perform on the job while heightening feelings of well-being."[47]

Testosterone

"I'm taking natural testosterone as a cream, one percent," says one woman in an Internet newsgroup. "My husband takes the gel, 5 percent, twice a day. He didn't want the patch because of skin irritation. Both of us are extremely satisfied. Very anti-depressant, energizing, and of course this is a very sexy hormone. Fabulous orgasms."

Just as many women have discovered estrogen replacement therapy, both men and women are now discovering the advantages of replacing testosterone. Many are not waiting to get definitive results from research studies before they begin treatment.

Johns Hopkins University is one of the places where research on hormone replacement therapy has been going on for some time. Thus far, the findings are promising. "Testosterone supplementation for normal, healthy older men might some day rival that of estrogen for women," says Adrian Dobs, M.D., associate professor of medicine and director of the endocrinology and metabolism clinical studies unit at Johns Hopkins.[48]

Dr. William Regelson agrees. "My prediction is that testosterone for midlife men will soon be as common as estrogen is for women. About one-third of all men will experience a significant midlife decline in testosterone that can affect their physical and emotional health."[49]

Newsweek magazine's cover story in September, 1996, headlined "Testosterone" and asked in its lead article: "Super-Hormone Therapy: Can It Keep Men Young?" The article quoted Dr. Regelson as saying "By restoring hormones we run low on after forty," which he calls super-hormones, "it is possible to slow and even reverse the aging process."[50]

Although still in the experimental stages, here are some of the preliminary findings on testosterone:

- *Builds muscle*—In a number of small-scale studies, there is evidence that aging men who take testosterone increase their lean body mass. "'The potential to alter body composition, which truly helps men in terms of function, is really exciting,' says Dr. Dobs."[51]

- *Shrinks a potbelly*—"A Swedish study of twenty-three men showed those taking testosterone saw their pot-bellies diminish, though their total body fat didn't."[52]

- *Protects the heart*—Recent research indicates that men who have heart attacks tend to have low testosterone levels. "Gerald B. Phillips, M.D., who compared testosterone levels of a number of men undergoing x-ray exams of their blood vessels, found that lower hormone levels accompanied higher degrees of heart disease. 'The hormone may help protect the heart by raising the HDL cholesterol level,' says Dr. Phillips." HDL is the "good kind" of cholesterol.[53]

- *Builds stronger bones*—"The risk for a broken bone doubles every five years after age fifty, when hormone levels begin to drop. And men [with lowered testosterone levels] tend to have a higher bone-snapping risk compared with normal men. One study showed that 59 percent of men with hip fractures had very low testosterone levels."[54]

The Super-Hormone Revolution: Cautious Optimism

In his book, *The Super-Hormone Promise*, Dr. Regelson describes an optimistic view of what men can expect in midlife and beyond. "It is a revolution that started because people are beginning to realize that they no longer have to accept the conventional wisdom that from middle age on their health and their mind and their looks must deteriorate."[55]

He believes, as do many physicians, that the traditional approach of simply attempting to treat the individual symptoms of aging as they arise is insufficient. "These physicians recognize that now, for the first time, science has the tools to extend life while also enhancing the quality of life by preventing and even reversing the ravages of aging. These physicians realize that there is absolutely no reason that we cannot live to be 90, 100, 110, and perhaps even to our potential maximum life span of 120, in strong, healthy bodies."[56]

Yet before you run out and stock up on the latest hormones for health, I recommend you look at both the benefits and the risks. All substances have both positive and negative effects, and to focus too much attention on the positive without looking at the negative will get us into trouble.

One of the drawbacks of taking testosterone, for instance, is that it may stimulate the growth of the prostate gland, which is a problem that is of increasing importance to men as we move through the Male Menopause Passage.

In the July 1997 issue of the *Harvard Men's Health Watch*, the editors reviewed the research on four hormones that tend to decline as men age—Human Growth Hormone, DHEA, Testosterone, and Melatonin—and asked, "Can replacement doses of any of them slow the aging process or improve health?" Their conclusion was that more study was needed before they would recommend that men take these hormones on a regular basis.[57]

If you do decide to explore hormone replacement, I recommend you work closely with a reputable physician who is not afraid of looking at new possibilities, but who will be cautious about prescribing powerful substances, such as hormones, without careful study.

Protecting Your Prostate

Many men are not aware that they have a prostate gland until it gives them trouble. "This gland, whose secretions lubricate the lining of the urethra and condition the environment for sperm, surrounds the urethra just below the bladder, a strategic position," says Andrew Weil, M.D. "Younger men often suffer from inflammations and infections of this gland; those in middle age develop urinary difficulties due to enlarged prostates; and the elderly are at risk for prostate cancer."[58]

The good news, according to Patrick C. Walsh, M.D., urologist-in-chief at the Johns Hopkins Medical Center, is that most prostate trouble can be prevented and, if caught early enough, all prostate problems can be cured, even cancer.

Early recognition and prompt treatment is the key. If you are like me, most of us put off our yearly exams, even though we know they are important. The American Cancer Society estimates that in 1997 more than 300,000 Americans will be told they have prostate cancer, and deaths from prostate cancer in the United States were more than 41,000 in 1996.[59]

Yet two easy tests can save your life. "After age fifty, and for the rest of their lives, men need a yearly prostate check up," say Patrick Walsh, M.D., and Janet Farrar Worthington, authors of *The Prostate*. "This involves a digital rectal examination—when a doctor's gloved finger is inserted in the rectum to feel for a knot or lump, swelling, or anything else out of the ordinary—and something called a PSA test, a highly sensitive blood test that catches trace amounts of a protein called prostate-specific antigen."[60]

A new blood test could help predict possible cases of prostate cancer up to ten years before the disease can be diagnosed, a six year jump on current methods, according to researchers at the Johns Hopkins University School of Medicine.

The new test involves a different way of monitoring the enzyme PSA in a man's blood. "Currently, most physicians test for total PSA only, which when measured repeatedly over time, can predict prostate cancer up to four years before clinical diagnosis," said James Fozard of the National Institute on Aging. "This study, however, shows that measuring the ratio of free to total PSA repeatedly over time may lead to predictions of prostate cancer up to ten years before clinical diagnosis of prostate cancer."[61]

Additional breakthroughs have come from researchers at the National Center for Human Genome Research, Johns Hopkins University and Umea University in Sweden, who have recently identified the location of the first major gene that predisposes men to prostate cancer. They have found that the number of prostate cancer cases varies widely among different ethnic groups, with African-American men suffering the highest incidence rate in the world.[62]

If you have other members of your family who have had prostate cancer, you may be at a higher than average risk and will want to be sure you get tested regularly.

After age fifty, most men begin to develop an enlarged prostate, a condition called benign prostatic hypertrophy (BPH). As the gland enlarges, it squeezes the urethra, often causing increased urinary frequency, a weaker flow, and difficulty getting started. The current medical treatment of choice, a drug called finasteride (Proscar) has significant drawbacks. According to Andrew Weil, M.D., "It's expensive, sometimes causes impotence, can take up to a year to have an effect, and works for only 30 percent of patients."

Fortunately, there is a better alternative. According to Weil, M.D., "European studies have shown that extract of saw palmetto—made from the berries of a plant native to the American Southeast—reduces the size of the prostate in only four to six weeks. And it's effective 90 percent of the time!"[63] I have followed Dr. Weil's advice, and it has helped reduce the number of times I wake up at night to urinate.

Michael B. Schachter, M.D., author of *The Natural Way to a Healthy Prostate*, agrees that saw palmetto is very beneficial and suggests additional supplements that research has shown to be helpful in treating and preventing prostate problems.[64] "The single most important nutrient for a healthy prostate is zinc," says Dr. Schachter. "The normal prostate contains up to ten times more zinc than any other organ of the body. Zinc deficiency, which is common among Americans, may cause prostate enlargement."[65]

Dr. Weil recommends a number of simple things we can do to prevent prostate problems from ever occurring, including the following:

- Drink lots of water (your urine should be light in color).

- Have an active sex life, but practice moderation. (You will have to determine the frequency of ejaculation that is best for you.)

- Eat plenty of soy foods. The phytoestrogens found in soy may block the negative effects of testosterone on the prostate.

- Reduce the amount of saturated fat in your diet. According to a study done at Stanford Medical School, men who eat more than 30 grams a day of saturated fat (mostly from meat and dairy) have twice the risk of prostate cancer as do men who eat only 11 grams of saturated fat a day.

- Eat meals rich in tomatoes. A recent study conducted by the Harvard School of Public Health shows a 20 percent reduction in prostate cancer risk in men who eat tomatoes or tomato sauce four times a week and a 50 percent reduction in those who eat ten servings a week.[66]

Our Bodies, Ourselves: The Birth of the Male Health Center

"If men knew as much about their bodies as they do about their cars, they'd be a lot better off," says Kenneth A. Goldberg, M.D. "We need to get men to realize that they are going to die if they don't make some pretty serious changes in the way they run their lives."[67] This recognition formed the seed of a dream for a center that would speak to the specific needs of men.

In 1989, Dr. Goldberg opened the Male Health Center in Dallas, Texas, the first center in the country specializing in treating male health problems. The purpose of the center is to help men live healthy and active lives. The center's strategies for improving men's health include early diagnosis and treatment of health problems, support during and after care, and education for men about their bodies so that future health problems can be avoided.

Dr. Goldberg was one of the first male practitioners in the country to focus on male menopause and recognized that many men between the ages of thirty-five and sixty-five experienced sexual dysfunction that, if left untreated, caused great problems for a man and his family.

"Looking back, I guess I'm just about a perfect example of how to get impotent," Cliff Davison, age sixty-five, told Dr. Goldberg. "I ate badly and I was too busy at work to get any exercise. Well, it caught up with me in a big way. When I was about sixty, everything seemed to start falling apart.

"First, I had a prostate problem that required an operation, and nine months after that, I had a heart attack. At the same time—even before—see, I was having some problems in the bedroom. I was interested in sex, and I could get an erection. But it wouldn't stay around long enough to satisfy my wife.

"After a couple of failures, I started avoiding sex. I'd go to bed early or late, or I'd try not to touch her. We didn't talk about it. It was like part of our life together just shut down."[68]

Cliff Davison is typical of thousands of men that have been treated at Dr. Goldberg's center for impotence and other sexual difficulties. "At the Male Health Center, I see many men so shattered by impotence that they can't even make eye contact with me. Then, as they progress toward sexual health, a miraculous change comes over them. They talk differently; they even walk differently. As one of my patients recently told me, trouble in bed can affect almost every aspect of our lives."[69]

"About 80 percent of all men with a potency problem respond to an injection of prostaglandin EI or a combination of prostaglandin EI, papaverine, and phentolamine—all drugs that relax smooth muscle in the penis," says Dr. Goldberg. "The needle is the tiniest made, and it is inserted in an area with very few nerve endings. Although any sensible man would be apprehensive before his first injection, most find that it's not uncomfortable," Dr. Goldberg says.[70]

"One man who has been quite satisfied with injection therapy originally came to me after he suffered damage to the nerves that control erection during an emergency abdominal surgery," Dr. Goldberg remembers. "He'd been unable to have an erection for seven years and had simply given up on sex, losing his marriage along the way. In my office, he responded immediately to prostaglandin E I, and his first question to the nurse on hand was, 'How often can I use this stuff?' (About three times a week is the answer.) Sporting an erection that he called 'a twelve on a scale of ten,' he had a second question: 'Where's the phone? I want to call my girlfriend.'"[71]

Dr. Goldberg tells men and their families that each situation is different. There is no one approach that is right for every man, yet every sexual problem can be treated. He chooses from a wide assortment of the latest technologies available, beginning with a complete physical examination and including psychological counseling, trial doses of yohimbine, vacuum devices, penile injections, revascularization surgery, penile implants, and hormone supplementation.[72]

"One of the most common misconceptions about impotence," says Dr. Goldberg, "is that it is often caused by low levels of sex hormones. The fact is, however, that inadequate testosterone is very rarely the cause. It might be a contributing factor, especially in older men, but there is usually some other psychophysiological basis for an inability to get or stay erect."[73]

Dr. Goldberg has demonstrated that a multi-modality approach is best in treating male menopause. He knows that helping a man recover his full sexual potential requires that he help him develop healthy habits in all aspects of his life.

One of the things that distinguishes Dr. Goldberg's center from the host of clinics that are springing up to deal with men's sexual dysfunctions is that it deals with more than the return of the erection. Dr. Goldberg believes that to be effective, programs have to focus on the man himself, not just his parts. "We see sixty to eighty men a day at the clinic," Dr. Goldberg told me recently.

"Each man is unique and no problem exists in isolation. For instance, I'm meeting with an endocrinologist today to look at the ways in which osteoporosis is linked to other changes associated with male menopause."[74]

Although the miracles of modern medicine can be of great help to men going through the Male Menopause Passage, there is much more that men can do using practices that go back thousands of years. These practices are increasingly becoming recognized and accepted by the scientific community. "In ancient Egypt, Greece, India, and China, physicians knew that a patient's emotions matter," says a report in the University of California at Berkeley *Wellness Letter*, "and that lifting the spirits plays an important role in relieving pain and curing illness. Song, dance, and ceremony were part of the physician's tool kit."[75] We'll explore some of these ancient-modern solutions in the next chapter.

Notes Chapter 8

1. Simone de Beauvoir, *The Coming of Age* (New York: G. P. Putnam's Sons, 1972), 539.

2. Psalms 31: 9–12.

3. Sharon R. Curtin, *Nobody Ever Died of Old Age* (Boston: Little, Brown and Company, 1972), 195–96.

4. Benedict Carey, "Hooked on Youth: The Latest Anti-Aging Drug Is Cheap, Convenient, and Makes Some People Feel Like Kids Again. So What's the Catch?," *Hippocrates*, February 1996, 39.

5. Ibid., 40.

6. Ibid., 42.

7. Walter M. Bortz II, M.D., *Dare To Be 100* (New York: Fireside, 1996), 18.

8. Quoted by Michael Lynberg, *The Path with Heart* (New York: Ballantine, 1989), 20.

9. Ibid., 17.

10. Ibid.

11. Zalman Schachter-Shalomi and Ronald S. Miller, *From Age-ing to Sage-ing: A Profound New Vision of Growing Older* (New York: Warner Books, 1995), 107.

12. Donovan Webster, "Erections 'R' Us," *Men's Health*, June 1996, 108.

13. Henry A. Feldman et al., "Impotence and Its Medical and Psychosocial Correlates: Results of the Massachusetts Male Aging Study," *Journal of Urology* 151 (January 1994): 58.

   Steven Lamm and Gerald Secor Couzens, M.D., *Younger at Last: The New World of Vitality Medicine* (New York: Simon and Schuster, 1997), 59.

14. Wilhelm Stekel, M.D., *Impotence in the Male* (New York: Liveright, 1927), 1.

15. Kenneth Goldberg, *How Men Can Live as Long as Women: Seven Steps to a Longer and Better Life* (Fort Worth, TX: The Summit Group, 1993), 172–73.

   Feldman, 54–61.

16. Webster, 108, 110.

17. Feldman, 54–61.

18. Reported by Jane E. Brody, "Impotence: More Options, More Experts, More Success," *New York Times*, 9 August 1995.

19. Ibid.

20. Stephen M. Auerbach, M.D., presentation at the Men's Health Conference, Scottsdale, Ariz., 18–19 November 1996.

21. Alan P. Brauer, M.D., correspondence with author, 19 June 1997.

22. Ibid.

23. Theresa L. Crenshaw, M.D., *The Alchemy of Love and Lust: Discovering Our Sex Hormones and How They Determine Who We Love, When We Love, and How Often We Love* (New York: G. P. Putnam's Sons, 1996), 286.

24. Ibid., 287.

25. Ibid., 286–87.

26. Ibid.

27. Joan Borysenko, *A Woman's Book of Life: The Biology, Psychology, and Spirituality of the Feminine Life Cycle* (New York: Riverhead Books, 1996), 251–52.

28. Crenshaw, 288.

29. Ibid., 288–89.

30. Ibid., 291.

31. Ronald Klatz and Carol Kahn, *Grow Young with HGH: The Amazing Medically Proven Plan to Reverse Aging* (New York: HarperCollins, 1997), 11.

32. Quoted in Crenshaw, 291.

33. William Regelson, M.D., and Carol Colman, *The Super-Hormone Promise: Nature's Antidote to Aging* (New York: Simon and Schuster, 1996), 210.

34. Ibid., 201.

35. Crenshaw, 291.

36. Russel J. Reiter, Ph.D., and Jo Robinson, *Melatonin Revolution: Your Body's Natural Wonder Drug* (New York: Bantam Books, 1996), 4.

37. Ibid., 129.

38. Ibid., 6.

39. Ibid.

40. Regelson and Colman, 221–22.

41. Crenshaw, 211.

42. Ibid., 212.

43. Regelson and Colman, 40–41.

44. Crenshaw, 80.

45. J. F. Flood, J. E. Morely, and E. Roberts. Pregnenolone sulfate enhances post-training memory processes when injected in very low doses into the limbic system structures: the amygdala is by far the most sensitive. Proceedings National Academy of Sciences, 1995, 92: 10806–10810.

46. Will Block, "Questions and Answwers," *Life Enhancement*, March 1997, 27.

47. Regelson and Colman, 103.

48. Quoted in Greg Gutfeld, "Test-Driving Testosterone," *Men's Health*, November 1994, 50.

49. Regelson and Colman, 25.

50. Quoted in Geoffrey Cowley, "Attention Aging Men: Testosterone and Other Hormone Treatments Offer New Hope for Staying Youthful, Sexy and Strong," *Newsweek*, 16 September 1996, 70.

51. Reported in Gutfeld, 50.

52. Ibid., 51.

53. Ibid., 50–51.

54. Ibid., 52.

55. Regelson and Colman, 17.

56. Ibid.

57. "The Aging Male: Can Hormones Help?" *Harvard University's Men's Health Watch* 1, no. 12 (July 1997).

58. Andrew Weil, M.D., "Protecting Your Prostate," *Andrew Weil's Self Healing Newsletter* 1, no. 4, (1995): 2–3.

59. Reported in Leon Jaroff, "The Man's Cancer," *Time*, 1 April 1996.

60. Patrick C. Walsh, M.D., and Janet Farrar Worthington, *The Prostate: A Guide for Men and the Women Who Love Them* (Baltimore: Johns Hopkins University Press, 1995), xv, xvi.

61. Quoted in "Prostate Cancer," *Washington Post*, 1 January 1997, sec. A, p. 2.

62. National Institute of Health press release, 21 November 1996, reported by *Men's Healthline*.

63. Andrew Weil, M.D., "Protecting Your Prostate," *Andrew Weil's Self Healing Newsletter* I, no. 4 (1995): 2-3.

64. Michael B. Schachter, M.D., correspondence with author, 17 April 1997.

65. Michael B. Schachter, M.D., *The Natural Way to a Healthy Prostate* (New Canaan, CT: Keats Publishing, Inc., 1995).

66. For an excellent summary of simple approaches to prostate health, I highly recommend Dr. Weil's newsletter *Self Healing*, particularly Vol. I, no. 4.

67. Quoted in Armin Brott "Getting to the Heart of the Men's Health Crisis: Genetics, Ignorance, and Fear Are a Prescription for Early Death," *San Francisco Examiner*, 24 May 1994, sec. C, p. I.

68. Goldberg, 136.

69. Ibid., 139.

70. Ibid., 172–73.

71. Ibid., 174.

72. Ibid., 180.

73. Ibid., 168,

74. Kenneth Goldberg, M.D., interview with author, 7 September 1996.

75. University of California, Berkeley, *Wellness Letter*, September 1996, 2.

9

Sex and Love on the Second Mountain: The Joys and Pleasures of Intimacy in Later Life

Just when I thought I had finally gotten comfortable with what it means to be a man and what a woman really wants, the ground beneath me began to shift, and I was thrown off balance. Carlin and I had been married ten years and had settled into a nice routine. I had the major money-making role with a career that often took me on the road.

Carlin's career brought in less money and allowed her to spend time at home with the children. Although our marriage was far from the traditional one of our parents, it was stable and satisfying. We were both making our way through the Menopause Passage.

After recovering from surgery to remove an adrenal tumor, I decided that I wanted to relax more and work less. We moved to the country, and to my surprise, I loved the slower pace. I could spend hours splitting wood and prided myself on spending quality time in the hammock each day. Where in the past, I loved to travel, now I had no interest in exotic places. I just wanted to stay at home.

Carlin, on the other hand, began to expand her work. She found she was becoming increasingly sought after as a counselor and spiritual mentor. She began to travel more and deepened her work with women. Even her time at home was much more demanding. She planted a city-block-sized garden and became a farmer with tasks that needed to be accomplished each day and throughout the seasons. She watered, fertilized, weeded, planted, and harvested. She terraced the hillside and pounded in iron re-bar to shore up the boards that held her fruit trees. She put in an irrigation system that had to be monitored and cleaned periodically.

She was so busy I had to remind her that we needed to take time for us. That used to be her role. Now it was me who was suggesting a day to ourselves. I was the one who read relationship articles and books to get clues about keeping our marriage alive and well. We seemed nearly to have reversed roles.

Men and Women: The Menopause Passage and the Second Half of Life

The Menopause Passage, for both men and women, involves the descent down the mountain of First Adulthood and through the valley below. Its purpose is to prepare us for the ascent up the second mountain so that we can fully engage life's later years, what Swiss psychologist Carl Jung called "the afternoon of life."[1]

Much of the discomfort that is associated with this time of life comes from the growing pains we experience. The degree of pain is proportional to the degree to which we cling to the past and refuse to embrace the future. One of the most surprising, and for some the most difficult, aspects of this change has to do with the shift in polarities between male and female.

Between the time we are born and the beginnings of adolescence, males and females are very much alike. The hormonal changes that begin as we reach puberty force males and females to diverge. Evolutionary psychologists believe that males and females become most different from each other during the reproductive years.[2]

Professor David Gutmann, author of *Reclaimed Powers*, believes that these differences are necessary so that children get the kind of parenting they need in order to grow up and become successful adults. He says that children need both physical and emotional security and that these needs are best served when one parent is in charge of each of these vital functions.[3]

Whether we have children during these years or not, our evolutionary heritage creates men and women who tend to separate roles along gender lines. However, in the postreproductive years, we can reclaim the parts of ourselves we had to deny in the service of our biologically driven need to provide support for the next generation.

"As a consequence," says Gutmann, "postparental men and women can reclaim the sexual bimodality that was hitherto repressed and parceled out between husband and wife. Because the restoration of sexual bimodality will no longer interfere with proper parenting, senior men and women can reclaim, for themselves, those aspects of self that were once disowned inwardly, though lived out externally, vicariously, through the spouse."[4] In the process, we become more like what our partners used to be like.

In midlife, the man seems to be drawn back toward home, back toward the center. He is drawn by what anthropologist Angeles Arrien calls the "magnetic" dimension of life. He feels more rooted, less interested in going outward, more content with staying put. The woman is driven by the opposite, "dynamic" dimension. The adventurer in her begins to assert itself, and she wants to move outward toward the periphery.

In their attempt to break out of traditional sex roles, some men and women reversed roles in their twenties and thirties with the woman going out and expressing the dynamic aspect of her nature, while the man became the "house-husband" and took on the more magnetic aspects of life. In these situations, the midlife change of directions brings the woman back home and the man moves outward. Whatever the primary mode was during First Adulthood, the complementary aspect begins to assert itself during Second Adulthood.

However, we live in a society that values the dynamic dimension much more than the magnetic. Women who embrace the dynamic aspects of themselves, though it may cause discomfort for those they are close to, are generally respected. Men, on the other hand, who embrace the magnetic aspects of life, are often shamed. This is frequently added to the shame men feel about themselves from the previous period of their lives.

During the reproductive years, men are often shamed for being away from home too much, always working, never emotionally available for their wives and children. Now, in the second half of life, they are often shamed for not being adventurous enough and being too emotionally dependent on their families.

The shame becomes a disease that destroys a man's sense of self-worth as it destroys the love, trust, and respect that is necessary for men and women to move successfully through the Male Menopause Passage.

Yet the experience of coming home for men does not need to be a shaming experience, though it can be difficult one. For a couple who ride with the changes and keep their communication open, it can be one of the most transformative experiences of their lives. For Ruth and Jeremy, it began as a major life crisis.

"It was a bigger disruption to our lives than the birth of our first child," says Ruth, describing her husband Jeremy's retirement. "He had been working since he was a teenager, and all of a sudden he had no role, no title, no job definition. He became very dependent on me, almost like a child," Ruth continued, remembering those first few months. "He couldn't think clearly. He lost his initiative and needed me to show him how things worked around the house. It just wasn't like him."

"Though we had both worked through most of our married life, the house was always my domain," Ruth acknowledged. "When Jeremy came home, he tried to take over. It's understandable really. He's used to being in charge, particularly when he is around women.

"He's spent forty years being surrounded by secretaries, research assistants, and waitresses; all female, all focused on being supportive of his needs.

"I got sick for three months and finally took a trip to visit friends. One told me I ought to leave Jeremy. But I didn't want to do that. I knew he needed to find his own structure, and he finally did.

"He joined a men's group and began to hear stories of men's pain. One day he came home crying. I had never seen him cry before. I asked him about it, and his response touched my heart. He told me he was thinking about himself when he was nine years old. I could tell he was remembering the pain of what he didn't receive from his father."

"For the first time in my life," says Jeremy, "I really felt I had something to offer younger men. I could listen to them without judgment. I could hug them with genuine warmth. Young men would call me and we would spend hours on the phone, mostly just sharing feelings.

"We would often meet for breakfast at a local cafe. I think I found my calling. I've become a mentor. I love Ruth for being supportive, for not putting me down when I was struggling. Having men who could give me support and men who I could give support to is a great gift."

Reclaiming Male Magnetism and Reintegrating Our Full Sexuality

In a society that overvalues the out-flowing dynamic dimension and often denigrates the magnetic inward dimension, whoever expresses this inward flow will often be shamed. During the reproductive years, "women's work," associated with home and family, was often devalued. The man's work outside the home was often afforded a status higher than it deserved because he "worked," he controlled the money, thought of himself as king of the castle, and expected instant respect; since she didn't "work," was merely a housewife, she didn't get paid, and often viewed herself as "less than" the man.

Yet, being a mother has its own rewards, and though the world of outside work may be seen as more valuable than "staying home," it clearly has merit to the family and society. But what is the role of older men who want to stay home? What value do they have if they're not working outside or raising their children? Are they just old bums, sitting around telling each other stories about their glory days, or is there a more important role for older men?

We can learn a lot that can help us by turning to the experiences of men in indigenous cultures throughout the world. Unlike our modern industrial society, many of these cultures have a long history of respect for older men and the roles they play in nurturing the community.

In traditional societies throughout Africa, for example, one of the prime roles of older men is as "Peacemaker." Anthropologist Paul Spencer found this role is prevalent among the Samburu of East Africa (an offshoot tribe of the bellicose Masai), as well as the Zulu, the Nyakyusa, and the Lele of Central Africa. They recognize that the young men must express their aggression, but they also recognize that the role of elder males is to channel and control it.

Professor David Gutmann, who has written extensively about these societies, says, "While the old men of these tribes might recognize that the intemperate young man is the best vessel for the collective aggression of the group, they also recognize that this aggression must be physically removed from the vulnerable precincts of the intimate community."[5]

In studying other indigenous cultures, two other roles arise as important for men. Elder males, in addition to their role in keeping order in the community, attend to the community's spiritual needs and provide mentoring for the young males.

As anthropologist Austin Shelton describes the roles of the Nsukka Ibo men of Nigeria, "The older man reaches a stage of life in which he leaves farming and manual labor to the young, on the grounds that he must now devote his energies to more important matters—maintaining order and justice in the clan, keeping his people under the protection of God and the ancestors, and teaching the young the correct ways of human relationships."[6]

All three of these roles—Peacemaker, Spirit Guide, and Mentor—involve a return of the magnetic dimension in men's lives. They return from their work on the periphery and take up a new position at the center. Women, meanwhile, have the opportunity to exercise the dynamic dimension and move outward more vigorously. This often affects the emotional balance in the relationship, where each begins to become what the other once was.

In evaluating cross-cultural data from around the world, Gutmann says that a significant sex-role turnover takes place as men begin to own, as part of themselves, the qualities of *"sensuality, affiliation,* and *maternal tendencies—*in effect, the *'femininity'* that was previously repressed in the service of productivity and lived out vicariously through the wife."

"By the same token, across societies," continues Gutmann, "we see the opposite effect in women....They generally become more *domineering, independent, unsentimental,* and *self-centered."*[7]

There is a hormonal basis for this midlife gender crossover. As estrogen levels drop for women, the testosterone/estrogen ratio increases. On the other hand, as testosterone levels drop for men, the estrogen/testosterone ratio increases. As a result, men become gentler and more introspective, while women become more testy and outgoing.

In describing women during their reproductive years, Theresa L. Crenshaw, M.D., says, "Normal levels of estrogen generally produce a sense of well-being, the need to be intimate and to be held."[8] According to William Regelson, M.D., "In premenopausal women, blood levels of estradiol [the main estrogen produced by the ovaries] average about 200 picograms per milliliter. After menopause that number drops to under 30 pc/ml. and the ovaries literally shut down."[9]

"Ironically," Dr. Regelson continues, "older men produce more estrogen and have higher levels of estrogen in their brains than postmenopausal women do."[10] This increase in estrogen in men going through the Menopause Passage could help account for their increased desire to hold and be held and their greater interest in expanding their sexuality to include more time for nongenital play and intimacy.

As my wife, Carlin, and I move through the Menopause Passage, these are exactly the changes we notice in ourselves and each other. It is the source of our greatest joy and also the source of our greatest conflict.

When I have done something I feel is particularly romantic and caring that Carlin doesn't seem to notice, my feelings get easily hurt. When I feel conflict between us, I often feel it is because she is being too "domineering, independent, unsentimental, and self-centered."

Was I really like that in my First Adulthood? When I think about it, I have to admit I was. The real problem, I believe, is that both men and women have difficulty recognizing and accepting these changes. We seem to have two models of relationship for later life. One is to try and hold on to our old roles. The other is to shed our roles completely and take on a "unisex" model where each partner tries to do and be everything.

The result is often a relationship that breaks under the stress of rigid sex roles that no longer fit the needs of each person or a relationship where the partners shed sex roles altogether and become "elder twins."

When couples complain that the sex has gone out of their relationship, it is often because they don't feel "manly" or "womanly." They develop an asexual relationship, where maleness and femaleness are seen as relics from a sexist society and are best done away with. It often serves to relieve the inevitable tensions of a long-term committed relationship but sacrifices the juicy sensuality that comes from gender differences.

Just as many older women are embracing the dynamic dimension of life, men need to embrace the magnetic. They need to recognize that the magnetic dimension, which is so important for men as they move through the Male Menopause Passage, is not superficial or weak. The magnetic-based roles of Peacemaker, Spirit Guide, and Mentor are important and strong roles for men in the second half of life.

I don't believe men will feel fulfilled in Second Adulthood by holding on, exclusively, to the dynamic roles that served them well in the first half of life. Nor will they feel fulfilled by denying their masculine selves, merging with their partners, and trying to be "nice guys." And it won't happen alone. Men need other men if they are going to be successful in the second half of life.

The truth is the newly emerging "magnetic man" will be eaten alive by the newly emerging "dynamic woman" unless he gets a great deal of support from the community of men.

I have found that women today have little sympathy for simpering men who cannot find their masculinity and hope women will take care of them. An elder woman's mothering instincts can still be tapped when their grown children (or grandchildren) are in danger, when their friends need help, or when the community needs a fierce protector. But with their husbands and lovers, they do indeed tend to exhibit their older-woman dynamism. They can be hard-edged and flinty. They don't have a lot of patience for men who aren't sure of their masculinity and who act like good old boys or frightened children.

It's the reason I have been in a men's group for the past eighteen years and intend to be in one the rest of my life. It's the only way possible for me to match the energy of the older woman in my life. If we are going to have a relationship based on mutual respect and love, I have found I need a continual infusion of male energy that I can only get when I am in the presence of other men.

But men are drawn to men at midlife for deeper reasons than the male support needed to stand up to strong women. They hunger to feel a connection with guys, a remembrance of a wonderful time long ago when they were more at home in their bodies and souls. I still remember that time of my life when I was ten or eleven, before hormonal shifts changed the world for me and girls became the focus of my hopes and dreams. I remember when Jack, Lester, David, and I were the center of a group of guys who hung together and loved each other totally and unself-consciously.

In some ways, we were at our best and brightest when we were ten. We were strong and rowdy, but we weren't afraid to love our buddies or sing their praises. Nothing felt better than knowing you had a place in the group, you fit, you belonged. Much of our hunger and rage towards women, I believe, results from our not having an intimate connection with guys in our lives.

As we move through the reproductive years, with their thrills of victory and agonies of defeat, we must recapture the feeling of being a man among men. The best of what we can become at fifty—rough and tough and playful, romantic and wide-eyed, committed heart to heart with a group of guys, idealistic and unafraid—recalls the best of who we were at ten.

Germaine Greer, in her book on menopause, *The Change*, connects these two periods of life and calls on women going through the Menopause Passage to remember the girl she used to be. "The passionate, idealistic, energetic young individual who existed before menstruation can come on earth again if we let her," Greer counsels. She goes on to offer a perspective that is as valuable to men as it is to women. "We might develop better strategies for the management of the difficult transition if we think of what we are doing not as denial of the change or postponement of the change, but as acceleration of the change, the change back into the self you were before you became a tool of your sexual and reproductive destiny. You were strong then, and well, and happy, until adolescence turned you into something more problematical, and you shall be well and strong and happy again."[11]

Rather than trying to recapture the competitive edge of the dating and mating years, what men at midlife really need to remember is the joy of affiliation they felt in those golden years when being part of "our gang" was about the best thing a guy could ever hope to achieve.

It is the reason you see elder males in cultures that respect this time of life hanging out with their peers—telling jokes, having fun, eating and drinking, singing, dancing, and telling stories. These cultures recognize the importance, particularly in Second Adulthood, for the genders to have time and space to be separate and for the guys to support each other and act like ten year olds again.

These cultures know that inevitable tensions build up between men and women, which are relieved when men can be with other men and women can be with other women. Men and women today have a lot to learn from these traditional cultures with their ancient practices, which have been honed for thousands of years.

Back to the Future: Food, Sex, God, and Healing

In chapter 8, we were told by one of the most prestigious health newsletters in the country that song, dance, and ceremony were once part of the physician's tool kit. Is there any relevance today to these ancient practices that on the surface seem pretty distant from modern scientific study of sex and love in Second Adulthood?

Angeles Arrien is a healer who is convinced that the old ways are not only still relevant to modern times, but may be even more needed now than ever before. She is a cross-cultural anthropologist, author, educator, corporate consultant, and one of the most perceptive and vibrant people I have ever met.

"Healers throughout the world," says Arrien, "recognize the importance of maintaining or retrieving the four universal healing salves: storytelling, singing, dancing, and silence."[12] Indigenous cultures, throughout human history, believed that when we stop singing, stop dancing, are no longer enchanted by stories, or become uncomfortable with silence, we experience soul loss, which opens the door to discomfort and disease. "The gifted healer," Arrien reminds us, "restores the soul through use of the healing salves."[13]

It has long been recognized that these healing salves (just the sound of the word makes me want to spread it all over my body and soul) are critical for our ongoing peace and well-being, particularly as we approach the end of the twentieth century.

Margaret Mead described the importance of these healing salves to a planet that is destroying itself through our addictive practice of consumption. "Prayer does not use any artificial energy," says Mead, "it doesn't burn up any fossil fuel, it doesn't pollute. Neither does song, neither does love, neither does the dance."[14] Some native peoples add to Mead's statement when they say, "the Great Spirit must have loved stories, because he made a lot of people."

One of the most universal aspects of storytelling is its connection to the sensual pleasures of food and drink, which become increasingly important as we move through the Male Menopause Passage. David Gutmann says of these needs, "In later life, food is sexy, the erotic keynote of healthy later life."[15]

He goes on to describe a scene in a retirement home where the residents are given democratic jurisdiction over their menus and where the political discussions are lively:

"Senators are elected every six years, presidents of the United States every four and food items are voted onto and off the menu every two years at the Hebrew Home in the Bronx. Senatorial and presidential elections are considered relatively inconsequential compared with what the residents of the home eat. 'A bum senator we can live with,' said one of the nineteen voting members making a speech at the meeting, where tasting, debating and balloting took place. 'Ratatouille we cannot.'

"Nothing is more important to people here than meals," said Marcus Solot, a member of the Food Committee. "It's just about all anyone talks about."[16]

We might think this focus on food is simply the result of older people who have lost their role in life and have little to occupy themselves. However, this is not the case. Dr. Gutmann has found this same desire in cultures throughout the world. "Despite varying cultural conventions regulating the distribution and value of food in later life," says Gutmann, "the rate of increase in oral concerns with age appears to be a cross-cultural constant, a universal."[17]

This oral need seems to be particularly prevalent among elder males. "Time does take away from older men their edge, their genital and phallic appetites for dominance, victory, and successful agency, but it gives back an extended range of hitherto closeted pleasures, those of the table and the community of companions, literally those who take bread together."[18]

Eating together and telling our life stories may be one of the most important things a man can do to keep his sexual vigor alive in later life. It's what connects us with ourselves, our friends, our community, and our God. If God loves those who tell good stories, there must be a special pleasure God receives when we tell good stories in the company of good food and good men.

Arrien believes that the most successful healers of the community are those who use their storytelling skills to greatest advantage. "Many shamans and medicine people are gifted storytellers," says Arrien. "Such people are called 'shapeshifters,' because they have the capacity to shift the shape of an individual's story, or even to shift the shape of their own physical appearance. A shaman who has this ability is considered a healing catalyst and change agent. Contemporary shape-shifters are the gifted medical people, therapists, ministers, counselors, and others who assist people through life transitions."[19]

As we move through the Male Menopause Passage and enter Second Adulthood, remembering our story, particularly our own love story, becomes vital to our health and well-being. "The capacity to attend to our own life story," Arrien concludes, "permits us to reopen the heart and connect to the other universal healing salves. This in turn allows us to experience the human resource of love, the most powerful healing force on Mother Earth."[20] But many of us have become disconnected. Sex and love seem absent or separated from each other.

Sex: Is It the Reason We "Can't Get No Satisfaction"?

It was billed as the most important and accurate sex survey in more than 40 years, "surpassing all previous sexuality surveys—including Kinsey, Masters and Johnson, and the Hite Report." Conducted by researchers under the auspices of the University of Chicago, the findings were published in two volumes, one for the general public, (*Sex in America: A Definitive Study*), the other for social scientists, counselors, and health professionals (*The Social Organization of Sexuality*).

Published in 1994, the chapter titles of the popular version give an idea of the material covered: "Sex in America," "The Sex Survey," "Who Are Our Sex Partners," "Finding a Partner," "How Many Sex Partners Do We Have?," "Practices and Preferences," "Masturbation and Erotica," "Homosexual Partners," "Sexually Transmitted Diseases," "AIDS," "Forced Sex," and "Sex and Society."

As I read through the material, I wondered, where are love and intimacy discussed? The index gave few listings for "love" and none for "intimacy." More space was given to a discussion of "forced sex" and "rape." The lack of information on love and intimacy, in this "definitive" study on sex in America, surprised me.

It seems that sex in America has become like white sugar— highly refined, very intense, found everywhere, compulsively sought after, and ultimately empty of nourishment. Sex, according to author George Leonard who has written extensively on the subject, has become "an activity, a field of study, an entity that somehow seems to exist almost entirely separated from the rest of life."[21]

As preoccupied with sex as we have become, most people do not realize that the concept of "human sexual behavior" was unknown until fairly recent times. Nowhere in nature does "sex" exist as an activity apart. According to Leonard, "The very idea that something called 'sex' could be perceived, experienced, and studied as being distinct from the rest of life would have been incomprehensible to people of earlier centuries."[22]

Could it be that our concentration on sex to the exclusion of love, commitment, and spiritual development is at the root of much of our difficulty as we move through the Male Menopause Passage?

After studying the modern field of human sexuality for more than twenty-five years, George Leonard offers the following recommendations. "For starters, I think we need to discard the entire idea encoded in the present usage of the word 'sex,'" says Leonard, "along with the dangerous trivialization, fragmentation, and depersonalization of life that it encourages. We need to reconnect the bedroom with the rest of our lives, with society, and nature, and perhaps with the stars."[23]

When sex becomes separated from love, intimacy, companionship, creative play, and healing, it loses its meaning. Couples who complain that their sex life has become boring, dull, predictable, and infrequent usually suffer from a lack of sexual richness. Sex, separated from life, is like a symphony orchestra that can play only one note.

Love, Sex, and Intimacy: Using the Power of Relationship to Heal Your Body and Soul

Although we have been led to believe that "sex" is as old as creation, we have seen that it is actually quite recent in origin. "Love," we are also told, is a modern invention that goes back a few hundred years to the troubadours and the courtly love traditions in Europe. Yet anthropologists who have studied human cultures have come to a different conclusion.

"Contrary to common belief, love is not a recent invention of the Western leisure classes," says psychologist David Buss, who conducted the most in-depth study of human mating ever undertaken, encompassing more than 10,000 people from thirty-seven cultures worldwide. "People in all cultures experience love and have coined specific words for it," Buss found. "Its pervasiveness convinces us that love, with its key components of commitment, tenderness, and passion, is an inevitable part of the human experience, within the grasp of everyone."[24]

How have men and women, as we approach the end of the millennium, become so confused about the place of sex and love in our lives? Psychologist Paul Pearsall believes that the problem results from following the mistaken advice of what he calls "the sex syndicate." He feels that the most popular approaches to sex therapy are incomplete, focusing on technique over connection, individual happiness over relationship health. "The result of the sex establishment's firm control over the definition of good sex has created a bondage of self-pleasure," says Pearsall. "There is little discussion of the meaning of sex or the healing nature of long and enduring relationships....Turn on rather than tune in seems to be the sex establishment message."[25]

Like so many respected healers, Dr. Pearsall is not afraid to share the core experience that led to his own sexual healing. "I had never known such helplessness and terror," Pearsall remembers. "I was blind and unable to move. Even my eyelids would not open in response to my efforts to cling to my tenuous connection with the world. I had just been taken to intensive care following surgery for cancer that had spread through my body and into my bones. I struggled to breathe and to move any part of my body, and I felt totally isolated and alone.

"I heard the words of a doctor pronouncing, 'I think we've lost him.' At that terrible moment, I felt the miraculous effects of sexual healing...."

"At my time of helplessness and isolation, my wife, Celest, brought me back from death's door and reconnected me with life. I felt the warmth of her breath against my cheek, the wetness of her tears falling gently on my eyelids, and the soothing and reassuring comfort of her fingers tracing along my arms, chest, and the scars that lined my abdomen. 'I love you. I'm here. You'll make it, sweetheart. We'll make it together like we always do,' she cried softly in my ear."

His wife's love gave him something that modern medicine, with all its technological wizardry, could not. It gave him a reason to live. "Like the electric paddles that shock a heart back to normal rhythm and bring a patient back to life, my wife's words seemed to be the catalyst for a flood of memories we had made together," said Pearsall. "As I lay near death, it was not my life that passed before my eyes—it was our life."[26]

Out of Dr. Pearsall's personal and professional experiences, he created a new field of study that he calls psychoneurosexuality (PNS). He defines it as the "study of the relationships among the brain in our skull, the mind as it exists throughout our body, the immune system that communicates with these systems, and the sexual system that expresses this entire health organization to another person."[27]

"A primary assumption of PNS is that sexual healing is pentamerous—that is, it involves five key connections." Pearsall describes his five-sided approach as follows:

- *Self-esteem*—A connection with Self
- *Intimacy*—A connection with someone significant in your life
- *Coherence*—A connection with someone who shares your beliefs in a higher purpose and meaning
- *Mindfulness*—A connection with the current moment
- *Sensuality*—A sensual connection with the physical body of yourself and someone you love as an intense physical expression and manifestation of all five levels of connection.[28]

In his book, *Sexual Healing*, Pearsall offers specific tools for healing our sexual selves that are valuable for all people, but particularly valuable to men and women in Second Adulthood. During this stage of our lives, we need to move beyond the more procreative focus of our early years and embrace the co-creative aspects of our later years.

Let's take a closer look at the way sexual healing expresses itself through the five factors that are at the core of Pearsall's approach.

1. Self-esteem

We connect with ourselves when our sexuality is an expression of who we are, rather than an expression of who we think we should be. We can allow ourselves to say "no" to sexuality that is limiting or abusive. We can say "yes" to sexuality that contributes to our health, the health of our partner, and the health of society.

2. Intimacy

We make a healing connection through sex with another person only when we are true to ourselves, honest, and respectful with our partner. We reach out sexually as an expression of love, not in an attempt to relieve tension or in an attempt to get our partner to love us.

I have found that sex without intimacy is abusive to all those involved. We hunger to feel our souls touch, yet often settle for less. Sexual intimacy must be based first and foremost on intimacy.

3. Coherence

Sexual healing occurs when we have sex with another person with whom we share common values and philosophy of life. Making love is an expression of our belief in the meaning of life. In his autobiography, *Memories, Dreams, and Reflections*, psychologist Carl Jung wrote, "Meaningless is equivalent to illness."[29] Sex without meaning adds to our aloneness.

4. Mindfulness

This concept means being aware of the present moment. It means allowing our sexual feelings to rise and fall in their own rhythm. It means being present to our partner and not fantasizing about being somewhere else or doing something else. It means "slow hands and an easy touch."

Paul Pearsall reminds us that "the sex of sexual healing is a slow, lingering, peaceful sex in which—at least for one moment—the eternity represented by the merging of the past and the future into the present moment is celebrated with someone we love."[30]

5. Sensuality

Our skin is our largest sense organ, and touching is healing. We need to relearn how to touch those we love. To do that we need to relearn how to touch ourselves. Most of us only touch ourselves when we masturbate or when we are criticizing our latest flaw.

"My stomach's too big, my arms are too small, my skin is getting droopy," we think to ourselves as we pull and poke at our bodies. Even when we touch ourselves sexually, it is rarely an expression of self-love and enjoyment. Usually, it is no more than a release of tension or an expression of our disappointment that we aren't sharing ourselves with a loving partner.

Pearsall concludes with these words: "Sexual healing involves a sensual connection on the molecular level, with every sense and cell merging in a melodic dance of molecules made healthier through our intimacy with our lover."[31]

Becoming a Sexual Shaman

When I looked up the word "shaman" in my Funk and Wagnalls dictionary, it was defined as "A North American Indian medicine man." Actually, shamanism derives its name from the indigenous religion of northern Asia. But the idea of a spiritual tradition that links people to the natural world is as old as humankind.

Although there is much in pop psychology that offers quick fix solutions to our modern problems and glorifies or trivializes native traditions, there seems to be an increasing body of scientific evidence that supports the belief that many of the ancient practices are valuable to modern times. Shamanic practices may not provide direction for building bridges, buses, or bombs, but they can give us help in healing our sexual selves.

"There have been shamans throughout history in all parts of the world," says Dr. Pearsall. "To become a sexual shaman or healer requires learning two special skills practiced by all shamans: playful joy in living with others and sensual activity and movement throughout the life cycle."[32]

After thirty-two years practicing the healing arts, I have found the following seven steps useful in developing yourself as a sexual shaman:

1. Eat Food for Life.

When conditions of life for any animal population deviate from those to which it has genetically adapted, biological maladjustment and disease are inevitable. The human species is no exception. Discordance between our current lifestyle and the one in which we evolved over the last three million years has promoted the chronic and deadly "diseases of civilization," the heart attacks, strokes, cancer, diabetes, emphysema, hypertension, cirrhosis, and like illnesses that cause 75 percent of all mortality in the United States. This discrepancy between how we evolved and how we presently live is particularly apparent in the food we presently consume.[33]

As much as we would like to deny it, there is much truth to the old adage that "we are what we eat." But with so much hype about this miracle diet or that one, it is difficult to know what path to follow. It might make sense to begin by asking the question, "what was the human body designed to eat?" Since the basic elements of our body design have not changed in the three million years our ancestors have lived on the planet, we can look to see what diet humans ate before we began eating the modern American diet.

Three modern day scientists have tackled the problem. S. Boyd Eaton, M.D., is a radiologist. Marjorie Shostak is an anthropologist and author of the classic *Nisa: The Life and Words of a Kung Woman.* Melvin Konner, M.D., Ph.D., is one of the leading experts in the emerging field of evolutionary psychology and the author of *The Tangled Wing: Biological Constraints on the Human Spirit.* Together they have written *The Paleolithic Prescription* that can tell us about the fuel the human body was designed to run on.

Compared to our present diet, the diet of our paleolithic ancestors was low in saturated fat and salt. Water was the major, and usually the only, beverage. Refined sugar—mainly honey— was available only seasonally. And roughage, or dietary fiber, was consumed in large quantities from wild, noncultivated plant foods—a major component of this diet.[34]

Although meat was enjoyed when available, it made up only a small percentage of the diet, and the meat that was eaten was much lower in fat than our present diet and was, of course, free of additives.[35]

"The whole of man's hunting endeavor must be understood as a symbolic, cultural, and social activity," says social scientist Paul Shepard, author of *The Tender Carnivore and the Sacred Game.* "Though he is a highly capable social predator on large, dangerous mammals, he is singularly without the nutritional necessity of eating meat. He is a polished runner and stalker who eats meat as a sacrament."[36]

Other modern scientists have validated the value of this ancient diet, basically vegetarian with some meat added. The traditional Asian diet, with its foundation of rice or other grains, an abundance of vegetables, fruits, beans, and legumes, a limited amount of meat and other animal foods, and virtually no dairy products, is pretty close to what our ancestors ate.

Research shows that the traditional Asian diet is far healthier than ours. The proof? People in Asian countries experience lower rates of heart disease, cancer, and diabetes than we do in the United States. In Japan, the result is the highest life expectancy in the world. The United States is twenty-sixth in longevity.[37]

To become a sexual shaman, eat like your ancestors: Plant foods first. If you like meat, eat wild game you kill yourself or meat from organically raised animals, not the hormone laced meat you buy in most stores.

2. Take Vitamins to Prevent Disease.

Are you as confused as I am about vitamins? Given the poor quality of our diet, it makes sense to take something for health, but what? One of the most respected physicians in the country, Andrew Weil, M.D., offers a straightforward approach that makes sense.

"I take a simple antioxidant formula every day," says Dr. Weil, "10,000 international units (IU) of mixed carotenoids (including lycopene), vitamin E (800 IU), selenium (200 mcg), and vitamin C (2,000 mg two or three times a day). I do this because there is abundant evidence that regular use of antioxidants reduces risk of cancer and heart disease, retards aging, and protects against toxic injury."

Weil notes that it is difficult to get all of what we need from our modern diet, even when we eat healthy. "I also take some supplemental zinc (30 mg a day), because I eat a mostly vegetarian diet, which is low in this mineral, and I take 80 mg of coenzyme Q a day, a supplement that increases aerobic capacity and protects heart muscle."[38]

These recommendations offer a basic formula that makes sense for most people. Other things can be added, depending on individual needs. New information is being learned all the time. Consult the resource section at the back of the book for ways to learn more about vitamin supplements that really work.

To become a sexual shaman, don't rely on food alone, but take supplements that are proven to be effective.

3. Exercise for Health

Exercise has been a part of our lives since the beginning. "Our genetic constitution has been selected to operate within a milieu of vigorous, daily, and lifelong physical exertion," say Eaton, Shostak, and Konner. "The exercise boom is not just a fad; it is a return to 'natural' activity—the kind for which our bodies are engineered and which facilitates the proper function of our biochemistry and physiology."[39]

Physical fitness has three main components: cardiorespiratory (aerobic) endurance, muscular strength, and flexibility.

"Good cardiorespiratory endurance means that activities requiring stamina (such as soccer, swimming, running, and basket-ball) can be maintained for relatively prolonged periods....People who do systematic exercise significantly improve their aerobic fitness," our three experts remind us, "reduce their percentage of body fat, lower their blood pressure and pulse, lower their 'bad' LDL-cholesterol values, increase their proportion of 'good' HDL-cholesterol, lower their blood sugar and insulin levels, and lower their level of serum triglycerides."[40]

Muscular strength usually peaks between the ages of twenty and thirty and declines steadily thereafter. Yet regular exercise can reduce the rate of decline. Strong muscles guard against injuries, and exercise helps keep our bones strong and protects us against osteoporosis.

Yet the most important aspect of our exercise program should be flexibility. Flexible bodies are limber, supple, and graceful. And, we might add, sexy at any age. One of the prime problems men have as they age is with their backs.

Anyone who has ever had a back go out, and that seems to be most all of us over fifty, knows it's difficult to feel sexy when it hurts to move.

"There's definitely a strong connection between good back flexibility and great sex," says James White, Ph.D., professor emeritus at the University of California, San Diego. "A lover with a stiff back is an oxymoron."[41] The good news is that a little stretching goes a long way.

"As we get older, sexual intercourse becomes less vigorous. Keeping your back flexible and abdominals strong can make things lively again, simply because it makes a man's body able to accommodate the thrusting and positioning required," says White.[42]

I have found daily yoga stretches (which my wife, Carlin, taught me) to be very helpful. "It's important to incorporate a sensible strength-building program as a complement to your flexibility program," says exercise physiologist Daniel Kosich, Ph.D. "Although it doesn't strike men as 'manly,' yoga provides an excellent combination of both strength and flexibility exercises—and can be just as tough as any competitive sport."[43]

Earlier in the book, we noted that impotence is a problem for many men as they age. However it seems to be of much less concern for physically fit men. Several years ago, Walter Bortz, M.D., did a survey on the sex habits of men over seventy who belong to the Fifty-Plus Fitness Association. "Of thirty-eight members, average age seventy-five, 58 percent still rated their sex lives as good or very good, another 23 percent fair, and only 19 percent reported their sex lives as poor."[44]

Research on the general population of men over the age of forty found that over half had experienced problems with impotence. Staying physically fit seems to be one of the best things a man can do to keep his sexuality alive and healthy.

To become a sexual shaman and enjoy sex, love, and intimacy into your seventies and beyond—exercise, exercise, exercise.

4. Find the Ancient Herbs for High Level Sex

I first met James Green six years ago at a conference we were both speaking at in San Francisco. His topic, "Why Can't I Call A Guy-necologist," was immediately intriguing. He began his talk with a topic of interest to everyone—the penis. His opening description told me I was in the presence of a man of wisdom who didn't take himself too seriously. "That notorious organ that no one trusts," his sonorous voice boomed to the lecture hall. "TV's perennially censored flesh; Hollywood's most unphotogenic performer; the surgeon's first male target; one of a male's most vulnerable possessions; Phallus officinalis; (In some circles, Phallus vulgaris); shaker and mover; the great stimulator of whispers, wonder and lengthy guesses."[45]

Green says that by profession he is a holistically oriented herbalist. But as I got to know Green, I found he was much more. He had a unique understanding of men and how to help us return to the roots of our health. "Herbal medicine is 'people's medicine,'" says Green. "It is the oldest branch of planetary medicine, suggesting itself to all animals instinctively."[46]

My wife, Carlin, is an herbalist and has long known about the values of these healing substances, as have many of her women friends. But men seem to be slow to recognize the benefits of herbs.

"Why are males slower to respond to the benefits of herbal medicine," Green asked in his talk. "Possibly the male, in general, requires and prefers medicine that is suitable for his more swashbuckling attitude about life. He requires medicine that is heroic in nature, not one that is nutritional. He seeks a medicine that is designed to be efficient in acute crises, not necessarily one that is preventive in nature."[47]

Though this dynamic approach may be helpful in the first half of life, the more magnetic way that is expressed in herbal medicine is particularly appropriate for men moving through the Male Menopause Passage. "A man's change of life is not a loss of his manlihood, his sex appeal or his maleness," says Green. "Through this normal transition a male's strength becomes more supportive of life in general....While a male's menopause is not as hormone altering as the female's, it can call for similar herbs to facilitate rebalance during these changes in life. A combination of herbs for a man experiencing male menopause will do well to include:

- Wild Yam for hormone building assistance;

- Black Cohosh for a relaxant and normalizer;

- Saw Palmetto for a reproductive system nutrient;

- Damiana as a prostate tonic, anti-depressant and nutrient for sluggish sexual organs;

- St. John's Wort and Oat for nerve tonics to help deal with any depression and other stress due to the changes."[48]

To become a sexual shaman and enjoy high level sex, find the male herbals that are right for you.

5. Embrace Self-Love and the Joys of Celibacy

For most men, the idea of celibacy is about as appealing as death and dismemberment. But I have found it has been a very valuable part of my life, not as a life-long practice, but as one to be embraced at important times.

We can learn a lot, though, from those who have made it an enduring practice, the monks and nuns who are fully aware of themselves as sexual beings but who express their sexuality in a celibate way. They manage to sublimate their sexual energies toward a purpose other than sexual intercourse and procreation. Most celibate clergy lead morally impeccable lives, full of love and joy.

I first discovered the value of celibacy when Carlin's Menopause Passage resulted in long periods where we didn't have intercourse. I found I could either fight the process by fantasizing about other women, masturbating incessantly, and making demands on Carlin for sex when she wasn't ready, or I could learn to enjoy the times where I could channel my sexual energy into my work or my art.

I must admit I didn't often do a good job of accepting the times we didn't have intercourse, but when I was able to relax into this state of being, there was such a deep sense of power and purpose that it made me want to engage more fully.

"Any marriage has times of separation, ill health, or just plain crankiness, times during which sexual intercourse is ill advised," says poet and author Kathleen Norris. "And it is precisely the skills of celibate friendship—fostering intimacy through letters; conversation, performing mundane tasks together (thus rendering them pleasurable), savoring the holy simplicity of a shared meal, or a walk together at dusk—that can help a marriage survive the rough spots. When you can't make love physically, you figure out other ways to do it."[49]

The bonus is that rather than letting your desire for sexual intercourse define your relationship, you allow your love for yourself and your partner to lead the way.

To become a sexual shaman, embrace the times when genital sex is not the right thing to do, and find more expansive expressions of intimacy and love.

6. Learn to Love the One You're With

Our evolutionary desires to procreate and pass on our genetic heritage keep us lusting for the perfect partner. When we are single, we hunger for a mate. When we are with a mate, we often hunger for someone else. In the first half of life, the draw to make babies often provides the glue that sticks us together.

In Second Adulthood, chemistry alone is not nearly enough to keep marriages alive. We need to make a conscious choice to love the one we're with if we are to experience the spiritual joys of a relationship that lasts until the end of time.[50]

I can't tell you how much time I've wasted questioning myself. "Is this the right person? Am I getting enough love? Is the love I have to give being received? Should we stay together?" It finally dawned on me that, in the words of poet Mignon McLaughlin, "No one has ever loved anyone the way everyone wants to be loved."[51]

Those words have helped me continue to make a conscious choice to be with and learn the majesty of love with the person I am with. It isn't easy. But it's the best game in town. "It is important to remember that we are, each of us, angels with only one wing," says author Luciano de Crescenzo. "And we can only fly embracing each other."[52]

To become a sexual shaman, find a partner and practice loving the one you're with. It is the most difficult and rewarding activity on the face of the planet.

7. Accept That You Have Twenty-Four Hour Access to the Best Healers in the World.

Every author wants to be a healer. In some way, we hope our words will make a difference in your life and that what has worked for us may be of value to you. As a counselor for thirty-two years, I believe my skills can be helpful to many people. I, too, read books and go for counsel. All can be helpful.

But there is an even better source. There are healers that are available whenever you want them, know the answers to all your questions, can help you decide what is right for you and what is best for your family, friends, community, and the planet.

Are you interested in meeting them? Let me tell you about my first encounter. It was 1973, I was approaching my thirtieth birthday, and it seemed like everything in my body was falling apart. I got the appropriate pills from my doctor, but I felt I needed something more. I found it in a book by Mike Samuels, M.D., and Hal Bennett called *The Well Body Book*.

"Your body is a three million year old healer," according to Samuels and Bennett. "Over three million years of evolution on this planet it has developed many ways to protect and heal itself. . . . You have all the knowledge, tools, materials, and energy necessary to keep yourself healthy."[53]

I still remember the morning nearly twenty-five years ago when I first contacted my healers. I did a meditation and saw in my mind's eye a male figure and a female figure who represented the male and female lines of my heritage. I asked for their guidance.

These inner healers have been my main source of support every day since then. You, too, have healers that reside within. They carry the evolutionary wisdom of what has worked to keep your ancestors alive.

Remember, none of your direct ancestors died childless. Every ancestor going back through three million years of evolutionary history knew in every cell of their body what to do to survive. You, too, have that wisdom. You may be out of touch with it, but it is still there waiting to guide you. Ask these internal healers the answers to your questions and be guided by the inner knowing of their response.

To become a sexual shaman, engage your three-million-year-old healers and listen to what they have to tell you.

It will be those who have become sexual shamans who will be the leaders we need to insure the survival of ourselves, our children, our communities, and the fragile planet we all share.

Notes Chapter 9

1. Quoted in Brian Chichester, Perry Garfinkel, and the Editors of Men's Health Books, *Stress Blasters: Quick and Simple Steps to Take Control and Perform under Pressure* (Emmaus, PA: Rodale Press, Inc., 1997), 94.

2. See David M. Buss, *The Evolution of Desire: Strategies of Human Mating,* and Helen E. Fisher, *Anatomy of Love: The Natural History of Mongamy, Adultery, and Divorce* for excellent discussions of the evolution of male and female differences.

3. David Gutmann, *Reclaimed Powers: Toward a New Psychology of Men and Women in Later Life* (New York: Basic Books, 1987), 185–214.

4. Ibid., 203.

5. Ibid., 85.

6. Quoted in Gutmann, 87.

7. Gutmann, 203.

8. Theresa L. Crenshaw, M.D., *The Alchemy of Love and Lust: Discovering Our Sex Hormones and How They Determine Who We Love, When We Love and How Often We Love* (New York: G. P. Putnam's Sons, 1996), 172.

9. William Regelson, M.D., and Carol Colman, *The Super-Hormone Promise: Nature's Antidote to Aging* (New York: Simon and Schuster, 1996), 159.

10. Ibid.

11. Germaine Greer, *The Change: Women, Aging and the Menopause* (New York: Ballantine, 1991), 53–55.

12. Angeles Arrien, *The Four-Fold Way: Walking the Paths of the Warrior, Teacher, Healer and Visionary* (San Francisco: Harper San Francisco, 1993), 54.

13. Ibid.

14. Quoted in Arrien, 55.

15. Gutmann, 114.

16. Ibid., 114

17. Ibid., 115.

18. Arrien, 56.

19. Ibid.

20. Ibid.

21. George Leonard, *The End of Sex: Erotic Love after the Sexual Revolution* (New York: Bantam Books, 1984), 11.

22. Ibid., 98.

23. Ibid., 13.

24. David M. Buss, *The Evolution of Desire: Strategies of Human Mating* (New York: Basic Books, 1994), 2.

25. Paul Pearsall, Ph.D., *Sexual Healing: Using the Power of an Intimate, Loving Relationship to Heal Your Body and Soul* (New York: Crown Publishers, 1994), 103.

26. Ibid., 1–2.

27. Ibid., 3.

28. Ibid., 5–7.

29. Quoted in Pearsall, 6.

30. Ibid., 6–7.

31. Ibid., 7.

32. Ibid., 208.

33. S. Boyd Eaton, M.D., Marjorie Shostak, and Melvin Konner, M.D., Ph.D., *The Paleolithic Prescription: A Program of Diet and Exercise and a Design for Living* (New York: Harper and Row, 1988), 7.

34. Ibid., 45.

35. Ibid., 74–75.

36. Paul Shepard, *The Tender Carnivore and the Sacred Game* (New York: Charles Scribner's Sons, 1973), 128.

37. *Women's Health Advocate*, February 1996.

38. Andrew Weil, M.D., "Protecting Your Prostate," *Andrew Weil's Self Healing Newsletter* 1, no. 1 (1995).

39. Eaton, Shostak, and Konner, 168.

40. Ibid., 179.

41. Quoted in Bert Trott, "Flex Appeal," *Men's Confidential: Health, Sex, and Fitness News for Men*, August 1994, 1.

42. Ibid., 1.

43. Ibid., 2.

44. Walter Bortz II, M.D., *Dare to Be 100* (New York: Fireside, 1996), 235.

45. First heard in James Green's San Francisco lecture and detailed in his book, *The Male Herbal: Health Care for Men and Boys* (Freedom, CA: The Crossing Press, 1991), 115.

46. Ibid., 9.

47. Ibid., 4.

48. Ibid., 41.

49. Kathleen Norris, "Celibate Passion," *The New Age Journal*, August 1996, 44.

50. See Timothy Miller, *How to Want What You Have: Discovering the Magic and Grandeur of Ordinary Existence* (New York: Henry Holt and Company, 1995) for a book which will help you practice this lost art.

51. Quoted in Pearsall, 88.

52. Ibid., 171.

53. Mike Samuels, M.D., and Hal Bennett, *The Well Body Book* (New York: Random House, 1973), I.

10

The End of the Sibling
Society and the Return
of the Prodigal Father

Be ashamed to die until you have won some victory for humanity.

—*Horace Mann*

Peter Pan and the Lost Fathers

I was tired from a long day of writing but had agreed to
accompany my wife to a local production of *Peter Pan*. In our
small town, the theater events draw the community together.
What is portrayed on stage often reflects the issues with which
the community is wrestling.

We all know the story. Three children with somewhat stuffy
English parents encounter Peter Pan, the kid who never wants to
grow up. With a little help from Tinkerbell's pixie dust, the children are able to fly with Peter to Never-Never Land. There they
have many adventures with the Lost Children, fighting the treacherous Captain Hook. In the end, missing their parents and their
real home, Wendy and the boys return to live happily ever after.

But reading the original play, written by J. M. Barrie in 1902,
it is clear that the play is not about children, but about a boy who

never wants to grow up, about the lost boys in the society, and about loss of fatherhood that is such an integral part of our modern urban life.

As the play opens, the children, Wendy, John, and Michael, are playing "family," pretending to be parents talking with their children. Their portrayal of their father is not flattering. They talk about him as though he were a distant relative.

When Barrie describes the family father, John Darling, just prior to his appearance in the play, we understand why the children see him as distant. "He is really a good man as breadwinners go," says Barrie of the father. But like fathers today, he must leave his family each day and engage work that demeans the spirit.

Barrie's description of John Darling could apply to millions of working men in contemporary society who are dehumanized at work and patronized at home. "In the city where he sits on a stool all day, as fixed as a postage stamp, he is so like all the others on stools that you recognize him not by his face but by his stool, but at home the way to gratify him is to say that he has a distinct personality."[1]

Think about the shame that is generated in a man who is invisible at work and ridiculed at home? We've seen him for years in the Sunday funnies—Dagwood Bumstead—and recognize him on television as Roseanne's brow-beaten husband, Dan, and the incompetent, macho fool of a father, Tim-the-tool-man-Taylor on *Home Improvement*.

As they leave for a party, father gets mad at the dog, Nanna, who is better than any nursemaid at keeping track of the children, and puts her out of the house. When the parents return from their business dinner to find the children gone, it is clear that Father is to blame.

As the kids fly away to Never-Never Land, I think about all the fatherless children I know. I think about the single moms stretching to make ends meet, driving themselves to destruction trying, unsuccessfully, to be both mother and father. I think of the men who long for their children, but don't seem to be able to bridge the gap back to them after a divorce. And I think about the children who bond so closely with their mothers there often is not room for a father to connect.

I think about my own family and the father who left when I was five. Like my mother, I felt abandoned. My mother and I were very close before he left and drew even closer afterwards. I remember humming along with her as she sang about how she got along without him before and how we would get along without him now.

I wonder whether moms and kids draw closer together because they believe that eventually dad will leave, and so they unconsciously begin preparing themselves for his expected departure. Or do dads unconsciously begin to withdraw because they feel unneeded, unwanted, and believe that eventually mom and the kids will push them out? I often see these cycles of withdrawal in marriages. Both partners begin to withdraw, fearing the other is withdrawing, and they end up bringing about the very thing they feared most. David Blankenhorn, in his book *Fatherless America*, offers one view on the disintegration of the American family:

Men in general, and fathers in particular, are increasingly viewed as superfluous to family life: either expendable or as part of the problem.

Though the boys in Never-Never Land have many great adventures, they miss their mothers. All the lost boys talk about mothers—things they remember—what she looked like, how she smelled, how much she loved them. Not one of the lost boys ever mentions their fathers. Where are the fathers, I wondered? Well, if they were perceived at all like Wendy, John, and Michael's father—inept, incompetent, unfeeling, and stupid—I could understand why none of them remembered their fathers with respect and kindness.

Meanwhile, back at the empty house where Father and Mother mourn their lost children, the parents wait and wonder. Mother is lighthearted and is sure if she keeps her faith (and keeps the window open) the children will return.

The father is, literally, in the doghouse. He blames himself for having been so insensitive to Nanna, the dog, the night the children are taken. He is beside himself with shame and recrimination. We see him scrunched up tight, his head peering out of the little doghouse door where it is clear he has been eating (probably dog food) and sleeping (snuggled up with his bone) since the children left.

I've seen a lot of men like this father. They are hardworking, caring men. They grew up at a time when the world was simpler. They knew if they got a good job, they could attract a good woman. If they could attract a good woman, they could have regular sex and loving children would likely follow. And if they were very good providers and caring partners, the sex would not end after the birth of the last child.

They would take off time from work to be involved in their family's activities and become pillars of the community. When the kids were grown, mom and dad could reclaim their identities as adults, have time for themselves, and travel to interesting and exotic places.

But their present reality does not conform to the dream they had growing up. They are still hardworking, caring men, but they have become lost in a world where all the rules seem to have changed. Loyalty at work no longer guarantees steady employment, and they are now fearful of losing their livelihood. Without a solid foundation in the world of work, they feel more like "flying boys," as therapist and author John Lee called them, than real men.

Without feeling worthwhile in the world of work, their approach to women becomes tentative or harsh. Even when they have found "a good woman," they are fearful they could lose her at any time. Women now seem to want so much more and need so much less from them. Terrified of making a fatal mistake, these men go through life with their heads down, trying in vain to avoid the mine fields.

Why do men act like flying boys? Perhaps it is because they are afraid they will be destroyed by the mine fields of life as they come down to earth. If they continue to fly, they will remain perpetual adolescents, absentminded, disconnected, but alive. Most choose life, but like the father in *Peter Pan*, they pay dearly for living with their heads in the clouds. Nothing they do seems right. Shame radiates from them like heat off the desert sand.

In *Peter Pan*, Father, like Mother, grieves the children's absence and longs for their return. Absentmindedly, he asks Mother to close the window. She reminds him with a scowl that the window must always remain open so the children will have a place to return. "Oh, yeah, I forgot," he says with his head hanging low.

I hear the audience groan. I know what many of the women are thinking. "Typical man. Pretends he cares about the kids, but in truth, he's just a selfish boob who only cares about his own comfort." I know, too, what many of the men are thinking. "I love our children as much as she does, but I make one little mistake, forget one little detail, and all my good deeds are forgotten."

When Wendy and the boys arrive, the first thing they do is find Mother. Hugs and kisses are given and received. No one seems to notice that Father is not around. When Wendy finally stumbles upon him sleeping in the doghouse, she hardly recognizes him. His greetings to the children are stilted. The love and longing he feels seems swallowed in fear and guilt. No hugs and kisses are given or received. Wendy remembers the lost children she has brought back with her and directs Father to go downstairs and see to their needs.

This scene is a common one in contemporary society. Fathers and children may not have been in contact for some time. Perhaps the mother and father are divorced and the children only come for visits. Maybe the father is working double shifts to pay the bills and appears like a ghost in his own home. When there is a coming together, the interaction is forced and uncomfortable for fathers and children. Both want more closeness, but both are afraid of rejection. Too many hurts. Too much anger. Too much guilt. Too many fears. According to David Blankenhorn in *Fatherless America:*

When a man does not live with his children and does not get along with the mother of his children, his fatherhood becomes essentially untenable, regardless of how he feels, how hard he tries, or whether he is a good guy. Almost by definition, he has become de-fathered.

What kids need are fathers who know how to love and support them. What fathers need are elder males who can teach them what it means to be a father, how to love and live with the mother of their children, and how to hold on to their dignity in a world that is rapidly changing.

Pseudo-Elders and the Tragedy of Fatherless Fathers

In the movie *Falling Down*, which we discussed in chapter 3, we are heartened by the arrival of the "hero," Sergeant Prendergast, played to perfection by Robert Duvall. We chuckle with him as he scans a graffiti scarred billboard beside the freeway showing a scantily clad beauty. He's a man who can appreciate sex, but he's not a sexist. He exhibits zen-like calm in the face of the frustrated, angry motorists. He is cool, clear, and incisive. He shows he knows how to handle an emergency as he helps the beat cop push Menopause Man's car off the freeway without having to wait for the tow-truck, which will take hours to arrive.

Back at the station house, he jokes easily with the rowdy police officers, stands firm with his boss on his decision to retire, and is caring and respectful of the female police officers. Here, we believe, we have found a true elder. Our hearts are hopeful that not only will he be able to find Menopause Man (played by Michael Douglas), who is out rampaging through the city, but he will be able to give the grandfatherly care and support Menopause Man needs if he is to do the right thing for his family.

But like so many men we encounter in our culture, Prendergast is not a true elder. He is an adult child masquerading as an elder. He has a strong facade, but he is a child inside an adult's body.

We get the first clue about his deeper nature when his wife calls, for the third time. The wife is frightened for her husband's

safety. Her constant needs for reassurance are met with conde-
scending replies. "Yes, dear," he tells her. "You're right, dear. Of
course, honey. I'll take care of everything, sweety." He seems to
love her like the child he believes she has become, and like many
parents today, he is totally intimidated by her demands.

The picture on the billboard when Prendergast first arrives
makes more sense now, as we remember that the graffiti is a drawing of a little man nestled between the breasts of a twenty foot tall
woman. The word circle coming from his mouth says, "Help me!"

Like many pseudo-elders in our society, this one is very nice
and very dangerous. He drips assurance, compassion, and care.
He believes in equality, women's rights, and social justice. His
young feminist partner both loves and respects him.

But he is not what he seems. He walks like a man, talks like
a man, acts like a man, even serves as a male role model for
others. But he is not a man. He is a damaged man-child made to
look like a man. And like many men in society today, he will kill
you with kindness, and you will never know what hit you. He will
explode with rage, but disappear in the smoke. He's a time bomb,
and he is deadly.

Pseudo-elders are difficult to detect until they explode and
we have nearly forgotten what a real elder is like. In his absence,
we accept what we can get. So, we clap when Prendergast finally
stands up to his wife's pleas for his attention, cuts off her
demands, and tells her, "I'll be home when I'm done, and I want
dinner on the table." We fail to notice that he has now gone from
passive to aggressive. He still has no clue about what his wife needs.

We cheer when he breaks in the front door of Menopause
Man's house, but fail to notice that his female partner takes the
more dangerous position in the back. We bow our heads in grat-
itude for his daring rescue of the little girl, but fail to notice that
he has just killed her father because he would rather have a macho
gun battle than shoot the man in the leg and cart him off to get
the help he needs.

What Menopause Man desperately needs is a true elder, a
father figure who can listen to his pain, hold him in his arms,

help him grieve the loss of his job, his wife, and his home, and teach him how to become the man he so desperately wants to be.

But like so many other men, Menopause Man's father is nowhere in evidence. How is he supposed to know how to live with an adult woman when he has no man to emulate? How is he supposed to know how to be a father to his daughter when his own father never learned how to be a father to his son? What can we expect from fatherless fathers?

What's sad is that most of the people in the theater audience cheered the film's ending. They believed that the hero had successfully triumphed and that another real life American drama was happily resolved. They failed to notice that another single mother would have to raise her child alone; that another needed father was permanently eliminated from the face of the earth; that another older woman was told to forget her fears about the violent world in which she lives and content herself with getting food on the table for her hungry man; and that another pseudo-elder thinks he's found his lost manhood because he was able to browbeat his wife into silence and have a duel to the death with a younger male.

My Father's Wisdom: If Life Is a Baseball Game, Men Are Striking Out

It is said that what doesn't kill you, makes you stronger. That was certainly true of my father. I think his love of baseball helped. Whenever I would come by to visit him in his little apartment in San Francisco, the first thing he would tell me was how his Giants were doing. He was always happy when the Giants were winning, but he never seemed to be unhappy if they lost. He loved the game of baseball, and he loved the game of life.

Though my father left when I was five, he survived a midlife breakdown, made peace with his family, and in his later years, became a role model for me and a shining example of a true elder. After he retired from the business of acting and writing, he became a street puppeteer and devoted the rest of his life to bringing words of wisdom to anyone who would stop long enough to listen to his puppets talk.

He was somewhat of legend on the streets of San Francisco. I could never go out to lunch or dinner with him without getting stopped, usually by nice-looking women in their twenties or thirties, toting a little child with them. "Oh, Tommy, my mother used to take me to see your puppet shows when I was just a little girl. Will you put on a show for my daughter?" He always had his puppets with him, carried in two big plastic bags. He never refused a puppet show.

A few days before he died at age eighty-nine, I came over to walk with him to the opening of the new San Francisco library. He was an avid reader. Books nourished his spirit, and libraries were his temples of worship. But baseball always took precedence over reading, and the Giants game was on the radio. (He never watched television, because he believed it dulled the senses and destroyed the imagination.)

After the game ended, we began the journey to the library. He stopped at the local Farmers' Market and bought a bouquet of flowers—he wanted to offer them as a "thank you" to all the people who had made the library possible.

The only thing that noticeably changed as he approached ninety was that he walked more slowly. His grip was as strong as ever as he held my arm. It took us nearly two hours to cover the mile-and-a-half distance to the library, but his step never faltered. After laying the flowers near the steps of the library entrance, we sat down to rest before making the return trip.

As we gazed across the civic center square, my Dad seemed to be lost in thought. "What are you thinking about?" I ventured, giving him a pat on the knee. He was rail thin and all bones. "Baseball!" he replied. We both smiled and were silent for a long time. He finally continued. "In order to win the game," his voice was strong, such a contrast to his weakening body, "you have to touch all three bases and make it home." I waited for more of his wisdom. "I'm ready to go home now." He was already leveraging himself off the bench and getting to his feet.

As we walked back to his apartment, and increasingly over the next week, I pondered his words. They took on deeper meaning when he was hospitalized the following Wednesday. He was having difficulty breathing, but the doctors and nurses said he'd be fine.

Two days after entering the hospital, he told his nurse, "it's time." When she asked, "time for what?," he simply repeated himself and asked if she would leave him alone for ten minutes, then return. The nurse shrugged and left.

When she came back as requested, he had stopped breathing. If it could ever be said of a man, "he did it his way," it was my dad. The *San Francisco Chronicle* ran a nice story: "Requiem for a Puppet Man." We gathered at his apartment in the Tenderloin—family, friends, and community. We shed our tears, paid our respects, and shared stories about my father's life.

I thought a lot about his last words and the baseball diamond after he passed. What had I learned? To win the game you have to step up to the plate—no one wins by sitting on the bench. You don't have to be perfect. In fact, being successful three times out of ten gives you a .300 batting average, and that is plenty good enough.

I thought about the men in our society. It seemed to me that too many had poor coaches or no coaches at all. No one told them they did not need to be perfect. They never learned how to swing a bat and so struck out time after time. Even those who got an occasional hit did not seem to know how to get around the base paths back to home plate.

If midlife is second base, it seems that men are dropping out of the game at three crucial points. First, many young males never make it to second base. In ever increasing numbers, they die from drugs, guns, and gang violence. Second, many adult males are so terrified of getting old they deny the aging process, refuse to make the turn at second, and end up alone in left field. Third, many men at midlife see no value in elderhood and allow themselves to decline physically, emotionally, and spiritually. They lack a clear purpose for their later years. They often give up, live lives of quiet desperation, and die before their time. They never make it past third base.

Our present focus on the problems of youth—drugs, violence, venereal disease, teen pregnancy—puts the cart before the horse and treats the symptoms of our societal crisis while ignoring the root causes. We must begin at "third base" and help older men successfully complete the Menopause Passage. They need help learning to heal their shame and reclaim their passion and purpose.

If fathers are increasingly absent from the lives of children, the cause may well be the absence of forty to sixty-five-year-old elders from the lives of fathers. Recent findings from the emerging field of evolutionary psychology demonstrate that without the active involvement of these "emeritus parents," even the healthiest nuclear families are doomed to failure.

According to David Gutmann, professor of psychiatry and education and director of the Older Adult Program at Northwestern University, without the presence of elders, "the unbuffered nuclear family does appear to be increasingly incapable of raising children who can avoid addictions, who do not need cults or charismatic totalitarian leaders, who can grow up to be parental in their own right."[2]

In other words, we are failing to raise viable children who will grow up to raise viable children. Though many would like to deny it, that is a prescription for species extinction. It certainly will not happen overnight. It may take many generations to occur. But what is at stake here is not only the survival of the American family, but the survival of the human race.

Put simply, without men who have successfully completed the Male Menopause Passage and become true leaders, fathers will not have the support necessary to return to responsible parenthood. Without the active involvement of fathers in our society, children will continue to feel lost and increasingly ashamed to be part of the human race. More and more are choosing to kill and to die.

Too many men embrace death because they have given up on life. They have come to believe that not only is their male passion, potency, and power superfluous in today's world, but that it is harmful. Many have checked out because they believe, consciously or unconsciously, that the world would be better off without them.

The Return of the Forgotten Elder

Many men have reached the bottom. They have accepted society's view that they are useless. They have opted for a slow slide down the hill towards old age and death, or they cling desperately to their lost youth. Like angry adolescents the world over, they say "fuck you" to the rest of society and withdraw into alcohol, work, and sexual fantasy.

They have allowed themselves to be eaten alive by women who are enraged by their passivity, women who desperately throw deadly verbal darts at their hearts hoping against hope that these men still have the guts to stand up to them. But more often than not, these men simply look down sheepishly as their life blood drips slowly away. They whine at their wives for being so mean to them and pray for their mythical mommies to return and save them from the wicked witches of the world.

But something is beginning to change. Men are starting to come together. They are meeting in football stadiums, marching to the Capitol, and returning to their communities with something important they must do.

An old Balinese legend might help us recognize what is afoot when the elders come out of hiding:

"It is said that once upon a time the people of a remote mountain village used to sacrifice and eat their old men. A day came when there was not a single old man left, and the traditions were lost. They wanted to build a great house for the meetings of the assembly, but when they came to look at the tree-trunks that had been cut for that purpose no one could tell the top from the bottom: if the timber were placed the wrong way up, it would set off a series of disasters. A young man said that if they promised never to eat the old men any more, he would be able to find a solution. They promised. He brought his grandfather, whom he had hidden; and the old man taught the community to tell top from bottom."[3]

For the first time in a long time, men are standing up for themselves, each other, their families, and their communities. Realizing they can't stand alone, they are creating new connections.

They are finding that eldering is a team sport, not a solo performance. For those who are willing to make the journey, the Male Menopause Passage is a training program for becoming part of that team. It is a lot more rigorous than Marine boot camp. But all it requires is a few good men who are ready for the challenge and a few good women who can stand with these new world elders.

The Million Man March and the Promise Keepers: What We Can Learn from a Yoruba Priestess and an Unrepentant Lesbian Yid

"When I heard they were getting together, I wondered, What the hell are they going to talk about?" said writer Iyanla Vanzant as she watched the gathering of a million African-American men from her home fifteen miles from the Capitol.

"I saw my father out there on that mall, although he has been dead for eleven years." Vanzant, who is also a Yoruba Priestess practiced in African spirituality, recalls that lifechanging day. "I saw my former husband out there. He too has been on the other side for quite some time. My brother was there. My son was there. In fact, all the men in my life I have ever told, 'Do something! Just do something!' were out there, whether or not they were present. I saw them making an effort, taking a step to do something for themselves. It made me proud. It made me humble. It scared me to death!"[4]

And what did they talk about? Iyanla Vanzant had waited a long time to know, but she would have to wait a little longer. "I cooked for them and waited for them to come home—my mate, my son-in-law and his cousins and their friends, my longtime childhood friends and their friends and their children....I waited for my four-year-old grandson to come home and share his experiences. I was excited."

What she heard when they finally did return surprised her and gave her profound hope. "It never crossed my mind that they would talk about what they have done and no longer want to do," she writes, obviously deeply touched.

"I never imagined they would explore the topics of father-hood, husbandhood, manhood, and selfhood. My mama never told me that men talked like that. I never heard my daddy talk about anything like that. Surely it was unimaginable that one million Black men would come together to talk about righting themselves, getting closer to God, or being better men for the sake of the women and children."[5]

But talk they did, and the talk translated into action for many. Men were on the move, and women could begin to let go of the male burden they had carried for so long. For some, the experience was wonderful and also disorienting. "The gathering of a million Black men helped me realize how long I have been the man in my life," says Vanzant, echoing a theme I have heard from hundreds of women. "I have been doing all the things I wanted a man to do for me and with me. While doing is not an activity exclusively reserved for men, women have been doing their part and the man's part for so long, we leave little room for them to show up in our lives."

For women who have had to do it all, the return of the prodigal father does not always feel like a blessing. "That I had been asked to stay home and not do was frightening," Vanzant recalls. "It created conflict in my brain. My personal affirmation, 'Can't no man tell me what to do!' pounded in my mind. How dare they! was my next thought. But then I remembered the language. Atone..."[6]

Something different was going on with these men than had occurred in recent memory. "Atonement is not the language used when malice or deception is intended," Vanzant reasoned. "They could have called it a day of strength or a day of pride. They did not. Atonement is a spiritual concept indicating a conscious intent to seek redemption....Many Black women have had their hearts broken or abused and their egos damaged by Black men.

Many of us have not forgiven them for it. In many instances, our egos are not ready to forgive."[7]

Like Iyanla Vanzant, Donna Minkowitz is a woman writer who has sustained her share of wounds at the hands of men. When she was asked by *Ms.* magazine to go undercover and infiltrate a Promise Keepers men's gathering, she leaped at the chance. "After a *Ms.* editor phoned, pretending to be my mom, and registered me (her teenage evangelical son), all I needed was a couple of trips to a boys' clothing store and a costume emporium, and *presto!* a pint-size Promise Keeper."[8]

You would think that a woman named Minkowitz who identifies with the philosophy of *Ms.* magazine and describes herself as "an unrepentant lesbian Yid" would have little in common with a stadium full of 50,000 right-wing Christian men who follow the philosophy of Promise Keepers founder Bill McCartney, the former University of Colorado football coach.

Promise Keepers has mushroomed from 4,200 conference attendees in 1991 to well over 1,000,000 in 1996. Though the organization has a position paper saying that it believes homosexuality "violates God's design," is opposed to abortion, is lead by men who identify easily with the Christian-right, and views "family" in a way that tries to return to the pre-liberation days of the 1950s, something much larger emerges when men, focused on healing themselves, come together.

"On a personal level, I'm breathing easier here than I have at any other Christian-right event I've covered," says Minkowitz. "There's much less hatred in the air," she says, "because there is so much emphasis on the men changing themselves." Atonement is a word that fits this group of men, as well as those Iyanla Vanzant saw in Washington.

There are also a lot more men of color present than at other men's gatherings. "Groups of black teenagers sit together, wearing identical T-shirts with the name of their Bible study group," Minkowitz recalls. "Latinos perk up when one speaker makes fun of Anglos who massacre Spanish. Roughly a quarter of this Florida audience are men of color—which can be interpreted variously, as a poor showing in an intensely multiracial state, or a tremendous success, given the long racial divisions among protestant evangelicals in the U. S."[9]

One of the main speakers, T. D. Jakes, an intense West Virginian, tells the crowd: "There are many ways of dealing with conflict. We can go to war, we can beat our chests and brag about our own strength and power, and fight. But the greatest enemy I've ever had to fight is the enemy in me."[10]

Over and over, men are urged to show their emotions, to let go of their anger, to reevaluate how they treat the women in their lives. "Six of the eight major speakers emphasize that men's fear of being seen as weak or unimportant—in effect, their fear of being equated with women—can become a terrible obstacle in all their relationships," says Minkowitz as the day's events begin to wind down. "I'm struck by how close it all sounds to feminism."[11]

The final speaker of the day says that one of the most important lessons of the weekend is that the power of God comes only through intimate relationship with His Son. "Maybe he really meant intimate relationship with anybody's son," Minkowitz wonders. "In a society where men are trained to reject and humiliate one another, it's no wonder that simply getting close to other men can feel divine. Watching these men blossom, I start to wonder if the key to men not oppressing women is for them to stop oppressing the woman inside."[12]

I've found it takes more than a weekend with men to reverse the internal and external oppression. What is needed is an initiation into the world of elderhood, a sacred ceremony that honors the passage of men into Second Adulthood, that marks the transition that male menopause brings about, that allows men to fully embrace their power, and that challenges them to become mentors to the young men of the future.

New Warriors and Sterling Men: On the Road to Elderhood

As a recent graduate of the New Warrior Training Adventure, I was invited to join with men from all over the country, as well as Edmonton, Canada, and London, England, for the tenth anniversary of the New Warriors. I had known one of the founders, Bill Kauth, as a fellow brother in the men's movement for many years, and I was anxious to get an overview of what the organization had been doing and where it was going.

Kauth is a gentleman in his fifties, with white hair and beard, who looks more like the king of the elves than the originator and co-founder of an organization of new warriors. My correspondence with Kauth gives some insight into the philosophy of the New Warriors:

We are an order of men called to reclaim the sacred masculine, for our time, through initiation, training, and action in the world.

Some of the action programs I heard about were exactly the kinds that I believe men need to engage in if they are going to be the kind of men that matter in the world. Examples include the Hales Franciscan Mentoring Project in Chicago, the Boot Camp project in Houston, the Inner-City Youth program in Milwaukee, and the Alternative Sentencing Project in San Diego.

When my own men's group, which had been meeting regularly for fifteen years, felt we needed something to revitalize our midlife energy, I suggested we do the New Warrior weekend together. I felt it would give us an opportunity to know each other in a deeper way and share an initiatory experience into manhood that most of us never had.

We flew down to San Diego, one of twenty-three centers throughout the country, and drove into the surrounding mountains to a wonderful spot near Mt. Palomar. The weekend was transformative, for us as a group and for each of us individually. It was a true initiation, a rite of passage, a celebration of manhood, and an opportunity to fully develop our life-purpose.

During one experience, I was able to heal old wounds I still carried from being raised by a single mother who, with my father absent from the time I was five, made me the "special man" in her life. As a child, I both relished the unique position I occupied and felt overwhelmed by the emotional incest that occurred when I became "the love" of my mother's life. Letting go of the rage and confusion I had carried for so long was one more block removed from being able to be the strong, gentle man that I had longed to become.

The day after I returned from the weekend, I got a call from my nineteen-year-old son, Aaron. As we talked about what was going on in our lives, he seemed down. On the other hand, I was overflowing with my experience of the men's weekend. "I've never heard you so enthusiastic about anything before," he told me over the phone. "You've done a lot of men's events. If your experience was that good, I want to go."

As luck, or the workings of the gods, would have it, there was a new center opening up in Portland, Oregon, where Aaron lived. After a personal interview with Bill Kauth, Aaron was accepted to attend, and I was accepted as one of the volunteer staff. Watching my son being mentored by older men and participating with him in his own rite of passage was one of the most moving and valuable experiences of my life.

If my own weekend helped me feel the power of initiation, to feel deeply accepted as a man, the weekend with Aaron helped me recognize how important older men are in the lives of younger men.

Aaron and I had inherited each other when Carlin and I got together. He already had a father, and I already had children. It wasn't clear what the nature of this "step" relationship should be. In my tentative way, I tried to be a supportive presence in Aaron's life without going over the line and being intrusive.

Though I was not aware of it until my own initiatory weekend, fears from my own childhood made me overly sensitive to not violate Aaron's or Carlin's boundaries. I wanted to be careful I did not do anything that might be interpreted by Aaron as trying to replace his father, and I did not want to do anything that might be interpreted by Carlin as trying to replace her as his principal parent. I also had a concern that over-involvement with Aaron might make my other children feel they were being pushed aside.

During the weekend, more happened than I could begin to share, but in a very emotional encounter, Aaron told me honestly that he felt I had failed him as a father. "I wanted more of you," he told me. "I didn't want a step-father, I wanted a father. Why can't a boy have two fathers?" he asked with tears in his eyes.

I realized that my own fears from the past had limited my ability to give Aaron all of myself. I see many men who are in the position of fathers, mentors, and teachers hold themselves back because they are unsure of how much they should give. Aaron was telling me, "Don't be afraid. Give all you've got. I need you. I love you." We were both in tears, as were the men who were holding us in their loving embrace.

A year later, I was listening while another man cried openly as he told about his experiences in a community of men. "That's the Center we helped keep alive," said Howard, a man I had recently met at a friend's wedding, pointing to a beautifully crafted structure across the street from where we had parked. "I still remember the night we first met. A group from the community had asked the support of the Sterling Men to help revitalize the local youth center, but they weren't sure whether anyone would show up on that rainy November night. Gradually the room began to fill with men until there was an overflow crowd."

Howard stopped talking and gazed across at the building as if remembering the volunteer work of the hundreds of people who came together to make a dream into a reality. "Women and kids got to see what men can do when they are told they are needed and offered a challenge big enough to engage their heart and soul," Howard said as he nodded his head and smiled.

I knew immediately that I wanted to be part of such a community and was told it began by attending the Sterling Men's Weekend. "My God, not another weekend," I thought as I rolled my eyes to the heavens. "Haven't I done enough of those?" Two hours later, I was seated with Howard at a local delicatessen looking over the application form.

After providing my vital statistics, the application asked me to "list three major changes you would like to have occur in your life as a direct result of taking the Sterling Men's Weekend. Use the purpose of the Weekend as a guide." Howard read the purpose of the weekend out loud:

Purpose of the Sterling Men's Weekend: To engage in the process of locating the source of your power and discovering and dissolving the barriers between you and manifesting that power, so that you experience total freedom as only a man can, and with that freedom be the man you always wanted to be.

I felt good making my commitment to the weekend, and I also felt scared. I had known about Justin Sterling's work for years. In fact, my friend Bill Kauth told me that he and one of the other founders had gone to the Sterling Institute when they were developing the New Warrior Weekend.

I had a strong reaction to Justin when I first met him. He's flamboyant and charismatic, with a cutting wit and confrontational style. He's absolutely dedicated to teaching men and women how to have relationships that work. After I completed my own weekend, my wife thought highly enough about the changes she saw in me to sign up for the Women's Weekend.

When Sterling talked about what we must do to raise healthy children, most of the men squirmed with discomfort while acknowledging the truth of the challenge he put before us. It was clear that like the African-American men in Washington and the men of the Promise Keepers, we had much to atone for and much to give. By the time the weekend was completed, I was in tears. I felt I had learned some valuable lessons about sex in the second half of life, accepted the legacy of my father, and been freed from the spectre of death that had been with me since I had witnessed a boyhood friend drown in the river when I was seven years old.

I also felt overwhelmed with the work that needed to be done if we were going to save the world by teaching men how to become the men they have always wanted to be, rather than the aging boys that most of us have settled for becoming. I thought of my four sons and two grandsons. I thought about my daughter and three granddaughters. I hoped I could make a difference in their lives and in the lives of others' sons and daughters.

I thought of the world we live in—a world dominated by Peter Pans, pseudo-elders, and Monster Boys. I thought of the Wendys of the world who treat their mates like little brothers; who pray every night that these perpetual adolescents will grow up and become men, and who cry every morning when they realize that a woman will always fail when she tries to teach a boy what it means to be a man.

When I looked again at the men who had shared the weekend with me and at my sponsor who had helped pave the way for me, I knew that there was important work that each man alive today was called upon to do. A man working alone today is likely to be enchanted by a Peter Pan, seduced by a pseudo-elder, and murdered by a Monster Boy. The only hope for our own survival and for the survival of our children, grandchildren, and the future of our planet is for men to work together. I returned to my community, joined a men's team, and felt tears of joy as my teammates and I watched 240 new men complete their own weekend initiation. One of the men was my third son, Evan.

I had suggested that Evan attend the Sterling Men's Weekend because, like so many men, he felt disconnected from the source of his own power. He was a successful man, with a wife and three children, but something was missing. There seemed to be a hole in his soul, and his self-esteem, self-acceptance, and self-love were shaky. "I try and do all the right things," he told me, "but I don't think I really know what a man is. My self-worth rises and falls depending on how those I care about feel about me."

I see that a lot with men today. They look good on the outside, but they feel that some essence of manhood is missing in them. Most have grown up without caring, involved fathers in their lives. Few of them have had the opportunity to be mentored by an older adult male. They long for what has been lost. "Such hungry sons hang around older men like the homeless do around a soup kitchen," says author and poet Robert Bly. "Like the homeless, they feel shame over their condition, and it is nameless, bitter, unexpungeable shame."[13]

It is the shame that often keeps men isolated. Yet one that can be overcome as men take the risk to reach out to each other and find strength in our roots. Even though we may not have had a good connection with our fathers or grandfathers, there is still wisdom we can draw from our ancestors.

The Wisdom of the Ancestors and Return of Indigenous Elders

"When we trace back our lineage far enough, we find that all human beings come from tribal or indigenous roots," says Malidoma Patrice Somé, a modern day elder with roots that reach back to his native Dagara tribe in West Africa.[14]

"Each of us still carries in our very bones the deep memory of those roots and an innate understanding of the need for ritual within a thriving village community," says Somé.[15]

I first met Somé, whose name he told me means "be friends with the stranger," in a small town in California, a block from the church where we held the service for my mother following her death. The call of the ancestors was on my mind when I joined him and his wife Sobonfu for a weekend experience in ritual community. During the time we were in community together, I learned about the necessity of joining the first and second halves of our lives as we join the wisdom of the indigenous and modern worlds.

Somé is a midlife man who is well-versed in the two worlds. Having grown up in the lap of his grandfather, a powerful tribal elder, his life was to radically change at a very young age. "When I was four years old," Somé remembers, "my childhood and my parents were taken from me when I was literally kidnapped from my home by a French Jesuit missionary who had befriended my father."[16]

"For the next fifteen years I was in a boarding school, far away from my family, and forced to learn about the white man's reality." At the age of twenty, Somé escaped and returned to his village after a treacherous journey through the jungle. After sixteen years, no one remembered him except his mother. "I no longer fit into the tribal community," Somé remembers. "I risked my life to undergo the Dagara initiation and thereby return to my people." His initiation, rather than bringing him back to stay in his native home, confirmed his true destiny—to be a bridge between the old world and the new world.[17]

Somé returned to the West to complete his education: a doctorate in political science from the Sorbonne in Paris and a Ph.D. in literature from Brandeis University in Boston. "So I am a man of two worlds," Somé concludes, "trying to be at home in both of them—a difficult task at best."[18]

Somé's journey is one all men at this time of life are being asked to make, each in his own way. We all need to integrate the two halves of our own lives, as well as the ancient and modern worlds of which we are a part. Somé offers powerful support for this rite of passage.

"You've first got to look at the two cultures as two sides of the same coin," says Somé. "Each side needs the other in order to be itself. The modern world is overinflated with materialism, whereas Africa has suffered greatly from colonial imperialism. One of their major challenges is day-to-day survival, due to famine and ecological imbalance. In my village, I once heard a starving man say, 'My hunger can be traced to someone who has overeaten somewhere.'"[19]

For those of us moving through the Menopause Passage, we must now pay attention to the spiritual hunger of Second Adulthood, otherwise the material hunger of First Adulthood will consume us. This shift from the material to the spiritual seems to have been necessary for people throughout human history. Yet each of us moves through our lives within a particular historical context. The social reality our parents and grandparents had to deal with was vastly different from the one we face today.

There are two major challenges that are unique to those of us moving through the Male Menopause Passage as we approach the end of the twentieth century. First, we must recognize that our disconnection from the earth, each other, and ourselves has created a crisis that is endangering the survival of the human species. Whether we prosper or perish will likely be decided by the actions we undertake over the next fifty years.

Second, we now know that it is possible to live the second half of life with the health and vitality of the first. Those of us who are between the ages of forty-five and sixty have within our power to live productive lives of service until we are ninety to 120 years old. Think what we could do with those years if men didn't just get older, but went through an initiation that could tap into the wisdom of our ancestors.

"Initiation," says Malidoma Somé, "gives you a clear direction for your life by confirming the purpose you have set for yourself prior to being born. The initiation process makes it clear to your psyche that your life is worth living for that ideal. Needless to say, if you don't get it then, something within you begins to rattle. And it turns you into a rather unstable person who is extremely temperamental and probably driven to excess."[20]

One of the most powerful expressions of what happens to modern men who are not initiated is given by the playwright, Eugene O'Neill. In his autobiographical work, *A Long Day's Journey into Night*, he comes to grips with his slide into addiction and loss of manhood that so many men experience today.

"It was a great mistake, my being born a man. I would have been much more successful as a sea gull or a fish. As it is, I will always be a stranger who never feels at home, who does not really want and is not really wanted, who can never belong, who must always be a little in love with death."[21]

This is one view of what lies ahead in Second Adulthood. It is the view that accepts Monster Boy Masculinity as our model for manhood and Peter Pan as our guide to old age. However, there is another option open to us. The Male Menopause Passage is an opportunity to begin an initiation into a different kind of manhood, one that is modeled after the man your ancestors always wanted you to be and guided by mentors like Bill Kauth, Justin Sterling, and Malidoma Somé.

The man initiated in this way might paraphrase O'Neill by proclaiming to the world:

"It was a great gift, my being born a man. I am a highly successful brother to the sea gull and the fish. As it is, I will always be a partner connected to my home, who truly wants to serve, and whose service is truly wanted, who will forever belong, and who must always be a little in love with life."

Chapter 10 Notes

1. J. M. Barrie, *Peter Pan* (London: Samuel French, Inc., 1928), 9–10.

2. David Gutmann, *Reclaimed Powers: Toward a New Psychology of Men and Women in Later Life* (New York: Basic Books, 1987), 7.

3. Recounted in Simone de Beauvoir, *The Coming of Age* (New York: G. P. Putnam's Sons, 1972), 77.

4. Iyanla Vanzant, *The Spirit of a Man: A Vision of Transformation for Black Men and the Women Who Love Them* (New York: HarperCollins, 1996), 34.

5. Ibid., 33.

6. Ibid., 35.

7. Ibid., 34.

8. Donna Minkowitz, "In the Name of the Father," *Ms.*, November–December 1995, 64.

9. Ibid., 67.

10. Quoted in Minkowitz, 67.

11. Minkowitz, 67.

12. Ibid., 68.

13. Robert Bly, *Iron John: A Book about Men* (New York: Addison-Wesley, 1990), 94.

14. Malidoma and Sobonfu Somé, workshop presentation, Fairfax, Calif., 14 November 1995.

15. Ibid.

16. Malidoma Patrice Somé, *Of Water and the Spirit: Ritual, Magic, and Initiation in the Life of African Shaman* (New York: G. P. Putnam's Sons, 1994), 2.

17. Ibid., 2–3.

18. Ibid., 3.

19. Malidoma Patrice Somé, "Ambassador of the Ancestors: An Interview with Malidoma Somé," interview by Virginia Lee in *Common Ground*, Fall 1996, 144.

20. Ibid.

21. Eugene O'Neill, *Long Day's Journey into Night* (New Haven, CT: Yale University Press, 1989), 153–54.

Epilogue

With the book nearly finished, I am taking a break to reflect on the past and the future. When I began to write *Male Menopause* in 1993, I thought I had a pretty good idea of what I wanted to say. But, like a child who has its own wisdom, the book took on its own character as it grew. I had thought, for instance, that male menopause and female menopause were vastly different and there would be no need to talk to women about what was going on during their changes of life. The book quickly told me I was wrong. There is much in this book I had not expected to find when I began. There is much more that has not yet been discovered.

Since things are changing rapidly, I have tried to give you the most up-to-date information I could find. There are three additional resources I have provided that I hope you will find useful:

1. A full index so you can locate and review topics of particular interest to you.

2. A complete bibliography of the books, magazines, and journals I used to develop information for *Male Menopause*.

3. A resource section of people and organizations that may be helpful on your journey.

If you learn of new resources, I would like to hear from you. I am putting together a directory of professionals who specialize in providing services to those going through the Male Menopause Passage. If you offer such services and would like to be included, please send me information on your work.

As with any new field of study, there will be a host of "leading experts" who will want to tell you what to do to live longer and healthier as you move through the Male Menopause Passage. I suggest you listen to those who make sense to you, but look to your inner healers for ultimate wisdom.

As one of my mentors, Sir Laurens van der Post, reminds us: "The age of the leaders has come and gone. Every man must be his own leader now. You must remove your projection, and contain the spirit of the time in your own life and your own nature, because to go the old way and follow your leader is a form of psychological imprisonment."[1]

My wife, Carlin, attended a protest vigil in a town just north of us. She and other friends from the community went in support of some of the last old growth redwoods alive on the face of the planet. These old trees have a lot to teach us, and whether they are allowed to live out their full life span may tell us something about our own prospects for the future.

Living among big trees, I find I often go to them for their wisdom. They have a way of connecting with my core. If I am able to be a mentor to those younger than me, it is because I have elders who share their wisdom so I can pass it on. The trees are my elders, and I honor their spirit as my family and friends do their best to save them from those who would kill them before their time. There are not many elders left. We would do well to listen to those few who remain.

The old ones also mentor my friend Joseph Jastrab, a longtime naturalist and wilderness guide. "I find myself walking the same wooded trails over and over again," Joseph tells me. "This allows me frequent visits with a few trees with whom I've become closely acquainted. I watch how they handle themselves in the wind, admire their steadfast grounding in the earth, the strength and flexibility of trunk and limb. Through it all, they stand.

"They invite me to do likewise. I waver. I want 'to keep my options open.' I can imagine no envy in them for my ability to wander across the earth in search of my place. None whom I've met have given me the slightest inclination that they would trade places with me. That's the thing about trees, they don't trade places. They belong. They live forever at home."

If there is anything I have learned writing this book, it is that each of us is a special being, and each must find the place where we belong. Each passage we move through has the ability to free us to be more fully ourselves, to know our purpose, and discover our place in the community of all spirits.

As Joseph says, the trees are "elders that return me to myself during times when fear causes me to forget. Everything about these beings suggests I will have to belong to somewhere, to something, to someone before I will be truly free, fully belong."

The Male Menopause Passage teaches us that we are both elders and youngsters, teachers and students. Beyond the experts, before the leaders, were the trees. I offer you these final words from my friend and fellow tree-brother, Joseph Jastrab. May they serve to guide you as they have me as we face our past and open to our future:

"Trees die at home. They fall on the very same ground that gave rise to their birth. Like the king of ancient times who offered himself as sacrifice so his blood would renew the soil and thus insure a healthy crop to feed his people, trees follow their generative destiny to the end.

"The sight of a young, green sapling growing from the body of one of its elders always gives me pause for reflection. I am both the sapling that grows from the sacrifice of those who have come before me, and I am the elder for those whose experience reflects a lighter shade of green than mine. What have I gained from my ancestors; from all the life that has come before me? What do I have to give to the unborn?

"Somewhere, in the silence between these two questions, is the truth of who I am, and the possibility of freedom."[2]

Epilogue Notes

1. A conversation with Sir Laurens van der Post, in New Dimensions, October-December, 1994.

2. Quotes from Joseph Jastrab are from a conversation with Joseph Jastrab and written in Wingspan: Journal of the Male Spirit, August 1996.

Resources
Bibliography
Index

Resources

Organizations for Support and Networking

Many of the World Wide Web addresses in this section can be accessed directly from the *Male Menopause* website at www.malemenopause.com.

Aging
National Institute on Aging
800-222-2225 (8:30–5 EST)

AIDS
National CDC HIV/AIDS Hotline
800-342-2437 (24-hour hotline)

Alternative Medicine
Office of Alternative Medicine
U. S. Government
9000 Rockville Pike
Building 51, Room 5B-37
Mailstop 2182
Betheseda, MD 29892
888-644-6226 (8:30–5 EST)

American Holistic Medical Association
6728 Old McLean Village Drive
McLean, VA 22101

Physicians Committee for Responsible Medicine
5100 Wisconsin Ave. NW, Suite 404
Washington, DC 20016
202-686-2210

Alzheimer's Disease
Alzheimer's Association
800-272-3900 (8–5 CST)

Arthritis
Arthritis Foundation
800-283-7800 (24-hour recording)

Cancer
American Cancer Society
800-227-2345 (24-hour recording)

Career Management
The Venture Hill Project's Career Management Group
PO Box 9568
Santa Rosa, CA 95405-1568
707-526-7441
email: hlagarde@wco.com

Developed by Howard LaGarde, this project operates from a context of "Lives Well Lived" and supports men (and women) in developing careers that balance personal, interpersonal, and planetary needs.

Cosmetic/Reconstructive Surgery
American Society of Plastic and Reconstructive Surgeons
800-635-0635 (8:30–4:30 CST)

Drugs/Alcohol

National Clearinghouse for Alcohol and Drug Information
800-729-6686 (8–7 EST)

Ecology and Cultural Renewal

Museletter
Richard Heinberg
1433 Olivet Rd.
Santa Rosa, CA 95401
707-542-5452
website: www.igc.org/museletter
email: rheinberg@igc.org

A wonderful monthly newsletter for $15 per year (12 issues) that explores the roots of our heritage back to hunter/gatherer times and offers hopeful alternatives for the future.

Environment and Health

Environmental Health Clearinghouse
800-643-4794 (9–8 EST)

Eyes

National Eye Institute
301-496-5248 (8:30–5 EST)

Grandparenting

Foundation for Grandparenting
7 Avenida Visto Grande
Suite B7-160
Santa Fe, NM 87505
www.grandparenting.org

Hearing

National Institute on Deafness and Other Communication Disorders
800-241-1044 (8:30–5 EST)

Heart

American Heart Association
800-AHA-USAI (8:30–4:30 local time)

Herbal Information

California School of Herbal Studies
James Green and James Snow Codirectors
PO Box 39
Forestville, CA 95436
707-887-7457

James Green who is author of *The Male Herbal* has also written the *Herbal Medicine-Makers Handbook*.

Incontinence

The Simon Foundation for Continence
800-237-4666 (24-hours)

Jed Diamond

Jed Diamond, Director
Third Age Wellness Center
34133 Shimmins Ridge Rd.
Willits, CA 95490
email: jedd1221@aol.com
website: www.thirdagewellness.com

Information on other books, booklets, tapes, seminars, and trainings by Jed Diamond; updated information on male menopause and men; programs for people in the Third Age of Life (40+).

Life Enhancement Information and Products

Arbonne International
15 Argonaut
Aliso Viejo, CA 92656
800-ARBONNE
949-837-8415
FAX: 949-770-2610

email: customerservicearbonne.com
website: www.arbonne.com

Arbonne International offers premium, Swiss-formulated skin care, beauty, and personal care products. Arbonne features an expanding line of nutrition products based on the latest advances in science and nutrition. Arbonne has twenty years of experience providing products that are pure, safe, beneficial, and unparalleled in quality, integrity, and effectiveness.

Smart Publications Update
PO Box 4667
Petaluma, CA 94955
707-769-8308
FAX: 707-763-3944
website: www.smart-publications.com

The Smart Publications Update is stuffed with valuable information on how to take the next steps toward a healthier, fuller life including: where to obtain the nutritional supplements discussed in this book and other articles you may find of great interest and value. Contact them for a free copy and please mention Jed Diamond so they know you were referred by me.

Longevity and Health

American Academy of Anti-Aging Medicine
1341 W. Fullerton, Suite 111
Chicago, IL 60614
773-528-4333
FAX: 773-528-5390
email: A4M@worldhealth.net
website: www.worldhealth.net

Longevity Institute International
89 Valley Rd.
Montclair, NJ 07042
973-746-3533
FAX: 201-746-4385

Lung

American Lung Association
800-LUNG-USA (9–4:30 EST)

Medication

Center for Drug Evaluation and Research
301-827-4573 (8–4:30 EST)

Men's Health

Will Courtenay, Ph.D., LCSW
Men's Health Consulting
2811 College Avenue, Suite 1
Berkeley, CA 94705-2165
800-WELL-MEN
FAX: 415-453-6599
email: courtenay@menshealth.org
website: www.menshealth.org

Men's Health Network
Ronald K. Henry, Esq., Director
310 D Street, N.E.
Washington, DC 20002
202-543-6461
email: mensnet@capaccess.org

Men's Health Doctors

Stephen Auerbach, M.D.
400 Newport Center Dr., Suite 501
Newport Beach, CA 92660
949-644-7200
FAX: 949-644-7937

Terry A. Kupers, M.D.
#8 Wildwood Avenue
Oakland, CA 94610
510-654-8333
email: kupers@igc.apc.org

The Male Health Center
Kenneth A. Goldberg, M.D.
5744 LBJ Freeway, Suite 100
Dallas, TX 75240
972-490-MALE

Marshall E. Noel, M.S., M.D.
Canterbury Women's Health Care & California
    Endometriosis Institute
5677 N. Fresno, Suite 101
Fresno, CA 93710
209-432-5677

Stephen B. Strum, M.D.
Healing Touch Oncology
Specializing in Prostate Cancer
9808 Venice Blvd., Suite 503
Culver City, CA 90232
310-827-7707

Donald C. Thompson, Ph.D., M.D.
Whole Person Medicine
1121 West 1st North St.
Morristown, TN 37816
423-581-6367

TotalCare Medical Center
Alan P. Brauer, M.D.
630 University Avenue
Palo Alto, CA 94301
650-329-8001

Finding a Knowledgeable Doctor in Your Area

Male menopause is still a new specialty. In addition to those doctors listed above, you may want to contact a doctor who is a member of the International College of Advanced Longevity Medicine (ICALM) or the American College for Advancement in Medicine (ACAM). All members of these professional organizations are skilled and knowledgeable in the prescription and use of natural hormones and other alternative compounds.

For a referral, contact:

ICALM
1407-B North Wells St.
Chicago, IL 60610
888-855-5050
FAX: 708-579-3097

ACAM
23121 Verdugo Dr., Suite 204
Laguna Hills, CA 92653
800-532-3688
website: www.acam.org

Men's Initiation and Mentoring

New Warrior Network
Drury Heffernan
New Warrior Network
Box 230
Malone, NY 12953-0230
800-870-4611
email: dhnwmtl@aol.com

An order of men called to reclaim the sacred masculine for our time, through initiation, training, and action in the world.

Sterling Institute of Relationship
695 Rand Avenue
Oakland, CA 94610
510-836-1400

Dedicated to transforming the quality of people's relationships to produce the partnership and the context necessary for the transition to a true global community.

Men's Issues

Men's Rights, Inc. (MR Inc.)
Fred Hayward, Executive Director
Box 163180
Sacramento, CA 95816
916-484-7333

A nonprofit corporation that raises public awareness about all men's issues. Their egalitarian philosophy is: equal rights for men and women...no exceptions.

National Organization of Circumcision Information Resource Centers
PO Box 2512
San Anselmo, CA 94979-2512
415-488-9883

Provides the most accurate and up-to-date information on the effects of circumcision on males. Sponsors international conferences on both male and female circumcision worldwide.

National Organization to Halt the Abuse and Routine Mutilation of Males (NOHARMM)
PO Box 460795
San Francisco, CA 94146
415-826-9351

A national, non-violent direct-action network of men organized against routine infant circumcision.

Men/Fathers Hotline
512-472-3237

A crisis line for men and fathers

Wingspan: Journal of the Male Spirit
414-695-8815

An international quarterly journal with wide-ranging focus on various aspects of the men's movement.

Men's Resources on the World Wide Web
General Information:
MenWeb
www.vix.com/menmag

MenWeb features interviews with best-selling authors, insightful articles, men's stories, poems, and a wealth of information on men's growth and personal development. Website for *Men's*

Voices, successor to *M.E.N. Magazine*, the content is wide-ranging but also has a "men's movement" and Jungian focus. Areas on fathers, relationships, fathering, men's groups, and other topics.

Men's Issues Page
www.vix.com/pub/men/index.html

An encyclopedic index of men's issues resources. The most complete index and archive of men's articles, issues, organizations, books, and resources.

Menstuff, The National Men's Resource
www.menstuff.org

A calendar listing international, national, and regional men's conferences, workshops, and gatherings.

Started in 1982 by Gordon Clay, they have the most complete calendar of men's events in the country. They list over 2,600 men's services and 1,700 books broken down by 60 major categories.

Manhood Online (Australia)
www.hothouse.com.au/hotworksmanhoodonline.htm

This site centers on the work of Steve Biddulph, author of Australian bestseller *Manhood*. Their "Manzine" has lots of interesting articles. The site also serves as a coordinating point for Men's Work around Australia. A calendar listing national and regional men's events and a resource catalog round out the offerings.

Crisis, Grief, and Healing: Men and Women
www.webhealing.com

This is a place men and women can browse to understand and honor the many different paths to heal strong emotions. It has a special emphasis on how men often grieve differently. Tom Golden, LCSW of Washington, DC, is an internationally known psychotherapist, author, and speaker on the topic of healing from loss.

M.A.L.E: Men Assisting, Leading and Educating
www.malesurvivor.org

M.A.L.E. is dedicated to helping male survivors of sexual abuse to heal.

Vietnam Veterans Page
www.vietvet.org/index.htm

This is an interactive online forum for Vietnam veterans and their families and friends to exchange information, stories, poems, songs, art, pictures, and experiences in any publishable form.

Health Information:

The Male Health Center
www.malehealthcenter.com

The Male Health Center in Dallas, Texas, founded by Dr. Ken Goldberg has an excellent website on important aspects of male health.

CaP CURE: The Association for the Cure of Cancer of the Prostate
www.capcure.org

The Association for the Cure of Cancer of the Prostate, CaP CURE, is a nonprofit public charity dedicated to finding a cure for prostate cancer by rapidly funding promising basic and clinical research.

Prostatitis Home Page
www.msn.fullfeed.com/prosfnd

An excellent resource concerning prostatitis and other problems associated with the prostate gland, sponsored by the Prostatitis Foundation.

University of Michigan Prostate Cancer Home Page
www.cancer.med.umich.edu/prostcan/prostcan.html

A professional prostate cancer resource page.

Conditions Men Get, Too (US FDA Page)
www.fda.gov/fdac/features/695_men.html

Describes how men are affected by osteoporosis, breast cancer, and eating disorders—diseases traditionally thought of as "women's diseases."

Circumcision Information and Resource Pages
www.cirp.org/CIRP

The Circumcision Information and Resource Pages provide information about all aspects of the genital surgery known as circumcision. The Circumcision Reference Library contains technical material, medical and historical articles, and statistics. The Circumcision Information Pages contain a more readable collection of information, suitable for parents and educators. This site also has links to information on the rights of the child, religious issues, and related issues.

Fathering Information:

Fathering Magazine
www.fathermag.com

An online magazine of articles, information, and links for fathers.

FatherNet
www.cyfc.umn.edu/fathernet

FatherNet has a wide range of articles for fathers and research and policy papers going back to 1991. It also has the electronic continuation of Family Re-Union III: The Role of Men in Children's Lives, a national conference on family policy moderated by Vice President Al Gore and cosponsored by the Consortium and the Tennessee Department of Human Services.

National Center for Fathering
www.fathers.com

Today's Father magazine provides an online presence and a wealth of tips and information on fathering. The mission of the National Center for Fathering is to inspire men to be better fathers and to develop practical resources to prepare dads for nearly every fathering situation.

The Divorce Page
www.divorcesupport.com

Dean Hughson has put together an excellent Web page on the emotional, practical, and legal problems that come up for men in divorce. It also has practical advice (e.g., how to sleep, eating well, cheap airline tickets to see the kids) and many valuable links.

Fathers' Rights and Equity Exchange (F.R.E.E.)
www.vix.com/pub/free/index.html

F.R.E.E.'s Director, Anne Mitchell, herself a single parent, is a 1992 graduate of Stanford Law School, a member of the California bar, and has been a fathers' rights advocate since 1987. F.R.E.E.'s Advisory Board includes author Dr. Warren Farrell, and author/journalists Asa Baber and Cathy Young.

United Fathers Forum
www.enol.com/~uff/uff.htm

Information on legislation and resources related to fathers' rights.

Men's Organizations:

Men's Rights, Inc.
www.mens-rights.org

Men's Rights, Inc. was founded by Fredric Hayward. It sponsors a Men's Rights ERA Project, "Equal rights for men and women...no exceptions," headed by Dave Ault in Seattle.

National Coalition of Free Men
www.ncfm.org

The National Coalition of Free Men (NCFM) is a nonprofit educational organization that examines the way sex discrimination affects men. It also tries to raise public consciousness about little-known, but important topics dealing with the male experience. In addition NCFM sponsors a variety of "men's rights" projects.

New Warrior Network
www.nwn.org

New Warrior offers opportunities for men to experience male initiation so that they can become mentors to younger men.

Metamorphosis: Transformation in Action
www.nom.org/pubs/mmorph

A book of men's stories, poems, photography, and art that reflects the lives of many of the members of The Nation of Men, a San Francisco Bay-area confederation of men's groups.

Certified Male Magazine (Australia)
www.pnc.com.au/~pvogel/cm

Certified Male is a journal of men's issues, published in Australia as a forty page magazine. Topics covered include men's stories, men's rights, masculism, men and feminism, the men's movement, men's groups, fathers and fathering, parenting, boys' education, men's health, domestic violence, gender, relationships, family law, divorce, child support and custody, sexuality, discrimination, sex roles, gender politics, and many other issues examined from a male perspective.

Websites for Regional Men's Centers:

Florida Men's Resource Site
www.wp.com/floridamenssite

Sponsored by the Orlando Men's Council. Created by James Bracewell, executive assistant forum manager of the Men's Forum on The Microsoft Network.

Vancouver (Canada) M.E.N.
www.netlegal.com/vancouvermen

Vancouver Men's Evolvement Network: Men supporting each other through life's journey.

Nation of Men
www.nom.org

The Nation of Men is devoted to supporting men, men's teams, and community. Hosted by the South Bay (San Francisco Bay Area) chapter, one of three active NOM chapters. Their site also hosts the online version of their book *Metamorphosis: Transformation in Action*, mentioned earlier.

Menopause

Menopause Access Hotline
800-222-4767 (For Information)

Mental Health

Grief Recovery Helpline
800-445-4808 (9–5 PST)

National Institute of Mental Health
301-443-4513 (8:30-4:30 EST)

Mind/Body Healing

Mind/Body Medical Institute
110 Francis Street
Boston, MA 02215
617-632-9525

Founded and directed by Herbert Benson, M.D., the Institute offers information and resources on mind/body healing.

Neurological Disorders

National Institute of Neurological Disorders and Stroke
301-496-5751 (8:30–5 EST)

Nutrition and Health

EarthSave
Box 68
Santa Cruz, CA 95062
502-589-7676

Founded by John Robbins, EarthSave promotes the benefits of plant-based food choices for optimal health, environmental preservation, and a more compassionate world.

American Dietetic Association Nutrition Hotline
800-366-1655 (experts: 9–4 CST; recording: 8–8 CST)

Osteoporsosis

National Osteoporosis Foundation
202-223-2226 (8:30–5:30 EST)

Parenting

National Institute of Child Health and Human Development
301-496-5133 (8–5 EST)

Pheromones

Athena Institute for Women's Wellness
Winnifred Cutler, Ph.D., President
610-827-2200

PMS (Pre-Menstrual Syndrome)

PMS Access
800-222-4767 (For information)
800-558-7046 (For referrals to physicians in your area 9–5 CST)

Prostate

The Prostatitis Foundation

This nonprofit group, formed by men frustrated with their treatment, has been lobbying Congress, organizing researchers, and disseminating information. The foundation offers the following resources:

Prostatitis Information Packet. For $2, you will receive a packet of information, including a lab-test worksheet that is very helpful in getting a proper diagnosis. Foundation Membership. For a $25 tax-deductible donation, you will receive a year of research updates. Write to:

The Prostatitis Foundation
Information Distribution Center
Parkway Business Center, 2929 Ireland Grove Rd.
Bloomington, IL 61704

Internet Newsgroup. You can join a supportive group of men exchanging the latest information on prostatitis by subscribing to sci.men.prostate.prostatis.

Us-Too International
1010 Jorie Blvd., Suite 124
Oak Brook, IL 60521
800-808-7866

This prostate-cancer support network boasts more than 440 groups throughout America.

National Prostate Cancer Coalition, Inc.
3709 W. Jetton Avenue
Tampa, FL 33629

Rare Diseases

National Organization for Rare Disorders
800-999-6673 (9–5 EST; 24-hour recording)

Stroke

American Heart Association Stroke Connection
800-553-6321 (8:30–5 CST)

Urologic Disorders

American Foundation for Urologic Disease
300 W. Pratt St., Suite 401
Baltimore, MD 21201
410-468-1800 (8:30–5 EST)

Wellness

Ardell Wellness Report
Don Ardell, Ph.D., Publisher
345 Bayshore Blvd., #414
Tampa, FL 33606
813-251-4567
donardell@earthlink.net

Readers can obtain a sample copy by sending a SASE and $.55 postage to this address.

Women's Health

Mind/Body Health Sciences, Inc.
Joan Borysenko, M.D., Director
393 Dixon Rd.
Boulder, CO 80302
303-440-8460

Dr. Christiane Northrup's Health Wisdom for Women Newsletter
Phillips Publishing, Inc.
7811 Montrose Rd.
Potomac, MD 20897-5924
800-804-0935

Women's Health Advocate Newsletter
PO Box 420235
Palm Coast, FL 32142-0235
800-829-5876

Women's International Pharmacy
Wallace L. Simons, R.Ph., Director
Natural hormone therapy by prescription only.
800-279-5708

Women's Health Watch
164 Longwood Ave.
Boston, MA 02115
800-829-5921

A newsletter of information for enlightened choices from the Harvard Medical School.

Please let us know if there are changes we need to make in this list or other resources that should be added in future editions.
Send to:
Jed Diamond
34133 Shimmins Ridge Rd.
Willits, CA 95490

Bibliography

Abraham, I. L., and H. V. Krowchuk. "Unemployment and Health: Health Promotion for the Jobless Male." *Nursing Clinics of North America* 21, no. I (1986): 37–47.

Abramson, Paul R., and Steven D. Pinkerton. *With Pleasure: Thoughts on the Nature of Human Sexuality.* New York: Oxford University Press, 1995.

"The Aging Male: Can Hormones Help?" *Harvard University's Men's Health Watch* I, no. 12 (July 1997): 1+.

Aldercreutz, H. "Western Diet and Western Diseases: Some Hormonal and Biochemical Mechanisms and Associations." *Scandinavian Journal of Clinical Laboratory Investigation* 50, Supp. 201 (1990): 3–23.

Altman, R. *The Prostate Answer Book.* New York: Warner Books, 1993.

American Cancer Society. *Cancer Facts and Figures: 1994.* Atlanta: American Cancer Society, 1994.

———. *Cancer Prevention Study 11: Fact Card.* Atlanta: American Cancer Society, 1988.

———. *Cancer: What You Eat Could Put You at Risk.* Atlanta: American Cancer Society, 1993.

American Heart Association. *Heart and Stroke Facts.* Dallas: American Heart Association, 1994.

American School Health Association. *The National Adolescent Student Health Survey: A Report on the Health of America's Youth.* Oakland, CA: Third Party Publishing, 1989.

Anderson, B. A. "Male Age and Fertility—Results From Ireland Prior to 1911." *Pop. Index* 41 (1975): 561–66.

Anderson, Barrie, M.D. et al. *The Menopause Book.* New York: Hawthorn Books, 1977.

Andres, R., D. Muller, and J. D. Sorkin. "Long-Term Effects of Change in Body Weight on All-Cause Mortality." *Annals of Internal Medicine* 119, no. 7, (1993): 737–43.

Annest, J. L. et al. "National Estimates of Nonfatal Firearm-Related Injuries: Beyond the Tip of the Iceberg." *JAMA* 273, no. 22 (1995): 1749–55.

Antonucci, T. C., and H. Akiyama. "An Examination of Sex Differences in Social Support among Older Men and Women." *Sex Roles* 17, no. 11/12 (1987): 737–49.

Ardell, Donald B. *High Level Wellness: An Alternative to Doctors, Drugs and Disease.* Berkeley, CA: Ten Speed Press, 1986.

Armstrong, B. et al. "Diet and Reproductive Hormones: A Study of Vegetarian and Non-Vegetarian Postmenopausal Women." *Journal of the National Cancer Institute* 67 (1981): 761–67.

Arrien, Angeles. *The Four-Fold Way: Walking the Paths of the Warrior, Teacher, Healer and Visionary.* San Francisco: Harper San Francisco, 1993.

Bagatelli, C. J., and W. J. Bremner. "Androgens in Men—Uses and Abuses." *Drug Therapy* 334 (1996): 707–14.

Baker, Carolyn. "The Hag and the Dark Feminine: An Interview with Carolyn Baker." By Bert H. Hoff. *M.E.N. Magazine,* October 1996.

Baker, H. W. G. et al. "Changes in the Pituitary Testicular System with Age." *Clinical Endocrinology* 5 (1976): 349–72.

Balswick, J. O., and C. Peek. "The Inexpressive Male: A Tragedy of American Society." *Family Coordinator* 20 (1971): 363–68.

Barbach, Lonnie. *The Pause: Positive Approaches to Menopause.* New York: Signet, 1994.

Barnard, Neal, M.D. *Eat Right, Live Longer.* New York: Harmony Books, 1995.

Barrett-Coonor, E., K. T. Khaw, and S. S. Yen. "A Prospective Study of Dehydroepiandrosterone Sulfate, Mortality and Cardiovascular Disease." *New England Journal of Medicine* 315 (1986): 1519–24.

Barrie, J. M. *Peter Pan.* London: Samuel French, Inc., 1928.

Barry, Dave. *Dave Barry Turns 40.* New York: Fawcett, 1990.

Bartecchi, C. E., T. D. MacKenzie, and R. W. Schrier. "The Global Tobacco Epidemic." *Scientific American,* May 1995, 44+.

Bartlik, Barbara, M.D., and Helen Singer Kaplan, M.D., Ph.D. Introduction to *The Hormone of Desire: The Truth about Sexuality, Menopause, and Testosterone,* by Susan Rako, M.D. New York: Harmony Books, 1996.

Batten, Mary. *Sexual Strategies: How Females Choose Their Mates.* New York: G. P. Putnam's Sons, 1992.

Beavam, Colin, and Anita Leclerc. "Pssst—Wanna Feel Young Again?" *Esquire,* June 1996, 50+.

Belloc, N. B. "Relationship of Health Practices and Mortality." *Preventive Medicine* 2 (1973): 67–81.

Belloc, N. B., and L. Breslow. "Relationship of Physical Health Status and Health Practices." *Preventive Medicine* I (1972): 409–21.

Bendvold, E. "Semen Quality in Norwegian Men over a 20 Year Period." *International Journal of Fertility* 34 (1989): 401–4.

Benson, Herbert. *The Relaxation Response.* New York: William Morrow, 1975.

Benson, Herbert, and Marg Stark. *Timeless Healing: The Power and Biology of Belief.* New York: Scribner, 1996.

Benton, D. et al. "The Impact of Long-Term Vitamin Supplementation on Cognitive Functioning." *Psychopharmacology* 117 (1995): 298–305.

Berger, Richard, M.D. "New Name, Treatments for Impotence." *Health News* 2, no. 17 (1996): 3+.

Berkman, L. F. "Assessing the Physical Health Effects of Social Networks and Social Support." *Annual Review of Public Health* 5 (1984): 413–32.

Berkman, L. F., and L. Breslow, eds. *Health and Ways of Living: The Alameda County Study.* New York: Oxford University Press, 1983.

Berkman, L. F., L. Breslow, and D. Wingard. "Health Practices and Mortality Risk." In *Health and Ways of Living,* edited by L. F. Berkman and L. Breslow. New York: Oxford University Press, 1983.

Berlan, J. "Case of the Falling Sperm Count." *National Review,* June 1995, 45+.

Berlin, J. A., and G. A. Colditz. "A Meta-Analysis of Physical Activity in the Prevention of Coronary Heart Disease." *American Journal of Epidemiology* 132 (1990): 612–28.

Berman, Morris. *Coming to Our Senses: Body and Spirit in the Hidden History of the West.* New York: Bantam Books, 1990.

Bhasin, S. et al. "The Effects of Supraphysiologic Doses of Testosterone on Muscle Size and Strength in Normal Men." *New England Journal of Medicine* 335 (1996): 1–7.

Biesele, Megan. *Women Like Meat: The Folklore and Foraging Ideology of the Kalahari Ju/'hoan.* Bloomington, IN: University of Indiana Press, 1993.

Birkenhager-Gillesse, E. G., J. Derkson, and A. M. Lagaay. "Dehydroepi-androsterone Sulphate (DHEAS) in the Oldest, Old, Aged 85 and Over." *Annals of the New York Academy of Sciences* 719 (1994): 543–52.

Bishop, D.T. et al. "The Effect of Nutritional Factors on Sex Hormone Levels in Male Twins." *Genetic Epidemiology* 5 (1988): 43–59.

Blair, A. et al. "Physical Fitness and All-Cause Mortality: A Prospective Study of Healthy Men and Women." *JAMA* 262, no. 17 (1989): 2395–401.

Blair, S. N. et al. "Body Weight Change, All-Cause Mortality, and Cause-Specific Mortality in the Multiple Risk Factor Intervention Trial." *Annals of Internal Medicine* 119, no. 7, (1993): 749–57.

Blankenhorn, David. *Fatherless America: Confronting Our Most Urgent Social Problem.* New York: Basic Books, 1995.

Blazer, D. G. "Social Support and Mortality in an Elderly Community Population." *American Journal of Epidemiology* 115, no. 5 (1982): 684–94.

Block, G., W. F. Rosenberger, and B. H. Patterson. "Calories, Fat and Cholesterol: Intake Patterns in the U. S. Population by Race, Sex, and Age." *American Journal of Public Health* 78, no. 9 (1988): 1150–55.

Block, Will. "Answers and Questions." *Life Enhancement,* March 1997, 27.

Bly, Robert. *Iron John: A Book about Men.* New York: Addison-Wesley, 1990.

———. *The Sibling Society.* Reading, MA: Addison-Wesley, 1996.

———. "The Gifts of Growing Old: An Interview with Robert Bly." *Utne Reader,* May-June 1996, 58+.

Boor, M. "Relationships between Unemployment Rates and Suicide Rates in Eight Countries, 1962–1976." *Psychological Reports* 47 (1980): 1095–101.

Booth, A., and J. M. Dabbs. "Testosterone and Men's Marriages." *Social Forces* 72 (1993): 463–77.

Booth, A. et al. "Testosterone, and Winning and Losing in Human Competition." *Hormones & Behavior* 23 (1989): 556–71.

Borek, Carmia, Ph.D. *Maximize Your Health Span with Antioxidants.* New Canaan, CT: Keats Publishing, 1995.

Bortz, Walter M., II, M.D. *Dare to Be 100.* New York: Fireside, 1996.

Borysenko, Joan. *Minding the Body, Mending the Mind.* New York: Addison-Wesley, 1987.

———. *A Woman's Book of Life: The Biology, Psychology, and Sprituality of the Feminine Life Cycle.* New York: Riverhead Books, 1996.

Bostofte, E., J. Serup, and H. Rebbe. "Has the Fertility of Danish Men Declined During the Years in Terms of Semen Quality? A Comparison of Semen Quality Between 1952 and 1972." *International Journal of Fertility* 28 (1972): 92–95.

Bostwick, David G., M.D., Gregory T. MacLennan, M.D., and Thayne R. Larson, M.D., for the American Cancer Society. *Prostate Cancer: What Every Man—and His Family—Needs to Know.* New York: Villard, 1996.

Bouchard, C. et al. *Exercise, Fitness and Health: A Consensus of Current Knowledge.* Champaign, IL: Human Kinetics Books, 1990.

Bovbjerg, V. E. et al. "Spouse Support and Long-Term Adherence to Lipid-Lowering Diets." *American Journal of Epidemiology* 141 (1995): 451–60.

Brecher, Edward M., and the Editors of Consumer Reports Books. *Love, Sex, and Aging.* Boston: Little, Brown, and Company, 1984.

Bremner, W., M. V. Vitiello, and P. N. Prinz. "Loss of Circadian Rhythmicity in Blood Testosterone Levels with Aging in Normal Men." *Journal of Clinical Endocrinology and Metabolism* 56 (1983): 1278–81.

Breslow, L., and J. E. Enstrom. "Persistence of Health Habits and Their Relationship to Mortality." *Preventive Medicine* 9 (1980): 469–83.

Bridges, William. *Job Shift: How to Prosper in a Workplace without Jobs.* New York: Addison-Wesley, 1994.

Budoff, Penny Wise. *No More Hot Flashes.* New York: G. P. Putnam's Sons, 1983.

Bureau of Labor Statistics. *Employment and Earnings: January, 1991.* Washington, DC: Bureau of Labor Statistics, 1991.

Burger, Julian. *The Gaia Atlas of First Peoples: A Future for the Indigenous World.* New York: Anchor Books, 1990.

Burris, A. S. et al. "Testosterone Therapy is Associated with Reduced Tactile Sensitivity in Human Males." *Horm. Behav.* 25 (1991): 195–205.

Buss, David M. *The Evolution of Desire: Strategies of Human Mating.* New York: Basic Books, 1994.

Busse, E. W., and G. L. Maddox, eds. *The Duke Longitudinal Studies of Normal Aging 1955-1980: An Overview of History, Design, and Findings.* New York: Springer Publishing Company, 1985.

Camaho, T. C., and J. Wiley. "Health Practices, Social Networks, and Changes in Physical Health." In *Health and Ways of Living,* edited by L. F. Berkman and L. Breslow. New York: Oxford University Press, 1983.

Carani, C. et al. "Effects of Androgen Treatment in Impotent Men with Normal and Low Levels of Free Testosterone." *Arch. Sex. Behav.* 19 (1990): 223–34.

Carey, Benedict. "Hooked on Youth: The Latest Anti-Aging Drug Is Cheap, Convenient, and Makes Some People Feel Like Kids Again. So What's the Catch?" *Hippocrates,* February 1996, 39+.

Carruthers, Malcolm. *Maximising Manhood: Beating the Male Menopause*. London: HarperCollins, 1997.

Castleman, Michael. *Sexual Solutions: An Informative Guide*. New York: Simon and Schuster, 1980.

Centers for Disease Control and Prevention. "Emergency Department Surveillance for Weapon-Related Injuries—Massachusetts, November 1993–April 1994." *JAMA* 273, no. 22 (1995): 1746–47.

Centers for Disease Control. *Hepatitis Surveillance*. Report no. 56. Atlanta: Centers for Disease Control, 1995.

———. "Physical Fighting among High School Students: United States, 1990." *Morbidity and Mortality Weekly Report* 41, no. 6 (1992): 91–94.

———. "Prevalence of Sedentary Lifestyle: Behavioral Risk Factor Surveillance System, United States, 1991." *Morbidity and Mortality Weekly Report* 42, no. 29 (1993): 576–79.

———. "Public Health Focus: Physical Activity and the Prevention of Coronary Heart Disease." *Morbidity and Mortality Weekly Report* 42, no. 35 (1993): 669–72.

———. "Selected Behaviors That Increase Risk for HIV Infection, Other Sexually Transmitted Diseases, and Unintended Pregnancy among High School Students—United States, 1991." *Morbidity and Mortality Weekly Report* 41, no. 50 (1992): 945–50.

———. "Selected Tobacco-Use Behaviors and Dietary Patterns among High School Students: United States, 1991." *Morbidity and Mortality Weekly Report* 41, no. 14 (1992): 760–72.

———. "Surveillance for Smoking-Attributable Mortality and Years of Potential Life Lost, by State: United States, 1990." *Morbidity and Mortality Weekly Report* 43, no. SS–1 (1994): 1–7.

Cetron, Marvin and Owen Davies. *Cheating Death: The Promise and the Future Impact of Trying to Live Forever*. New York: St. Martin's Press, 1998.

Challem, Jack. "The War on Aging." *Natural Health*, March–April 1997, 91+.

Cheever, John. *The Journals of John Cheever*. New York: Alfred A. Knopf, 1991.

Chen, I. "Hormone Replacement for Men?" *Hippocrates*, 1994, 22+.

Chen, Ingfei. "Should Men Have Hormone Replacement Therapy?" *Business First—Louisville*, 12 December 1994, 35.

Chichester, Brian, Perry Garfinkel, and the Editors of Men's Health Books. *Stress Blasters: Quick and Simple Steps to Take Control and Perform under Pressure*. Emmaus, PA: Rodale Press, Inc., 1997.

Chopra, Deepak, M.D. *Ageless Body, Timeless Mind: The Quantum Alternative to Growing Old*. New York: Harmony Books, 1993.

————. *Return of the Rishi: A Doctor's Search for the Ultimate Healer.* Boston: Houghton Mifflin, 1988.

Church, Paul, M.D., and Peta Gillyatt. "Impotence: No Need to Suffer in Secret." *Harvard Health Letter,* May 1996, 4+.

Clark, Etta. *Growing Old Is Not for Sissies: Portraits of Senior Athletes.* Corte Madera, CA: Pomegranate Calendars and Books, 1986.

Clayton, Craig, and Virginia McCullough. *A Consumer's Guide to Alternative Health Care.* Holbrook, MA: Adams, 1995.

Cohen, Jessica. "The Healing Touch." *Longevity,* January 1994, 26+.

Coles, Stephen, M.D. "CoQ-10 and Life Span Extension." *Journal of Longevity Research* I, no. 5 (1995).

Collins, Gary R., and Timothy E. Clinton. *Baby Boomer Blues.* Dallas: Word Publishing, 1992.

Coney, Sandra. *The Menopause Industry: How the Medical Establishment Exploits Women.* Alameda, CA: Hunter House, 1994.

Cooper, Kenneth, M.D. *It's Better to Believe.* Nashville, TN: Thomas Nelson Publishers, Inc.: 1995.

Corney, R. H. "Sex Differences in General Practice Attendance and Help Seeking for Minor Illness." *Journal of Psychosomatic Research* 34, no. 5 (1990): 525–34.

Cose, Ellis. *A Man's World: How Real Is Male Privilege—And How High Is Its Price?* New York: HarperCollins, 1995.

Courtenay, Will H. In review for publication. "Behavioral Factors Associated with Male Disease, Injury, and Death: Evidence and Implications for Prevention." *American Journal of Preventative Medicine.*

————. In revision for publication. "Constructions of Masculinity and Their Influence on Men's Well-Being: A Theory of Gender and Health." *Social Science and Medicine.*

Cousins, Norman. *Anatomy of An Illness.* New York: Bantam Books, 1981.

Cowley, Geoffrey. "Attention Aging Men: Testosterone and Other Hormone Treatments Offer New Hope for Staying Youthful, Sexy and Strong." *Newsweek,* 16 September 1996, 68+.

————. "My Month on DHEA: One Man's Experiment with Hormone Therapy." *Newsweek,* 16 September 1996, 74.

Cranton, Elmer M., M.D., and James P. Frackelton, M.D. "Growth Hormone to Reverse Aging." *Alternative Medicine,* June 1995.

Crenshaw, Theresa L., M.D. *The Alchemy of Love and Lust: Discovering Our Sex Hormones and How They Determine Who We Love, When We Love, and How Often We Love.* New York: G. P. Putnam's Sons, 1996.

Crenshaw, Theresa L., and James P. Goldberg. *Sexual Pharmacology.* New York: Norton, 1996.

Crenshaw, Theresa L., James P. Goldberg, and W. C. Stern. "Pharmacologic Modification of Psychosexual Dysfunction." *Journal of Sexual and Marital Therapy* 13 (1987): 239–52.

Crosse, Royda. *Why Women Live Longer Than Men: And What Men Can Learn From Them.* San Francisco: Jossey-Bass, 1997.

Cucca, S. "[The Thymopause: An Immunological Climacteric]." *Minerva Med* 74 (1983): 1241–45. Language: Italian.

Curcio, C. A., S. J. Buell, and P. D. Coleman. "Morphology of the Aging Central Nervous System: Not All Downhill." In *Advances in Neurogerontology: The Aging Motor System,* edited by J. A. Mortimer, F. J. Prozzola, and G. I. Maletta. New York: Praeger, 1982.

Curtin, Sharon R. *Nobody Ever Died of Old Age.* Boston: Little, Brown and Company, 1972.

Cutler, Blayne. "Marketing to Menopausal Men." *American Demographics,* March 1993, 49.

Cutler, Winnifred B., Ph.D. *Love Cycles: The Science of Intimacy.* New York: Villard Books, 1991.

Cwikel, J. M. et al. "Mechanisms of Psychosocial Effects on Health: The Role of Social Integration, Coping Style, and Health Behavior." *Health Education Quarterly* 15 (1988): 151–73.

Dabbs, M., D. de la Rue, and P. M. Williams. "Testosterone and Occupational Choice: Actors, Ministers and Other Men." *Journal of Personality and Social Psychology* 59 (1990): 1261–65.

Darrach, B. "The War on Aging." *Life,* October 1992, 32+.

Davidson, J. M., C. A. Camargo, and E. R. Smith. "Effects of Androgen on Sexual Behavior in Hypogonadal Men." *Journal of Clinical Endocrinology and Metabolism* 48 (1979): 955–58.

Davidson, J. M. et al. "Hormonal Changes and Sexual Function in Aging Men." *Journal of Clinical Endocrinology and Metabolism* 57 (1983): 71–79.

Dawkins, Richard. *The Selfish Gene.* Oxford: Oxford University Press, 1976.

de Beauvoir, Simone. *The Coming of Age.* New York: G. P. Putnam's Sons, 1972.

De Lignieres, B. "Transdermal Dihydrotestosterone Treatment of Andropause." *Annals Of Medicine* 25, no. 3 (1993): 235–41.

Dean, Ward, and John Morgenthaler. *Smart Drugs and Nutrients: How to Improve Your Memory and Increase Your Intelligence Using the Latest Discoveries in Neuroscience.* Santa Cruz, CA: B&J Publications, 1990.

Dean, Ward, John Morgenthaler, and Steven W. Fowkes. *Smart Drugs II: The Next Generation—New Drugs and Nutrients to Improve Your Memory and Increase Your Intelligence.* Santa Cruz, CA: B&J Publications, 1990.

Degler, Carl N. *In Search of Human Nature: The Decline and Revival of Darwinism in American Social Thought.* Oxford: Oxford University Press, 1991.

Denke, M. A., C. T. Sempos, and S. M. Grundy. "Excess Body Weight: An Underrecognized Contributor to High Blood Cholesterol Levels in White American Men." *Archives in Internal Medicine* 153 (1993): 1093–103.

Department of Health and Human Services. "Advance Report of Final Mortality Statistics, 1991." *Monthly Vital Statistics Report* 42, no. 2. Hyattsville, MD: Public Health Service, 1993.

———. *Healthy People 2000: National Health Promotion and Disease Prevention Objectives.* DHHS Publication no. [PHS] 91-50212. Washington, DC: U. S. Government Printing Office, 1991.

———. *Highlights from Wave 1 of the National Survey of Personal Health Practices and Consequences: United States, 1979.* DHHS Publication no. [PHS] 81-1162. Hyattsville, MD: Public Health Service, 1981.

———. *Vital and Health Statistics: Health Promotion and Disease Prevention, United States, 1990.* DHHS Publication no. [PHS] 93-1513. Hytattsville, MD: Public Health Service, 1993.

Department of Justice. *National Crime Victimization Survey: Criminal Victimization—1993.* Publication no. NCJ-151658. Washington, DC: U. S. Government Printing Office, 1995.

———. *Sourcebook of Criminal Justice Statistics—1993.* Publication no. NCJ-148211. Washington, DC: U. S. Government Printing Office, 1994.

Deslypere, J. P., and A. Vermuelen. "Leydig Cell Function in Normal Men: Effect of Age, Life Style, Residence, Diet and Activity." *Journal of Clinical Endocrinology and Metabolism* 59 (1984): 955–62.

Deslypere, J. P. et al. "Influence of Age on Pulsatile Hormone Release and Responsiveness of the Gonadotrophs to Sex Hormone Feedback in Men." *Journal of Clinical Endocrinology and Metabolism* 64 (1987): 68–73.

DeVita, E. "The Hormone Craze." *American Health,* January–February 1996, 73.

Diamond, Irene, and Gloria Feman Orenstein, eds. *Reweaving the World: The Emergence of Ecofeminism.* San Francisco: Sierra Club Books, 1990.

Diamond, Jared. "Why Women Change." *Discover,* July 1996, 131+.

————. *The Third Chimpanzee: The Evolution and Future of the Human Animal.* New York: HarperCollins, 1992.

Diamond, Jed. *The Warrior's Journey Home: Healing Men, Healing the Planet.* Oakland, CA: New Harbinger Publications, 1994.

Dilman, Vladimir, and Ward Dean. *The Neuroendocrine Theory of Aging and Degenerative Disease.* Pensacola, FL: Center for Bio-Gerontology, 1992.

"Do Men Go through Menopause?" *Consumer Reports On Health,* October 1993, 105+.

Douglass, William Campbell, M.D. "A Neglected Hormone—Testosterone for Men and Women, Part I." *Second Opinion,* March 1995, 1+.

————. "A Neglected Hormone—Testosterone for Men and Women, Part II." *Second Opinion,* April 1995, 1+.

Downes, Peggy et al. *The New Older Woman.* Berkeley: Celestial Arts, 1996.

Durning, Alan. *How Much is Enough? The Consumer Society and the Future of the Earth.* New York: W. W. Norton and Company, 1992.

————. *This Place On Earth: Home and the Practice of Permanence.* Seattle, WA: Sasquatch Books, 1996.

Eaton, S. Boyd, M.D., Marjorie Shostak, and Melvin Konner, M.D., Ph.D. *The Paleolithic Prescription: A Program of Diet and Exercise and a Design for Living.* New York: Harper and Row, 1988.

EDK Associates. *The ABCs of STDs.* New York: EDK Associates, 1995.

Einstein, Albert. *The World As I See It.* Secaucus, NJ: Citadel Press, 1976.

Eisler, Riane. *The Chalice and the Blade.* San Francisco: Harper and Row, 1988.

Elder, G. H., and J. K. Liker. "Hard Times in Women's Lives: Historical Influences across Forty Years." *American Journal of Sociology* 88 (1994): 481–89.

Elia, Irene. *The Female Animal.* New York: Henry Holt and Company, 1986.

Ellenberg, Daniel, and Judith Bell. *Lovers for Life: Creating Lasting Passion, Trust and True Partnership.* Santa Rosa, CA: Aslan Publishing, 1995.

Enstrom, J. E., L. E. Kanim, and L. Breslow. "The Relationship between Vitamin C Intake, General Health Practices, and Mortality in Alameda County, California." *American Journal of Public Health* 76 (1986): 1124–30.

Epstein, Randi Hutter. "Do Men Go through Menopause?" *Frontiers,* July 1992, 31.

Ericksen, K. P., and K. F. Trocki. "Behavioral Risk Factors for Sexually Transmitted Diseases in American Households." *Social Science and Medicine* 34, no. 8 (1992): 843–53.

————. "Sex, Alcohol, and Sexually Transmitted Diseases: A National Survey." *Family Planning Perspectives* 26 (1994): 257–63.

Fahey, Thomas D. "The Male Mid-Life Crisis:Viropause: Myth or Reality?" *Muscle and Fitness,* May 1994, 160+.

Farrell, Warren. *Why Men Are the Way They Are.* New York: McGraw-Hill, 1986.

Farrow, J. A., and P. Brissing. "Risk for DWI: A New Look at Gender Differences in Drinking and Driving Influences, Experiences and Attitudes among New Adolescent Drivers." *Health Education Quarterly* 17, no. 2 (1990): 312–21.

Fausto-Sterling, Anne. *Myths of Gender: Biological Theories about Women and Men.* New York: Basic Books, 1985.

Feldman, Henry A. et al. "Impotence and Its Medical and Psychosocial Correlates: Results of the Massachusetts Male Aging Study." *Journal of Urology* 151 (January 1994): 54–61.

Fields, Rick. *The Code of the Warrior: In History, Myth, and Everyday Life.* New York: HarperCollins, 1991.

Fisher, Helen, Ph.D. *Anatomy of Love: The Natural History of Monogamy, Adultery, and Divorce.* New York: W. W. Norton and Company, 1992.

————.*The Sex Contract: The Evolution of Human Behavior.* New York: William Morrow and Company, 1982.

Fleming, R. et al. "Mediating Influences of Social Support on Stress at Three Mile Island." *Journal of Human Stress* 8 (1982): 14–22.

Flieger, Ken. "Testosterone: Key to Masculinity and More." *FDA Consumer,* May 1995, 27+.

Ford, Richard. *Independence Day.* New York: Alfred A. Knopf, 1995.

French, Sean. Untitled. *New Statesman and Society,* 7 April 1995, 51.

Frey, Chris. *Men at Work: An Action Guide to Masculine Healing.* Dubuque, IA: Islewest Publishing, 1997.

Friday, Nancy. *The Power of Beauty.* New York: HarperCollins, 1996.

Friedan, Betty. *The Fountain of Age.* New York: Simon & Schuster, 1993.

————. *The Second Stage.* New York: Summit Books, 1981.

Gaby, Alan R., M.D. *Preventing and Reversing Osteoporosis: Every Woman's Essential Guide.* Rocklin, CA: Prima Publishing, 1993.

Gelles, R. J., and M. A. Straus. *Intimate Violence.* New York: Simon and Schuster, 1988.

Gerzon, Mark. *Listening to Midlife: Turning Your Crisis into a Quest.* Boston: Shambhala, 1996.

Gillette, Douglas M. *Primal Love: Reclaiming Our Instincts for Lasting Passion.* New York: St. Martin's Press, 1995.

Gilligan, James. *Violence: Our Deadly Epidemic and Its Causes.* New York: G. P. Putnam's Sons, 1996.

Gillyatt, Peta. "How to Answer Your Own Medical Questions." *Harvard Health Letter,* July 1996.

Gilroy, D., ed. *How Men Stay Young.* Emmaus, PA: Rodale Press, 1991.

Ginsburg J., and B. O'Reilly. "Climacteric flushing in a man." Letter. *British Medical Journal, Clinical Research Ed,* 23 July 1983.

Gittleman, Ann Louise. *Super Nutrition For Men And the Women Who Love Them.* New York: M. Evans and Company, 1996.

Glantz, Kalman, and John K. Pearce. *Exiles From Eden: Psychotherapy from an Evolutionary Perspective.* New York: W. W. Norton and Company, 1989.

Goldberg, Kenneth. *How Men Can Live as Long as Women: Seven Steps to a Longer and Better Life.* Fort Worth, TX: The Summit Group, 1993.

Goldman, J. E., N. V. Calingasan, and G. E. Gibson. "Aging and the Brain." *Current Opinion in Neurology* 7, no. 4 (1994): 287–93.

Gordon, James S., M.D. *Manifesto for a New Medicine: Your Guide to Healing Partnerships and the Wise Use of Alternative Therapies.* New York: Addison-Wesley, 1996.

Gottlieb, N. H., and L. W. Green. "Life Events, Social Network, Life-Style, and Health: An Analysis of the 1979 National Survey of Personal Health Practices and Consequences." *Health Education Quarterly* 11 (1984): 91–105.

Gottman, John. *Why Marriages Succeed or Fail.* New York: Simon and Schuster, 1994.

Gouchie, C., and D. Kimura. "The Relationship between Testosterone Levels and Cognitive Ability Patterns." *Psychoneuroendocrinology* 16 (1991): 323–34.

Gould, Stephen Jay. *Full House: The Spread of Excellence From Plato to Darwin.* New York: Harmony Books, 1996.

Graham, Stedman. *You Can Make It Happen: A Nine-Step Plan For Success.* New York: Simon & Schuster, 1997.

Gray, A. et al. "Age, Disease, and Changing Sex Hormone Levels in Middle-Aged Men: Results of the Massachusetts Male Aging Study." *Journal of Clinical Endocrinology and Metabolism* 73, no. 5 (1991): 1016–25.

Green, James. *The Male Herbal: Health Care for Men and Boys.* Freedom, CA: The Crossing Press, 1991.

Greenberger, Dennis and Christine A. Padesky. *Mind Over Mood: Change How You Feel by Changing the Way You Think.* New York: The Guilford Press, 1995.

Greenwood, Sadja. *Menopause Naturally: Preparing for the Second Half of Life.* Volcano, CA: Volcano Press, 1984.

Greer, Germaine. *The Change: Women, Aging and the Menopause.* New York: Ballantine, 1991.

Gruninger, U. J. "Patient Education: An Example of One-to-One Communication." *Journal of Human Hypertension* 9, no. 1 (1995): 15–25.

Gurian, Michael. *The Wonder of Boys: What Parents, Mentors and Educators Can Do to Shape Boys into Exceptional Men.* New York: G. P. Putnam's Sons, 1996.

————. "The Wonder of Boys: An Interview with Michael Gurian." By Bert H. Hoff. *M.E.N. Magazine,* October 1996.

Gutfeld, Greg. "Is Testosterone in Your Future?" *Prevention,* October 1994, 68+.

————. "Test-Driving Testosterone." *Men's Health,* November 1994, 50+.

Gutmann, David. *Reclaimed Powers: Toward a New Psychology of Men and Women in Later Life.* New York: Basic Books, 1987.

Haidl, G., F. M. Koehn, and W. B. Schill. "[The Aging Male from the Andrological Viewpoint]." *Hautarzt* 45, no. 9 (1994): 599–604. Language: German.

Haisin, D. S., B. F. Grant, and J. Weinflash. "Male/Female Differences in Alcohol-Related Problems: Alcohol Rehabilitation Patients." *International Journal of the Addictions* 23, no. 5 (1988): 547–48.

Hallowell, Edward. *Worry: Controlling It and Using It Wisely.* New York: Pantheon Books, 1997.

Hamer, Dean and Peter Copeland. *Living With Our Genes: Why They Matter More Than You Think.* New York: Doubleday, 1998.

————. *The Science of Desire: The Search for the Gay Gene and the Biology of Behavior.* New York: Simon and Schuster, 1994.

Hammarstrom, A. "Health Consequences of Youth Unemployment: Review from a Gender Perspective." *Social Science and Medicine* 38, no. 5 (1994): 699–709.

Hardiman, P. J., P. D. Abel, and J. Ginsburg. "Peripheral Vascular Effects of Gonadotropin Releasing Hormone Agonists in Men." *Journal of the North American Menopause Society* 2 (1995): 159–61.

Harman, S. M., and M. R. Blackman, for the American Society of Andrology. "Is There an Andropause, the Analog to Menopause, and If

So, What Tissues Are Affected and How?" *Handbook of Andrology.* Lawrence, KS: Allen Press, 1995. 72–75.

Hayflick, Leonard. *How and Why We Age.* New York: Ballantine, 1994.

"Heart Healthy Testosterone?" *Consumer Reports On Health,* November 1994, 125.

Heinberg, Richard. *Memories and Visions of Paradise: Exploring the Universal Myth of a Lost Golden Age.* Wheaton, IL: The Theosophical Publishing House, 1995.

————. *A New Covenant with Nature.* New York: Quest Books, 1996.

————. "Touch, Talk, Pleasure, and Violence." *Muse Letter,* October 1996.

Hennenfent, Bradley R., M.D., *The Prostatitis Syndromes.* Bloomington, IL: The Prostatitis Foundation, 1996.

Hill, Aubrey M. *Viropause/Andropause: The Male Menopause: Emotional and Physical Changes Mid-Life Men Experience.* Far Hills, NJ: New Horizon Press, 1993.

————. *Testosterone: New Ways to Revitalize Your Life with Male Hormone Therapy.* Sacramento, CA: Prima Publishing, 1997.

Hillman, James. *The Soul's Code: In Search of Character and Calling.* New York: Random House, 1996.

————. *Kinds of Power: A Guide to Its Intelligent Uses.* New York: Doubleday, 1995.

Hitchcox, Lee, D. C. *Long Life Now: Strategies for Staying Alive.* Berkeley, CA: Celestial Arts, 1996.

Hite, Shere. *Women as Revolutionary Agents of Change: The Hite Reports and Beyond.* Madison, WI: University of Wisconsin Press, 1994.

Hixon, M. E. "Aging and Heart Failure." *Progress in Cardiovascular Nursing* 9, no. I (1994): 4–12.

Ho, S. C. "Health and Social Predictors of Mortality in an Elderly Chinese Cohort." *American Journal of Epidemiology* 133, no. 9 (1991): 907–21.

Hodes, Richard. "The NIA's Position on Growth Hormone Replacement Therapy in Adults, with Comments by Edmund Y. Chein." *Journal of American Geriatrics Society* 42 (1994): 1208–11.

Hoffman, Andrew R., Steven A. Lieberman, and Gian Paolo Ceda. "Growth Hormone Therapy in the Elderly: Implications for the Aging Brain." *Psychoneuroendocrinology* 17, no. 4 (1992): 327–33.

Hoffman, Edward. *The Right to Be Human: A Biography of Abraham Maslow.* Los Angeles: Jeremy P. Tarcher, Inc., 1988.

Hogshire, Jim. "Take Two and See Me in the Morning." *GQ,* July 1995, 62+.

Holinger, P. C. "Violent Deaths among the Young: Recent Trends in Suicide, Homicide, and Accidents." *American Journal of Psychiatry* 136, no. 9 (1979): 1144–47.

House, J. D., K. R. Landis, and D. Umberson. "Social Relationships and Health." *Science* 241 (1988): 540–45.

House, J. S., C. Robbins, and H. L. Metzner. "The Association of Social Relationships and Activities with Mortality: Prospective Evidence from the Tecumseh Community Health Study." *American Journal of Epidemiology* 116, no. 1 (1982): 123–40.

Hung, J. et al. "Association of Sleep Apnea with Myocardial Infarction in Men." *Lancet* 336 (1990): 261–64.

Huselid, R. F., and M. L. Cooper. "Gender Roles as Mediators of Sex Differences in Adolescent Alcohol Use and Abuse." *Journal of Health and Social Behavior* 33 (1992): 348–62.

Huyghe, P. "The Hormone Whose Time Has Come." *Hippocrates* 7/8 (1994): 22–25.

Ikeda, Y. et al. "Testosterone or GnRH Treatment Improved Impaired Response of Plasma Vasopressin Stimuli in Men with Hypogonadism." Endocrine Society 72nd Meeting Abstracts, 1995.

Irving, John. *The Water Method Man.* New York: Ballantine, 1972.

Irwin, M. et al. "Partial Sleep Deprivation Reduces Natural Killer Cell Activity in Humans." *Psychosomatic Medicine* 56 (1994): 493–98.

Ivker, Robert, M.D., and Edward Zorensky. *Thriving: The Complete Mind/Body Guide for Optimal Health and Fitness for Men.* New York: Crown Publishers, 1997.

Jackson, Phil, and Hugh Delehanty. *Sacred Hoops: Spiritual Lessons of a Hardwood Warrior.* New York: Hyperion, 1995.

Jacobelli, A. "[The Male Climacteric. Endocrinologic Profile and Therapeutic Prospectives]." *Clinica Terapeutica* 112, no. 2 (1985): 155–61. Language: Italian.

Jamison, Kay Redfield. *An Unquiet Mind: Memoir of Moods and Madness.* New York: Vintage Books, 1996.

———. *Touched With Fire: Manic-Depressive Illness and The Artistic Temperment.* New York: Free Press, 1993.

Janczewski, Z., L. Bablok, and A. Smith. "[Clinical Course of Andropause]." *Polski Tygodnik Lekarski* 44, no. 7–8 (1989): 173–75. Language: Polish.

———. "[Functional Gonadal Reserve in a Climacteric Male]." *Polski Tygodnik Lekarski* 44, no. 7–8 (1989): 176–78. Language: Polish.

Janeway, Elizabeth. *Man's World, Woman's Place: A Study in Social Mythology.* New York: Dell, 1971.

Janiger, O., and P. Goldberg. *A Different Kind of Healing: Doctors Speak Candidly about Their Successes with Alternative Medicine.* New York: Putnam, 1993.

Jaroff, Leon. "The Man's Cancer." *Time,* 1 April 1996.

————. "New Age Therapy (Research on Anti-Aging Pill)." *Time,* 23 January 1995, 52.

Jastrab, Joseph. *Sacred Manhood, Sacred Earth: A Vision Quest into the Wilderness of a Man's Heart.* New York: HarperCollins, 1994.

Jenkins, Tom. "Male Menopause: Myth or Monster." *Vibrant Life,* November–December 1995.

Johnson, A. R., and J. P. Jarow. "Is Routine Endocrine Testing of Impotent Men Necessary?" *Journal of Urology* 147 (1992): 1542–44.

Johnson, L. "Spermatogenesis and Aging in Humans." *Journal of Andrology* 7 (1986): 331–54.

Johnson, Sonia. *Going Out of Our Minds: The Metaphysics of Liberation.* Freedom, CA: The Crossing Press, 1987.

Jones, Dan. *What Makes a Man a Man.* Austin, TX: Mandala Books, 1993.

Jorgensen, Jens O. L. et al. "Three Years of Growth Hormone Treatment in Growth Hormone-Deficient Adults: Near Normalization of Body Composition and Physical Performance." *European Journal of Endocrinology* 130 (1994): 224–28.

Kabat-Zinn, Jon. *Wherever You Go, There You Are.* New York: Hyperion, 1994.

————. *Full Catastrophe Living: Using the Wisdom of Your Body and Mind to Face Stress, Pain, and Illness.* New York: Delacort, 1990.

————. "Moment to Moment: An Interview with Jon Kabat-Zinn." *Common Ground,* Spring 1997, 146+.

Kaiser, F., and J. E. Morley. "Gonadotropins, Testosterone and the Aging Male." *Neurology of Aging* 15 (1994): 559–63.

Kaiser, F. E. "Sexuality and Impotence in the Aging Man." *Clinics in Geriatric Medicine* 7, no. 1 (1991): 63–72.

Kandrack, M., K. R. Grant, and A. Segall. "Gender Differences in Health Related Behavior: Some Unanswered Questions." *Social Science and Medicine* 32, no. 5 (1991): 579–90.

Kaplan, G. A. et al. "Mortality among the Elderly in the Alameda County Study: Behavioral and Demographic Risk Factors." *American Journal of Public Health* 77 (1987): 307–12.

Kaplan, H. B. "Social Psychology of the Immune System: A Conceptual Framework and Review of the Literature." *Social Science and Medicine* 33, no. 8 (1991): 909–23.

Kauth, Bill. *A Circle of Men: The Original Manual for Men's Support Groups.* New York: St. Martin's Press, 1992.

Kazantzakis, Nikos. *Zorba the Greek.* New York: Simon and Schuster, 1952.

Keen, Sam. *Fire in the Belly: On Being a Man.* New York: Bantam Books, 1991.

Kendig, Frank, and Richard Hutton. *Life Spans: Or How Long Things Last.* New York: Holt, Rinehart and Winston, 1979.

Kent, Debra. "Prayer: More Potent Than Penicillin." *Country Living,* Spring/Summer 1997, 38+.

Kent, J. Z., and A. B. Acone. "Plasma Testosterone Levels and Aging in Males." In *Androgens in Normal and Pathological Conditions,* edited by A. Vermeulen and D. Exley. *International Congress Series* 101 (1966): 730–35.

Kessler, R. C. et al. "Lifetime and 12-Month Prevalence of DSM-III-R Psychiatric Disorders in the United States: Results from the National Comorbidity Survey." *Archives of General Psychiatry* 51 (1994): 8–19.

Key, M. R. *Male/Female Language.* Metuchen, NJ: Scarecrow Press, 1975.

Key, T. et al. "Testosterone, Sex Hormone Binding Gobulin, Calculated Free Testosterone and Oestradiol in Male Vegans and Omnivores." *British Journal of Nutrition* 64 (1990): 111–19.

Keyes, Ken. *Your Road Map to Lifelong Happiness: A Guide to the Life You Want.* Coos Bay, OR: Love Line Books, 1995.

Kimbrell, Andrew. *The Masculine Mystique: The Politics of Masculinity.* New York: Ballantine, 1995.

Kinsey, A. C. et al. *Sexual Behavior in the Human Male.* Philadelphia: W. B. Saunders Company, 1948.

Kipnis, Aaron, and Elizabeth Herron. *Gender War, Gender Peace: The Quest for Justice between Women and Men.* New York: William Morrow and Company, Inc., 1994.

Kirschbaum, C. et al. "Sex-Specific Effects of Social Support on Cortisol and Subjective Responses to Acute Psychological Stress." *Psychosomatic Medicine* 57 (1995): 23–31.

Klatz, Ronald, and Carol Kahn. *Grow Young with HGH: The Amazing Medically Proven Plan to Reverse Aging.* New York: HarperCollins, 1997.

Klatz, Ronald, and Robert Goldman. *Stopping the Clock.* New Canaan, CT: Keats Publishing, Inc., 1996.

Kopera, H. "Sex Hormones and the Brain." In *Sex and the Brain*, edited by J. Durden-Smith and D. DeSimone. New York: Arbor House, 1983.

Korten, David C. *When Corporations Rule the World.* West Hartford, CT: Kumerian Press, 1995.

Koster, Anne, Kim Solstad, and Vibeke Porsdal. "[The Lay Concept of the Climacteric Among Middle-Aged Danes]." *Nordic Journal Of Psychiatry* 49, no. 1 (1995): 63–67. Language: Danish.

Kramer, Jonathan, and Diane Dunaway. *Why Men Don't Get Enough Sex and Women Don't Get Enough Love.* New York: Pocket Books, 1990.

Kraus, J. F., and C. Conroy. "Mortality and Morbidity from Injuries in Sports and Recreation." *Annual Review of Public Health* 5 (1984): 163–92.

Krause, W. "[Do We Need the Concept of Male Climacteric?]." *Fortschr Med* 113, no. 4 (1995): 32+. Language: German.

————. "[The Male Menopause. A Case for Dermatological Andrology]." *Hautarzt* 45, no. 9 (1994): 593–98. Language: German.

Kurtz, Ernest, and Katherine Ketcham. *The Spirituality of Imperfection: Storytelling and the Journey to Wholeness.* New York: Bantam Books, 1994.

Lamm, Steven, M.D., and Gerald Secor Couzens. *The Virility Solution.* New York: Simon & Schuster, 1998.

————. *Younger at Last: The New World of Vitality Medicine.* New York: Simon and Schuster, 1997.

Lane, J. D. et al. "Cardiovascular Effects of Caffeine and Stress in Regular Coffee Drinkers." *Psychophysiology* 24 (1994): 157–64.

Lawlor, Robert. *Earth Honoring: The New Male Sexuality.* Rochester, VT: Park Street Press, 1989.

Lawren, Bill. "Testosterone: Whose Turn-on?" *Omni,* May 1994, 28.

Lear, Martha Weinman. "Is There a Male Menopause?" *New York Times Magazine,* 28 January 1973, 19.

Lee, John R., M.D., and Virginia Hopkins. *What Your Doctor May Not Tell You about Menopause: The Breakthrough Book on Natural Progesterone.* New York: Warner Books, 1996.

Leger, D. "The Cost of Sleep Related Accidents: A Report for the National Commission on Sleep Disorders Research." *Sleep* 17, no. 1 (1994): 84–93.

Leigh, B. C., M. T. Temple, and K. F. Trocki. "The Sexual Behavior of U. S. Adults: Results from a National Survey." *American Journal of Public Health* 83, no. 10 (1993): 1400–8.

Leigh, I. M., C. C. Hsieh, and R. S. Paffenbarger. "Exercise Intensity and Longevity in Men: The Harvard Alumni Health Study." *JAMA* 273, no. 15 (1995): 1179–84.

Leigh, J. P., and J. F. Fries. "Associations among Healthy Habits, Age, Gender, and Education in a Sample of Retirees." *International Journal of Aging and Human Development* 36, no. 2 (1993): 139–55.

Lejeune, H., H. Dechaud, and M. Pugeat. "[Evolution of the Hypothalamo-Pituitary-Testicular Axis With Aging]." *Contraception Fertilite Sexualite* 19, no. 11 (1991): 951–57. Language: French.

Leonard, George. *The End of Sex: Erotic Love after the Sexual Revolution.* New York: Bantam Books, 1984.

Lepore, S. J., K. A. Allen, and G. W. Evans. "Social Support Lowers Cardiovascular Reactivity to an Acute Stressor." *Psychosomatic Medicine* 55 (1993): 518–24.

Levay, Simon. *The Sexual Brain.* Cambridge, MA: MIT Press, 1993.

Levine, Judith. *My Enemy, My Love: Man-Hating and Ambivalence in Women's Lives.* New York: Doubleday, 1992.

Levinson, Daniel J. *The Seasons of a Man's Life.* New York: Ballantine, 1978.

———. *The Seasons of a Woman's Life.* New York: Alfred A. Knopf, 1996.

Levy, A. "Why Flush? (Hot Flashes in Men)." Commentary. *Lancet* 347, no. 8994 (1996): 73.

Lewis, Robert A. et al. "Developmental Transitions in Male Sexuality." *Counseling Psychologist* 7, no. 4 (1978): 15–18.

Lex, B. W. "Some Gender Differences in Alcohol and Polysubstance Users." *Health Psychology* 10 (1991): 121–32.

Liebowitz, M. R. *The Chemistry of Love.* Boston: Little, Brown, 1983.

Lonnquist, L. E., G. L. Weiss, and D. L. Larsen. "Health Value and Gender in Predicting Health Protective Behavior." *Women and Health* 19, no. 2/3 (1992): 69–85.

Lookingbill, D. P. et al. "Clinical and Biochemical Parameters of Androgen Action in Normal Healthy Caucasian Versus Chinese Subjects." *Journal of Clinical Endocrinology and Metabolism* 72 (1991): 1242–48.

Los Angeles Times, 6 November 1986–5 December 1993.

Love, Patricia, with Jo Robinson. *The Emotional Incest Syndrome: What to Do When a Parent's Love Rules Your Life.* New York: Bantam Book, 1990.

Love, Susan M., M.D., and Karen Lindsey. *Dr. Susan Love's Hormone Book.* New York: Random House, 1997.

Lynburg, Michael. *The Path with Heart.* New York: Ballantine, 1989.

Males, Mike A. *The Scapegoat Generation: America's War on Adolescents.* Monroe, ME: Common Courage Press, 1996.

Mander, Jerry. *In the Absence of the Sacred: The Failure of Technology and the Survival of the Indian Nations.* San Francisco: Sierra Club Books, 1991.

Manheimer, Ronald J. *The Second Middle Age: Looking Differently at Life Beyond 50.* Detroit: Visible Ink Press, 1995.

Marin Independent Journal, 22 March 1991.

Marcus, R. "Should All Older People Be Treated with Growth Hormone?" *Drugs and Aging,* 8 January 1996, 1.

Martin, G. R., D. B. Danner, and N. K. Holbrook. "Aging—Causes and Defenses." *Annual Review of Medicine* 44 (1993): 419–29.

Martin-Du Pan, R., S. Martin-Du Pan, and P. Sindelar. "[Andropause, Male Climacteric and Crisis of the Fifties: Should Androgens Be Administered?]." *Rev Med Suisse Romande* 115, no. 3 (1995): 257–62. Language: French.

Masters, William H., Virginia E. Johnson, and Robert C. Kolodny. *Heterosexuality.* New York: HarperCollins, 1994.

Matsumoto, Alvin M. "'Andropause'—Are Reduced Androgen Levels in Aging Men Physiologically Important?." Editorial; Comment. *Western Journal of Medicine* 159, no. 5 (1993): 618–20.

———. "Effects of Chronic Testosterone Administration in Normal Men: Safety and Efficacy of High Dosage Testosterone and Parallel Dose Dependent Suppression of Luteinizing Hormone, Follicle Stimulating Hormone and Sperm Production." *Journal of Clinical Endocrinology and Metabolism* 70 (1990): 282–87.

McCartney, Bill. *What Makes a Man? 12 Promises That Will Change Your Life.* Colorado Springs, CO: Navpress, 1992.

McFadden, Cyra. "Is There Really a Male Menopause?" *New Choices,* July–August 1994, 44+.

McGill, M. E. *The McGill Report on Male Intimacy.* New York: Holt Reinhart, 1985.

McGinnis, J. M., and W. H. Foege. "Actual Causes of Death in the United States." *JAMA* 270, no. 18 (1993): 2207–12.

McKinlay, J. B., C. Longcope, and A. Gray. "The Questionable Physiologic and Epidemiologic Basis for a Male Climacteric Syndrome: Preliminary Results From the Massachusetts Male Aging Study [USA]." *Maturitas* 11, no. 2 (1989): 103–16.

McLure, R. D., R. Oses, and M. L. Ernst. "Hypogonadal Impotence Treated by Transdermal Testosterone." *Urology* 37 (1991): 224–28.

Mead, Margaret. *Male and Female.* New York: William Morrow and Company, 1949.

Meadows, Kenneth. *The Medicine Way: A Shamanic Path to Self Mastery.* Longmead, UK: Element Books, 1990.

Medina, John J. *The Clock of Ages: Why We Age—How We Age—Winding Back the Clock.* Cambridge: Cambridge University Press, 1996.

Meichenbaum, D., and D. C. Turk. *Facilitating Treatment Adherence: A Practitioner's Guidebook.* New York: Plenum, 1987.

Men's Confidential, Editors. "Boost Your Sex Drive: Hidden Factors in Your Everyday Life May be Driving Down Your Sex Drive." *Men's Confidential Newsletter: Health, Sex, and Fitness for Men,* December 1993, 11+.

————. "Gender Benders: How to Combat the New Breed of Chemicals That is Threatening to Destroy Manhood as We Know It." *Men's Confidential Newsletter: Health, Sex, and Fitness for Men,* October 1994, 11+.

————. "Healing the Prostate: As Many as 50 Percent of American Men Will Develop a Prostate Infection. Here's How to Make the Most of the Latest Treatments to Speed Recovery." *Men's Confidential Newsletter: Health, Sex, and Fitness for Men,* June 1996, 1+.

————. "Insider Trading: Prostate-Cancer Support Groups Offer Much More Than a Shoulder to Cry On: They Put You on the Fast Track to Recovery." *Men's Confidential Newsletter: Health, Sex, and Fitness for Men,* August 1995, 11+.

————. "Libido-Lifters." *Men's Confidential Newsletter: Health, Sex, and Fitness for Men,* August 1996, 1+.

————. "Low-Fat Diet Protects Prostate." *Men's Confidential Newsletter: Health, Sex and Fitness for Men,* December 1995, 7.

————. "The Male G-Spot: How to Add Power to Your Orgasms and Strength to Your Erections by Harnessing the Secrets of the Prostate." *Men's Confidential Newsletter: Health, Sex, and Fitness for Men,* May 1996, 8+.

————. "Natural Erection Boosters: New Research Uncovers Herbal Products That Produce Harder, Stronger, Longer-Lasting Erections." *Men's Confidential Newsletter: Health, Sex and Fitness for Men,* April 1996, 1+.

————. "Preserve Your Potency: Researchers Have Discovered Over Half of All Men Develop Erectile Problems as They Age. Here Are 10 Ways You Can Keep from Joining Their Ranks." *Men's Confidential Newsletter: Health, Sex, and Fitness for Men,* July 1994, 11+.

———. "Psyching Up: Many Men Who See Urologists for Erectile Problems Would Be Better Served by a Short Course in Performance Anxiety." *Men's Confidential Newsletter: Health, Sex, and Fitness for Men*, June 1995, 1+.

———. "Saw Salvation: A Centuries-Old Herbal Remedy May Be More Effective at Shrinking Enlarged Prostates Than the Best New Drugs." *Men's Confidential Newsletter: Health, Sex, and Fitness for Men*, September 1995, 1+.

———. "Solo Sex Straight Talk." *Men's Confidential Newsletter: Health, Sex and Fitness for Men*, January 1996, 10+.

Menkveld, R. et al. "Possible Changes in Male Fertility over a 15 Year Period." *Archives of Andrology* 27 (1986): 143–44.

Mermall, J. et al. "Temporal (Circadian) and Functional Relationship Between Prostate-Specific Antigen and Testosterone in Healthy Men." *Urology* 46 (1995): 45–52.

Merriggiola, M.C. et al. "Testosterone Enanthate at a Dose of 200mg/week decreases HDL Cholesterol Levels in Healthy Men." *International Journal of Andrology* 18 (1995): 237–42.

Meyer, Alfred. "Patching up Testosterone." *Psychology Today*, March–April 1997, 54+.

Michael, Robert T., John H. Gagnon, Edward O. Laumann, and Gina Kolata. *Sex in America: A Definitive Survey.* New York: Warner Books, 1994.

Miedzian, Myriam. *Boys Will Be Boys: Breaking the Link between Masculinity and Violence.* New York: Doubleday, 1991.

Miller, Alice. *For Your Own Good: Hidden Cruelty in Child Rearing and the Roots of Violence.* New York: Farrar, Strauss, Giroux, 1983.

Miller, Timothy. *How to Want What You Have: Discovering the Magic and Grandeur of Ordinary Existence.* New York: Henry Holt and Company, 1995.

Minkowitz, Donna. "In the Name of the Father." *Ms.*, November–December 1995, 64+.

Mitscherlich, Alexander. *Society without the Father: A Contribution to Social Psychology.* Translated by Eric Mosbacher. New York: HarperCollins, 1969.

Mittleman et al. "Triggering of Acute Myocardial Infarction by Heavy Physical Exertion: Protection against Triggering by Regular Exertion." *New England Journal of Medicine* 328, no. 4 (1993): 253–56.

Moir, Anne, and David Jessel. *Brain Sex: The Real Difference between Men and Women.* New York: Carol Publishing Group, 1991.

Moldofsky, H. et al. "Effects of Sleep Deprivation on Human Immune Function." *Federation of American Societies for Experimental Biology Journal* 3 (1989): 1972–77.

Monath, J. R. et al. "Physiologic Variations of Serum Testosterone within the Normal Range Do Not Affect Serum Prostate-Specific Antigen." *Urology* 46 (1995): 58–61.

Money, J., and A. A. Ehrhardt. *Man and Woman, Boy and Girl.* Baltimore: Johns Hopkins University Press, 1972.

Montagu, A. *Touching: The Human Significance of Skin.* New York: Harper and Row, 1986.

Montanini, V. et al. "Age-Related Changes in Plasme Dehydroepiandrosterone Sulfate, Cortisol, Testosterone and Free Testosterone Circadian Rhythms in Adult Men." *Hormone Research* 29, no. 1 (1988): 1–6.

Montouri, Alfonso, and Esabella Conti. *From Power to Partnership: Creating the Future of Love, Work, and Community.* San Francisco: Harper San Francisco, 1993

Moore, Robert, and Douglas Gillette. *The Warrior Within: Accessing the Knight in the Male Psyche.* New York: William Morrow, 1992.

Morales, Arlene J. et al. "Effects of Replacement Dose of Dehydroepi-androsterone in Men and Women of Advancing Age." *Journal of Clinical Endocrinology and Metabolism* 78, no. 6 (1994).

"More Than Hot Flushes." Editorial. *Lancet* 338, no. 8772 (1991): 917+.

Morgenthaler, John, and Dan Joy. *Better Sex through Chemistry: A Guide to the New Prosexual Drugs.* Petaluma, CA: Smart Publications, 1994.

Morris, Desmond. *Bodywatching: A Field Guide to the Human Species.* London: Capse, 1985.

Muhlenkamp, A. F., and Sayles. "Self-Esteem, Social Support, and Positive Health Practices." *Nursing Research* 35, no. 6 (1986): 334–38.

Murphy, M. R. et al. "Changes in Oxytocin and Vasopressin Secretion During Sexual Activity in Men." *Journal of Clinical Endocrinology and Metabolism* 65 (1987): 738–41.

Murphy, S. et al. "Sex Hormones and Bone Mineral Density in Elderly Men." *Bone Mineral* 20 (1993): 133–40.

Murray, Michael T., M.D. *The Healing Power of Herbs: The Enlightened Person's Guide to the Wonders of Medicinal Plants.* Rocklin, CA: Prima, 1995.

Myss, Carolyn. *Anatomy of the Spirit.* New York: Harmony Books, 1996.

Nadler, Holly. "My Life As A Man." *Utne Reader,* May–June 1994, 134+.

Nankin, H. R. et al. "The Aging Leydig Cell: III Gonadotropin Stimulation in Men." *Journal of Andrology* 2 (1981): 181–218.

National Institute for Occupational Safety and Health. *Fatal Injuries to Workers in the United States, 1980–1989: A Decade of Surveillance.* NIOSH, no. 93–108. Cincinnati: National Institute for Occupational Safety, 1993.

National Institute of Health. *Older and Wiser: The Baltimore Longitudinal Study of Aging.* NIH Publication no. 89-2797. Washington, DC: U. S. Government Printing Office, September 1989.

National Institute on Drug Abuse. *National Household Survey on Drug Abuse: Population Estimates 1991.* DHHS Publication no. [ADM] 92-1887. Washington, DC: U. S. Government Printing Office, 1992.

National Safety Council. *Accident Facts, 1992 Edition.* Itasca, IL: National Safety Council, 1992.

————. *Accident Facts, 1994 Edition.* Itasca, IL: National Safety Council, 1994.

National Sleep Foundation. *National Stress Survey, March 1995.* Washington DC: National Sleep Foundation, 1995.

Neaves, W. B. et al. "Leydig Cell Numbers, Daily Sperm Production and Serum Gonadotropin Levels in Aging Men." *Journal of Clinical Endocrinology and Metabolism* 59 (1984): 756–63.

Nesse, Randolph M., and George C. Williams. *Why We Get Sick: The New Science of Darwinian Medicine.* New York: Times Books, 1994.

Neugarten, B. L. "The Awareness of Middle Age." In *Middle Age and Aging,* edited by B. L. Nuegarten. Chicago: University of Chicago Press, 1968.

New York Times. *The Downsizing of America: The Reporters of the New York Times.* New York: Random House, 1996.

New York Times, 20 May 1992–30 August 1995.

Nichols, M. "The Sperm Scare." *MacLean's,* 1 April 1996, 50+.

Nichols, M. E. "Age-Related Changes in the Neurological Examination of Healthy Sexagenarians, Octogenarians and Centenarians." *Journal of Geriatric Psychiatry and Neurology* 7 (1994): 1–7.

Nieschlag, E., and E. Michel. "Reproductive Functions in Grandfathers." In *Aging, Reproduction and the Climacteric,* edited by L. Mastriani and A. Paulsen. New York: Plenum Press, 1981.

Nieschlag, E. et al. "Reproductive Function in Young Fathers and Grandfathers." *Journal of Clinical Endocrinology and Metabolism* 55 (1982): 676–81.

Norris, Kathleen. "Celibate Passion." *New Age Journal,* August 1996.

Notman, Malkah, M.D. "Is There a Male Menopause?" In *The Menopause Book,* edited by Louisa Rose. New York: Hawthorne Books, 1977.

Nouwen, Henri, and Walter J. Gaffney. *Aging: The Fulfillment of Life.* New York: Doubleday and Company, Inc., 1976.

O'Brien, M. K., K. Petrie, and J. Raeburn. "Adherence to Medication Regimens: Updating a Complex Medical Issue." *Medical Care Review* 49, no. 4 (1992): 435–54.

O'Carroll, Bancroft J. "Testosterone Therapy for Low Sexual Interest and Erectile Dysfunction in Men: A Controlled Study." *British Journal of Psychiatry* 145 (1984): 146–51.

O'Neil, M. K., W. J. Lance, and J. J. Freeman. "Sex Differences in Depressed University Students." *Social Psychiatry* 20 (1985): 186–90.

O'Neill, Eugene. *Long Day's Journey into Night.* New Haven, CT: Yale University Press, 1989.

Okin, Susan Moller. *Justice, Gender, and the Family.* New York: Basic Books, 1989.

Oppenheim, M. *The Man's Health Book.* Englewood Cliffs, NJ: Prentice Hall, 1994.

Ornstein, R., and D. Sobel. *Healthy Pleasures.* Reading, PA: Addison-Wesley, 1989.

Ornstein, Robert. *The Evolution of Consciousness: The Origins of the Way We Think.* New York: Touchstone, 1991.

Ortegay Gasset, Jose. *Meditations on Hunting.* New York: Macmillan Publishing Company, 1985.

Osser, S., P. Liedholm, and J. Randstram. "Depressed Semen Quality. A Survey After Two Decades." *Archives of Andrology* 12 (1984): 113–16.

Pacific Sun, 17 July 1996.

Paffenbarger, R. S. et al. "The Association of Changes in Physical-Activity Level and Other Lifestyle Characteristics with Mortality Among Men." *New England Journal of Medicine* 328 (1993): 538–45.

Papadakis, M. A. et al. "Growth Hormone Replacement in Healthy Older Men Improves Body Composition But Not Functional Ability." *Annals of Internal Medicine* 124 (1996): 1–4.

Papolos, Demitri, M.D., and Janice Papolos. *Overcoming Depression: The Definitive Resource for Patients and Families Who Live With Depression and Manic-Depression.* New York: HarperCollins, 1997.

Pascale, P. J., and W. J. Evans. "Gender Differences and Similarities in Patterns of Drug Use and Attitudes of High School Students." *Journal of Drug Education* 23, no. 1 (1993): 105–16.

Pate, R. R., Ph.D. et al. "Physical Activity and Public Health: A Recommendation From the Centers for Disease Control and Prevention and the American College of Sports Medicine." *JAMA* 273, no. 5 (1995): 403.

Patterson, James, and Peter Kim. *The Day America Told the Truth: What People Really Believe about Everything That Really Matters.* New York: Prentice Hall, 1991.

Pearce, Joseph Chilton. *Evolution's End: Claiming the Potential of Our Intelligence.* San Francisco: Harper San Francisco, 1992.

Pearsall, Paul, Ph.D. *Sexual Healing: Using the Power of an Intimate, Loving Relationship to Heal Your Body and Soul*. New York: Crown Publishers, 1994.

Pearson, Durk, and Sandy Shaw. *Life Extension: A Practical Scientific Approach*. New York: Warner Books, 1982.

Peterson, Peter G. *Will America Grow up Before It Grows Old?* New York: Random House, 1996.

Phillips, G. B. "The Variability of the Serum Estradiol Level in Men: Effects of Stress (College Examinations), Cigarette Smoking, and Coffee Drinking on the Serum Sex Hormone and Other Hormone Levels." *Steroids* 57 (1992): 135–41.

Pierpaoli, Walter, and William Regelson, with Carol Colman. *The Melatonin Miracle*. New York: Simon and Schuster, 1995.

Powell, K. E. et al. "Physical Activity and Chronic Diseases" *American Journal of Clinical Nutrition* 49 (1989): 999–1006.

Powell, K. E. et al. "Physical Activity and the Incidence of Coronary Heart Disease." *Annual Review of Public Health* 8 (1987): 253–87.

Preusser, D. F., A. F. Williams, and A. K. Lund. "Characteristics of Belted and Unbelted Drivers." *Accident Analysis and Prevention* 23, no. 6 (1991): 475–82.

Prohaska, T. R. et al. "Health Practices and Illness Cognition in Young, Middle Aged and Elderly Adults." *Journal of Gerontology* 40 (1985): 569–78.

"Putting the 'Men' into Menopause." *Week in Germany*, 15 July 1994, 7.

Raines, H. *Fly Fishing through the Midlife Crisis*. New York: Morrow, 1993.

Rako, Susan, M.D. *The Hormone of Desire: The Truth about Sexuality, Menopause, and Testosterone*. New York: Harmony Books, 1996.

Rakowski, W. "Personal Health Practices, Health Status, and Expected Control over Future Health." *Journal of Community Health* 11, no. 3 (1986): 189–203.

Rapp, P. R., and W. C. Heindel. "Memory Systems in Normal and Pathological Aging." *Current Opinion in Neurology* 7 (1994): 294–98.

Razak, Ariska. "Toward a Womanist Analysis of Birth." In *Reweaving the World: The Emergence of Ecofeminism*, edited by Irene Diamond and Gloria Feman Orenstein. San Francisco: Sierra Club Books, 1990.

Real, Terrence. *I Don't Want to Talk about It: Overcoming the Secrecy of Male Depression*. New York: Scribner, 1997.

Redaihs, M. H., J. S. Reis, and N. S. Creason. "Sleep in Old Age: Focus on Gender Differences." *Sleep* 13, no. 5 (1990): 410–24.

Regelson, W. et al. "Hormonal Intervention: 'Buffer Hormones' or 'State Dependency': The Role of Dehydroepiandrosterone (DHEA), Thyroid Hormone, Estrogen, and Hypophysectomy in Aging." *Annals of the New York Academy of Science* 521 (1988): 260–73.

Regelson, William, M.D., and Carol Colman. *The Super-Hormone Promise: Nature's Antidote to Aging.* New York: Simon and Schuster, 1996.

Reiter, Russel J., Ph.D., and Jo Robinson. *Melatonin Revolution: Your Body's Natural Wonder Drug.* New York: Bantam Books, 1995.

Reiter, T. "Testosterone Implantation: A Clinical Study of 240 Implantations in Aging Males." *Journal of the American Geriatric Society* II (1963): 540–50.

Reitz, Rosetta. *Menopause: A Positive Approach.* Radnor, PA: Chilton Book Company, 1977.

"Researchers Certain of Male Menopause and Its Treatments." *Early Prime,* CNN, 17 November 1995.

Reyner, A., and Horne. "Gender- and Age-Related Differences in Sleep Determined by Home-Recorded Sleep Logs and Actimetry from 400 Adults." *Sleep* 18, no. 2 (1995): 127–34.

Ridley, Matt. *The Red Queen: Sex and the Evolution of Human Nature.* New York: Macmillan Publishing Company, 1993.

Rifkin, Jeremy. *The End of Work.* New York: G. P. Putnam's Sons, 1995.

Rimm, E. B. et al. "Body Size and Fat Distribution as Predictors of Coronary Heart Disease among Middle-Aged and Older U. S. Men." *American Journal of Epidemiology* 141, no. 12 (1995): 1117–27.

Rivara, F. P. et al. "Epidemiology of Childhood Injuries." *American Journal of Diseases of Children* 136 (1982): 502–6.

Robbins, John. *Reclaiming Our Health: Exploding the Medical Myth and Embracing the Source of True Healing.* Tiburon, CA: H. J. Kramer, Inc., 1996.

Robertson, Joel with Tom Monte. *Natural Prozac: Learning to Release Your Body's Own Anti-Depressants.* San Francisco: Harper SanFrancisco, 1997.

Robins, L. N. et al. "Lifetime Prevalence of Specific Psychiatric Disorders in Three Sites." *Archives of General Psychiatry* 41 (1984): 949–58.

Roelofs, W. L. "Chemistry of Sex Attraction." *Proc. Natl. Acad. Sci. U. S. A.* 92 (1995): 44–49.

Rose, M. R., and T. J. Nusbaum. "Prospects for Postponing Human Aging." *FASEB Journal* 8, no. 12 (1994): 925–28.

Ross, C. E., and C. E. Bird. "Sex Stratification and Health Lifestyle: Consequences for Men's and Women's Perceived Health." *Journal of Health and Social Behavior* 35 (1994): 161–78.

Rossi, J. S. "Stages of Change for 15 Health Risk Behaviors in an HMO Population." Paper presented at the 13th annual scientific sessions of the Society of Behavioral Medicine, New York, NY, March 1992.

Roszak, Theodore, Mary E. Gomes, and Allen D. Kanner. *Ecopsychology: Restoring the Earth, Healing the Mind.* San Francisco: Sierra Club Books, 1995.

Rothenberg, David. "Out on a Limb." *Fortune News,* Spring 1983.

Rubin, L. B. *Intimate Strangers.* New York: Harper and Row, 1983.

Rudman, Daniel, M.D. et al. "Relations of Endogenous Anabolic Hormones and Physical Activity to Bone Density and Lean Body Mass in Elderly Men." *Clinical Endocrinology* 40 (1994): 653–61.

Rudman, Daniel, M.D. et al. "Effects of Human Growth Hormone in Men Over 60 Years Old." *New England Journal of Medicine* 323, no. 1 (1990): 1–6.

Rusting, R. L. "Why Do We Age?" *Scientific American,* June 1992, 130+.

Ryan, George. *Reclaiming Male Sexuality: A Guide To Potency, Vitality, and Prowess.* New York: M. Evans and Company, 1997.

Ryback, David. *Look 10 Years Younger, Live 10 Years Longer: A Man's Guide.* New York: Prentice Hall, 1995.

Sahelian, Ray, M.D. "Melatonin: The Natural Sleep Medicine." *Total Health,* August 1995, 30+.

———. "The Fountain of Youth—The Never Ending Quest." *Muscular Development and Fitness,* January 1996, 48.

Samuels, Mike, M.D., and Hal Bennett. *The Well Body Book.* New York: Random House, 1973.

Sand, Gayle. *Is It Hot in Here or Is It Me?* New York: HarperCollins, 1993.

San Francisco Examiner, 24 May 1994.

Sarafin, T. A., and D. E. Bredesen. "Is Apoptosis Mediated by Reactive Oxygen Species?" *Free Radical Research* 21, no. 1 (1994): 1–8.

Sasano, M., and S. Ishyo. "Vascular Patterns of the Human Testes with Special Reference to its Senile Changes." *Tohaku J. Exp. Med.* 99 (1969): 269–80.

Schachter, Michael B., M.D. *The Natural Way to a Healthy Prostate.* New Canaan, CT: Keats Publishing, Inc., 1995.

Schachter-Shalomi, Zalman, and Ronald S. Miller. *From Age-ing to Sage-ing: A Profound New Vision of Growing Older.* New York: Warner Books, 1995.

Schaef, Anne Wilson. *Native Wisdom for White Minds.* New York: Ballantine, 1995.

Schenk, Roy U., and John Everingham. *Men Healing Shame: An Anthology.* New York: Springer Publishing Company, 1995.

Schiavi, R. C. et al. "Aging, Sleep Disorders and Male Sexual Function." *Biological Psychiatry* 30, no. 1 (1991): 15–24.

Schneider, H. D. "[Sexuality in Old Age]." *Schweizerische Rundschau fur Medizin Praxis* 83, no. 10 (1994): 267–72. Language: German.

Schneider, Jennifer, and Burt Schneider. *Sex, Lies, and Forgiveness: Couples Speaking Out on Healing From Sex Addiction.* Center City, MN: Hazelden, 1991.

Schoenbach, V. J. et al. "Social Ties and Mortality in Evans County, Georgia." *American Journal of Epidemiology* 123, no. 4 (1986): 577–91.

Schoenborn, C. A. "Health Habits of U. S. Adults, 1985: The 'Alameda 7' Revisited." *Public Health Reports* 101, no. 6 (1986): 571–80.

Schroder. "Androgens and Carcinoma of the Prostate." In *Testosterone, Action, Deficiency, Substitution,* edited by E. Nieschlag and H. M. Behre. Berlin: Springer Verlag, 1990.

Seals, D. R., J. A. Taylor, and M. D. Esler. "Exercise and Aging: Autonomic Control of the Circulation." *Medicine and Science in Sports and Exercise* 26, no. 5 (1994): 568–76.

Seeman, T. E. et al. "Social Network Ties and Mortality among the Elderly in the Alameda County Study." *American Journal of Epidemiology* 126 (1987): 714–23.

Segell, Michael. "The New Softness. (Why Men Become More Intimate and Nurturing in Later Life)." *Esquire,* April 1996, 51.

Seligman, Daniel. "Testosterone Power." Review of *Why Men Rule: A Theory of Male Dominance,* by Steven Goldberg. *National Review,* 4 April 1994, 64+.

Seligmann, Jean. "Testosterone Wimping Out." *Newsweek,* 3 July 1995, 61.

Serdula, M. K. et al. "Relationship between Drug Use and Sexual Behaviors and the Occurrence of Sexually Transmitted Diseases among High-Risk Male Youth." *Sexually Transmitted Diseases* 20, no. 6 (1993): 307–13.

Shafer, M. A. et al. "Relationship between Drug Use and Sexual Behaviors and the Occurrence of Sexually Transmitted Diseases among High-Risk Male Youth." *Sexually Transmitted Diseases* 20, no. 6 (1993): 307–13.

Shandler, Nina. *Estrogen: The Natural Way—Over 250 Easy and Delicious Recipes for Menopause.* New York: Villard, 1997.

Sheehy, Gail. *Passages: Predictable Crises of Adult Life.* New York: E. P. Dutton and Company, 1976.

———. *Pathfinders.* New York: Bantam Books, 1982.

———. *Menopause: The Silent Passage.* New York: Random House, 1991.

———. "The Unspeakable Passage. Is There a Male Menopause?" *Vanity Fair,* April 1993, 164+.

————. "What You Should Know about Male Menopause." *Reader's Digest*, August 1993, 114+.

————. *New Passages: Mapping Your Life across Time*. New York: Random House, 1995.

————. *Understanding Men's Passages: Discovering the New Map of Men's Lives*. New York: Random House, 1998.

Shepard, Paul. *The Tender Carnivore and the Sacred Game*. New York: Charles Scribner's Sons, 1973.

Sherrod, D. "The Bonds of Men." In *The Making of Masculinities*, edited by H. Brod. Winchester, MA: Allen and Unwin, 1987.

Sherven, Judith and James Sniechowski. *The New Intimacy: Discovering the Magic at the Heart of Your Differences*. Deerfield Beach, Florida: Health Communications, 1997.

Shye, D. et al. "Gender Differences in the Relationship between Social Network Suport and Mortality: A Longitudinal Study of an Elderly Cohort." *Social Science and Medicine* 41, no. 7 (1995): 78–80.

Skalka, Patricia. *The American Medical Association Guide to Health and Well-Being after Fifty*. New York: Random House, 1984.

Skolnick, Andrew A. "Is 'Male Menopause' Real or Just an Excuse? (Medical News and Perspectives)." *JAMA* 268, no. 18 (1992): 2486.

Small, Meredith F. *What's Love Got to Do with It? The Evolution of Human Mating*. New York: Doubleday, 1995.

Smeeding, T. M. "Children and Poverty: How the U. S. Stands." *Forum for Applied Research and Public Policy*, Summer 1991, 6.

Snowdon, D. A. et al. "Is Early Menopause a Biological Marker of Health and Aging?" *American Journal of Public Health* 79 (1989): 709–14.

Solomon, M. F. *Lean On Me: The Power of Positive Dependency in Intimate Relationships*. New York: Simon and Schuster, 1994.

Solstad, K., and K. Garde. "Middle-Aged Danish Men's Ideas of a Male Climacteric—and of the Female Climacteric." *Maturitas* 15 (1992): 7–16.

Solstad, Kim. "[Male Climacteric: a Useful Concept?]." *Nordisk Sexologi* 8, no. 4 (1990): 241–49. Language: Danish.

Somé, Malidoma Patrice. "Ambassador of the Ancestors: An Interview with Malidoma Somé." By Virginia Lee. *Common Ground*, Fall 1996, 144+.

————. *Of Water and the Spirit: Ritual, Magic, and Initiation in the Life of an African Shaman*. New York: G. P. Putnam's Sons, 1994.

Soules, Michael R., and William J. Bremner. "The Menopause and Climacteric: Endocrinologic Basis and Associated Symptomatology." *Journal of the American Geriatrics Society* 30, no. 9 (1982): 547–61.

Spark, R. F., R. A. White, and P. B. Connolly. "Impotence Is Not Always Psychogenic. Newer Insights into Hypothalamic-Pituitary-Gonadal Dysfunction." *JAMA* 243 (1980): 750–55.

Sprinivasan, G., E. Campbell, and N. Bashirelahi. "Androgen, Estrogen, and Progesterone Receptors in Normal and Aging Prostates." *Microsc. Res. Tech.* 30 (1995): 293–304.

Steele, B. F., and C. B. Pollock. "Psychiatric Study of Abusing Parents." In *The Battered Child*, edited by Ray E. Helfer and C. Henry Kempe. Chicago: University of Chicago Press, 1966.

Stein, Murray. *In Midlife*. Dallas, TX: Spring Publications, 1983.

Steinfeld, A. D., and C. Reinhardt. "Male Climacteric after Orchiectomy in Patient With Prostatic Cancer." *Urology* 16, no. 6 (1980): 620–22.

Stekel, Wilhelm, M.D. *Impotence in the Male*. New York: Liveright, 1927.

Sterling, A. Justin. *What Really Works with Men*. New York: Warner Books, 1992.

Stephenson, June. *Men Are Not Cost-Effective*. New York: HarperCollins, 1995.

Strouse, William, and Neil Howe. *Generations: The History of America's Future, 1584-2069*. New York: William Morrow, 1991.

Struck, H. J. "[Biomechanics and Aging]." *Zeitschrift fur Gerontologie* 24, no. 3 (1991): 121–28. Language: German.

Stukane, Eileen. "Testosterone, the Other Hormone." *Cosmopolitan*, February 1995, 120+.

Swerdloff, Ronald S., and Christina Wang. "Androgen Deficiency and Aging in Men." *Western Journal of Medicine* 159: 579–85.

Swimme, Brian, and Thomas Berry. *The Universe Story: From the Primordial Flaring Forth to the Ecozoic Era, A Celebration of the Unfolding of the Cosmos*. San Francisco: Harper San Francisco, 1992.

Symons, Donald. *The Evolution of Human Sexuality*. Oxford: Oxford University Press, 1979.

Szarvas, F. "[The Male Climacteric from the Practical Viewpoint]." *Wiener Medizinische Wochenschrift* 142, no. 5–6 (1992): 100–3. Language: German.

Tannen, Deborah. *You Just Don't Understand: Women and Men in Conversation*. New York: William Morrow and Company, 1990.

Tavris, Carol. *The Mismeasure of Woman: Why Women Are Not the Better Sex, the Inferior Sex, or the Opposite Sex*. New York: Simon and Schuster, 1992.

Tenover, J. S. et al. "The Effect of Aging in Normal Men on Bioavailable Testosterone and Luteinizing Hormone: Response to Clomiphene Citrate." *Journal of Clinical Endocrinology and Metabolism* 65 (1987): 1118–25.

Tenover, Joyce S. "Androgen Administration to Aging Men." *Endocrinology and Metabolism Clinics of North America* 23, no. 4 (1994): 877–92.

————. "Effects of Testosterone Supplementation in the Aging Male." *Journal of Clinical Endocrinology and Metabolism* 75 (1992): 1092–98.

Terkel, Studs. *Coming of Age: Passion, Power and the Old.* New York: New Press, 1995.

Thomas, B. S. "The Effectiveness of Selected Risk Factors in Mediating Gender Differences in Drinking and its Problems." *Journal of Adolescent Health* 17, no. 2 (1995): 91–98.

Thompson, Keith. *To Be a Man: In Search of the Deep Masculine.* New York: G. P. Putnam's Sons, 1991.

Toffler, Alvin. *Power Shift: Knowledge, Wealth, and Violence at the Edge of the 21st Century.* New York: Bantam, 1990.

Tomer, Y., B. Lunenfeld, and M. Berezin. "[Andropause: Myth or Reality]?" *Harefuah* 128, no. 12 (1995): 785–88. Language: Hebrew.

Travis, John, and Regina Sara Ryan. *Wellness Workbook.* Berkeley, CA: Ten Speed Press, 1988.

Travis, John. "Treating Old Age with Testosterone." *Science News,* 1 July 1995, 15.

Trott, Bert. "Flex Appeal." *Men's Confidential: Health, Sex, and Fitness News for Men,* August 1994.

Tsitouras, P. D., and T. Bulat. "The Aging Male Reproductive System." *Endocrinology and Metabolism Clinics of North America* 24 (1995): 297–315.

Tsitouras, P. D., C. E. Martin, and S. M. Harman. "Relationship of Serum Testosterone to Sexual Acitivity in Healthy Elderly Men." *Journal of Gerontology* 37 (1982): 288–93.

Turnbull, Colin M. *The Human Cycle.* New York: Simon and Schuster, 1983.

Umberson, D. "Gender, Marital Status and the Social Control of Health Behavior." *Social Science and Medicine* 34, no. 8 (1992): 907–17.

Umberson, D., C. B. Wortman, and R. C. Kessler. "Widowhood and Depression: Explaining Long-Term Gender Differences in Vulnerability." *Journal of Health and Social Behavior* 33 (1992): 10–24.

University of California, Berkeley. *Wellness Letter,* September 1996.

"Upper Limits on Male Fertility." *Muscle & Fitness,* December 1994, 44.

Urban, R. J. "Neuroendocrinology of Aging in the Male and Female." *Endocrinology and Metabolism Clinics of North America* 21, no. 4 (1992): 921–31.

U. S. Bureau of the Census, Dept. WP/94. *World Poplulation Profile.* Washington, DC, 1994.

U.S. Bureau of the Census. *Statistical Abstract, 1985.* Washington, DC, 1985.

———. *Statistical Abstract, 1990.* Washington, DC, 1990.

———. *Statistical Abstract, 1996.* Washington, DC, 1996.

U. S. Department of Health and Human Services. National Center for Health Statistics. *Vital Statistics of the United States, 1995.*

U. S. Department of Justice. Federal Bureau of Investigations. *Uniform Crime Reports, 1989.*

———. *Uniform Crime Reports, 1996.*

Valemaki, M. et al. "Sex Hormones and Adrenocortical Steroids in Men Acutely Intoxicated With Ethanol." *Alcoholism* 1 (1984): 89–93.

———."The Pulsative Secretion of Gonadotropin and Growth Hormone and the Biological Activity of Luteinizing in Men Acutely Intoxicated With Ethanol." *Alcoholism: Clinical and Experimental Research* 14 (1990): 928–31.

Van Biema, David. "Emperor of the Soul." *Time,* 24 June 1996, 65+.

Van Horn, L. V. et al. "Diet, Body Size, and Plasma Lipids-Lipoproteins in Young Adults: Differences by Race and Sex." *American Journal of Epidemiology* 133, no. 1 (1991): 9–23.

Vanzant, Iyanla. *The Spirit of a Man: A Vision of Transformation for Black Men and the Women Who Love Them.* New York: HarperCollins, 1996.

Varenhorst, E., T. Frodin, and G. Alund. "Climacteric Flushing in a Man." Letter. *Br Med J* (Clin Res Ed) 287, no. 6395 (1983): 838–39.

Ventura, Michael. *Letters at 3 AM: Reports on Endarkenment.* Dallas, TX: Spring Publications, 1993.

Verbrugge, L. M. "Unveiling Higher Morbidity for Men: The Story." In *Social Structures and Human Lives,* edited by M. W. Riley. Newbury Park, CA: Sage, 1988.

Vermeulen, A. "Andropause, Fact or Fiction?" In *The Modern Management of the Menopause: A Perspective for the 21st Century. Proc. of the VII International Congress on the Menopause,* edited by G. Berg and M. Hammar, International Congress Symposium and Seminar Series 8, Stockholm, Sweden, June 1993. Pearl River, NY: Parthenon Publishing Group, 1994.

———. "Biological Manifestations of the Andropause." *Fiziologicheskii Zhurnal* (Kiev) 36, no. 5 (1990): 90–93. Language: Russian.

————. "[Do hormones determine our fate?]." *Verhandelingen—Koninklijke Academie voor Geneeskunde Van Belgie* 56, no. 1 (1994): 5–16. Language: Dutch.

————. "Environment, Human Reproduction, Menopause, and Andropause." *Environmental Health Perspectives* 101 Suppl 2 (1993): 91–100.

————. "The Male Climacterium." *Annals Of Medicine* 25, no. 6 (1993): 531–34.

————. "[Neuroendocrinological Aspects of Aging]." *Verhandelingen—Koninklijke Academie voor Geneeskunde Van Belgie* 56, no. 4 (1994): 267–80. Language: Dutch.

Vermeulen, A., and J. Belaisch. "[The Endocrine Substrate of the Andropause]." *Contraception Fertilite Sexualite* 20, no. 5 (1992): 561–66. Language: French.

Vermeulen, A., and J. M. Kaufman. "[Aging of the Hypothalamo-Pituitary-Testicular Axis in Men]." *Hormone Research* (Basel) 43, no. 1–3 (1995): 25–28. Langue: French.

Vermeulen, A., and J. P. Deslypere. "Intratesticular Unconjugated Steroids in Elderly Men." *Journal Of Steroid Biochemistry* 24 (1986): 1079–89.

Vermeulen, A., J. P. Deslypere, and J. M. Kaufman. "[Andropause: Myth or Reality]." *Contraception Fertilite Sexualite* 17, no. 5 (1989): 473–77. Language: French.Vermeulen, A., J. P. Deslypere, and K. De Meirlier. "A New Look to the Andropause Altered Function of the Gonadotrophs." *Journal of Steroid Biochemistry* 32, no. 1B (1989): 163–66.

Vermeulen, A., T. Stoica, and L. Verdonck. "The Apparent Free Testosterone Concentration, An Index of Androgenicity." *Journal of Clinical Endocrinology and Metabolism* 33 (1971): 759–67.

Vigderhous, G., and G. Fishman. "The Impact of Unemployment and Familial Integration on Changing Suicide Rates in the U. S. A., 1920–1969." *Social Psychiatry* 13 (1978): 239–48.

Vittachi, Anuradhu. *Earth Conference One.* Boston: Shambhala, 1989.

Wainstein, C., G. Burgos, and G. Pineda. "[Hormones Levels in the Male Climacteric]." *Rev Med Chil* 111, no. 6 (1983): 564–66. Language: Spanish.

Wallis, Claudia. "Faith and Healing." *Time,* 24 June 1996, 58+.

Walsh, Patrick C., M.D., and Janet Farrar Worthington. *The Prostate: A Guide for Men and the Women Who Love Them.* Baltimore: Johns Hopkins University Press, 1995.

Washington Post, 1 January 1997.

Webster, Donovan. "Erections 'R' Us." *Men's Health,* June 1996, 108+.

Weil, Andrew, M.D. *Health and Healing.* Boston: Houghton Mifflin, 1983.

————. *Roots of Healing: The New Medicine.* Carlsbad, CA: Hay House, Inc., 1997.

————. "Protecting Your Prostate." *Andrew Weil's Self Healing Newsletter* I, no. 4 (1995): 2–3.

Weiner, Bernard. *Boy into Man: A Father's Guide to Initiation of Teenage Sons.* San Francisco: Transformation Press, 1992.

Weiss, Daniel Evan. *The Great Divide: How Females and Males Really Differ.* New York: Poseidon Press, 1991.

Weissfeld, J. L., J. P. Kirscht, and B. M. Brock. "Health Beliefs in a Population: The Michigan Blood Pressure Survey." *Health Education Quarterly* 17, no. 2 (1990): 141–55.

Wertheimer, Neil. *Total Health for Men: How to Prevent and Treat the Health Problems That Trouble Men Most.* Emmaus, PA: Rodale Press, 1995.

"White Male Paranoia." *Newsweek,* 29 March 1993, cover.

Whybrow, Peter C., M.D. *A Mood Apart: The Thinker's Guide to Emotion and Its Disorders.* HarperPerrenial, 1998.

Wilber, Ken. *A Brief History of Everything.* Boston: Shambhala, 1996.

————. *Sex, Ecology, Spirituality: The Spirit of Evolution.* Boston: Shambhala, 1995.

Williams, D. G. "Gender, Masculinity-Femininity, and Emotional Intimacy in Same-Sex Friendship." *Sex Roles* 12, no. 5/6 (1985): 587–600.

Williams, R. B., M.D. et. al. "Prognostic Importance of Social and Economic Resources among Medically Treated Patients with Angiographically Documented Coronary Artery Disease." *JAMA* 267, no. 4 (1992): 522–23.

Willich, S. N. et al. "Physical Exertion as a Trigger of Acute Myocardial Infarction." *New England Journal of Medicine* 329, no. 23 (1993): 1684–90.

Wilmer, Harry A., M.D. *Practical Jung: Nuts and Bolts of Jungian Psychotherapy.* Wilmette, IL: Chiron Publications, 1987.

Winawer, S. J., and M. Shike. *Cancer Free: The Comprehensive Cancer Prevention Program.* New York: Simon and Schuster, 1995.

Winn, R. L., and N. Newton. "Sexuality in Aging: A Study of 106 Cultures." *Arch. Sex. Behav.* 11, no. 4 (1982).

Winters, S. J., R. S. Sherins, and P. Troen. "The Gonadotropic Suppressive Activity of Androgens is Increased in Elderly Men." *Metabolism* 33 (1984): 1052–59.

Women's Health Advocate, February 1996.

Wood, W. B., and T. E. Johnson. "Aging: Stopping the Clock." *Current Biology* 4, no. 2 (1994): 151–53.

Yasavage, J. A. et al. "Plasma Testosterone Levels, Sexuality and Age." *Biol. Psychiatry* 20 (1985): 199–228.

Yen, S. S., and R. B. Jaffe. *Reproductive Endocrinology: Physiology, Pathophysiology, and Clinical Management.* Philadelphia: Saunders, 1991.

Yen, S. S. C., A. J. Morales, and O. Khorram. "Replacement of DHEA in Aging Men and Women." In *Dehydroepiandrosterone (DHEA) and Aging,* edited by F. Bellino et al. *Annals of the New York Academy of Sciences* 774 (1995): 128–42.

Zuckerman, M. *Behavioral Expressions and Biosocial Bases of Sensation Seeking.* New York: Cambridge University Press, 1994.

————. "Sensation Seeking: A Comparitive Approach to a Human Trait." *The Behavioral and Brain Sciences* 7 (1984): 413–71.

————. "Sensation Seeking and Sports." *Personality and Individual Differences* 4, no. 3 (1983): 285–93.

Index

About the Author

Jed Diamond is director of the Third Age Wellness Center, which offers health services for men and women over the age of forty. He is also a member of the International Society for the Study of the Aging Male, dedicated to improving the quality of life for men throughout the world.

Diamond has been a licensed psychotherapist for thirty-four years, and is a nationally recognized educator and trainer in the area of men's health. His work has lent his expertise on the nation's top shows and the world's most prestigious publications, including *Good Morning America, CBS Up-to-the-Minute, National Public Radio, The View with Barbara Walters, The Wall Street Journal,* and *USA Today.* He is also the host of the public television special based on this book.

Diamond received his masters degree in social work from the University of California at Berkeley, where he now teaches courses for professionals in addiction studies. Jed and his wife, Carlin, live in northern California and conduct relationship workshops together throughout the country. He is the father of five grown children and four grandchildren.

If you would like to know about Jed's other books, booklets, and tapes or would like to know about upcoming workshops and training events, you may contact him at:

34133 Shimmins Ridge Rd.

Willits, CA 95490